ANNUAL EDITIONS

The Family 11/12

Thirty-Seventh Edition

W9-BAG-423

EDITOR

Kathleen R. Gilbert
Indiana University

Kathleen Gilbert is a professor in the Department of Applied Health Science at Indiana University. She received a BA in Sociology and an MS in Marriage and Family Relations from Northern Illinois University. Her PhD in Family Studies is from Purdue University. Dr. Gilbert's primary areas of interest are loss and grief in a family context, trauma and the family, family process, and family diversity. She has published several books and articles in these areas.

McGraw-Hill

Connect
Learn
Succeed™

ANNUAL EDITIONS: THE FAMILY, THIRTY-SEVENTH EDITION

Published by McGraw-Hill, a business unit of The McGraw-Hill Companies, Inc., 1221 Avenue
of the Americas, New York, NY 10020. Copyright © 2011 by The McGraw-Hill Companies, Inc.
All rights reserved. Previous edition(s) © 2010, 2009, and 2008. No part of this publication may be
reproduced or distributed in any form or by any means, or stored in a database or retrieval system,
without the prior written consent of The McGraw-Hill Companies, Inc., including, but not limited
to, in any network or other electronic storage or transmission, or broadcast for distance learning.

Some ancillaries, including electronic and print components, may not be available to customers
outside the United States.

Annual Editions® is a registered trademark of The McGraw-Hill Companies, Inc.
Annual Editions is published by the **Contemporary Learning Series** group within
The McGraw-Hill Higher Education division.

1 2 3 4 5 6 7 8 9 0 WDQ/WDQ 1 0 9 8 7 6 5 4 3 2 1 0

ISBN 978–0–07–805077–0
MHID 0–07–805077–4
ISSN 1092–4876

Managing Editor: *Larry Loeppke*
Developmental Editor: *Dave Welsh*
Permissions Coordinator: *DeAnna Dausener*
Senior Marketing Communications Specialist: *Mary Klein*
Project Manager: *Robin A. Reed*
Design Coordinator: *Margarite Reynolds*
Buyer: *Sandy Ludovissy*
Cover Graphics: *Kristine Jubeck*

Compositor: Laserwords Private Limited
Cover Images: Hill Street Studios/Getty Images (inset); Jon Boyes/Photographer's Choice/Getty
Images (background)

Library in Congress Cataloging-in-Publication Data
Main entry under title: Annual Editions: The Family. 2011/2012.
  1. The Family—Periodicals. I. Gilbert, Kathleen R., *comp.* II. Title: The Family.
658'.05

www.mhhe.com

Editors/Academic Advisory Board

Members of the Academic Advisory Board are instrumental in the final selection of articles for each edition of ANNUAL EDITIONS. Their review of articles for content, level, and appropriateness provides critical direction to the editors and staff. We think that you will find their careful consideration well reflected in this volume.

ANNUAL EDITIONS: The Family 11/12
37th Edition

EDITOR

Kathleen R. Gilbert
Indiana University

ACADEMIC ADVISORY BOARD MEMBERS

Preface

In publishing ANNUAL EDITIONS we recognize the enormous role played by the magazines, newspapers, and journals of the public press in providing current, first-rate educational information in a broad spectrum of interest areas. Many of these articles are appropriate for students, researchers, and professionals seeking accurate, current material to help bridge the gap between principles and theories and the real world. These articles, however, become more useful for study when those of lasting value are carefully collected, organized, indexed, and reproduced in a low-cost format, which provides easy and permanent access when the material is needed. That is the role played by ANNUAL EDITIONS.

The purpose of *Annual Editions: The Family 11/12* is to bring to the reader the latest thoughts and trends in our understanding of the family, to identify current concerns as well as problems and potential solutions, and to present alternative views of family processes. The intent of this anthology is to explore intimate relationships as they are played out within the family and, in doing this, to reflect the family's evolving function and importance. The articles in this volume are taken from professional journals as well as other professionally oriented publications and popular lay publications aimed at both special populations and a general readership. The selections are carefully reviewed for their currency and accuracy.

In the current edition, a number of new articles have been added to reflect reviewers' comments on the previous edition. As the reader, you will note the tremendous range in tone and focus of these articles, from first-person accounts to reports of scientific discoveries as well as philosophical and theoretical writings. Some are more practical and applications-oriented, while others are more conceptual and research-oriented.

This anthology is organized to address many of the important aspects of family and family relationships. The first unit takes an overview perspective and looks at varied perspectives on the family. The second unit examines the beginning steps of relationship building as individuals go through the process of exploring and establishing connections. In the third unit, means of finding and maintaining a relationship balance, romantic as well as for other intimate relationships, are examined. Unit 4 is concerned with crises and ways in which these can act as challenges and opportunities for families and their members. Finally, the fifth unit takes an affirming tone as it looks at family strengths and ways of empowering families.

Annual Editions: The Family 11/12 is intended to be used as a supplemental text for lower-level, introductory marriage and family or sociology of the family classes, particularly when they tie the content of the readings to essential information on marriages and families, however they are defined. As a supplement, this book can also be used to update or emphasize certain aspects of standard marriage and family textbooks. Because of the provocative nature of many of the essays in this anthology, it works well as a basis for class discussion about various aspects of marriages and family relationships. This edition of *Annual Editions: The Family* contains web sites that can be used to further explore topics addressed in the articles. These sites are cross-referenced by number in the *topic guide.*

I would like to thank everyone involved in the development of this volume. My appreciation goes to those who sent in article rating forms and comments on the previous edition as well as those who suggested articles to consider for inclusion in this edition. To all of the students in my Marriage and Family Interaction class who have contributed critiques of articles, I would like to say thanks.

Anyone interested in providing input for future editions of *Annual Editions: The Family* should complete and return the postage-paid *article rating form* at the end of this book. Your suggestions are much appreciated and contribute to the continuing quality of this anthology.

Kathleen R. Gilbert
Editor

Contents

Preface   **iv**

Correlation Guide   **xii**

Topic Guide   **xiii**

Internet References   **xvi**

UNIT 1
Evolving Perspectives on the Family

Unit Overview   **xviii**

1. **Marriage and Family in the Scandinavian Experience,** David Popenoe, *Society,* May/June 2006

   In this article, the author compares U.S. and Scandinavian **societal expectations and attitudes regarding marriage and the family.** Legal and social differences are addressed, and many surprising similarities are identified. For example, although the **marriage rate** is much lower in Sweden than in the United States, the breakup rate of relationships involving a commitment is much the same.   **2**

2. **The Significant Dynamic Relationship between Globalization and Families,** Bahira Serif Trask

   We live in an increasingly globalized world, with different countries and cultures influencing each other. Often the focus in on "big picture" concerns like the economy and politics. This article focuses on the day-to-day **decisions that families make** with regard to **work** issues, **gender roles, child rearing,** and **care of the elderly,** and moving and migration.   **7**

3. **Interracial Families,** Carol Mithers, *Ladies' Home Journal,* July 2006

   The number of **mixed-race marriages** has grown sevenfold from 1970 to 2000. The implications of this change for **managing relationships** and **socializing children** are discussed.   **12**

4. **Family Partnerships,** JoBeth Allen, *Educational Leadership,* September 2008

   Partnerships between **families and schools** help to facilitate learning among children. They also increase respect for the **family's strengths** and abilities as well as awareness of **cultural variations in families.**   **14**

UNIT 2
Exploring and Establishing Relationships

Unit Overview   **18**

Part A. Love and Sex

5. **This Thing Called Love,** Lauren Slater, *National Geographic,* February 2006

   What we recognize as **passionate love or infatuation** share a chemical profile that is surprisingly similar to that of obsessive-compulsive disorder. In order for relationships to last, we **cannot depend on retaining feelings of passionate love** throughout the duration of the relationship.   **20**

The concepts in bold italics are developed in the article. For further expansion, please refer to the Topic Guide.

6. **24 Things Love and Sex Experts Are Dying to Tell You,** Ellise Pierce,
Redbook, June 2006

Fourteen experts share with readers their advice on love, sex, and *intimate relationships.* Their down-to-earth suggestions range from "*how to use compliments*" to "when to (and not to) sweep problems under the rug." Don't knock it until you've tried it twice.   **26**

Part B. Finding a Life Partner

7. **Against All Odds,** Anne Kingston, *Maclean's,* August 24, 2009

This article asks: "Is it crazy to **marry** someone you've known only a few weeks?" Perhaps a better question to ask would be if *"instant relationships"* stand much of a chance of long-term success?   **30**

8. **The Expectations Trap,** Hara Estroff Marano, *Psychology Today*
March/April 2010

Many of the **expectations we have for what a potential partner** can and should do are culturally determined. We may blame our partners for our unhappiness, and continue seek "the one." **Choosing the right partner is important,** but by looking at oneself and one's expectations, **it is possible to become the right partner.**   **33**

9. **On-Again, Off-Again,** Elizabeth Svoboda, *Psychology Today,*
March/April 2008

Some couples seem trapped in a *relationship cycle of breaking up and making up.* This article addresses possible explanations for this phenomenon as well as ways of *breaking the cycle,* either by choosing to stay in the relationships or leaving for good.   **39**

Part C. Pregnancy and the Next Generation

10. **Fats, Carbs and the Science of Conception,** Jorge E. Chavarro, Walter C.
Willett, and Patrick J. Skerrett, *Newsweek,* December 10, 2007

Sperm meets egg—the simple fact of **conception.** Yet, the reality of conception is that it is a complicated and amazing process that is responsive to a variety of behavioral and other *choices on the part of the parents.* This article addresses specific influences: diet, exercise and weight control.   **41**

11. **Not Always 'the Happiest Time,'** Lisa Miller and Anne Underwood,
Newsweek, April 24, 2006

The Constitution of the United States identifies the *right to procreate* as a fundamental human right. Yet there is almost no public policy in the United States regarding *reproductive rights and access to reproductive technology.* The provocative article discusses this thorny issue and the results are thought provoking.   **47**

12. **Truth and Consequences at Pregnancy High,** Alex Morris, *New York Magazine,* May 18, 2009

The rate of unmarried teen *parenting* in the United States is rising, after a decade of decline. Approximately 60 percent of *adolescent* moms drop out of *school* and 64 percent live in a *culture* of poverty. Most have no *health* care, eat junk food, and live dangerously during *pregnancy.* Response to an online survey showed that 20 percent of girls in the United States want to become teen moms. This article describes the negative outcomes for these *women.*   **49**

13. **Baby Survival Guide: 7 Truths That'll Keep You Sane,** Maura Rhodes,
Parenting.com, December/January 2009

Raising an infant can be highly stressful. This article presents seven truths about rearing babies that, if followed, can *help parents stay sane* and *benefit the babies* they are raising.   **54**

The concepts in bold italics are developed in the article. For further expansion, please refer to the Topic Guide.

UNIT 3
Family Relationships

Unit Overview   56

Part A. Marriage and Other Committed Relationships

14. **Contributing to the Debate over Same-Sex Marriage,** Gwendolyn Puryear Keita, *Monitor on Psychology,* April 2009, Vol. 40, No. 4
Dr. Gwendolyn Puryear Keita, APA Executive Director for the Public Interest, provides the position of the American Psychological Association regarding the major impact of stigma on well-being, the **benefits of marriage,** and the **lack of difference between lesbian and gay parents and heterosexual parents.**   58

15. **Can Marriage Be Saved?,** Frank Furstenberg, *Dissent,* Summer 2005
The author assures his readers that the institution of **marriage** is not in trouble. He argues that although there are other issues that affect all marriages, the focus should be on resources, as the often cited unhealthy marriage and family trends occur only among the most socially disadvantaged.   60

16. **The Polygamists,** Scott Anderson, *National Geographic,* February 2010, Vol. 217, No. 2
This intimate look inside a fundamentalist **polygamist community** describes attitudes, standards, and beliefs related to plural marriage from the insiders' perspective of members of the community.   64

Part B. Relationships between Parents and Children

17. **Good Parents, Bad Results,** Nancy Shute, *U.S. News & World Report,* June 23, 2008
Parents often struggle to provide needed **structure for their children.** This article presents **eight common mistakes** made by parents as they rear their children.   69

18. **Do We Need a Law to Prohibit Spanking?,** Murray Straus, *Family Focus,* June 2007
A substantial body of evidence documents the **harmful effects of spanking,** yet few recognize this. Therefore, Straus argues for a law to prohibit spanking.   73

19. **Children of Lesbian and Gay Parents: Psychology, Law and Policy,** Charlotte J. Patterson, *American Psychologist,* November 2009
Does **parental sexual orientation** affect **child development?** After years of research, little difference in children has been found between parents living in a same-sex and those living in an opposite-sex relationship. This article argues that sexual orientation should not be used as a sole or even significant criterion for determining child custody.   75

20. **Minding the Kids,** Meg Caddoux Hirschberg, *Inc.,* March 2010
Running one's own business can be challenging and time consuming. This article discusses the challenges of **rearing young children** while also **establishing and maintaining a family business.** Children are often more aware of what is going on than parents know, but parents need to know that their children's awareness may be misinformed and inaccurate.   79

21. **Mother, Damnedest,** Terri Apter, *Psychology Today,* January/February 2010
Living with a difficult mother can be trying and leave lasting scars. This article addresses the question, 'What are your obligations to a parent who is smothering or **abusive?**' Suggestions for ways of dealing with **dominating parents** are provided.   81

The concepts in bold italics are developed in the article. For further expansion, please refer to the Topic Guide.

Part C. Other Family Relationships

22. **The Forgotten Siblings,** Sally Young, *Australian & New Zealand Journal of Family Therapy,* 2007

    In studying families, we often lose sight of **siblings** and aspects of siblinghood (including **sibling rivalry** as well as **sibling loyalty**). Yet siblings maintain a powerful influence on each other that extends throughout life, even if physical contact is broken off.   **85**

23. **Four Myths about Older Adults in America's Immigrant Families,** Judith Treas, *Generations,* Vol. XXXII, No. 4, 2009

    Many assumptions are held regarding the lives of **older adults** in America's **immigrant families.** This article addresses four myths held about older adults in such families and **counter these myths with fact.**   **92**

UNIT 4
Challenges and Opportunities

Unit Overview   **96**

Part A. Abuse and Neglect

24. **Recognizing Domestic Partner Abuse,** *Harvard Women's Health Watch,* September 2006

    This brief article provides a concise description of the **risk factors for domestic partner abuse,** as well as suggestions for **how to help** someone whom you suspect is in an abusive relationship.   **99**

25. **Domestic Abuse Myths,** Raina Kelley, *Newsweek Web Exclusive,* March 9, 2009

    Even when it involves rich and privileged celebrities, incidents of **domestic violence** are accompanied by myths and mistaken assumptions about choices both parties make. Domestic violence is, in fact, underlain by elements of **power, control, and domination.**   **101**

26. **The Fatal Distraction: Forgetting a Child in the Backseat of a Car Is a Horrifying Mistake. Is It a Crime?,** Gene Weingarten, *The Washington Post,* April 3, 2009

    Each year, **children die** as a result of being left in an overheated vehicle. Is this **neglect** and should these **parents be punished**? Gene Weingarten writes about this horrific occurrence and asks readers to consider whether it could happen to them.   **103**

Part B. Substance Abuse

27. **Children of Alcoholics,** Cara E. Rice et al., *The Prevention Researcher,* November 2006

    Children of alcoholic parents have a variety of risk factors for developing substance abuse as well as other negative outcomes. This article identifies protective factors that may reduce the risks children of alcoholic parents face.   **105**

28. **Impact of Family Recovery and Pre-Teens and Adolescents,** Virginia Lewis and Lois Allen-Byrd, *The Prevention Researcher,* November 2006

    Beginning with the introduction to the concept of **family recovery,** this article explores its stages and three distinct types of **alcoholic families** in recovery. The primary focus, however, is the impact family recovery has on pre-teens and adolescents who are the "forgotten" family members in this radical and traumatic long-term process.   **110**

The concepts in bold italics are developed in the article. For further expansion, please refer to the Topic Guide.

Part C.   Infidelity

29. Love but Don't Touch, Mark Teich, *Psychology Today,* March/April 2006

Often seen as less serious than a **sexual affair,** when one's partner has an **emotional affair** it can have a devastating effect on a **couple's relationship.** Emotional affairs may not even involve sexual contact and may not be seen as *"cheating"* by the party who is involved in the affair. Yet, the recovery from the **deceit and violation of trust** that is an integral element of an emotional affair can be just as challenging.   **115**

30. Is This Man Cheating on His Wife?, Alexandra Alter, *The Wall Street Journal Online,* August 10, 2007

Second Life, a 3D virtual world, allows "residents," using avatars (visual representations of themselves), to interact and build relationships with other residents. This article depicts what happens when one spouse *"cheats" on his wife* in his second life while he neglects his wife in real life.   **119**

Part D.   Economic Concerns

31. The Opt-Out Myth, E. J. Graff, *Columbia Journalism Revue,* March/April 2007

E.J. Graff explains why the media reports that upper-class women are opting out of the labor market to raise children in substantial numbers are myths. The proportion of women, even mothers, in the labor force is increasing, not decreasing. The consequences and policy implications of the truth are immense.   **122**

32. Making Time for Family Time, Tori DeAngelis, *Monitor on Psychology,* January 2008

As they **start their lives** together, **couples** must confront issues associated with bringing their **home and work lives** together. DeAngelis provides a list of helpful recommendations from early-career experts on how to deal with the complexities of this topic.   **126**

33. Mother (and Father), Can You Spare a Dime?, Dan Kadlec, *Money,* January 2009

Economic changes are taking place that put **middle-aged parents** in a bind. Should they **lend money** to their **adult children?** This article addresses issues related to lending to one's adult children and ways in which parents can avoid problems if they do lend.   **128**

34. Rise of the Desperate House Husband, Gaby Hinsliff, *New Statesman,* December 21, 2009—January 3, 2010

Increasingly, changes in the economy have resulted in a **reversal of roles for some couples,** in which the husband becomes the primary caregiver while the wife is the family breadwinner. Yet, these changes, which mirror those that occurred during the Great Depression, may not be permanent.   **130**

35. Trust and Betrayal in the Golden Years, Kyle G. Brown, *The Globe and Mail,* January 27, 2007

Kyle Brown points out the problems confronted by many older persons when they turn over the control of their finances and property to their children. **Exploitation and abuse of elders by their children** has become more widespread than ever imagined. Moreover, there are numerous and often insurmountable difficulties confronted by older persons attempting to resolve these problems.   **132**

Part E.   Illness and Caregiving in the Family

36. Dealing *Day-to-Day* with Diabetes: A Whole Family Experience, Karen Giles-Smith, *Today's Dietitian,* November 2007

Chronic illnesses like diabetes are a "never-ending" story with which **families must learn to cope. Parents may have more difficulty** with the necessary changes that must be made, but families can successfully adjust and **thrive in the face of ongoing care.**   **134**

The concepts in bold italics are developed in the article. For further expansion, please refer to the Topic Guide.

37. The Positives of Caregiving: Mothers' Experiences Caregiving for a Child with Autism, Michael K. Corman, *Families in Society: The Journal of Contemporary Social Services,* Vol. 90, No. 4, 2009

Although much research on autism focuses on stress and coping, the study reported in this article addresses *resilience exhibited by mothers providing care* to an autistic child. Mothers identify experiences that are appraised in a positive, even joyous, light. Practical implications are included. **138**

Part F. Death and the Family

38. Bereavement after Caregiving, Richard Schulz, Randy Herbert, and Kathrin Boerner, *Geriatrics,* January 2008

Approximately 20 percent of *bereaved caregivers* will experience a number of psychiatric symptoms. The authors identify prebereavement *risk factors* and *preventive strategies* as well as *diagnostic and treatment strategies* that can be implemented post-loss. **146**

39. Love, Loss—and Love, Karen Springen, *Newsweek,* December 3, 2007

The *death of a child* is one of the most painful losses, possibly the most painful, that can occur to an adult. Life is never "normal" again—or at least the normal that parents knew before. *Parents struggle with the reality of their loss,* dealing with a myriad of emotions and questioning whether they should try again. Yet, it is possible for *parents to reconcile themselves to their loss* and to, again, welcome a child into their lives. **149**

40. A Family Undertaking, Holly Stevens, *Christian Century,* October 6, 2009

Home funerals, a common occurrence in the long past, provide families with one last opportunity to *provide care to a loved one.* Providing an opportunity for *families to be creative* in how they honor their loved one; family members often describe these as healing. **150**

Part G. War, the Stress of Separation

41. Stressors Afflicting Families during Military Deployment, Gina M. Di Nola, *Military Medicine,* May 2008, Vol. 173, Issue 5

This article discusses factors that affect U.S. *military families* during the time that a *parent is deployed.* The experience is highly *stressful for families,* and Family Readiness Groups (FRG), which provide a *variety of services* to the families, are described. **152**

42. Children of the Wars, Lawrence Hardy, *American School Board Journal,* January 2008

When *parents are on active duty, children face tremendous stress* and potentially overwhelming fear. Will their parent come back? With repeated deployments, children re-experience these fears. Adults can and should provide *comfort and support* for them, and this article describes ways in which this can be done. **155**

Part H. Divorce and Remarriage

43. A Divided House, Mark Teich, *Psychology Today,* May/June 2007

An unfortunate and painful result of a *divorce* may be one parent attempting (and sometimes succeeding) to turn the children against the other parent. This article depicts the effects of this *alienation of a child's affection* and presents ways in which parents might try to repair the break. **158**

44. Civil Wars, Christopher Munsey, *Monitor on Psychology,* November 2007

The divorce, itself, isn't necessarily the problem for children whose parents *divorce.* This article describes how psychologists, working as *parenting coordinators,* help parents to work through the details of their divorce while also managing their emotions, which makes the experience easier for the *children.* **162**

45. Estranged Spouses Increasingly Waiting out Downturn to Divorce, Donna St. George, *Washington Post,* Monday, March 22, 2010

Divorce is often difficult, and the *current economy* makes it doubly so. Estranged couples now find themselves trapped in houses they are unable to sell, protecting their financial interests as they attempt to co-exist with their *estranged, even ex-spouse.* **164**

The concepts in bold italics are developed in the article. For further expansion, please refer to the Topic Guide.

UNIT 5
Families, Now and into the Future

Unit Overview   **166**

46. Get a Closer Look, Ira Wolfman, *Writing,* November/December 2005

Family interviews can add to one's *understanding of family members* and can be fun and informative, but they take some preparation and planning. This article describes how one might go about doing such an interview.   **168**

47. The Joy of Rituals, Dawn Marie Barhyte, *Vibrant Life,* November/December 2006

Families are strengthened through rituals and this article presents a variety of *strategies for strengthening families* through rituals.   **170**

48. Sustaining Resilient Families for Children in Primary Grades, Janice Patterson and Lynn Kirkland, *Childhood Education,* Fall 2007

Resilient families share certain characteristics. This article catalogues characteristics of resilient families; makes suggestions for ways of *strengthening families;* and discusses the importance of *family traditions and routines,* the value of children's literature for *family communication,* and the role of *community in the family.*   **172**

49. Where Is Marriage Going?, Anthony Layng, *USA Today,* January 2009

Expectations about *"traditional" marriage* are tied to a surprisingly recent, and culturally specific, version of marriage. This article discusses the *evolution of marriage* and suggests that marriage will continue to change and adapt to the demands of current society.   **178**

Test-Your-Knowledge Form   **180**
Article Rating Form   **181**

The concepts in bold italics are developed in the article. For further expansion, please refer to the Topic Guide.

Correlation Guide

The *Annual Editions* series provides students with convenient, inexpensive access to current, carefully selected articles from the public press. **Annual Editions: The Family 11/12** is an easy-to-use reader that presents articles on important topics such as *family composition, love and sex, family stressors,* and many more. For more information on *Annual Editions* and other *McGraw-Hill Contemporary Learning Series* titles, visit www.mhhe.com/cls.

This convenient guide matches the units in **Annual Editions: The Family 11/12** with the corresponding chapters in three of our best-selling McGraw-Hill Family textbooks by DeGenova et al., Ferguson, and Cherlin.

Annual Editions: The Family 11/12	Intimate Relationships, Marriages, and Families, 8/e by DeGenova et al.	Shifting the Center: Understanding Contemporary Families, 4/e by Ferguson	Public and Private Families: An Introduction, 6/e by Cherlin
Unit 1: Evolving Perspectives on the Family	**Chapter 1:** Intimate Relationships, Marriages, and Families in the Twenty-First Century **Chapter 2:** Family Backgrounds and How They Influence Us **Chapter 9:** Work, Family Roles, and Material Resources	**Chapter 1:** Introduction to the Study of Families **Chapter 2:** Historical Changes and Family Variations **Chapter 3:** Courtship, Dating, and Power **Chapter 4:** Marriage, Cohabitation, and Partnership **Chapter 5:** Motherhood and Fatherhood **Chapter 10:** Families, Work, and Carework	**Chapter 1:** Public and Private Families **Chapter 2:** The History of the Family **Chapter 3:** Gender and Families **Chapter 4:** Social Class and Families **Chapter 6:** Sexualities **Chapter 7:** Cohabitation and Marriage
Unit 2: Exploring and Establishing Relationships	**Chapter 1:** Intimate Relationships, Marriages, and Families in the Twenty-First Century **Chapter 5:** Attracting and Dating **Chapter 6:** Love and Mate Selection **Chapter 7:** Qualities of a Successful Marriage	**Chapter 3:** Courtship, Dating, and Power **Chapter 4:** Marriage, Cohabitation, and Partnership	**Chapter 3:** Gender and Families **Chapter 6:** Sexualities **Chapter 7:** Cohabitation and Marriage
Unit 3: Family Relationships	**Chapter 1:** Intimate Relationships, Marriages, and Families in the Twenty-First Century **Chapter 2:** Family Backgrounds and How They Influence Us **Chapter 9:** Work, Family Roles, and Material Resources **Chapter 10:** Power, Decision Making, and Communication **Chapter 13:** Parent-Child Relationships **Chapter 14:** Parents and Extended Family Relationships	**Chapter 1:** Introduction to the Study of Families **Chapter 2:** Historical Changes and Family Variations **Chapter 3:** Courtship, Dating, and Power **Chapter 4:** Marriage, Cohabitation, and Partnership **Chapter 6:** Parents and Parenting, Children and Childrearing	**Chapter 1:** Public and Private Families **Chapter 2:** The History of the Family **Chapter 5:** Race, Ethnicity, and Families **Chapter 7:** Cohabitation and Marriage **Chapter 9:** Children and Parents **Chapter 10:** The Elderly and Their Families **Chapter 13:** Remarriage and Stepfamilies
Unit 4: Challenges and Opportunities	**Chapter 10:** Power, Decision Making, and Communication **Chapter 13:** Parent-Child Relationships **Chapter 14:** Parents and Extended Family Relationships **Chapter 15:** Conflict, Family Crises, and Crisis Management **Chapter 16:** The Family and Divorce **Chapter 17:** Coming Together: Remarriage and Stepparenting	**Chapter 1:** Introduction to the Study of Families **Chapter 2:** Historical Changes and Family Variations **Chapter 8:** Divorce, Remarriage, and Blended Families **Chapter 9:** Families and Violence **Chapter 11:** Families and Poverty	**Chapter 3:** Gender and Families **Chapter 10:** The Elderly and Their Families **Chapter 11:** Domestic Violence **Chapter 12:** Divorce **Chapter 13:** Remarriage and Stepfamilies
Unit 5: Families: Now and into the Future	**Chapter 1:** Intimate Relationships, Marriages, and Families in the Twenty-First Century **Chapter 2:** Family Backgrounds and How They Influence Us	**Chapter 1:** Introduction to the Study of Families **Chapter 2:** Historical Changes and Family Variations **Chapter 5:** Motherhood and Fatherhood	**Chapter 1:** Public and Private Families **Chapter 2:** The History of the Family

Topic Guide

This topic guide suggests how the selections in this book relate to the subjects covered in your course. You may want to use the topics listed on these pages to search the Web more easily.

On the following pages a number of websites have been gathered specifically for this book. They are arranged to reflect the units of this Annual Editions reader. You can link to these sites by going to www.mhhe.com/cls

All the articles that relate to each topic are listed below the bold-faced term.

Abuse and neglect

18. Do We Need a Law to Prohibit Spanking?
21. Mother, Damnedest
24. Recognizing Domestic Partner Abuse
25. Domestic Abuse Myths
26. The Fatal Distraction: Forgetting a Child in the Backseat of a Car Is a Horrifying Mistake. Is It a Crime?
35. Trust and Betrayal in the Golden Years

Aging

23. Four Myths about Older Adults in America's Immigrant Families
35. Trust and Betrayal in the Golden Years

Bereavement

38. Bereavement after Caregiving
39. Love, Loss—and Love
40. A Family Undertaking

Biology

5. This Thing Called Love
10. Fats, Carbs and the Science of Conception
11. Not Always "the Happiest Time"
27. Children of Alcoholics

Caregiving

36. Dealing *Day-to-Day with* Diabetes: A Whole Family Experience
37. The Positives of Caregiving: Mothers' Experiences Caregiving for a Child with Autism
38. Bereavement after Caregiving

Childcare/Child rearing

2. The Significant Dynamic Relationship between Globalization and Families
20. Minding the Kids
42. Children of the Wars

Children

3. Interracial Families
4. Family Partnerships
15. Can Marriage Be Saved?
19. Children of Lesbian and Gay Parents
20. Minding the Kids
22. The Forgotten Siblings
27. Children of Alcoholics
28. Impact of Family Recovery and Pre-Teens and Adolescents
32. Making Time for Family Time
48. Sustaining Resilient Families for Children in Primary Grades

Communication

9. On-Again, Off-Again
29. Love but Don't Touch
44. Civil Wars
47. The Joy of Rituals

Dating

7. Against All Odds
8. The Expectations Trap
9. On-Again, Off-Again

Divorce

1. Marriage and Family in the Scandinavian Experience
43. A Divided House
44. Civil Wars
45. Estranged Spouses Increasingly Waiting out Downturn to Divorce

Emotions

5. This Thing Called Love
18. Do We Need a Law to Prohibit Spanking?
38. Bereavement after Caregiving
39. Love, Loss—and Love
47. The Joy of Rituals

Family forms

1. Marriage and Family in the Scandinavian Experience
2. The Significant Dynamic Relationship between Globalization and Families
3. Interracial Families
16. The Polygamists
49. Where Is Marriage Going?

Family interaction

18. Do We Need a Law to Prohibit Spanking?
20. Minding the Kids
21. Mother, Damnedest
41. Stressors Afflicting Families during Military Deployment
43. A Divided House
46. Get a Closer Look
47. The Joy of Rituals
48. Sustaining Resilient Families for Children in Primary Grades

Finances, family

1. Marriage and Family in the Scandinavian Experience
2. The Significant Dynamic Relationship between Globalization and Families
15. Can Marriage Be Saved?
31. The Opt-Out Myth
32. Making Time for Family Time
33. Mother (and Father), Can You Spare A Dime?
34. Rise of the Desperate House Husband
35. Trust and Betrayal in the Golden Years

Gay marriage

1. Marriage and Family in the Scandinavian Experience
14. Contributing to the Debate over Same-Sex Marriage
19. Children of Lesbian and Gay Parents

Gender roles

1. Marriage and Family in the Scandinavian Experience
2. The Significant Dynamic Relationship between Globalization and Families

Government roles

1. Marriage and Family in the Scandinavian Experience
16. The Polygamists
41. Stressors Afflicting Families during Military Deployment

Health

10. Fats, Carbs and the Science of Conception
11. Not Always "the Happiest Time"
12. Truth and Consequences at Pregnancy High
27. Children of Alcoholics
36. Dealing *Day-to-Day with* Diabetes: A Whole Family Experience
37. The Positives of Caregiving: Mothers' Experiences Caregiving for a Child with Autism
38. Bereavement after Caregiving

Infidelity

29. Love but Don't Touch
30. Is This Man Cheating on His Wife?

Intimacy

5. This Thing Called Love
6. 24 Things Love and Sex Experts Are Dying to Tell You
9. On-Again, Off-Again

Laws

1. Marriage and Family in the Scandinavian Experience
16. The Polygamists
18. Do We Need a Law Banning Spanking?
19. Children of Lesbian and Gay Parents
44. Civil Wars
45. Estranged Spouses Increasingly Waiting out Downturn to Divorce

Love

6. 24 Things Love and Sex Experts Are Dying to Tell You
7. Against All Odds
8. The Expectations Trap
9. On-Again, Off-Again

Marriage

1. Marriage and Family in the Scandinavian Experience
2. The Significant Dynamic Relationship between Globalization and Families
3. Interracial Families
14. Contributing to the Debate over Same-Sex Marriage
15. Can Marriage Be Saved?
16. The Polygamists
43. A Divided House
44. Civil Wars

Mate selection

3. Interracial Families
7. Against All Odds
9. On-Again, Off-Again

Mental health

5. This Thing Called Love
17. Good Parents, Bad Results
18. Do We Need a Law to Prohibit Spanking?
21. Mother, Damnedest
24. Recognizing Domestic Partner Abuse
25. Domestic Abuse Myths
27. Children of Alcoholics
28. Impact of Family Recovery and Pre-Teens and Adolescents
30. Is This Man Cheating on His Wife?
38. Bereavement after Caregiving
39. Love, Loss—and Love
41. Stressors Afflicting Families during Military Deployment
48. Sustaining Resilient Families for Children in Primary Grades

Military families

41. Stressors Afflicting Families during Military Deployment
42. Children of the Wars

Parent–adult child relationship

21. Mother, Damnedest
27. Children of Alcoholics
33. Mother (and Father), Can You Spare a Dime?

Parenting

17. Good Parents, Bad Results
18. Do We Need a Law to Prohibit Spanking?
19. Children of Lesbian and Gay Parents
20. Minding the Kids
22. The Forgotten Siblings
26. The Fatal Distraction: Forgetting a Child in the Backseat of a Car Is a Horrifying Mistake. Is It a Crime?
37. The Positives of Caregiving: Mothers' Experiences Caregiving for a Child with Autism
48. Sustaining Resilient Families for Children in Primary Grades

Pregnancy

10. Fats, Carbs and the Science of Conception
11. Not Always "the Happiest Time"

Race and culture

1. Marriage and Family in the Scandinavian Experience
2. The Significant Dynamic Relationship between Globalization and Families
3. Interracial Families
4. Family Partnerships

Reproduction

10. Fats, Carbs and the Science of Conception
11. Not Always "the Happiest Time"
12. Truth and Consequences at Pregnancy High

Resilience

18. Do We Need a Law to Prohibit Spanking?
36. Dealing *Day-to-Day with* Diabetes: A Whole Family Experience
37. The Positives of Caregiving: Mothers' Experiences Caregiving for a Child with Autism
39. Love, Loss—and Love
40. A Family Undertaking
42. Children of the Wars
48. Sustaining Resilient Families for Children in Primary Grades

School/Family

4. Family Partnerships
42. Children of the Wars

Sex

5. This Thing Called Love
6. 24 Things Love and Sex Experts Are Dying to Tell You

Siblings

22. The Forgotten Siblings

Social change

1. Marriage and Family in the Scandinavian Experience
2. The Significant Dynamic Relationship between Globalization and Families
3. Interracial Families
14. Contributing to the Debate over Same-Sex Marriage
15. Can Marriage Be Saved?
19. Children of Lesbian and Gay Parents
34. Rise of the Desperate House Husband
49. Where Is Marriage Going?

Spanking

17. Good Parents, Bad Results
18. Do We Need a Law Banning Spanking?

Spirituality in the family

47. The Joy of Rituals

Stress

24. Recognizing Domestic Partner Abuse
25. Domestic Abuse Myths
34. Rise of the Desperate House Husband
35. Trust and Betrayal in the Golden Years
36. Dealing *Day-to-Day with* Diabetes: A Whole Family Experience
39. Love, Loss—and Love
41. Stressors Afflicting Families during Military Deployment
42. Children of the Wars

Substance abuse

27. Children of Alcoholics
28. Impact of Family Recovery and Pre-Teens and Adolescents

Support

18. Do We Need a Law to Prohibit Spanking?
28. Impact of Family Recovery and Pre-Teens and Adolescents
36. Dealing *Day-to-Day with* Diabetes: A Whole Family Experience

41. Stressors Afflicting Families during Military Deployment
42. Children of the Wars
47. The Joy of Rituals

Technology

30. Is This Man Cheating on His Wife?

Values

1. Marriage and Family in the Scandinavian Experience
18. Do We Need a Law to Prohibit Spanking?
47. The Joy of Rituals
49. Sustaining Resilient Families for Children in Primary Grades

Work and family

1. Marriage and Family in the Scandinavian Experience
2. The Significant Dynamic Relationship between Globalization and Families
15. Can Marriage Be Saved?
31. The Opt-Out Myth
32. Making Time for Family Time
34. Rise of the Desperate House Husband

Internet References

The following Internet sites have been selected to support the articles found in this reader. These sites were available at the time of publication. However, because websites often change their structure and content, the information listed may no longer be available. We invite you to visit www.mhhe.com/cls for easy access to these sites.

Annual Editions: The Family 11/12

General Sources

AARP (American Association of Retired Persons)
www.aarp.org

This major advocacy group for older people includes among its many resources suggested readings and Internet links to organizations that deal with social issues that may affect people and their families as they age.

Encyclopedia Britannica
www.britannica.com

This huge "Britannica Internet Guide" leads to a cornucopia of informational sites and reference sources on such topics as family structure, the family cycle, forms of family organization, and other social issues.

Planned Parenthood
www.plannedparenthood.org

Visit this well-known organization's home page for links to information on the various kinds of contraceptives (including outercourse and abstinence) and to discussions of other topics related to sexual and reproductive health.

Social Science Information Gateway
http://sosig.esrc.bris.ac.uk

This is an online catalog of Internet resources relevant to social science education and research. Sites are selected and described by a librarian or subject specialist.

Sympatico: HealthyWay: Health Links
www1.sympatico.ca/Contents/health

This Canadian site, which is meant for consumers, will lead you to many links that are related to sexual orientation. *Sympatico* also addresses aspects of human sexuality as well as reproductive health over the life span.

UNIT 1: Evolving Perspectives on the Family

American Studies Web
www1.georgetown.edu/departments/american_studies

This site provides links to a wealth of resources on the Internet related to American studies, from gender to race and ethnicity to demography and population studies.

Anthropology Resources Page
www.usd.edu/anth

Many cultural topics can be accessed from this site from the University of South Dakota. Click on the links to find comparisons of values and lifestyles among the world's peoples.

UNIT 2: Exploring and Establishing Relationships

Bonobo Sex and Society
http://songweaver.com/info/bonobos.html

This site, accessed through Carnegie Mellon University, contains an article explaining how a primate's behavior challenges traditional assumptions about male supremacy in human evolution. This interesting site is guaranteed to generate much spirited debate.

Go Ask Alice!
www.goaskalice.columbia.edu/index.html

This interactive site of the Columbia University Health Services provides discussion and insight into a number of personal issues of interest to college-age people and those younger and older.

The Kinsey Institute for Research in Sex, Gender, and Reproduction
www.indiana.edu/~kinsey

The purpose of this Kinsey Institute website is to support interdisciplinary research in the study of human sexuality.

Mysteries of Odor in Human Sexuality
www.pheromones.com

This is a commercial site with the goal of selling a book by James Kohl. Look here to find topics of interest to nonscientists about pheromones. Check out the diagram of "Mammalian Olfactory-Genetic-Neuronal-Hormonal-Behavioral Reciprocity and Human Sexuality" for a sense of the myriad biological influences that play a part in sexual behavior.

The Society for the Scientific Study of Sexuality
www.sexscience.org

The Society for the Scientific Study of Sexuality is an international organization dedicated to the advancement of knowledge about sexuality.

UNIT 3: Family Relationships

Child Welfare League of America
www.cwla.org

The CWLA is the largest U.S. organization devoted entirely to the well-being of vulnerable children and their families. This site provides links to information about such issues as teaching morality and values.

Internet References

Coalition for Marriage, Family, and Couples Education
www.smartmarriages.com

CMFCE is dedicated to bringing information about and directories of skill-based marriage education courses to the public. It hopes to lower the rate of family breakdown through couple-empowering preventive education.

The National Academy for Child Development
www.nacd.org

The NACD, dedicated to helping children and adults reach their full potential, presents links to various programs, research, and resources into a variety of family topics.

National Council on Family Relations
www.ncfr.com

This NCFR home page leads to valuable links to articles, research, and other resources on issues in family relations, such as stepfamilies, couples, and children of divorce.

Positive Parenting
www.positiveparenting.com

Positive Parenting is an organization dedicated to providing resources and information to make parenting rewarding, effective, and fun.

SocioSite
www.pscw.uva.nl/sociosite/TOPICS/Women.html

Open this site to gain insights into a number of issues that affect family relationships. It provides wide-ranging issues of women and men, of family and children, and more.

UNIT 4: Challenges and Opportunities

Alzheimer's Association
www.alz.org

The Alzheimer's Association, dedicated to the prevention, cure, and treatment of Alzheimer's and related disorders, provides support to afflicted patients and their families.

Caregiver's Handbook
www.acsu.buffalo.edu/~drstall/hndbk0.html

This site is an online handbook for caregivers. Topics include medical aspects and liabilities of caregiving.

National Crime Prevention Council
www.ncpc.org

NCPC's mission is to enable people to create safer and more caring communities by addressing the causes of crime and violence and reducing the opportunities for crime to occur.

Widow Net
www.widownet.org

Widow Net is an information and self-help resource for and by widows and widowers. The information is helpful to people of all ages, religious backgrounds, and sexual orientation who have experienced a loss.

UNIT 5: Families, Now and into the Future

National Institute on Aging
www.nih.gov/nia

The NIA presents this home page that will take you to a variety of resources on health and lifestyle issues that are of interest to people as they grow older.

UNIT 1

Evolving Perspectives on the Family

Unit Selections

1. **Marriage and Family in the Scandinavian Experience,** David Popenoe
2. **The Significant Dynamic Relationship between Globalization and Families,** Behira Sherif Trask
3. **Interracial Families,** Carol Mithers
4. **Family Partnerships,** JoBeth Allen

Key Points to Consider

- How do marriages and families compare in Sweden and the United States? Do you see trends they share in common? What is the effect of globalization on families?

- What are your views on the changing nature of the American family? What are your thoughts on interracial families?

- What are your expectations for the family as an institution? How do personally held views of family influence policy? What might be the effect of this?

- How can schools and families collaborate to support student learning?

Student Website

www.mhhe.com/cls

Internet References

American Studies Web
   www1.georgetown.edu/departments/american_studies/
Anthropology Resources Page
   www.usd.edu/anth/

Digital Vision

Our image of what family is and what it should be is a powerful combination of personal experience, family forms we encounter or observe, and attitudes we hold. Once formed, this image informs decision making and interpersonal interaction throughout our lives and has far-reaching effects: On an intimate level, it influences individual and family development as well as relationships both inside and outside the family; on a broader level, it affects legislation as well as social policy and programming. In many ways, this image can be positive. It can act to clarify our thinking and facilitate interaction with like-minded individuals. It can also be negative, because it can narrow our thinking and limit our ability to see that other ways of carrying out the functions of family have value. Their very differentness can make them seem "bad." In this case, interaction with others can be impeded because of contrasting views. This unit is intended to meet several goals with regard to perspectives on the family: (1) to sensitize the reader to sources of beliefs about the "shoulds" of the family—what the family should be and the ways in which family roles should be carried out, (2) to show how different views of the family can influence attitudes toward community responsibility and family policy, and (3) to show how views that dominate one's culture can influence awareness of ways of structuring family life. In the first reading, "Marriage and Family in the Scandinavian Experience," David Popenoe explores the differences and similarities in marriage and family experiences in the United States and Sweden. These comparisons provide

© Blend Images/Alamy

information that may surprise the reader. Following this reading, Bahira Serif Trask's article on "The Significant Dynamic Relationship between Globalization and Families" addresses these and other aspects of the family in terms of the effect of globalization on the form and function of families. The nature of "Interracial Families" and children of these families is explored in the next reading.

Collaboration between families and the schools is the focus of the final reading in this unit, "Family Partnerships."

Marriage and Family in the Scandinavian Experience

DAVID POPENOE

Many Americans have long had a ready answer to America's family problems: We should become more like Scandinavia. Whether the issues are work-family, teen sex, child poverty, or marital break-up, a range of Scandinavian family and welfare policies is commonly put forth with the assertion that, if only these could be instituted in America, family life in our nation would be improved significantly. But what can we in the United States really learn from Scandinavia? The Scandinavian nations are so small and demographically homogeneous that the idea of simply transferring their social policies to this country must be viewed as problematic. Sweden, for example, the largest Scandinavian nation and the one featured in this essay, has only 9 million people compared to our population of nearly 300 million. And how well have these policies actually worked in Scandinavia? As this essay will make clear, some of the Scandinavian family policies have, indeed, been quite successful on their own home ground. Yet aside from the potential non-transferability of these policies, by focusing so much attention on them we may be overlooking some even more important aspects of the Scandinavian family experience.

Sweden and the United States

It is now well known that there has been a weakening of marriage and the nuclear family in advanced, industrialized societies, especially since the 1960s. What is not well known is the surprising fact that the two nations that lead in this weakening are Sweden and the United States—two nations that stand at almost opposite extremes in terms of their socioeconomic systems. Let us look at one telling statistical measure. Defining the nuclear family as a mother and father living together with their own biological children, a good measure of nuclear familism in a society is the percentage of children under the age of 18 who live with both biological parents. This percentage for the United States is 63, the lowest among Western industrialized nations. The second from lowest is Sweden, at 73!

How is this possible? At the one socioeconomic extreme, Sweden has the strongest public sector, the highest taxes, and is the most secular. At the other, the United States has the weakest public sector, the lowest taxes, and is the most religious. Could these fundamental factors be mostly irrelevant to family change? And if so, what key factors are involved? As we shall see, the answer to this intellectual puzzle is to be found largely in the realm of a postmodern trend shared by both nations. But first we need to consider other family differences between the two nations. Two key differences stand out: in the United States more people marry, but they also divorce in large numbers; in Sweden, fewer people marry, but the Swedish divorce rate is a little lower than in the United States.

Here is the recent statistical record, beginning with Sweden. The Swedish marriage rate by the late 1990s was *one of the lowest in the world;* indeed, one of the lowest marriage rates ever recorded and considerably lower than the rates of other Western European nations. (Number of marriages per 1000 unmarried women in 2002—Sweden: 17.5; U.S.: 43.4. Unless otherwise noted, all statistics in this essay were gathered or computed by the National Marriage Project from official statistical sources in each nation.) If this rate holds, only about 60 percent of Swedish women today will "ever marry," compared to over 85 percent in the United States. This is a quite recent development. Not so long ago the two nations were quite similar: For the generation marrying in the 1950s, the figure for Sweden was 91 percent and for the United States 95 percent.

Sweden's low marriage rate does not mean that Swedes are living alone; rather, they are living together outside of marriage—another area in which Sweden has been in the vanguard. In fact, Sweden leads the Western nations in the degree to which nonmarital cohabitation has replaced marriage. The United States, on the other hand, has a lower rate of nonmarital cohabitation than all but the Catholic nations of southern Europe. About 28 percent of all couples in Sweden are cohabiting, versus 8 percent of all American couples. In Sweden, virtually all couples live together before marriage, compared to around two-thirds of couples currently in America. Many couples in Sweden don't marry even when they have children. In a recent opinion poll, Swedish young adults were asked whether it was OK to cohabit even after having children; 89 percent of women and 86 percent of men answered "yes."

Why is the Swedish marriage rate so low relative to other nations? In brief, because religion there is weak, a left-wing political ideology has long been dominant, and almost all governmental incentives for marriage have been removed. First, the religious pressure for marriage in Sweden is all but gone (although of the marriages that do occur, many are for vague religious reasons). Any religious or cultural stigma in Sweden against cohabitation is no longer in evidence; it is regarded as irrelevant to question whether a couple is married or just living together. Second, the political left wing throughout Europe has generally been antagonistic to strong families, based on a combination of feminist concerns about patriarchy and oppression, an antipathy toward a bourgeois social institution with traditional ties to nobility and privilege, and the belief that families have been an impediment to full equality. Finally, unlike in the United States, all government benefits in Sweden are given to individuals irrespective of their intimate relationships or family form. There is no such thing, for example, as spousal benefits in health care. There is also no joint-income taxation for married couples; all income taxation is individual.

Turning to the United States, if Sweden stands out for having the lowest marriage rate, the United States is notable for having the world's highest divorce rate. Given the divorce rates of recent years, the risk of a marriage ending in divorce in the United States is close to 50 percent, compared to a little over 40 percent in Sweden. Why is the American divorce rate so high relative to other nations? Mainly because of our relatively high ethnic, racial and religious diversity, inequality of incomes with a large underclass, and extensive residential mobility, each of which is associated with high divorce rates. Revealingly, if one looks at the divorce rate of the relatively homogeneous and Scandinavian-settled state of Minnesota, it is only slightly higher than that of Sweden. (Number of divorces per 1000 married women in 2002—Sweden: 13.7; Minnesota: 14.7; United States: 18.4.)

Another big divorce risk factor in America is marrying at a young age; the average U.S. ages of first marriage today are 25 for women and 27 for men, versus 31 and 33 in Sweden. As a more consumer-oriented and economically dynamic society, in addition, there is probably something about this nation that promotes a more throw-away attitude toward life. And let us not overlook the dominant influence of Hollywood and pop culture in general, with their emphasis on feel good and forget the consequences.

Of course, if people don't marry, they can't divorce. And that is one reason why, by certain measures, Sweden has a lower divorce rate. But if couples just cohabit they certainly can break up, and that is what Swedish nonmarital couples do in large numbers. It is estimated that the risk of breakup for cohabiting couples in Sweden, even those with children, is several times higher than for married couples. By one indication, in the year 2000 there were two-and-one-half separations or divorces per 100 children among married parents, almost twice that number among unmarried cohabiting parents living with their own biological children, and three times that number among cohabiting couples living with children from a previous relationship. (A recent study found that 50 percent of children born to a cohabiting couple in the United States see their parents' union end by age five, compared to only 15 percent of children born to a married couple. [Wendy D. Manning, Pamela J. Smock, and Debamm Majumdar, "The Relative Stability of Cohabiting and Marital Unions for Children," *Population Research and Policy Review* 23 (2004): 135–159].)

Already one of the highest in Western Europe, the Swedish divorce rate has been growing in recent years, while the U.S. rate has been declining. If we consider this convergence of divorce rates, and count both cohabiting couples and married couples, *the total family breakup rate in the two nations today is actually quite similar.*

So why, in view of the similarity of overall family breakup rates, are more Swedish than American children living with their biological parents? This is especially surprising in view of the fact that the Swedish nonmarital birth percentage is much higher than that of the United States (56 percent in Sweden vs. 35 percent in the U.S.). The main reason is that far more nonmarital births in Sweden, about 90 percent, are actually to biological parents who are living together but have not married, compared to just 40 percent in the United States. The great majority of nonmarital births in the U.S., 60 percent, are to truly single, non-cohabiting mothers. This discrepancy reflects the far higher rate of births in the United States to teenagers, the stage of life at which the father is least likely to remain involved with the mother and child. (Births per 1000 girls ages 15–19 in 2002—United States: 43; Sweden: 5.) The relatively high U.S. teen birthrate, in turn, is commonly accounted for by more teen sexual activity combined with less use of contraceptives. There is also a discrepancy between the two countries in that the United States has about twice Sweden's rate of "unwanted" children.

Having sketched out these noteworthy differences in family structure between the United States and Sweden, together with some causal explanations for the differences, what are some reasonable conclusions that can be drawn from the Scandinavian family experience?

The Decline of Marriage

If a society deinstitutionalizes marriage, as Sweden has done through its tax and benefit policies and the secularization of its culture, marriage will weaken. In addition, because most adults still like to live as couples, human pair-bonding doesn't disappear when this happens. Rather, the institution of marriage is replaced by nonmarital cohabitation—marriage lite. Then, if one institutionalizes nonmarital cohabitation in the laws and government policies, as Sweden has also done, making it the virtual equivalent of marriage, marriage will decline still further.

In the modern world, people are reluctant to make strong commitments if they don't have to; it's easier to hang loose. The problem is that society ends up with adult intimate relationships that are much more fragile. It is, indeed, surprising that Sweden has such a high level of couple breakup, because it is the kind of society—stable, homogeneous, and egalitarian—where one would expect such breakups to be minimal. Yet the high breakup level is testimony to the fragility of modern marriage in which most of the institutional bonds have been stripped away—economic dependence, legal definitions, religious sentiments, and family pressures—leaving marriage and other pair-bonds held together solely by the thin and unstable reed of affection.

The losers in this social trend, of course, are the children. They are highly dependent for their development and success in life on the family in which they are born and raised, and a convincing mass of scientific evidence now exists pointing to the fact that not growing up in an intact nuclear family is one of the most deleterious events that can befall a child. In Sweden, just as in the United States, children from non-intact families—compared to those from intact families—have two to three times the number of serious problems in life. We can only speculate about the extent of psychological damage that future generations will suffer owing to today's family trends. That the very low marriage rate and high level of parental breakup are such non-issues in Sweden, something which few Swedes ever talk about, should be, in my opinion, a cause there for national soul searching.

All that said, however, there are other important conclusions one can draw from the Scandinavian family experience. What most Americans don't realize is that, in a strict comparison, Scandinavia is probably preferable to the United States today as a place to raise young children. In other writings I have suggested that the ideal family environment for raising young children has the following traits: an enduring two-biological parent family that engages regularly in activities together, has developed its own routines, traditions and stories, and provides a great deal of contact time between adults and children. Surrounded by a community that is child friendly and supportive of parents, the family is able to develop a vibrant family subculture that provides a rich legacy of meaning and values for children throughout their lives. Scandinavians certainly fall short on the enduring two-biological-parent part of this ideal (yet even there they are currently ahead of the United States), but on the key ingredients of structured and consistent contact time between parents and their children in a family-friendly environment, they are well ahead of us.

In America today, the achievement of this ideal family environment requires what many parents are coming to consider a Herculean countercultural effort, one that involves trying to work fewer hours and adopting the mantra of "voluntary simplicity" for those who can afford it; turning off the TV set and avoiding popular culture; seeking employment in firms that have family-friendly policies such as flexible working hours; and residing in areas that are better designed for children and where the cost of living is lower. Families in Scandinavia need not be so countercultural to achieve these goals because the traits of the ideal childrearing environment are to a larger degree already built into their societies.

The Scandinavian societies tend to be "soft" or low-key, with much more leisure time and not so much frantic consumerism and economic striving as in the United States. Perhaps one could even say that they practice "involuntary simplicity." The average American would probably find life in Scandinavia rather uncomfortable due to high taxes, strict government regulation, limited consumer choice, smaller dwelling units, social conformity, and a soft work ethic, not to mention possible boredom. There are also growing concerns about the quality of education in Scandinavia. Moreover, the Scandinavian system may ultimately prove to be so counterproductive for economic growth that it becomes unsustainable. At any one time more than 20 percent of working-age Swedes are either on sick leave, unemployed, or have taken early retirement, and the nation has recently sunk to one of the lowest per capita income levels in Western Europe! (Reported in Sweden's leading newspaper, *Dagen's Nyheter,* on August 23, 2004.) But in the meantime, and compared to other modern nations, the system seems particularly good for the rearing of young children.

The Scandinavian childrearing advantage is probably as much cultural as governmental, as much due to the way Scandinavians think about children as to specific welfare state policies (although the two are, of course, interrelated.) Scandinavian culture has always been more child centered than the more individualistic Anglo societies. The emphasis in Scandinavian culture on nature and the outdoor environment, conflict-aversion, and even social conformity happens to be especially child friendly. Children benefit from highly structured, stable, and low-conflict settings. There are in Scandinavia many statues of children and mothers in public parks (in place of war heroes!), and planned housing environments are heavily oriented to pedestrian access and children's play. Scandinavian children even have their own Ombudsmen who represent them officially in the government and monitor children's rights and interests. Interestingly, Minnesota—the most Scandinavian-settled U.S. state—was recently ranked the number one state in the nation for child well-being by the Kids Count Data Book. (Annie E. Casey Foundation, 2004, Baltimore, MD)

Scandinavian Family Policies

The Scandinavian concern for children, sometimes even smacking of "traditional family values," is expressed in some areas that should surprise those Americans who think only of "decadent welfare states." For example, all Swedish married couples with children aged 16 and younger, should they want a divorce, have a six-month waiting period before a divorce becomes final. Most American states make no distinction in their divorce laws between couples with children and those without. In vitro fertilization in Sweden can be performed only if the woman is married or cohabiting in a relationship resembling marriage, and completely anonymous sperm donations are not allowed, whereas the practice of "assisted reproduction" in America goes virtually unregulated. And no Swedish abortion can take place after the 18th week of pregnancy, except under special circumstances and only with permission from the National Board of Health. The laws permitting abortion are much more liberal in the United States. Some of these positions are made possible, of course, by the fact that the Scandinavian societies are more homogeneous, unified, and less rights-oriented than the United States.

Just as in the United States at least up until welfare reform, welfare policies in Scandinavia have not been drawn up with an eye toward encouraging marriage and limiting family breakup, a very serious problem as noted above. There are relatively few economic disincentives to becoming a single parent in Sweden, in fact probably fewer than in any other society in the world. Nevertheless, many Scandinavian welfare-state policies have brought significant benefits to children and to childrearing families. Scandinavian family leave policies, especially, seem highly desirable for young children. Almost all mothers in Sweden, for example, and far more than in the United States, are at home with their infants up until age one—which is the critical year for mother-child connection. They have one year off from their jobs at 80 percent or more of their salary (and an additional six months at reduced salary), with a guarantee of returning to their old jobs or an equivalent when they reenter the labor force. Recently, two months leave has been set aside solely for fathers to take; if they don't take it, the benefit is lost. Because of these family-leave policies very few Swedish infants under the age of one are in day care or other out-of-home child care arrangement, a quite different situation from the United States. In addition, to help defray the expenses of childrearing, all Swedish parents receive a non-means-tested child allowance and there is also a means-tested housing allowance.

Beyond these benefits, Scandinavian mothers and fathers have far more flex-time from their work to home with children during the growing-up years, and most women with young children work just part time. There are certainly fewer full-time, non-working, stay-at-home mothers in Sweden than in the United States, in fact almost none because it is economically prohibitive. But in actual parenting time—although good comparative data are unavailable—Sweden may well be in the lead. The larger number of stay-at-home moms in the United States is off-set by the larger number of full-time working mothers, many of whom return to work during their child's first year. It is of interest to note that many fewer Swedish women have top positions in the private sector than is the case in the United States, and this has long been a bone of contention for American feminists when they look at Sweden. By one recent analysis, only 1.5 percent of senior management positions are filled by women in Sweden, compared to 11 percent in the United States. The amount of time that Swedish mothers devote to child care clearly has affected their ability to rise in the private sector hierarchy of jobs, although this is off-set in some degree by their much stronger status in the public sector where a high percentage of the jobs are located.

As a result of welfare state policies child poverty in Sweden is virtually nonexistent (for the 1990s, 1 percent compared to 15 percent in the United States) and all children are covered by health insurance. These and related factors are doubtless of importance in placing Sweden at the top of the list of the best places in the world to live, surpassed only by Norway according to the Human Development Index prepared by the United Nations Development Program (2004), and based on income, life expectancy and education. The United States ranks well down the list, in eighth place, no doubt due in part to the fact that we have a different population mix than other nations.

Again, the two societies are such polar opposites, at least among Western nations, as we have indicated, that it is a mistake to think that what works in Sweden could necessarily be transplanted to the United States. Up to now, at least, the Scandinavian nations have had that strong sense of "brotherhood" or "sisterhood" that is required for a strong welfare state. The common sentiment has been that the high taxes are going for a good cause, "my fellow Swede." Indeed, the lack of outcry against high taxation in Scandinavia comes as a shock to most visiting Americans. To suggest that this communal spirit and attitude toward government and taxation could ever exist in the United States, with all its diversity and individualism, is to enter the realm of utopian thinking. Thus, it is unclear how many of these family policies could be implemented in the United States, and what their actual effect would be if they were.

This leaves us with a final conclusion from the Scandinavian family experience, a more general one. The fact that family breakdown has occurred so prevalently in both the United States and Scandinavia, two almost opposite socioeconomic systems, suggests that the root cause lies beyond politics and economics and even national culture in an overarching trend of modernity that affects all advanced, industrial societies. Basic to this trend is the growth of a modern form of individualism, the single-minded pursuit of personal autonomy and self-interest, which takes place at the expense of established social institutions such as marriage. It shows up in low marriage and high cohabitation rates in the Scandinavian societies, even though they are relatively communitarian. And it is expressed in high divorce and high solo parenting rates in the United States, despite our nation's relatively religious character.

One paramount family goal for modern societies today, put forward by many experts, is to create the conditions whereby an increasing number of children are able to grow up with their own two married parents. If this is a worthy goal, both Scandinavia and the United States have failed badly, and millions of children have been hurt. If we are to take seriously the record of recent history in these nations, the market economy on its own, no matter how strong, is unlikely to be of much help in achieving this goal. The wealthier we become, the weaker the family. But neither helpful, apparently, are the many governmental policies of the welfare state. They may help to soften the impact of family breakup, but the state appears relatively powerless to contain family decline and often even contributes to it. What we must look for, are ways to curtail the growth of modern individualism. While in Scandinavia the main thrust of such efforts probably should focus on resisting the anti-marriage influences of political ideologies and social policies, in the United States the issue is to find better ways to insulate marriage and the family from the pernicious effects of a self-interested market economy that is tethered increasingly to a coarsening popular culture.

DAVID POPENOE is co-director of the National Marriage Project at Rutgers, The State University of New Jersey. He is author of *War Over the Family, Disturbing the Nest,* and *Private Pleasure, Public Plight* all available from Transaction.

From *Society,* 43(4), May/June 2006, pp. 68–72. Copyright © 2006 by Springer Science and Business Media. Reprinted by permission.

The Significant Dynamic Relationship between Globalization and Families

BAHIRA SHERIF TRASK, PhD

Globalization is associated with profound changes for individuals and families in the United States and abroad. Some of these changes have been highlighted through the recent global economic recession. We are increasingly aware that economic downturns and governmental policies affect everyone's lives, often with unexpected consequences. Furthermore, rapid advances in communication and information technologies are changing the ways in which individuals connect, access information, and interact with each other. The farthest corners of the world now accessible, in ways that most of us were unable to imagine even just several years ago. All of these developments are related to globalization. Due to a number of factors however, in most people's minds, globalization remains primarily associated with economics and politics. In reality, globalization is closely related to both the major and day to day decisions that families make with respect to work issues, gender roles, the raising of children and care of the elderly, and moving and migration.

What Is Globalization?

Even though globalization is a complicated controversial phenomenon, there is some agreement that it refers to an economic and political process, and that it also entails a new form of connecting geographic and cultural distances. Globalization as a concept and a term, entered mainstream discussions in economics and political science from the mid-1990s onwards (Rodrik, 1997). With respect to globalization, of particular interest has been the flow of money and capital between countries, the changing role of governments vis a vis their citizenry, the increased movement and migration of individuals within and between countries, and the growth and expansion of multinational corporations and transnational organizations. However, despite the fact that individuals and families are affected by all of these issues, there has been remarkably little attention focused on the societal effects of globalization. This omission is important because it is specifically families, communities, and social life that are affected by globalization (Baars, Dannefer, Phillipson, & Walker, 2006).

Despite the lack of analyses of the effects of globalization on social life, individuals and families are directly and indirectly affected by globalizing processes all over the world. While family arrangements may vary, depending on place and time, some form of family or kin relationships characterize all societies. As individuals, families, communities, and societies increasingly become integrated into new complex globalized systems, their values, traditions, and relationships change (Parkin & Stone, 2004). Moreover, we often find that different groups of people react very differently to globalization. Globalization transmits new concepts about gender, work citizenship, identity, familial relationships, and women's and children's rights around the globe. In some cases, these concepts empower individuals and their families to change their lives, and in other cases, they are forced into situations that are disadvantageous and destructive. Also, in some places in the world, globalization is perceived as a form of enforced Westernization. The response to the assumption of dominance of Westernization is often nationalistic and fundamentalist. In an effort to preserve "traditional" values and beliefs, people turn back to what they believe are the authentic traditions and beliefs of their societies, sometimes even use violence to enforce their values.

Globalization and Migration

An important part of globalization is the movement of individuals within societies and across national borders. Migration is most commonly associated with seeking new work opportunities, but at times individuals and families migrate due to political and other social reasons. Specifically, international migration has led to a new type of family form, also known as transnational families. Transnational families are characterized by retaining roots in their home societies and simultaneously also creating new ties in their host countries. While proportionally to the world population, actual migration numbers are low (currently approximately 3 percent of the global population is on the move), modern migration has significant social effects. Most individuals migrate as families or in groups, and their residency in the new host society has a significant impact on both their country of origin, as well as the receiving society (Castles & Miller, 2003). For example, immigrants may be highly educated and possess important skills which benefit the receiving society but they also leave behind in their home countries what is commonly referred to as the "brain drain"—not enough highly educated people to take on important jobs that require education and skills, and could potentially improve the conditions in these countries. There are also other types of immigrants. For example, immigrants may be uneducated, poorer members of their home societies who leave and are then willing to take on the lowest level jobs in the host country. In either case, immigrants often send back extensive remittances (money to their relatives back home) that make a significant economic impact on their home societies.

Increasingly, transnational families are also associated with a phenomenon sometimes referred to as transnational mothering (Mortgan & Zippel, 2003). As service jobs in the industrialized world have multiplied, women from poorer countries are leaving their families behind in order to earn an income in other parts of the world. Women who leave their families to work abroad most often do this in order to help their families financially, and specifically to provide a future better life for their children. Many of these migrating women take on jobs associated with domestic labor such as cleaning houses and providing child and elder care. Most often women who migrate do so because there is a lack of economic opportunities in their home societies. However, this fact is often overlooked in political and academic discussions and analyses. Instead, because migrating women so often leave their children behind in their home countries, they are criticized and referred to as "negligent" or "uncaring" mothers by individuals in their host and home societies. Nevertheless, these women take on migration and its accompanying life styles and challenges and adapt their mothering styles with the hope of one day bettering the lives of their children. They usually make arrangements with their husbands (if there is a husband in the picture) and extended families to take care of their children while they are abroad. The growing phenomenon of transnational mothering illustrates that globalization can have significant impacts on family life that are not easily understood from a superficial perspective.

Globalization and Gender

As the migration example illustrates, globalization has had a profound effect on the lives of women, men, and children. It is worth noting that women as a group have been specifically and significantly impacted by globalizing processes. For example, for women around the world, there are today increasing chances for education, training, and work. In the West, specifically middle class women have seen new opportunities open up with respect to jobs, education, and equal rights over the last fifty years. Interestingly, in less developed countries, there has also been an increasing concern with the status of women. Some governments and international non-profits have set up training programs for poor and rural women in order to advance their lives. While these opportunities have not benefited all women, their very presence indicates that under the correct circumstances, globalizing forces can have positive effects on individuals' lives.

For the majority of women the world over, however, globalization has not necessarily improved their lives. Particularly

in the developing world, but also in parts of the industrialized world, we are increasingly seeing what is termed as the "feminization of the labor force." This term refers to the growing number of women who are working outside of the home in paid employment. Most of the time, these women are working in employment that is more flexible than traditional U.S. 8—5 jobs and in informal types of work that are part time and come without benefits. Both in the U.S. and other countries, this trend has been accompanied by a decrease in the types of jobs that have regularly been held by men—full time jobs with benefits for the whole family (Safa, 2002).

As an increasing number of women take on this type of work, and as more men lose their role as the primary breadwinner, gender roles and relationships are changing. We see this particularly in the United States, Canada, Australia, and Europe, where there has been an increase in new living arrangements such as cohabitation, a rising divorce rate, and out of wedlock births. Moreover, cross-cultural research reveals that as economic bonds in families are changing with an increased number of women working in the paid labor force, the concept of marriage is shifting in response. For example, as women are able to earn their own living, they are less likely to stay in destructive and abusive relationships, or they may choose not to marry at all. These changes have results in a global rise in divorce and an increase in female-headed households. As women's roles are changing, diverse family structures are becoming more common even in places such South East Asia and the Middle East, where cultural beliefs about traditional roles in families have long played a significant role in preserving certain aspects of those societies (Moghadam, 2003).

In a discussion about the changing roles of women and men, is also important to remember that millions of women worldwide do not have the same freedom with respect to making choices about their marriages, working outside of the home, and having control over their money, such as those that are available to middle class Western women. For many women, especially rural and low-income women, working outside of the home in the formal and informal labor force has not bettered their lives. Instead, these women now carry the double burden of working for pay and having to take care of the home, the children, the disabled, and the elderly.

Globalization has also had a serious impact on the roles of men. As a significant number of men have lost their jobs and their primary role as breadwinner/provider, they have had to adjust to new roles in the family. For example, middle class American men today are more likely to be involved with home responsibilities and child care than men in previous generations. However, these types of changes in family life have not necessarily occurred across the world. Instead, in some areas and in some cases, men have reacted with anger over the loss of what they perceive as their basic rights. In fact, there is some evidence that domestic violence rises in those places where men have been out of work for a significant period of time. Since most men the world over are raised to believe that men are to be the primary provider/breadwinner, when they lose that role, they may react in unexpected and at times violent ways. The clash of values that results from globalizing processes that draw women into the paid labor force conflicts with traditional values pertaining to the roles of women and men (Yan & Neal, 2006). Further, many of these conflicts are heightened through the spread of media and Internet images of the lives and rights of women in the West compared to those in other places.

Globalization and Children

While there is quite a bit of research on the relationship between globalization and women's changing roles, we know much less about the relationship between globalization and children. Globalization has produced and spread a popular vision of what childhood is supposed to be like, and what children should do with their time (Kuznesof, 2005). From a Western perspective, children need to be "protected" from harsh surroundings and complex situations, they should "play," and they ought to go to school. However, this concept of children and childhood does not fit neatly with the day to day realities of the lives of children in many parts of the world, raising complicated questions about universal concepts about the lives and rights of children.

Ideas about childhood and what children are like and what they are capable of are determined by the social context and the historical period in society in which they grow up. Historically, we have had very different beliefs about the capabilities of children. For example, during colonial times, children were raised very strictly and most children began learning a work related skill (usually through an apprenticeship) at a very young age (Malkki & Martin, 2003). In part, due to globalization, we have a very different situation today. Western, and specifically, American concepts about children and childhood are spreading to parts of the world where children live under very different conditions. For example, many contemporary children are growing up in war zones, areas ravaged by HIV/AIDS, and/or areas of extreme poverty. Under those conditions, children are unable to go to school and have no access to an easy, carefree childhood. Even here in the U.S., many children grow up in areas that are crime ridden and extremely poor. These conditions do not allow them to have the kind of childhood that is encouraged and promoted by so much of the current child pedagogy literature, raising complicated questions about the universal application of our ideas about children and childhood. What may be appropriate in one context, for example, for white middle class American children, may not be fit in any way the lives of street children in Brazil. While this was also true in the past, in the contemporary context information flows more easily between societies and places. And since the West tends to dominate information flows, we are increasingly setting the standard for what is appropriate—or at least what we feel is appropriate when it comes to children and childhood experiences.

Another complex issue arising out of our globalized context is the disputed topic of children's rights. Children's rights are closely related to debates on human rights, which many feel have been, by far, one of the most important aspects of a growing system of globally shared values (Kaufman, 2002). The concept of human rights encompasses the idea that the world's most vulnerable individuals including minorities, women, children, and the disabled should receive equal protection under the law. This is based on the idea that all people have a shared humanity, irrespective of their nationality. For much of recorded history, children from many societies were not accorded the status of being "fully human" and were allowed to be sold and exchanged as if they were possessions. However, over the course of the last century, this situation changed and culminated in the global adoption in 1989 of the Convention on the Rights of the Child. This convention entails the protection of the largest single group (children) that any legal document with respect to human rights has ever dealt with. By signing on, countries take on a legal obligation to ensure the "best interests of the child" and work towards the survival, development, and protection of their nations' children. According to the Convention, children have certain basic rights that include the right to life, to their own name and identity, to be raised within their own families or cultural groupings, to express their opinions, to be protected from abuse, and to have their privacy protected. Currently, the only two countries in the world that have not signed on to the Convention on the Rights of the Child are the United States and Somalia. Much of the opposition in the U.S. comes from individuals who believe that there are some basic conflicts between the Convention and the Constitution and due to the resistance of some religious and political conservatives. Moreover, certain factions in the U.S. worry that by signing on to an international legal document, the U.S. will be bound to external international control over what are deemed as domestic policies.

Closely related to the issue of children's rights is the complicated topic of child labor. Current statistics indicate that child labor is actually increasing instead of declining. The International Labor Organization (ILO) (2002) estimates that approximately 352 million five- to seventeen-year-olds around the globe work in some form, and that out of this group about two-thirds of young workers are defined as "child laborers." Most of these children work, primarily on family farms, in their families' households, in small manufacturing businesses, and in mining. Some children are also involved with the production of carpets, garments, furniture, textiles, and shoes (French & Wokutch, 2005). Included in the statistics on child labor are a small group of children around the world who live on the street and participate in a wide range of legal or illegal activities or are involved in prostitution.

Globalization and engagement with the Convention on the Rights of the Child has raised awareness about the issue of child labor. Images of children working in sweat shops and hard labor move across the Internet and the media easily and have raised, in particular, concerns in the West about the lives of children in other parts of the world. Even people who would usually not be that concerned with social justice issues have spoken out publicly and led crusades banning "third world labor practices." This has led to international boycotts of certain brands and corporations who supposedly rely on this type of exploitive behavior for the production of their goods. What is rarely understood in these debates is that there is a great deal of controversy about what constitutes child labor, and to what extent enforcing a Western type of childhood would actually benefit these children. Often the children who are engaged in child labor are doing so to support their families and kin groups because there is no other way for them to survive. For example, in certain parts of Africa, many children have lost both of their parents to the HIV/AIDS crisis. The only way for them and their siblings to make any kind of a living is for some members of the family, or even for all of them, to work at whatever employment is available. This is only one example, but it points to the fact that we need to be more sensitive about the contexts in which children live, and we need to allow for some variation in their personal circumstances.

The complexity of child labor disputes is further heightened by the conflicts over what exactly constitutes "work". There are some types of jobs such as working in mines that are clearly harmful to children's health. However, it is unclear if helping on the family farm is really physically and psychologically damaging to a teenager. Critics of universal labor laws argue that if a family's survival depends on children's work, and if they are not being placed in harm's way, it may actually have social and personal benefits to not enforce a uniform approach to child labor. In other words, we should institute some basic laws that ensure the safety of all children, but that with respect to work, certain types of labor should be permitted. Moreover, gender needs to be taken into account in these discussions. Often, depending on cultural context, it is girls who are taken out of school and asked to take over domestic responsibilities such as cooking and child care, while their mothers work outside of the home and their brothers go to school. Statistics on child labor often do not include these employed girls, because their duties are not understood to be "real work." However, it is clearly these girls, life chances that become permanently constrained due to their lack of education. Again, this indicates that we need to think carefully about enforcing universal concepts such as the rights of children and the prohibition of child labor. An approach that universalizes the needs, beliefs, and rights of all children can have unintended detrimental consequences, thus it is imperative that local conditions also be taken into account.

The Continuing Significance of Families

While this article has raised awareness about some of the complex issues that are faced by individuals and families, in a globalized context, it has also highlighted the fact that there is a close relationship between globalization and families. In all parts of the world, individuals, be they children or adults, still make decisions in the context of those that they consider to be family or they have a close, family-like bond to. Families act as a buffer between globalizing forces and the choices and challenges that individuals need to deal with (Edgar, 2004). However, globalization has varying effects and means different things depending on where people live and what their particular social, political, and economic situation is like. Globalization can allow individuals to be exposed to new ideas and resources; however, globalization can also mean that certain groups become poorer or are treated in a way that is not in synch with their particular culture or situation. Moreover, particularly in

non-Western concepts the whole family often functions specifically as an economic unit (Kelly, 2001). Decisions with respect to who works, what they do, and if they work near their home or in a far away locale is closely tied to family decision making and often family survival. Globalization has provided the venue for many people to seek out new opportunities. But it has also limited the options of others. For example, it is now possible for an unemployed nurse from the Philippines to find work in Hong Kong and send money back to her family. However, a family father from a small mid-Western industrial town may find that after twenty years of devoted employment, he is permanently laid off from his manufacturing site, because his job has been outsourced to China. Both of these trends are related to globalization, making it difficult to speak about globalization as either just a positive or a negative force in individuals' and families' lives. We can also not assume that globalization will lead to all families having similar lives and sharing the same tastes despite increasing global exposure to similar messages and goods. Instead, we need to realize that people live in very varied circumstances and that these local contexts are an important component for how global messages and products are received. Maybe most importantly, it is critical to understand that globalization is related to fast, intense social change. None of us are immune to these changes but our experiences will vary depending on where we live and what our particular circumstances may be.

References

Baars, J., Dannefer, D., Phillipson, C., & Walker, A. (2006). Introduction: Critical perspectives in social gerontology. In J. Baars, D. Dannefer, C. Phillipson, & A. Walker, (Eds.), *Aging, globalization and inequality: The new critical gerontology.* (pp. 1–16). Amityville, NY: Baywood Publishing.

Castles, S., & Miller, M. (2003). *The age of migration: International population movements in the modern world.* New York: Guilford Press.

Edgar, D. (2004). Globalization and Western bias in family sociology. In J. Scott, J. Treas, & M. Richards (Eds.), *The Blackwell companion to the sociology of families* (pp. 3–16). Malden, MA: Oxford University Press.

French, J.L., & Woktuch, R. E. (2005). Child workers, globalization, and international business ethics: A case study in Brazil's export-oriented shoe industry. *Business Ethics Quarterly, 15,* 615–640.

Kaufman, N. (2002). The status of children in international law. In N. Kauman & I. Rizzini, (Eds.), *Globalization and children: Exploring potentials for enhancing opportunities in the lives of children and youth,* (pp. 31–45.) New York: Springer.

Kelly, R.M. (2001). *Gender, globalization and democratization.* Lanham, MD: Rowman & Littlefield Publishers.

Kuznesof, E. (2005). The house, the street, global society: Latin American families and childhood in the twenty-first century. *Journal of Social History, 38,* 859–872.

Malkki, L., & Martin, E. (2003). Children and the gendered politics of globalization: In remembrance of Sharon Stephens. *American Ethnologist, 30,* 216–224.

Moghadam, V. (2003). A political explanation of the gendered division of labor in Japan. In M. Marchand & A. Runyan (Eds.),

Gender and global restructuring: Sightings, sites and resistances (pp. 99–115). London: Routledge.

Mortgan, K., & Zippel, K. (2003). "Paid to care: The origins and effects of care leave policies in Western Europe." *Social Politics: International Studies in Gender, State, and Society, 10,* 49–85.

Parkin, R., & Stone, L. (2004). *Kinship and family: An anthropological reader.* New York: Blackwell.

Rodrik, D. (1997). *Has globalization gone too far?* Washington, Institute for International Economics.

Safa, H. (2002). Questioning globalization: Gender and export processing in the Dominican Republic. *Journal of Developing Societies, 18,* 11–31.

Yan, R., & Neal, A. (2006). The impact of globalization on family relations in China. *International Journal of Sociology of the family, 32,* 113–125.

Interracial Families

Marriages between people of different races have mushroomed in the last three decades, and the children of these unions have a whole new point of view.

CAROL MITHERS

The growth of mixed-race marriage: According to the most recent Census figures, the percentage of couples who are interracial increased sevenfold from 1970 to 2000, and the number of children in interracial families quadrupled to 3.4 million. The most prevalent pairing is white men and Asian women. Among people under 30, interracial couples are at least 30 percent more common.

Changing attitudes: More than 300 years ago, Maryland was the first state to outlaw interracial marriage. In 1967 the Supreme Court ruled such laws unconstitutional but many states kept their statutes. Alabama didn't remove its law until 2000. Yet a 2003 poll showed that 86 percent of blacks, 79 percent of Latinos and 66 percent of whites would accept a child marrying someone of a different race.

Tracking the trend: In 2000 Americans could check more than one box for ethnicity and race, and about 7 million did. Estimates put the multiracial population even higher.

Representative family: Sandra and Steven Stites, of Kansas City, Missouri. Married 19 years, both are 46-year-old doctors with three children.

For the Stites children, an interracial life "is all they've ever known," says Sandra, and they are perfectly comfortable with it. Ailea says her friends have affectionately labeled her "half-rican." Her younger sister, Sierra, has dubbed herself a "wack," short for white-black.

Sandra and Steven became friends in 1982 when they were lab partners in an anatomy class at the University of Missouri-Columbia. "We met over a cadaver," Steven jokes. They didn't expect to marry. Steven had grown up in virtually all-white Independence, Missouri. Sandra's Kansas City neighborhood was black but she went to a mostly white private school and briefly dated a white boy. Still, after her first date with Steven, she told a friend, "He's perfect, except he's white."

The couple dated for four years. "It was important to me that we both loved the outdoors and musical theater," Steven says. "We had common ground, even if it didn't include race."

Sandra had concerns, however. "If we had kids, would they be accepted?" she remembers thinking at the time. "Would we be accepted?" They kept their relationship secret for two months. Once they went public, Sandra's fears were realized. Some classmates avoided them. Steven's father said that marrying Sandra would limit his career. Sandra's parents worried "because Steven was 'different.' "

By the time Sandra and Steven married, their parents had come around. "My father got to know Sandra," says Steven. "Most racism is based on a fear of difference. Once you learn that people aren't as different as you think, the fear goes away."

Once you learn that people aren't as different as you think they are, the fear goes away.

Sandra's family, too, discovered that Steven was less "different" than they'd thought. "His mother was from the South," says Sandra. "My grandfather would prepare food like collard greens and say, 'That boy won't eat this!' But this was food Steven knew."

When Ailea was born, in 1990, Steven and Sandra had already agreed they wanted their children to recognize their dual heritage. The children have contact with white culture in their neighborhood and school, and they are close to Sandra's parents, who live near the Stiteses' home, as well as her extended family in Dallas. "We want the kids to understand the struggles," says Sandra.

Not everyone is on board, though. Steven has an uncle who refuses to let the couple in his house. And while nobody looks twice at the Stites family in Kansas City, in the suburban malls, "we get what we call 'the triangle look,' " says Sandra. "Eyes go to Steven, then me, then the kids. And salespeople don't see us as a couple. Sometimes we pretend we're not together and then say, 'Your name is on my checkbook! How did that happen?'"

"What really rankles are the thoughtless remarks from strangers who see Sandra with her children. "They'll ask, 'Are you the nanny?'" Sandra says.

The Stiteses send their kids to a private school, though they picked one that is 17 percent nonwhite. When the children classified themselves on school forms, Ailea wrote "multiracial," Sierra picked "other," and James chose both African-American and white.

"Their generation doesn't see color the way it used to be seen," says Sandra. "When Ailea describes a guy she likes, she mentions the color of his eyes and skin and hair. She describes his looks, but it never occurs to her to mention his race at all."

From *Ladies' Home Journal,* by Carol Mithers, July 2006, pp. 102, 106. Copyright © 2006 by Carol Mithers. Reprinted with permission of the author.

Family Partnerships That Count

**How can schools meaningfully engage families
in supporting student learning?**

JoBeth Allen

Uptown High School's Mardi Gras Carnival, organized by the 21-person Parent Advisory Council, is a fun family event that raises nearly $1,000 each year.

Midtown Elementary teachers reach their goal of 100 percent participation in parent-teacher conferences, in which they strive to convey all the important information about programs, test scores, and grades in only 15 minutes.

Downtown Middle School draws more than half of its families to Technology Night. Parents walk through impressive exhibits of student projects and then enjoy refreshments in the cafeteria, converted to a student-run Cyberspace Café.

Which of these endeavors to "involve parents" contribute to student learning?

To start a conversation about this question at your school, you might want to gather a group of educators, students, and family members to brain storm a list of everything the school does to involve families. If you're like most schools, it will be an impressive list. Next, put each item in one of three categories: Builds Deep Relationships; Supports Student Learning; or Does Neither (But We Keep Doing It Anyway). Finally, examine the activities in the first two columns and ask, Which families are benefiting? Which families are not?

Contrary to the prevailing myth, when parents or guardians walk into school, their children's learning does not automatically increase. Mattingly, Radmila, McKenzie, Rodriguez, and Kayzar (2002) analyzed 41 parent involvement programs. They concluded that some things we count as parental that Count involvement—being room parents, signing behavior reports, attending PTA meetings, and so on—don't improve student achievement. So what does?

Henderson and Mapp (2002) examined 80 studies on parental involvement, preschool through high school, throughout the United States. They concluded that family involvement was likely to increase student achievement when that involvement was connected to academic learning. Let's look at three important approaches they identified: building respectful relationships, engaging families in supporting learning at home, and addressing cultural differences.

Building Respectful Relationships
Family Funds of Knowledge

Horses. That was the common thread Kathy Amanti noticed from home visits with three families in her multiage bilingual classroom. She learned that Carlos's father was teaching his sons how to care for and ride the family's three horses; that Fernando rode and cared for horses each summer when he stayed with his grandparents in Mexico; and that the Rivera family had gathered to watch a videotape of a relative riding in a horse race in Sonoyta, Mexico.

Surveying the rest of her class, Amanti found a great deal of interest in and knowledge about horses. Together, she and her students designed an interdisciplinary unit on horses, which included taking a field trip to Carlos's home, observing a parent shoeing a horse, and viewing the Riveras' video. Families were resources on individual projects as well, helping students study Spanish explorers; the history of saddles; local horse ordinances; horse anatomy; measurement (converting hands to inches and feet); and horse gestation and evolution.

Amanti was one of a group of teachers and professors who worked with Mexican and Yaqui Indian families in Tucson, Arizona (Gonzáles, Moll, & Amanti, 2005). These educators challenged the deficit model and developed a powerful alternative: learning about and incorporating family *funds of knowledge* into the classroom. Teachers studied the history of their border community. They visited homes and entered into conversations—*not* scripted interviews—centering on family and work history (border crossings, extended families, religious traditions, work experiences); household activities (gardening, home and car repair, caring for children, recreation); and parents' views of their roles (raising children, languages spoken at home, schooling).

The home visits enabled teachers and families to build *confianza* (mutual trust) and to create *reciprocity* (a healthy partnership in which teachers and parents give in ways that support one another and support the student). The teachers learned that all families have important experiences, skills, and knowledge that teachers can tap into. The teachers also became more knowledgeable about how their students learned outside school. For example, in many Mexican and Yaqui families, children are active participants and ask questions that guide their own learning, skills not always encouraged at school.

Throughout the year, teachers met in study groups to discuss what they learned and to create thematic units that built on their community's funds of knowledge. They learned that families had a wealth of knowledge about ranching, farming, mining, and construction. In the area of business, they knew about appraising, renting and selling, labor laws, and building codes. Household management acumen included budgeting, child care, cooking, and repair. Many had knowledge of both contemporary and folk medicine for people and animals. Religious knowledge included rituals; texts (especially the Bible); and moral and ethical understandings.

We've seen how Kathy Amanti incorporated family funds of knowledge into meaningful learning that went beyond the classroom. Here's another example of the way learning with and from families can support student achievement.

Teacher-Parent Partnerships for Learning

Antonio was 13, had a broad vocabulary, and was fluent in oral Spanish and English. He had been homeless for five years, and his family frequently moved. He stopped reading specialist Paula Murphy in the hall one day, asking, "I need help in reading. Can I go to your class?"

Paula started making home visits to Antonio's family at the shelter, at a friend's apartment, and at other temporary housing. She learned that his mother and stepfather helped him with homework; his mother wrote short stories, provided emotional support, and encouraged him to do well in school. Paula designed a reading program that actively involved his parents. She engaged in regular communication with the family. She also intervened with the district so Antonio could stay in her school when the family moved. In one year, Antonio's reading and writing skills improved significantly. Paula reflected,

> As a Puerto Rican . . . I felt that sharing the culture and the language of my Latino students was enough to understand their world. . . . I learned I know nothing about growing up poor, homeless, and in an environment of violence. . . . I learned of my responsibility to understand not only my students' ethnic culture, but their community culture as well. (Murphy, 1994, p. 87)

Although there is no substitute for the personal relationships and deep understanding of family knowledge developed in home visits, it's not always possible for teachers to visit every student's home on a regular basis. But there's another way of learning about a student's life outside of school—hand her a camera!

Photographs of Local Knowledge Sources (PhOLKS)

I was part of a teacher study group in Georgia that used photography to learn about family funds of knowledge (Allen et al., 2002). The PhOLKS group served a culturally, linguistically, and economically diverse student population. Educators in our group were African American, Colombian, and European American; Christian and Jewish; originally from the Northeast, Midwest, and South; with childhoods from poor to privileged. This diversity was essential in mediating our understanding of cultural differences.

With a small grant, we paid for three 35mm cameras, film, and processing for each classroom. We invited students to photograph what was important to them in their homes and neighborhoods. Teachers prepared students by analyzing photographic essays, sharing photographs of their own lives outside school, and inviting parents who enjoyed photography to help students learn how to see through the camera's eye. English as a second language teacher Carmen Urdanivia-English read from her photo-illustrated memoir about growing up in Colombia and then invited a reporter from the local Spanish-language newspaper to show students ways to document family and community histories.

Students took cameras home on a rotating schedule, charged with capturing their out-of-school lives. Teachers invited students and family members to write or dictate stories about their photos. Parents and guardians contributed descriptions, memories, poetry, letters, and personal stories.

Cyndy, a white teacher, worried about Kenesha, a black student who often slept in class. Other teachers at the school said her mother was never involved and had been in special education when she attended the school. When Kenesha took her photo journal home with an invitation to write about the pictures, her mother wrote,

> My daughter name is Kenesha. . . . She is very sweet all the teacher and people love her because she is understanding and nice, polite, sweet, listen, smart. She have her good days & bad days but she is the sweetest child you like to spend time with. . . . Members of the church love to hear her sing she sings so good you love her. She like to read and talk a lot. She loves dogs. She like to play with dolls. She love her new baby brother. (Allen et al., 2002, p. 317)

Cyndy and Kenesha's mother began communicating frequently through notes and phone calls. Mom wanted to know how Kenesha was doing. She promised to make sure Kenesha got more sleep.

One photograph, one invitation, and one letter did not change Kenesha's life. The family still struggled, and so did Kenesha—but now there was a partnership working together to teach her.

Engaging Families in Supporting Learning at Home

The parental support that made a difference for Antonio and Kenesha did not involve parents coming into the classroom, yet the parent-teacher-student relationships affected not only the students' participation in the classroom community but also their learning. That was also the case for the students of two primary-grade teachers with whom I worked in Georgia.

School-Home Reading Journals

I learned about genuine family-school partnerships from Betty Shockley and Barbara Michalove, 1st and 2nd grade teachers (respectively) who invited parents and other family members to join them in teaching their children to read and write.

Betty, Barbara, and I are European American, middle-class, experienced educators who joined in partnership with families in a high-poverty, predominantly black school. To connect home and school literacy learning, Betty and Barbara designed family-school connections including, among other practices, school-home reading journals.

Teachers and families exchanged reading journals all year. Children took home these spiral-bound or sewn notebooks two or three times a week along with books from the classroom libraries. Parents or others in the family sustained a remarkable commitment to read with their children, talk about the books, and write together in the journals.

Betty and Barbara honored the families' investment of time by responding to every entry, as we see from these excerpts from the journal of Lakendra's mother, Janice:

Janice: In the story "I Can Fly" Lakendra did very good. Her reading was very good. And maybe she's ready to move on to . . . a book with a few more words. If you think so also. (9/30)

Betty: I agree. She can read more difficult books but like everybody, young readers enjoy reading things that are easy for them too. (10/1)

Janice: In the story of the Halloween Performance, Lakendra seem to have some problems with many of the words. Maybe she get a story with too many difficult words for her right now. But still I enjoyed her reading. Thank You. Janice (10/2)

Betty: When you get ready to read together each night, you might begin by asking Lakendra, Do you want to read your book to me or do you want me to read to you? Sometimes after you read even a more difficult book, she may ask to read it after you. Let her be the leader. One of the most important things about sharing books together is talking about them together. Thanks. (10/3)

Janice: Lakendra was very excited about the books she chose to read to me. So excited she read them over and over again. And I was so pleased. Maybe last night she did want me to read the story to her I don't know but I will ask her from now on. Because she was a little upset that she didn't know a lot of the words. And I don't ever want her to feel pressured. Thanks. Janice (10/3) (Shockley, Michalove, & Allen, 1995, pp. 42–43)

This kind of extended written communication, which did not involve enlisting parents to solve discipline problems or to sign reading logs, established deep relationships that supported emerging readers and writers at home as well as at school in ways neither teacher nor parent could have accomplished alone. Without ever entering the school, parents became members of the classroom community.

Addressing Cultural Differences

We are all cultural beings shaped by time and place, religion and race, language and gender, and a host of other ongoing influences. In my work with educators, we use a number of strategies as a springboard for conversations among parents and teachers of diverse cultural backgrounds.

For example, drawing maps of childhood neighborhoods, or *memory maps* (Frank, 2003), might take place during a home visit, or in a classroom, or during a whole-school event such as a family night. Each participant draws an annotated map of his or her childhood neighborhood(s). Next, in small groups that include both teachers and families, participants walk one another through their neighborhood maps. Participants at one school had had very different childhood experiences: One of us made daily trips to the corner grocery store in Philadelphia; one rarely left the farm until he was in high school; one moved from a small town in Mexico and learned English at the Boys and Girls Club. We were amazed at the differences as well as the similarities (for example, "Back then it was safe for a child to go to the store alone").

Neighborhood maps may lead to stories of schooling. Each teacher and parent writes down or draws two memories of schooling, one positive and one negative. The sharing of these stories is often quite intense. It's important for parents to know that teachers have both kinds of memories; many parents may believe that all teachers had only positive, successful school experiences. Conversely, teachers need to learn about parents' positive memories as well as the "ghosts at the table," Sara Lawrence-Lightfoot's (2003) expression for those memories from their own schooling that haunt parents and hover over the conference table when parents and teachers try to talk about a student.

A third and potentially deeper exploration of cultural understanding occurs through developing cultural memoirs. Family members—including students—and teachers can ask themselves, Who am I as a cultural being and what are the influences in my life that have made me who I am? These are some ways to approach this project with families:

- *Read and discuss cultural memoirs.* A great place to start is by reading and discussing memoirs deeply contextualized in time and place, such as *All Over But the Shoutin',* by Rick Bragg (Pantheon, 1997), or *The*

16

House on Mango Street, by Sandra Cisneros (Vintage, 1989). Busy parents and teachers may appreciate shorter memoirs from popular magazines, television biopics, or radio broadcasts such as National Public Radio's StoryCorps.

- *Gather photographs and other cultural artifacts.* Go through those boxes, albums, and digital files asking, What were my cultural influences in terms of race, social class, gender, ethnicity, geographic region, religion, nationality, language/dialect, sexual orientation, schooling, physical or mental health or ability, and family structure?
- *Share cultural memoirs.* Create a form to represent your multicultured self, such as a poem, scrapbook, telenovela, photo essay, iMovie, or picture book. Some teachers and parents create classroom coffee house atmospheres and invite families in during the school day, in the evening, or on Saturday to share memoirs. Find out from parents what works for them, and consider holding two or three events so everyone can participate. You might plan one meeting for adults only, but remember that students love hearing their parents' and teachers' stories, too.

Educators and family members begin to understand cultural differences when they share their lives and make connections that build a foundation of respect and trust. When we make culture central to creating family-school partnerships, we acknowledge differences with respect, marvel at similarities, and open up dialogue about how to support each student as a unique learner.

Educators and family members begin to understand cultural differences when they share their lives.

A Starting Point

We've examined funds of knowledge, home visits, photography, reading journals, and other ways teachers have engaged families in creating positive learning experiences for students at home and in the classroom. Any of these practices could be a starting point. But let me suggest another logical place to start. Go back to that list you made of your school's parent involvement activities: Builds Deep Relationships; Supports Student Learning; Does Neither (But We Keep Doing It Anyway).

What are you already doing that you can build on? What might you do with your equivalent of Uptown High School's Mardi Gras Carnival—that fun tradition that doesn't really build relationships or support student learning? In addition to

striving for high parent participation in conferences as Midtown Elementary does, what if you held student-led conferences, focusing only on student learning? How could you involve parents in the preparation for a Technology Night event? Perhaps students could interview their parents and grandparents about changes in technology in their lifetimes, how they use technology in their jobs, and the pros and cons of various aspects of technology. Parents might engage with students in studying the effects of technology on global warming by surveying their home, work, and community settings to assess how much energy is used to run computers, cell phones, and other technologies.

How will you create opportunities *with* families?

How will you create opportunities *with* families that really improve and deepen student learning?

References

Allen, J., Fabregas, V., Hankins, K., Hull, G., Labbo, L., Lawson, H., et al. (2002). PhOLKS lore: Learning from photographs, families, and children. *Language Arts, 79*(4), 312–322.

Frank, C. (2003). Mapping our stories: Teachers' reflections on themselves as writers. *Language Arts, 80*(3), 185–195.

Gonzáles, N., Moll, L., & Amanti, C. (Eds.). (2005). *Funds of knowledge: Theorizing practices in households, communities, and classrooms.* Mahwah, NJ: Erlbaum.

Henderson, A., & Mapp, K. (2002). *A new wave of evidence: The impact of school, family, and community connections on student achievement.* Austin, TX: Southwest Educational Development Laboratory.

Lawrence-Lightfoot, S. (2003). *The essential conversation: What parents and teachers can learn from each other.* New York: Random House.

Mattingly, D. J., Radmila, P., McKenzie, T. L., Rodriguez, J. L., & Kayzar, B. (2002). Evaluating evaluations: The case of parent involvement programs. *Review of Education Research, 72*(4), 549–576.

Murphy, P. (1994). Antonio: My student, my teacher. *Language Arts, 1*(2), 75–88.

Shockley, B., Michalove, B., & Allen, J. (1995). *Engaging families: Connecting home and school literacy communities.* Portsmouth, NH: Heinemann.

JOBETH ALLEN is Professor, Department of Language and Literacy Education, University of Georgia, Athens; jobethal@uga.edu. She is the author of *Creating Welcoming Schools: A Practical Guide to Home-School Partnerships with Diverse Families* (Teachers College Press, 2007).

UNIT 2

Exploring and Establishing Relationships

Unit Selections

5.   **This Thing Called Love,** Lauren Slater
6.   **24 Things Love and Sex Experts Are Dying to Tell You,** Ellise Pierce
7.   **Against All Odds,** Anne Kingston
8.   **The Expectations Trap,** Hara Estroff Marano
9.   **On-Again, Off-Again,** Elizabeth Svoboda
10.   **Fats, Carbs and the Science of Conception,** Jorge E. Chavarro, Walter C. Willett and Patrick J. Skerrett
11.   **Not Always 'the Happiest Time',** Lisa Miller and Anne Underwood
12.   **Truth and Consequences at Pregnancy High,** Alex Morris
13.   **Baby Survival Guide: 7 Truths That'll Keep You Sane,** Maura Rhodes

Key Points to Consider

- What are key components to this thing we call "love"? How do we maintain a satisfying sexual relationship? What do you look for in a mate? Do you seem to struggle with lasting relationships? Why do you think this is so?

- Do you see children as a part of your life? Why or why not? What are the challenges of having a child?

Student Website

www.mhhe.com/cls

Internet References

Bonobo Sex and Society
   http://songweaver.com/info/bonobos.html
Go Ask Alice!
   www.goaskalice.columbai.edu/index.html
The Kinsey Institute for Research in Sex, Gender, and Reproduction
   www.indiana.edu/~kinsey/
Mysteries of Odor in Human Sexuality
   www.pheromones.com
The Society for the Scientific Study of Sexuality
   www.sexscience.org

By and large, we are social animals, and as such, we seek out meaningful connections with other humans. John Bowlby, Mary Ainsworth, and others have proposed that this drive toward deep connections is biologically based and is at the core of what it means to be human. However it plays out in childhood and adulthood, the need for connection, to love and be loved, is a powerful force moving us to establish and maintain close relationships. As we explore various possibilities, we engage in the complex business of relationship building. In doing this, many processes occur simultaneously: Messages are sent and received; differences are negotiated; assumptions and expectations are or are not met. The ultimate goals are closeness and continuity. How we feel about others and what we see as essential to these relationships play an important role in our establishing and maintaining relationships. In this unit, we look at factors that underlie the establishment of relationships as well as the beginning stages of relationships.

The first subsection takes a broad look at factors that influence the building of meaningful connections and at the beginning stages of adult relationships. The first essay, "This Thing Called Love" takes a cross-cultural perspective on the nature of romantic love. Among its interesting and controversial suggestions is that passionate love has a natural lifespan and shares characteristics with obsessive compulsive disorder. The next essay goes on to discuss "24 Things Love and Sex Experts Are Dying to Tell You"—key pieces of information for couples.

In the second subsection, several aspects of the choice of a mate are examined. "Against All Odds" explores the concept of "instant relationships" and "The Expectations Trap" examines the impact of expectations on the choice we make regarding life partners. "On-Again, Off-Again" examines a number of

© Blend Images/Getty Images

explanations for why some couples break up and make up, over and over again. Why does this happen and what can they do to break the cycle?

The third subsection looks at pregnancy and the next generation. "Fats, Carbs and the Science of Conception" explores new research on the role of diet, exercise, and weight control in fertility. The following article, "Not Always 'the Happiest Time'" looks at pregnancy and depression, long assumed to occur only after birth, if at all. This article addresses the potential that those at risk for depression are not protected and may, in fact, hide their depression out of shame. "Truth and Consequences at Pregnancy High" explores the impact, often life long, of having a child while in high school.

This Thing Called Love

LAUREN SLATER

My husband and I got married at eight in the morning. It was winter, freezing, the trees encased in ice and a few lone blackbirds balancing on telephone wires. We were in our early 30s, considered ourselves hip and cynical, the types who decried the institution of marriage even as we sought its status. During our wedding brunch we put out a big suggestion box and asked people to slip us advice on how to avoid divorce; we thought it was a funny, clear-eyed, grounded sort of thing to do, although the suggestions were mostly foolish: Screw the toothpaste cap on tight. After the guests left, the house got quiet. There were flowers everywhere: puckered red roses and fragile ferns. "What can we do that's really romantic?" I asked my newly wed one. Benjamin suggested we take a bath. I didn't want a bath. He suggested a lunch of chilled white wine and salmon. I was sick of salmon.

What can we do that's really romantic? The wedding was over, the silence seemed suffocating, and I felt the familiar disappointment after a longed-for event has come and gone. We were married. Hip, hip, hooray. I decided to take a walk. I went into the center of town, pressed my nose against a bakery window, watched the man with flour on his hands, the dough as soft as skin, pushed and pulled and shaped at last into stars. I milled about in an antique store. At last I came to our town's tattoo parlor. Now I am not a tattoo type person, but for some reason, on that cold silent Sunday, I decided to walk in. "Can I help you?" a woman asked.

"Is there a kind of tattoo I can get that won't be permanent?" I asked.

"Henna tattoos," she said.

She explained that they lasted for six weeks, were used at Indian weddings, were stark and beautiful and all brown. She showed me pictures of Indian women with jewels in their noses, their arms scrolled and laced with the henna markings. Indeed they were beautiful, sharing none of the gaudy comic strip quality of the tattoos we see in the United States. These henna tattoos spoke of intricacy, of the webwork between two people, of ties that bind and how difficult it is to find their beginnings and their elms. And because I had just gotten married, and because I was feeling a post wedding letdown, and because I wanted something really romantic to sail me through the night, I decided to get one.

"Where?" she asked.

"Here," I said. I laid my hands over my breasts and belly.

She raised her eyebrows. "Sure," she said.

I am a modest person. But I took off my shirt, lay on the table, heard her in the back room mixing powders and paints. She came to me carrying a small black-bellied pot inside of which was a rich red mush, slightly glittering. She adorned me. She gave me vines and flowers. She turned my body into a stake supporting whole new gardens of growth, and then, low around my hips, she painted a delicate chain-linked chastity belt. An hour later, the paint dry, I put my clothes back on, went home to film my newly wed one. This, I knew, was my gift to him, the kind of present you offer only once in your lifetime. I let him undress me.

"Wow," he said, standing back.

I blushed, and we began.

We are no longer beginning, my husband and I. This does not surprise me. Even back then, wearing the decor of desire, the serpentining tattoos, I knew they would fade, their red-clay color bleaching out until they were gone. On my wedding day I didn't care.

I do now. Eight years later, pale as a pillowcase, here I sit, with all the extra pounds and baggage time brings. And the questions have only grown more insistent. Does passion necessarily diminish over time? How reliable is romantic love, really, as a means of choosing one's mate? Can a marriage be good when Eros is replaced with friendship, or even economic partnership, two people bound by bank accounts?

Let me be clear: I still love my husband. There is no man I desire more. But it's hard to sustain romance in the crumb-filled quotidian that has become our lives. The ties that bind have been frayed by money and mortgages and children, those little imps who somehow manage to tighten the knot while weakening its actual fibers. Benjamin and I have no time for chilled white wine and salmon. The baths in our house always include Big Bird.

If this all sounds miserable, it isn't. My marriage is like a piece of comfortable clothing; even the arguments have a feel of fuzziness to them, something so familiar it can only be called home. And yet . . .

In the Western world we have for centuries concocted poems and stories and plays about the cycles of love, the way it morphs and changes over time, the way passion grabs us by our flung-back throats and then leaves us for something saner.

If *Dracula*—the frail woman, the sensuality of submission—reflects how we understand the passion of early romance, the *Flintstones* reflects our experiences of long-term love: All is gravel and somewhat silly, the song so familiar you can't stop singing it, and when you do, the emptiness is almost unbearable.

We have relied on stories to explain the complexities of love, tales of jealous gods and arrows. Now, however, these stories—so much a part of every civilization—may be changing as science steps in to explain what we have always felt to be myth, to be magic. For the first time, new research has begun to illuminate where love lies in the brain, the particulars of its chemical components.

Anthropologist Helen Fisher may be the closest we've ever come to having a doyenne of desire. At 60 she exudes a sexy confidence, with corn-colored hair, soft as floss, and a willowy build. A professor at Rutgers University, she lives in New York City, her book-lined apartment near Central Park, with its green trees fluffed out in the summer season, its paths crowded with couples holding hands.

Fisher has devoted much of her career to studying the biochemical pathways of love in all its manifestations: lust, romance, attachment, the way they wax and wane. One leg casually crossed over the other, ice clinking in her glass, she speaks with appealing frankness, discussing the ups and downs of love the way most people talk about real estate. "A woman unconsciously uses orgasms as a way of deciding whether or not a man is good for her. If he's impatient and rough, and she doesn't have the orgasm, she may instinctively feel he's less likely to be a good husband and father. Scientists think the fickle female orgasm may have evolved to help women distinguish Mr. Right from Mr. Wrong."

One of Fisher's central pursuits in the past decade has been looking at love, quite literally, with the aid of an MRI machine. Fisher and her colleagues Arthur Aron and Lucy Brown recruited subjects who had been "madly in love" for an average of seven months. Once inside the MRI machine, subjects were shown two photographs, one neutral, the other of their loved one.

What Fisher saw fascinated her. When each subject looked at his or her loved one, the parts of the brain linked to reward and pleasure—the ventral tegmental area and the caudate nucleus—lit up. What excited Fisher most was not so much finding a location, an address, for love as tracing its specific chemical pathways. Love lights up the caudate nucleus because it is home to a dense spread of receptors for a neurotransmitter called dopamine, which Fisher came to think of as part of our own endogenous love potion. In the right proportions, dopamine creates intense energy, exhilaration, focused attention, and motivation to win rewards. It is why, when you are newly in love, you can stay up all night, watch the sun rise, run a race, ski fast down a slope ordinarily too steep for your skill. Love makes you bold, makes you bright, makes you run real risks, which you sometimes survive, and sometimes you don't.

I first fell in love when I was only 12, with a teacher. His name was Mr. McArthur, and he wore open-toed sandals and sported a beard. I had never had a male teacher before, and I thought it terribly exotic. Mr. McArthur did things no other teacher dared to do. He explained to us the physics of farting. He demonstrated how to make an egg explode. He smoked cigarettes at recess, leaning languidly against the side of the school building, the ash growing longer and longer until he casually tapped it off with his finger.

What unique constellation of needs led me to love a man who made an egg explode is interesting, perhaps, but not as interesting, for me, as my memory of love's sheer physical facts. I had never felt anything like it before. I could not get Mr. McArthur out of my mind. I was anxious; I gnawed at the lining of my cheek until I tasted the tang of blood. School became at once terrifying and exhilarating. Would I see him in the hallway? In the cafeteria? I hoped. But when my wishes were granted, and I got a glimpse of my man, it satisfied nothing; it only inflamed me all the more. Had he looked at me? Why had he not looked at me? When would I see him again? At home I looked him up in the phone book; I rang him, this in a time before caller ID. He answered.

"Hello?" Pain in my heart, ripped down the middle. Hang up. Call back. "Hello?" I never said a thing.

Once I called him at night, late, and from the way he answered the phone it was clear, even to a prepubescent like me, that he was with a woman. His voice fuzzy, the tinkle of her laughter in the background. I didn't get out of bed for a whole day.

Sound familiar? Maybe you were 30 when it happened to you, or 8 or 80 or 25. Maybe you lived in Kathmandu or Kentucky; age and geography are irrelevant. Donatella Marazziti is a professor of psychiatry at the University of Pisa in Italy who has studied the biochemistry of lovesickness. Having been in love twice herself and felt its awful power, Marazziti became interested in exploring the similarities between love and obsessive-compulsive disorder.

She and her colleagues measured serotonin levels in the blood of 24 subjects who had fallen in love within the past six months and obsessed about this love object for at least four hours every day. Serotonin is, perhaps, our star neurotransmitter, altered by our star psychiatric medications: Prozac and Zoloft and Paxil, among others. Researchers have long hypothesized that people with obsessive-compulsive disorder (OCD) have a serotonin "imbalance." Drugs like Prozac seem to alleviate OCD by increasing the amount of this neurotransmitter available at the juncture between neurons.

Marazziti compared the lovers' serotonin levels with those of a group of people suffering from OCD and another group who were free from both passion and mental illness. Levels of serotonin in both the obsessives' blood and the lovers' blood were 40 percent lower than those in her normal subjects. Translation: Love and obsessive-compulsive disorder could have a similar chemical profile. Translation: Love and mental illness may be difficult to tell apart. Translation: Don't be a fool. Stay away.

Of course that's a mandate none of us can follow. We do fall in love, sometimes over and over again, subjecting ourselves, each time, to a very sick state of mind. There is hope, however, for those caught in the grip of runaway passion—Prozac. There's nothing like that bicolored bullet for damping down the sex drive and making you feel "blah" about the buffet. Helen

21

Fisher believes that the ingestion of drugs like Prozac jeopardizes one's ability to fall in love—and stay in love. By dulling the keen edge of love and its associated libido, relationships go stale. Says Fisher, "I know of one couple on the edge of divorce. The wife was on an antidepressant. Then she went off it, started having orgasms once more, felt the renewal of sexual attraction for her husband, and they're now in love all over again."

Psychoanalysts have concocted countless theories about why we fall in love with whom we do. Freud would have said your choice is influenced by the unrequited wish to bed your mother, if you're a boy, or your father, if you're a girl, Jung believed that passion is driven by some kind of collective unconscious. Today psychiatrists such as Thomas Lewis from the University of California at San Francisco's School of Medicine hypothesize that romantic love is rooted in our earliest infantile experiences with intimacy, how we felt at the breast, our mother's face, these things of pure unconflicted comfort that get engraved in our brain and that we ceaselessly try to recapture as adults. According to this theory we love whom we love not so much because of the future we hope to build but because of the past we hope to reclaim. Love is reactive, not proactive, it arches us backward, which may be why a certain person just "feels right." Or "feels familiar." He or she is familiar. He or she has a certain look or smell or sound or touch that activates buried memories.

Love and obsessive-compulsive disorder could have a similar chemical profile. Translation: Love and mental illness may be difficult to tell apart. Translation: Don't be a fool. Stay away.

When I first met my husband, I believed this psychological theory was more or less correct. My husband has red hair and a soft voice. A chemist, he is whimsical and odd. One day before we married he dunked a rose in liquid nitrogen so it froze, whereupon he flung it against the wall, spectacularly shattering it. That's when I fell in love with him. My father, too, has red hair, a soft voice, and many eccentricities. He was prone to bursting into song, prompted by something we never saw.

However, it turns out my theories about why I came to love my husband may be just so much hogwash. Evolutionary psychology has said good riddance to Freud and the Oedipal complex and all that other transcendent stuff and hello to simple survival skills. It hypothesizes that we tend to see as attractive, and thereby choose as mates, people who look healthy. And health, say these evolutionary psychologists, is manifested in a woman with a 70 percent waist-to-hip ratio and men with rugged features that suggest a strong supply of testosterone in their blood. Waist-to-hip ratio is important for the successful birth of a baby, and studies have shown this precise ratio signifies higher fertility. As for the rugged look, well, a man with a good dose of testosterone probably also has a strong immune system and so is more likely to give his partner healthy children.

Perhaps our choice of mates is a simple matter of following our noses. Claus Wedekind of the University of Lausanne in Switzerland did an interesting experiment with sweaty T-shirts. He asked 49 women to smell T-shirts previously worn by unidentified men with a variety of the genotypes that influence both body odor and immune systems. He then asked the women to rate which T-shirts smelled the best, which the worst. What Wedekind found was that women preferred the scent of a T-shirt worn by a man whose genotype was most different from hers, a genotype that, perhaps, is linked to an immune system that possesses something hers does not. In this way she increases the chance that her offspring will be robust.

It all seems too good to be true, that we are so hardwired and yet unconscious of the wiring. Because no one to my knowledge has ever said, "I married him because of his B.O." No. We say, "I married him (or her) because he's intelligent, she's beautiful, he's witty, she's compassionate." But we may just be as deluded about love as we are when we're *in* love. If it all comes down to a sniff test, then dogs definitely have the edge when it comes to choosing mates.

W hy doesn't passionate love last? How is it possible to see a person as beautiful on Monday, and 364 days later, on another Monday, to see that beauty as bland? Surely the object of your affection could not have changed that much. She still has the same shaped eyes. Her voice has always had that husky sound, but now it grates on you—she sounds like she needs an antibiotic. Or maybe you're the one who needs an antibiotic, because the partner you once loved and cherished and saw as though saturated with starlight now feels more like a low-level infection, tiring you, sapping all your strength.

Studies around the world confirm that, indeed, passion usually ends. Its conclusion is as common as its initial flare. No wonder some cultures think selecting a lifelong mate based on something so fleeting is folly. Helen Fisher has suggested that relationships frequently break up after four years because that's about how long it takes to raise a child through infancy. Passion, that wild, prismatic insane feeling, turns out to be practical after all. We not only need to copulate; we also need enough passion to start breeding, and then feelings of attachment take over as the partners bond to raise a helpless human infant. Once a baby is no longer nursing, the child can be left with sister, aunts, friends. Each parent is now free to meet another mate and have more children.

Biologically speaking, the reasons romantic love fades may be found in the way our brains respond to the surge and pulse of dopamine that accompanies passion and makes us fly. Cocaine users describe the phenomenon of tolerance: The brain adapts to the excessive input of the drug. Perhaps the neurons become desensitized and need more and more to produce the high—to put out pixie dust, metaphorically speaking.

Maybe it's a good thing that romance fizzles. Would we have railroads, bridges, planes, faxes, vaccines, and television if we were all always besotted? In place of the ever evolving technology that has marked human culture from its earliest tool use, we would have instead only bonbons, bouquets, and birth control. More seriously, if the chemically altered state induced by romantic love is akin to a mental illness or a drug-induced euphoria, exposing yourself for too long could result in psychological damage. A good sex life can be as strong as Gorilla Glue, but who wants that stuff on your skin?

Once upon a time, in India, a boy and a girl fell in love without their parents' permission. They were from different castes, their relationship radical and unsanctioned. Picture it: the sparkling sari, the boy in white linen, the clandestine meetings on tiled terraces with a fat, white moon floating overhead. Who could deny these lovers their pleasure, or condemn the force of their attraction?

Their parents could. In one recent incident a boy and girl from different castes were hanged at the hands of their parents as hundreds of villagers watched. A couple who eloped were stripped and beaten. Yet another couple committed suicide after their parents forbade them to marry.

Anthropologists used to think that romance was a Western construct, a bourgeois by-product of the Middle Ages. Romance was for the sophisticated, took place in cafés, with coffees and Cabernets, or on silk sheets, or in rooms with a flickering fire. It was assumed that non-Westerners, with their broad familial and social obligations, were spread too thin for particular passions. How could a collectivist culture celebrate or in any way sanction the obsession with one individual that defines new love? Could a lice-ridden peasant really feel passion?

Easily, as it turns out. Scientists now believe that romance is panhuman, embedded in our brains since Pleistocene times. In a study of 166 cultures, anthropologists William Jankowiak and Edward Fischer observed evidence of passionate love in 147 of them. In another study men and women from Europe, Japan, and the Philippines were asked to fill out a survey to measure their experiences of passionate love. All three groups professed feeling passion with the same searing intensity.

But though romantic love may be universal, its cultural expression is not. To the Fulbe tribe of northern Cameroon, poise matters more than passion. Men who spend too much time with their wives are taunted, and those who are weak-kneed are thought to have fallen under a dangerous spell. Love may be inevitable, but for the Fulbe its manifestations are shameful, equated with sickness and social impairment.

In India romantic love has traditionally been seen as dangerous, a threat to a well-crafted caste system in which marriages are arranged as a means of preserving lineage and bloodlines. Thus the gruesome tales, the warnings embedded in fables about what happens when one's wayward impulses take over.

Today love marriages appear to be on the rise in India, often in defiance of parents' wishes. The triumph of romantic love is celebrated in Bollywood films. Yet most Indians still believe arranged marriages are more likely to succeed than love marriages. In one survey of Indian college students, 76 percent said they'd marry someone with all the right qualities even if they weren't in love with the person (compared with only 14 percent

of Americans). Marriage is considered too important a step to leave to chance.

Studies around the world confirm that, indeed, passion usually ends. No wonder some cultures think selecting a lifelong mate based on something so fleeting is folly.

Renu Dinakaran is a striking 45-year-old woman who lives in Bangalore, India. When I meet her, she is dressed in Western-style clothes—black leggings and a T-shirt. Renu lives in a well-appointed apartment in this thronging city, where cows sleep on the highways as tiny cars whiz around them, plumes of black smoke rising from their sooty pipes.

Renu was born into a traditional Indian family where an arranged marriage was expected. She was not an arranged kind of person, though, emerging from her earliest days as a fierce tennis player, too sweaty for saris, and smarter than many of the men around her. Nevertheless at the age of 17 she was married off to a first cousin, a man she barely knew, a man she wanted to learn to love, but couldn't. Renu considers many arranged marriages to be acts of "state-sanctioned rape."

Renu hoped to fall in love with her husband, but the more years that passed, the less love she felt, until, at the end, she was shrunken, bitter, hiding behind the curtains of her in-laws' bungalow, looking with longing at the couple on the balcony across from theirs. "It was so obvious to me that couple had married for love, and I envied them. I really did. It hurt me so much to see how they stood together, how they went shopping for bread and eggs."

Exhausted from being forced into confinement, from being swaddled in saris that made it difficult to move, from resisting the pressure to eat off her husband's plate, Renu did what traditional Indian culture forbids one to do. She left. By this time she had had two children. She took them with her. In her mind was an old movie she'd seen on TV, a movie so strange and enticing to her, so utterly confounding and comforting at the same time, that she couldn't get it out of her head. It was 1986. The movie was *Love Story*.

"Before I saw movies like *Love Story*, I didn't realize the power that love can have," she says.

Renu was lucky in the end. In Mumbai she met a man named Anil, and it was then, for the first time, that she felt passion. "When I first met Anil, it was like nothing I'd ever experienced. He was the first man I ever had an orgasm with. I was high, just high, all the time. And I knew it wouldn't last, couldn't last, and so that infused it with a sweet sense of longing, almost as though we were watching the end approach while we were also discovering each other."

When Renu speaks of the end, she does not, to be sure, mean the end of her relationship with Anil; she means the end of a certain stage. The two are still happily married, companionable, loving if not "in love," with a playful black dachshund they bought together. Their relationship, once so full of fire, now seems to simmer along at an even temperature, enough to keep them well fed and warm. They are grateful.

"Would I want all that passion back?" Renu asks. "Sometimes, yes. But to tell you the truth, it was exhausting."

From a physiological point of view, this couple has moved from the dopamine-drenched state of romantic love to the relative quiet of an oxytocin-induced attachment. Oxytocin is a hormone that promotes a feeling of connection, bonding. It is released when we hug our long-term spouses, or our children. It is released when a mother nurses her infant. Prairie voles, animals with high levels of oxytocin, mate for life. When scientists block oxytocin receptors in these rodents, the animals don't form monogamous bonds and tend to roam. Some researchers speculate that autism, a disorder marked by a profound inability to forge and maintain social connections, is linked to an oxytocin deficiency. Scientists have been experimenting by treating autistic people with oxytocin, which in some cases has helped alleviate their symptoms.

In long-term relationships that work—like Renu and Anil's—oxytocin is believed to be abundant in both partners. In long-term relationships that never get off the ground, like Renu and her first husband's, or that crumble once the high is gone, chances are the couple has not found a way to stimulate or sustain oxytocin production.

"But there are things you can do to help it along," says Helen Fisher. "Massage. Make love. These things trigger oxytocin and thus make you feel much closer to your partner."

Well, I suppose that's good advice, but it's based on the assumption that you still want to have sex with that boring windbag of a husband. Should you fake-it-till-you-make-it?

"Yes," says Fisher. "Assuming a fairly healthy relationship, if you have enough orgasms with your partner, you may become attached to him or her. You will stimulate oxytocin."

This may be true. But it sounds unpleasant. It's exactly what your mother always said about vegetables: "Keep eating your peas. They are an acquired taste. Eventually, you will come to like them."

But I have never been a peas person.

I t's 90 degrees on the day my husband and I depart, from Boston for New York City, to attend a kissing school. With two kids, two cats, two dogs, a lopsided house, and a questionable school system, we may know how to kiss, but in the rough and tumble of our harried lives we have indeed forgotten how to *kiss*.

The sky is paved with clouds, the air as sticky as jam in our hands and on our necks. The Kissing School, run by Cherie Byrd, a therapist from Seattle, is being held on the 12th floor of a run-down building in Manhattan. Inside, the room is whitewashed; a tiled table holds bottles of banana and apricot nectar, a pot of green tea, breath mints, and Chapstick. The other Kissing School students—sometimes they come from as far away as Vietnam and Nigeria—are sprawled happily on the bare floor, pillows and blankets beneath them. The class will be seven hours long.

Byrd starts us off with foot rubs. "In order to be a good kisser," she says, "you need to learn how to do the foreplay before the kissing." Foreplay involves rubbing my husband's smelly feet, but that is not as bad as when he has to rub mine. Right before we left the house, I accidentally stepped on a diaper the dog had gotten into, and although I washed, I now wonder how well.

"Inhale," Byrd says, and shows us how to draw in air.

"Exhale," she says, and then she jabs my husband in the back. "Don't focus on the toes so much," she says. "Move on to the calf."

Byrd tells us other things about the art of kissing. She describes the movement of energy through various chakras, the manifestation of emotion in the lips; she describes the importance of embracing all your senses, how to make eye contact as a prelude, how to whisper just the right way. Many hours go by. My cell phone rings. It's our babysitter. Our one-year-old has a high fever. We must cut the long lesson short. We rush out. Later on, at home, I tell my friends what we learned at Kissing School: We don't have time to kiss.

A perfectly typical marriage. Love in the Western world.

Luckily I've learned of other options for restarting love. Arthur Aron, a psychologist at Stony Brook University in New York, conducted an experiment that illuminates some of the mechanisms by which people become and stay attracted. He recruited a group of men and women and put opposite sex pairs in rooms together, instructing each pair to perform a series of tasks, which included telling each other personal details about themselves. He then asked each couple to stare into each other's eyes for two minutes. After this encounter, Aron found most of the couples, previously strangers to each other, reported feelings of attraction. In fact, one couple went on to marry.

Novelty triggers dopamine in the brain, which can stimulate feelings of attraction. So riding a roller coaster on a first date is more likely to lead to second and third dates.

Fisher says this exercise works wonders for some couples. Aron and Fisher also suggest doing novel things together, because novelty triggers dopamine in the brain, which can stimulate feelings of attraction. In other words, if your heart flutters in his presence, you might decide it's not because you're anxious but because you love him. Carrying this a step further, Aron and others have found that even if you just jog in place and then meet someone, you're more likely to think they're attractive. So first dates that involve a nerve-racking activity, like riding a roller coaster, are more likely to lead to second and third dates. That's a strategy worthy of posting on Match.com. Play some squash. And in times of stress—natural disasters, blackouts, predators on the prowl—lock up tight and hold your partner.

In Somerville, Massachusetts, where I live with my husband, our predators are primarily mosquitoes. That needn't stop us from trying to enter the windows of each other's soul. When I propose this to Benjamin, he raises an eyebrow.

"Why don't we just go out for Cambodian food?" he says.

"Because that's not how the experiment happened."

As a scientist, my husband is always up for an experiment. But our lives are so busy that, in order to do this, we have to make a plan. We will meet next Wednesday at lunchtime and try the experiment in our car.

On the Tuesday night before our rendezvous, I have to make an unplanned trip to New York. My husband is more than happy to forget our date. I, however, am not. That night, from my hotel room, I call him.

"We can do it on the phone," I say.

"What am I supposed to stare into?" he asks. "The keypad?"

"There's a picture of me hanging in the hall. Look at that for two minutes. I'll look at a picture I have of you in my wallet."

"Come on," he says.

"Be a sport," I say. "It's better than nothing."

Maybe not. Two minutes seems like a long time to stare at someone's picture with a receiver pressed to your ear. My husband sneezes, and I try to imagine his picture sneezing right along with him, and this makes me laugh.

Another 15 seconds pass, slowly, each second stretched to its limit so I can almost hear time, feel time, its taffy-like texture, the pop it makes when it's done. Pop pop pop. I stare and stare at my husband's picture. It doesn't produce any sense of startling intimacy, and I feel defeated.

Still, I keep on. I can hear him breathing on the other end. The photograph before me was taken a year or so ago, cut to fit my wallet, his strawberry blond hair pulled back in a ponytail. I have never really studied it before. And I realize that in this picture my husband is not looking straight back at me, but his pale blue eyes are cast sideways, off to the left, looking at something I can't see. I touch his eyes. I peer close, and then still closer, at his averted face. Is there something sad in his expression, something sad in the way he gazes off?

I look toward the side of the photo, to find what it is he's looking at, and then I see it: a tiny turtle coming toward him. Now I remember how he caught it after the camera snapped, how he held it gently in his hands, showed it to our kids, stroked its shell, his forefinger moving over the scaly dome, how he held the animal out toward me, a love offering. I took it, and together we sent it back to the sea.

24 Things Love and Sex Experts Are Dying to Tell You

ELLISE PIERCE

At REDBOOK, we're dedicated to helping you get the most out of every part of your life—*especially* your love life. That's why we created the RED-BOOK Love Network, a brain trust of today's top authorities on relationships, to provide you with the best, most current info on the ins and outs, and ups and downs, of sex and love. Here, our experts share the essential pieces of advice every couple needs.

1 Never Underestimate the Power of a Compliment

"Every day, tell your partner about one thing they did that you appreciate. Everybody is quick to let their partner know what they didn't do right, and what made you angry. Make sure you balance this with what they do that pleases you. From the small things to the big things, the more you say 'Thank you,' the more of what makes you happy will come your way."

—Jane Greer, PhD, couples therapist and author of *Gridlock: Finding the Courage to Move On in Love, Work, and Life*

2 Sex: Just Do It

"Have sex—even when you don't want to! Many times, arousal comes before desire. Once you get going, you'll probably find yourself enjoying it. And the more you experience sex, the more your body will condition itself to want it. You'll feel more sensual and energized, and your partner will pick up on this sexy change."

—Laura Berman, PhD, director of the Berman Center in Chicago and author of *The Passion Prescription*

3 Listen More, Talk less

"Communication is 85 percent listening and 15 percent talking. The more you listen, the more you'll enhance communication. Try getting out of the house, taking a long walk without your cell phones, and just looking into your partner's eyes and listening to him. It's an amazing thing in a relationship when you truly feel listened to!"

—Neil Clark Warren, PhD, founder of eHarmony.com and author of *Falling in Love for All the Right Reasons*

4 Sweep Your Problems (The Little Ones) Under the Rug

"It really is okay to drop certain subjects and not even come back to them. People think this means you're avoiding key issues. But for everyday little things, successful couples agree to ignore the small problems. It's not worth the aggravation to insist on winning everything."

—David Wexler, PhD, executive director of the Relationship Training Institute in San Diego and author of *When Good Men Behave Badly*

5 Treat Your Love Like a Cherished Friendship

"The happiest couples relate to each other with respect, affection, and empathy. They choose their words carefully, avoiding the most poisonous relationship behaviors—criticism, defensiveness, contempt, and stonewalling—and feel emotionally connected."

—John Gottman, PhD, cofounder of the Gottman Institute in Seattle and author of *10 Lessons to Transform Your Marriage*

6 To Change Your Relationship, Change Yourself

"In most relationships, we think, I'm right, you're wrong, and I'll try to convince you to change. The truth is, if one person changes, the relationship changes. People say, 'Why do I have to change?' But when I show them how to tip over the first domino, their only question is, "Why did I wait so long?"

—**Michele Weiner-Davis, couples therapist and author of *The Sex-Starved Marriage***

7 Watch out for Harsh Comments—They Hit Harder than You Think

"When you're tired or frustrated, it's easy to slip into being critical of your partner. But remember, negative expressions and comments and behaviors hold much more weight than positive interactions. Make sure that for every one negative interaction, you have five positive interactions to counteract it—a touch, a laugh, a kiss, an act of love, a compliment."

—**Scott Haltzman, MD, Psychiatrist and author of *The Secrets of Happily Married Men***

8 Don't Knock It Till You've Tried It . . . Twice

"Try being adventurous in bed. Even if you don't like something, give it at least two chances before you give up on it—it may grow on you!"

—**Laura Berman, PhD**

9 Be the First to Offer the Olive Branch

"Often when there's a problem, each person will wait for the other to take the initiative to work things out. But the longer you wait, the more frustrated you both get and the worse you feel. Try making the first move to break a stalemate. It doesn't mean that you're giving in. You're getting the ball rolling, rather than being stuck."

—**Norman Epstein, PhD, marriage researcher and family therapist at the University of Maryland**

10 How to Be a Couple and Still Be Free

Give the love you want to get. "Put out lots of love and appreciation and doing your share, and you're much more likely to get it back. Put out demands and complaining, and you'll get that back too."

—**Tina B. Tessina, PhD, couples therapist and author of *How to Be a Couple and Still Be Free***

11 Fight for Your Love

"I've never seen a decent marriage where there wasn't a lot of conflict. Conflict is always the result of uniqueness, the differences between two people rubbing up against each other. Lots of people try to shut themselves down in order to avoid conflict, but any two people living full and vibrant lives are going to clash at some point. If you manage it carefully and thoughtfully, conflict can actually give your marriage a shot of energy. You can have a broader, fuller, more interesting relationship."

—**Neil Clark Warren, PhD**

12 Sex Matters; Couple Time Matters Even More

"Often couples focus on scheduling sex and working very hard on their sex life, and they don't get anywhere. But when they focus instead on spending time together—going to the movies, working on a project together—then often a better sex life will grow out of that."

—**Ian Kerner, PhD, sex therapist and author of *She Comes First* and *He Comes Next***

13 Don't Get Caught up in Right or Wrong

"It's easy to fall into a power struggle of who's right and who's wrong, but that prevents you from actually solving the real problem. You're not going to be punished for being wrong, so don't worry about who's right—work together to solve the problem."

—**Tina B. Tessina, PhD**

14 Feed Your Relationship

"People often make their own needs a first priority, and then say they can't get what they want out of the relationship. It's like going to your garden and saying,

'Feed me,' and you haven't put any plants in the ground. Make your relationship your first priority. Maybe your relationship needs more time, more vacation. Maybe you need to put in more positive statements or more moments of connection. Become partners in taking care of this relationship. If you get couples engaged in a mutual project, which is their relationship, no matter what they come up with, it's good. It's the working together that does it."

—Harville Hendrix, PhD, founder/
director of Imago Relationship
International and author of
Getting the Love You Want

15 Words Are Like Food—Nurture Each Other with Good Ones

"Say things such as 'I love you,' 'I really appreciate that,' 'I'd love to hear your thoughts about. . . you name it.' And use more empathetic words, like, 'It seems like you're struggling with this.' You'll communicate genuineness and respect, and make your partner feel loved."

—Alan Hovestadt, EdD, president of the
American Association for Marriage
and Family Therapy

16 Never Mind Equality; Focus on Fairness

"Everything doesn't have to be 50/50. Having a sense that each person is doing what's fair—even if it's not always equal—is what really makes a happy marriage. That applies not just to housework, but to the relationship itself."

—Barbara Dafoe Whitehead, PhD,
codirector of the National Marriage
Project at Rutgers University

17 Remember That You Were Partners before You Were Parents

"If you have children, don't forget about your own connection and relationship and put everything into the children. Make relating to each other one-on-one—not just as parents, but as lovers a priority."

—Lou Paget, sex educator
and author of *The Great Lover
Playbook*

18 Learn How to Communicate without Saying a Word

"We are profoundly affected by touch, both physically and emotionally. Happy couples touch each other frequently. A caring touch offers a simple acknowledgment of your partner, saying, 'Way to go' or 'I know that was difficult for you,' without words."

—Alan Hovestadt, EdD

19 Pay Back Your Partner Using His or Her Currency

"Each of us wants our mate to pay us back for our contributions, to give us positive reinforcement. But this payment needs to be in currency that we recognize. A wife may say, 'The way I show I care is that I make his bed every day,' but if he doesn't even notice that, it's ineffective. Get to know what your partner is looking for and make sure you speak his language."

—Scott Haltzman, MD

20 Draw on Your Successes as a Couple

"One way to bring out the best in a relationship is to focus on what you've done right in the past. For example, if you're trying to break a habit of bickering a lot, think back to a time when you were bickering but ended it differently, with humor or by dropping it or in some other way. Every couple has a big hat of experiences when they handled things well, and it's important to draw on this catalog of successes. Rather than just focusing on the times when things ended negatively."

—David Wexler, PhD

21 Dream a Big Dream for Your Relationship

"When two people dream a great dream for their marriage, they typically see their relationship take a dramatic step in the direction of that dream. Start dreaming big— envision where you want your lives and your relationship to be in 10 years. Then let yourself be inspired by these dreams to make whatever changes are necessary to live these dreams out."

—Neil Clark Warren, PhD

22 See Things through Each Other's Eyes

"A lot of conflict comes from always putting a negative spin on what your partner does. Instead of telling yourself that your partner is being thoughtless or irritating, try to think about it from the other person's point of view—ask yourself, What is going on inside that would make him or her act that way? The behavior might still be a problem, but being aware of your partner's intention can change how you view the problem, and make it easier to communicate about it."

—David Wexler, PhD

23 Cultivate Trust to Grow Intimacy

"Trust issues are like sparks in a dry forest—you want to deal with them as fast as you can, whether it's something major, like an affair, or something smaller, like a wife sharing intimate things about her marriage with her best friend. You have to remove the masons for lack of trust so that you can both feel safe sharing yourselves deeply."

—Neil Clark Warren, PhD

24 Never Lose Sight of the Romance

It's important to keep setting aside time for romance. It doesn't always mean that you have to go out for dinner or take a trip. Be imaginative. In fact, I think it's better to have little romantic episodes more often than to have one romantic blowout a year. You want this romantic feeling to be threaded through all your days, so it becomes part of the lifeblood of the marriage."

—Barbara Dafoe Whitehead, PhD

Against All Odds

ANNE KINGSTON

Last month, Jillian Harris packed up her bags and moved from Vancouver to Chicago to live with her fiancé, Ed Swiderski, whom she'd known all of nine weeks before giddily agreeing to marry him; they plan to wed within the year. The couple's warp-speed romance, one of several Harris was juggling on the last season of *The Bachelorette,* was served up like spray cheese on crackers to a fixated audience of millions. The 29-year-old gushed about her instant connection with the 30-year-old Swiderski on *Live with Regis and Kelly* in July: "We had that one date when everything came together," she said. "I knew I could not let him go ever."

As psychotic as that statement sounds, it's the linga franca of the whirlwind courtship, a phenomenon far more fascinating in reality than any on faux "reality" programming. Lately there's been a crop of them. Earlier this year, the 70-year-old writer Joyce Carol Oates married Charles Gross, a professor of psychology at Princeton less than a year after her husband of 47 years, with whom she'd had a happy marriage, died. In January, the *National Post* columnist Diane Francis wed John Beck, the CEO of the construction conglomerate Aecon Group, knowing him less than four months. The couple, both in their 60s, met at a dinner thrown by the conservative think tank the Fraser Institute, which, when you think about it, is the perfect forum for finding Mr. or Ms. Right: Beck, who arrived late, ended up in the only available empty chair, next to Francis. The opinionated pundit declines to comment on her personal life, but in an email response to a question from the *Globe and Mail* about the relationship's rapid progression, she wrote: "When it's right you just know it."

The French coined the term *coup de foudre* to describe the love-at-first-sight thunderbolt—fitting, given the impetuous history of its current first couple, 53-year-old Nicolas Sarkozy and 41-year-old Carla Bruni, the supermodel turned songstress. "I was in love at first sight," Bruni told *Vanity Fair* about meeting France's president at a dinner party in 2007. "I was really surprised by him, by his youth, his energy, his physical charm—which you could not actually see so much on television—his charisma." The pair wed in February 2008, less than three months after that fateful night. It was the first marriage for Bruni, who's famed for her sexual conquests, the third for Sarkozy, also known for making amorous leaps.

The certainty, that "I just knew" that underlines the whirlwind marriage, inspires wonder—and cynicism given the wreckage it can leave in its wake. Hollywood provides the most celebrated examples, the most madcap being Pamela Anderson's and Mötley Crüe member Tommy Lee's three-year nuptial spectacle that kicked off in a pheromone haze on a Mexican beach in 1995: Anderson, in a bridal bikini, married the drummer some 96 hours after they were introduced. Then there is the actress Kate Walsh, who crowed about becoming engaged to 20th Century Fox executive Alex Young in May 2007 after knowing him weeks. "I know—I'm literally living the dream," she told *People* magazine. "But you know when you know." The couple wed in September 2007; 15 months later, the marriage was kaput and Walsh is now living the nightmare of a messy public divorce.

Emily Yoffe, the Washington-based writer who's the "Prudence" of *Slate*'s popular advice column "Dear Prudence," believes the love-at-first-sight model can create pressure, and unrealistic expectations. "There are so many paths to falling in love," she says. She gets letters from people who say they're with a wonderful person and are the happiest they've ever been but don't feel the big romantic "This is it!" so common in chick flicks and reality shows: "And I can never be sure if it's 'You're in this genuine boredom' or 'You have this stupid Hollywood thing in your head about what it should be and you're going to miss what real life is.'"

Marriage counsellors too are critical of "instant" relationships, observing they're often animated by delusion and projection. "I see so much of the damage caused by people blindly connecting, rushing through the stages of commitment, and not creating the solid basis a true relationship needs," says Tina Tessina, a marriage therapist and author in Long Beach, Calif.

Programs like *The Bachelorette* foster the myth that love is an instantaneous emotion, says Mary-Lou Galician, who teaches media analysis and criticism at Arizona State University. "We all have had that feeling and then found out what a dreadful mistake it was," she says. "Real love takes time."

Still, enough inspiring examples exist that suggest a quick impulse to marry can be prescient, even shrewd. Exhibit A is lawyer, political operative and University of Toronto chancellor David Peterson and his wife, Shelley, an actress and author: the couple knew one another only 2½ months before they married in London, Ont., in January 1974. He was 29, she was 21. She didn't know what his religious background was, whether his grandparents were alive or whether or not he wanted children, Shelley Peterson admits: "There were a lot of things we hadn't figured out." Thirty-five years, three children and one grandchild later, the former Ontario premier calls the flight to the altar "the smartest thing I ever did." His wife is equally effusive: "I'm more in love with him now than I was then," she says. "I find that astonishing."

Peterson says he was smitten the first time he saw his future wife on stage. He finagled her phone number and called repeatedly. She had no interest in meeting him, she says: "I didn't need more men in my life." Finally she agreed to lunch. "I thought 'I'll just get this over with. One hour, that's it.'"

By the time the soup course came, David Peterson was "head over heels in love," he says: "She was perfect, gorgeous, funny." She too was taken: "I thought he was lovely and intriguing. I thought, 'This is somebody I need to get to know.'" Shelley Peterson speaks of their marriage as inevitable. "There wasn't a moment I wanted to marry him," she says. "It was more that there just wasn't any other thing to do except to marry him."

Waiting wasn't an option, he says: "How could you wait? It's like a cat catching a mouse: you just jump on it. Everyone knew she was perfect. The only question was whether I was good enough for her."

Her friends and family were less enthusiastic. "But I was quite sure," she says. "And on the other hand I felt that if it didn't turn out to be a good idea I could get out of it."

Catherine Burton, a marriage and family therapist in Dallas, has said that couples who move quickly because they've found someone with stellar spouse qualities—being even-tempered, respectful and thoughtful—tend to have stronger marriages. The Petersons' example supports this theory; they both speak of enduring qualities in the other. "I recognized a sincerity, a belief in humanity, an optimism—a lot of things that never change in a person," she says. He praises her character: "She's the most empathetic person, deeply moral, she has a deep knowledge of the world and what's important." Love flourishes only with mutual respect, they agree. They've told their own children never to settle for a relationship that isn't joyful and passionate. "We tell them it's far better to be alone than in an even slightly unhappy relationship," Shelley Peterson says.

But she knows luck played a part. "How would I know that David was all of the things I hoped he was?" she says. "I couldn't know that. I believe I was extraordinarily lucky that the wilful passion I felt as a 21-year-old didn't end in terrible disaster." Her husband agrees: "But there's also brains in it and you have to work on it."

Research on courtship, surprisingly, contradicts the conventional wisdom that the longer the courtship, the more stable the union. The expert in the field is Ted Huston, a professor of human ecology at the University of Texas who set up a project in 1978 that, for decades, followed 168 couples from their newlywed days. He concludes marital happiness is less a result of a courtship's length than its quality: harmonious courtships tend to presage happy marriages; turbulent ones foreshadow problems. He found that the closer a couple's courtship is to the average length of two years, four months, the more successful their marriage will be. Couples very quick or very slow to wed are more likely to divorce, though those who married in a whirlwind tended to remain married longer, which he attributes to the fact that they start off on such an emotional high they're reluctant to give it up. Those with more drawn-out courtships often

hope marriage will improve their relationship; when it doesn't, they quickly conclude it isn't going to work.

Tessina says she has seen successful marriages after quick courtships: "It can work, if both people are really committed to building a life together, and not just to 'being happy' or getting their own individual needs met," she says. Still, she tells couples to slow down and discuss the serious issues: "They can find out pretty quickly if they have enough shared values."

That's the advice Emily Yoffe gives as "Prudence." "My reaction is: 'What's the rush?'" she says. "Wait at least a year—you'll go through the seasons, you'll have had the holiday issues. Also, you'll want to have your first fight. Sometimes it takes quite a while for masks to drop."

Yet she made the marital leap almost as quickly as Bruni and Sarkozy did; she married *Washington Post* writer John Mintz in 1994 within four months of meeting him. She was 38, had never married, and was living in Los Angeles. Mintz was a 41-year-old widower, living in Washington. Their circles overlapped: Yoffe had lived in Washington and they had mutual friends. Yoffe had dated one of Mintz's friends in L.A. When he told her about Mintz's devotion to his wife during her long illness she was impressed. She didn't know at the time that the friend was turning to Mintz for advice when the relationship began to falter. Mintz, who'd been widowed and single for five years, found himself becoming intrigued by Yoffe. "After a while, John was thinking to himself, 'I have a conflict of interest here: she sounds perfect for me,'" Yoffe says with a laugh. When Yoffe and the friend stopped seeing one another, Mintz called her. After several conversations, he concocted a reason to visit L.A. for business. Yoffe recalls telling her mother that she wasn't sure she wanted to move back to Washington. "My mother said, 'What are you talking about? You haven't even gone out with him yet!' But she didn't understand what this was about, that the stakes were high," she says.

Their maturity was a benefit, Yoffe believes: "We just knew. But we knew in a way that had I been 24 I wouldn't have known." They also knew the attraction was more than lust: "We couldn't stop talking: it's one thing if you can't stop the other 'i-n-g'; that's great but it burns out fast."

Yoffe speaks of the easy comfort and calm many quick-to-marry couples experience, what some refer to as "being home," absent the common "Will he call me?" dating angst. "We were able to read one another and realize we're not on first-date best behavior. We got each other's jokes. I felt he got me, I got him." Six weeks later, standing in the dairy section of a Washington supermarket, they decided to marry. "For us there was a rush," she says. "We wanted to try to have kids. The clock was ticking." Today, the couple are the happily married parents of a 13-year-old daughter.

Older couples often know what they need from a partner, says Tessina, which can help them figure out more quickly if their relationship will succeed, though not always: "Some just repeat the same old mistakes." What counts more, she says, is "emotional maturity."

Yet having the clock ticking literally can spur couples on, as was the case with 61-year-old Shirley Griff, a real estate agent in Thorold, Ont., who married Bill Coates, also 61, in November

2007, six months to the day after they met through an online dating site. Griff's 30-year marriage ended in 2002. Coates, a professional stamp collector, was divorced after a 24-year marriage. They met for lunch at one o'clock. Griff recalls tearing herself away at 4:15 for a 4:30 appointment. "We just spent so much time together and have so much in common," she says. "We're two days apart in age. We're both Pisces." His devotion to his mother impressed her: "To me that's a sign he's going to be appreciative of you as well." He also clicked with her two adult children, who teased her about the suddenness of the wed-ding, she says, which in part was spurred by their desire that Coates's 92-year-old mother be there: "My daughter asked me: 'Are you pregnant, Mom?'"

Waiting didn't make sense, Griff says. "It didn't seem it would prove anything to us, like it would be any different."

Such is the logic from inside the whirlwind courtship. Outside it's another matter. Asked what he'd say to his children if they announced they were marrying someone they had known for a matter of weeks, the happily married David Peterson is adamant: "I'd tell them they were crazy."

The Expectations Trap

Much of the discontent couples encounter today is really culturally inflicted, although we're conditioned to blame our partners for our unhappiness. Yet research points to ways couples can immunize themselves against unseen pressures now pulling them apart.

HARA ESTROFF MARANO

Six years, ten months, and eight days into their marriage, Sam and Melissa blew apart. Everyone was stunned, most of all the couple themselves. One day she was your basic stressed-out professional woman (and mother of a 3-year-old) carrying the major financial burden of their household. The next day she was a betrayed wife. The affair Sam disclosed detonated a caterwaul of hurt heard by every couple in their circle and her large coterie of friends and family. With speed verging on inevitability, the public knowledge of their private life commandeered the driver's seat of their own destiny. A surge of support for Melissa as the wronged woman swiftly isolated Sam emotionally and precluded deep discussion of the conditions that had long alienated him. Out of respect for the pain that his mere presence now caused, Sam decamped within days. He never moved back in.

It's not clear that the couple could have salvaged the relationship if they had tried. It wasn't just the infidelity. "We had so many background and stylistic differences," says Sam. "It was like we came from two separate cultures. We couldn't take out the garbage without a Geneva Accord." Constant negotiation was necessary, but if there was time, there was also usually too much accumulated irritation for Melissa to tolerate. And then, opening a public window on the relationship seemed to close the door on the possibility of working through the disappointments, the frustrations, the betrayal.

Within weeks, the couple was indeed in discussions—for a divorce. At least they both insisted on mediation, not litigation, and their lawyers complied. A couple of months, and some time and determination later, they had a settlement. Only now that Sam and Melissa have settled into their mostly separate lives, and their daughter appears to be doing well with abundant care from both her parents, are they catching their respective breaths—two years later.

Americans value marriage more than people do in any other culture, and it holds a central place in our dreams. Over 90 percent of young adults aspire to marriage—although fewer are actually choosing it, many opting instead for cohabitation. But no matter how you count it, Americans have the highest rate of romantic breakup in the world, says Andrew J. Cherlin, professor of sociology and public policy at Johns Hopkins. As with Sam and Melissa, marriages are discarded often before the partners know what hit them.

"By age 35, 10 percent of American women have lived with three or more husbands or domestic partners," Cherlin reports in his recent hook. *The Marriage-Go-Round: The State of Marriage and the Family in America Today.* "Children of married parents in America face a higher risk of seeing them break up than children born of unmarried parents in Sweden."

With general affluence has come a plethora of choices, including constant choices about our personal and family life. Even marriage itself is now a choice. "The result is an ongoing self-appraisal of how your personal life is going, like having a continual readout of your emotional heart rate," says Cherlin. You get used to the idea of always making choices to improve your happiness.

The constant appraisal of personal life to improve happiness creates a heightened sensitivity to problems that arise in intimate relationships.

The heightened focus on options "creates a heightened sensitivity to problems that arise in intimate relationships." And negative emotions get priority processing in our brains. "There are so many opportunities to decide that it's unsatisfactory," says Cherlin.

It would be one thing if we were living more satisfied lives than ever. But just gauging by the number of relationships wrecked every year, we're less satisfied, says Cherlin. "We're carrying over into our personal lives the fast pace of decisions and actions we have everywhere else, and that may not be for the best." More than ever, we're paying attention to the most volatile parts of our emotional makeup—the parts that are too reactive to momentary events to give meaning to life.

> **More than ever, we're paying attention to the most volatile parts of our emotional makeup—parts that are too reactive to momentary events to give meaning to life.**

Because our intimate relationships are now almost wholly vehicles for meeting our emotional needs, and with almost all our emotions invested in one relationship, we tend to look upon any unhappiness we experience—whatever the source—as a failure of a partner to satisfy our longings. Disappointment inevitably feels so *personal* we see no other possibility but to hunt for individual psychological reasons—that is, to blame our partners for our own unhappiness.

But much—perhaps most—of the discontent we now encounter in close relationships is culturally inflicted, although we rarely interpret our experience that way. Culture—the pressure to constantly monitor our happiness, the plethora of choices surreptitiously creating an expectation of perfection, the speed of everyday life—always climbs into bed with us. An accumulation of forces has made the cultural climate hostile to long-term relationships today.

Attuned to disappointment and confused about its source, we wind up discarding perfectly good relationships. People work themselves up over "the ordinary problems of marriage, for which, by the way, they usually fail to see their own contributions," says William Doherty, professor of family sciences at the University of Minnesota. "They badger their partners to change, convince themselves nothing will budge, and so work their way out of really good relationships." Doherty believes it's possible to stop the careering disappointment even when people believe a relationship is over.

It's not going to happen by putting the genie back in the bottle. It's not possible to curb the excess of options life now offers. And speed is a fixture of the ongoing technological revolution, no matter how much friction it creates in personal lives. Yet new research points to ways that actually render them irrelevant. We are, after all, the architects of our own passions.

The Purpose of Marriage

Marriage probably evolved as the best way to pool the labor of men and women to enable families to subsist and assure that children survive to independence—and data indicate it still is. But beyond the basics, the purpose of marriage has shifted constantly, says Stephanie Coontz, a historian at Washington's Evergreen State College. It helps to remember that marriage evolved in an atmosphere of scarcity, the conditions that prevailed for almost all of human history. "The earliest purpose of marriage was to make strategic alliances with

---

Case Study
Stephen and Christina

Five years into his marriage, not long after the birth of his first son, most of Stephen G.'s interactions with his wife were not pleasant. "I thought the difficulties would pass," he recalls. "My wife, Christina, got fed up faster and wanted me to leave." He was traveling frequently and finances were thin; she'd gone back to school full-time after having worked until the baby was born. "Very few needs were being met for either of us. We were either yelling or in a cold war."

They entered counseling to learn how to co-parent if they indeed separated. "It helped restore our friendship: At least we could talk civilly. That led to deeper communication—we could actually listen to each other without getting defensive. We heard that we were both hurting, both feeling the stress of new parenthood without a support system of either parents or friends. We could talk about the ways we weren't there for each other without feeling attacked. It took a lot longer for the romance to return."

Stephen, now 37, a sales representative for a pharmaceutical company in San Francisco, says it was a time of "growing up. I had to accept that I had new responsibilities. And I had to accept that my partner, now 38, is not ideal in every way although she is ideal in many ways. But her short temper is not enough of a reason to leave the relationship and our two kids. When I wish she'd be different, I have to remind myself of all the ways she is the person I want to be with. It's not something you 'get over.' You accept it."

---

other people, to turn strangers into relatives," says Coontz. "As society became more differentiated, marriage became a major mechanism for adjusting your position."

It wasn't until the 18th century that anyone thought that love might have anything to do with marriage, but love was held in check by a sense of duty. Even through the 19th century, the belief prevailed that females and males had different natures and couldn't he expected to understand each other well. Only in the 20th century did the idea take hold that men and women should be companions, that they should be passionate, and that both should get sexual and personal fulfillment from marriage.

We're still trying to figure out how to do that—and get the laundry done, too. The hassles of a negotiated and constantly renegotiated relationship—few wish a return to inequality—assure a ready source of stress or disappointment or both.

From We to Me

Our mind-set has further shifted over the past few decades, experts suggest. Today, the minute one partner is faced with dissatisfaction—feeling stressed-out or neglected, having

Case Study
Susan and Tim

Susan Pohlman, now 50, reluctantly accompanied her workaholic husband on a business trip to Italy believing it would be their last together. Back home in Los Angeles were their two teenagers, their luxurious home, their overfurnished lives—and the divorce lawyer she had contacted to end their 18-year marriage.

They were leading such parallel lives that collaboration had turned to competition, with fights over things like who spent more time with the kids and who spent more time working. But knocked off balance by the beauty of the coast near Genoa toward the end of the trip, Tim asked, out of the blue, "What if we lived here?" "The spirit of this odd day overtook me," recalls Susan. At 6 P.M. on the evening before departure, they were shown a beautiful apartment overlooking the water. Despite knowing no Italian, they signed a lease on the spot. Two months later, with their house sold, they moved with their kids to Italy for a year.

"In L.A. we were four people going in four directions. In Italy, we became completely dependent on each other. How to get a phone? How to shop for food? Also, we had no belongings. The simplicity forced us to notice the experiences of life. Often, we had no idea what we were doing. There was lots of laughing at and with each other." Susan says she "became aware of the power of adventure and of doing things together, and how they became a natural bridge to intimacy."

Both Pohlmans found Italy offered "a more appreciative lifestyle." Says Susan: "I realized the American Dream was pulling us apart. We followed the formula of owning, having, pushing each other. You have all this stuff but you're miserable because what you're really craving is interaction." Too, she says, American life is exhausting, and "exhaustion distorts your ability to judge problems."

Now back in the U.S. and living in Arizona, the Pohimans believe they needed to remove themselves from the culture to see its distorting effects. "And we needed to participate in a paradigm shift: 'I'm not perfect, you're not perfect; let's not get hung up on our imperfections.'" But the most powerful element of their move could be reproduced anywhere, she says: "The simplicity was liberating."

---

consumer mind-set is a major portal through which destructive forces gain entry and undermine conjoint life.

"Marriage is for *me*" is the way Austin, Texas, family therapist Pat Love puts it. "It's for meeting *my* needs." It's not about what *I do,* but how it makes me *feel.*

Such beliefs lead to a sense of entitlement: "I deserve better than I'm getting." Doherty sees that as the basic message of almost every advertisement in the consumer culture. You deserve more and we can provide it. You begin to think: This isn't the deal I signed up for. Or you begin to feel that you're putting into this a lot more than you're getting out. "We believe in our inalienable right to the intimate relationships of our choice," says Doherty.

In allowing such free-market values to seep into our private lives, we come to believe that a partner's job is, above all, to provide pleasure. "People do not go into relationships because they want to learn how to negotiate and master difficulties," observes Brown University psychiatrist Scott Haltzman. "They want the other person to provide pleasure." It's partner as service provider. The pleasure bond, unfortunately, is as volatile as the emotions that underlie it and as hollow and fragile as the hedonic sense of happiness.

The Expectations Trap: Perfection, Please

If there's one thing that most explicitly detracts from the enjoyment of relationships today, it's an abundance of choice. Psychologist Barry Schwartz would call it an *excess* of choice—the tyranny of abundance. We see it as a measure of our autonomy and we firmly believe that freedom of choice will lead to fulfillment Our antennae are always up for better opportunities, finds Schwartz, professor of psychology at Swarthmore College.

Just as only the best pair of jeans will do, so will only the best partner—whatever that is. "People walk starry-eyed looking not into the eyes of their romantic partner but over their romantic partner's shoulder, in case there might be somebody better walking by. This is not the road to successful long-term relationships." It does not stop with marriage. And it undermines commitment by encouraging people to keep their options open.

Like Doherty, Schwartz sees it as a consequence of a consumer society. He also sees it as a self-fulfilling phenomenon. "If you think there might be something better around the next comer, then there will be, because you're not fully committed to the relationship you've got."

It's naïve to expect relationships to feel good every minute. Every relationship has its bumps. How big a bump does it have to be before you do something about it? As Hopkins's Cherlin says, if you're constantly asking yourself whether you should leave, "there may be a day when the answer is yes. In any marriage there may be a day when the answer is yes."

One of the problems with unrestrained choice, explains Schwartz, is that it raises expectations to the breaking point.

a partner who isn't overly expressive or who works too hard or doesn't initiate sex very often—then the communal ideal we bring to relationships is jettisoned and an individualistic mentality asserts itself. We revert to a stingier self that has been programmed into us by the consumer culture, which has only become increasingly pervasive, the current recession notwithstanding.

Psychologically, the goal of life becomes *my* happiness. "The minute your needs are not being met then you appropriate the individualistic norm," says Doherty. This accelerating

A sense of multiple alternatives, of unlimited possibility, breeds in us the illusion that perfection exists out there, somewhere, if only we could find it. This one's sense of humor, that one's looks, another one's charisma—we come to imagine that there will be a package in which all these desirable features coexist. We search for perfection because we believe we are entitled to the best—even if perfection is an illusion foisted on us by an abundance of possibilities.

If perfection is what you expect, you will always be disappointed, says Schwartz. We become picky and unhappy. The cruel joke our psychology plays on us, of course, is that we are terrible at knowing what will satisfy us or at knowing how any experience will make us feel.

> **A sense of multiple alternatives, of unlimited possibility, breeds in us the illusion that the perfect person is out there waiting to be found.**

If the search through all possibilities weren't exhausting (and futile) enough, thinking about attractive features of the alternatives not chosen—what economists call opportunity costs—reduces the potential pleasure in whatever choice we finally do make. The more possibilities, the more opportunity costs—and the more we think about them, the more we come to regret any choice. "So, once again," says Schwartz, "a greater variety of choices actually makes us feel worse."

Ultimately, our excess of choice leads to lack of intimacy. "How is anyone going to stack up against this perfect person who's out there somewhere just waiting to be found?" asks Schwartz. "It creates doubt about this person, who seems like a good person, someone I might even be in love with—but who knows what's possible *out* there? Intimacy takes time to develop. You need to have some reason to put in the time. If you're full of doubt at the start, you're not going to put in the time."

Moreover, a focus on one's own preferences can come at the expense of those of others. As Schwartz said in his 2004 book, *The Paradox of Choice: Why More Is Less,* "most people find it extremely challenging to balance the conflicting impulses of freedom of choice on the one hand and loyalty and commitment on the other."

And yet, throughout, we are focused on the partner we want to have, not on the one we want—or need—to be. That maybe the worst choice of all.

Disappointment—or Tragedy?

The heightened sensitivity to relationship problems that follows from constantly appraising our happiness encourages couples to turn disappointment into tragedy, Doherty contends.

Inevitably, images of the perfect relationship dancing in our heads collide with our sense of entitlement; "I'm entitled to the best possible marriage." The reality of disappointment becomes intolerable. "It's part of a cultural belief system that says we are entitled to everything we feel we need."

Through the alchemy of desire, wants become needs, and unfulfilled needs become personal tragedies. "A husband who isn't very expressive of his feelings can be a disappointment or a tragedy, depending on whether it's an entitlement," says Doherty. "And that's very much a cultural phenomenon." We take the everyday disappointments of relationships and treat them as intolerable, see them as demeaning—the equivalent of alcoholism, say, or abuse. "People work their way into 'I'm a tragic figure' around the ordinary problems of marriage." Such stories are so widespread, Doherty is no longer inclined to see them as reflecting an individual psychological problem, although that is how he was trained—and how he practiced for many years as an eminent family therapist. "I see it first now as a cultural phenomenon."

First Lady Michelle Obama is no stranger to the disappointment that pervades relationships today. In *Barack and Michelle: Portrait of an American Marriage,* by Christopher Anderson, she confides how she reached a "state of desperation" while working full-time, bringing in the majority of the family income, raising two daughters, and rarely seeing her husband, who was then spending most of his week away from their Chicago home as an Illinois state senator, a job she thought would lead nowhere while it paid little. "She's killing me with this constant criticism," Barack complained. "She just seems so bitter, so angry all the time." She was annoyed that he "seems to think he can just go out there and pursue his dream and leave all the heavy lifting to me."

But then she had an epiphany: She remembered the guy she fell in love with. "I figured out that I was pushing to make Barack be something I wanted him to be for me. I was depending on him to make me happy. Except it didn't have anything to do with him. I needed support. I didn't necessarily need it from Barack."

Certainly, commitment narrows choice. But it is the ability to remember you really do love someone—even though you may not be feeling it at the moment.

Commitment is the ability to sustain an investment, to honor values over momentary feelings. The irony, of course, is that while we want happiness, it isn't a moment-by-moment experience; the deepest, most enduring form of happiness is the result of sustained emotional investments in other people.

Architects of the Heart

One of the most noteworthy findings emerging from relationship research is that desire isn't just something we passively feel when everything's going right; it develops in direct response to what we do. Simply having fun together, for example, is crucial to keeping the sex drive alive.

But in the churn of daily life, we tend to give short shrift to creating positive experiences. Over time, we typically become more oriented to dampening threats and insecurities—to resolving conflict, to eliminating jealousy, to banishing problems. But the brain is wired with both a positive and negative motivational system, and satisfaction and desire demand keeping the brain's positive system well-stoked.

Even for long-term couples, spending time together in novel, interesting, or challenging activities—games, dancing, even conversation—enhances feelings of closeness, passionate love, and satisfaction with the relationship. Couples recapture the excitement of the early days of being in love. Such passion naturally feeds commitment.

From Michelle to Michelangelo

Important as it is to choose the right partner, it's probably more important to *be* the right partner. Most people are focused on changing the wrong person in the relationship; if anyone has to change in a relationship, it's you—although preferably with the help of your partner.

> **Important as it is to choose the right partner, it's probably more important to *be* the right partner. We focus on changing the wrong person.**

Ultimately, "Marriage is an inside job," Pat Love told the 2009 Smart marriages Conference. "It's internal to the person. You have to let it do its work." And its biggest job is helping individuals grow up. "Marriage is about getting over yourself. Happiness is not about focusing on yourself." Happiness is about holding onto your values, deciding who you are and being that person, using your particular talent, and investing in others.

Unfortunately, says Margin family therapist and *PT* blogger Susan Pease Gadoua, not enough people today are willing to do the hard work of becoming a more mature person. "They think they have a lot more choices. And they think life will be easier in another relationship. What they don't realize is that it will be the same relationship—just with a different name."

The question is not how you want your partner to change but what kind of partner and person you want to be. In the best relationships, not only are you thinking about who you want to be, but your partner is willing to help you get there. Psychologist Caryl E. Rusbult calls it the Michelangelo phenomenon. Just as Michelangelo felt the figures he created were already "in" the stones, "slumbering within the actual self is an ideal form," explains Eli Finkel, associate professor of psychology at Northwestern University and frequent Rusbult collaborator. Your partner becomes an ally in sculpting your ideal self, in bringing out the person you dream of becoming, leading you to a deep form of personal growth as well as long-term satisfaction with life and with the relationship.

It takes a partner who supports your dreams, the traits and qualities you want to develop—whether or not you've

Case Study
Patty and Rod

Patty NewBold had married "a really great guy," but by the time their 13th anniversary rolled around, she had a long list of things he needed to change to make the marriage work. At 34, she felt depressed, frantic—and guilty, as Rod was fighting a chronic disease. But she had reached a breaking point, "I read my husband my list of unmet needs and suggested a divorce," even though what she really wanted was her marriage back. "I wanted to feel loved again. But it didn't seem possible."

Newbold has had a long time to think about that list. Her husband died the next day, a freak side effect of his medications. "He was gone, but the list remained. Out of perhaps 30 needs, only one was eased by losing him. I was free now to move the drinking glasses next to the sink."

As she read through the list the morning after he died, she realized that "marriage isn't about my needs or his needs or about how well we communicate about our needs. It's about loving and being loved. *Life* is about meeting (or letting go of) my own *needs. Marriage* is about loving another person and receiving love in return. It suddenly became oh so clear that receiving love is something I make happen, not him." And then she was flooded with memories of all the times "I'd been offered love by this wonderful man and rejected it because I was too wrapped up in whatever need I was facing at the time."

Revitalized is "a funny word to describe a relationship in which one party is dead," she reports, "but ours was revitalized. I was completely changed, too," Everything she learned that awful day has gone into a second marriage, now well into its second decade.

articulated them clearly or simply expressed vague yearnings. "People come to reflect what their partners see in them and elicit from them," Finkel and Rusbult report in *Current Directions in Psychological Science*.

Such affirmation promotes trust in the partner and strengthens commitment. And commitment, Rusbult has found, is a key predictor of relationship durability. "It creates positive bias towards each other," says Finkel. "It feels good to achieve our goals. It's deeply satisfying and meaningful." In addition, it immunizes the relationship against potential distractions—all those "perfect" others. Finkel explains, "It motivates the derogation of alternative partners." It creates the perception—the illusion—that even the most attractive alternative partners are unappealing. Attention to them gets turned off—one oft he many cognitive gymnastics we engage in to ward off doubts.

Like growth, commitment is an inside job. It's not a simple vow. Partners see each other in ways that enhance their connection and fend off threats. It fosters the perception that the relationship you're in is better than that of others. It breeds the inclination to react constructively—by accommodation—rather than destructively when a partner does something inconsiderate. It even motivates that most difficult of tasks, forgiveness for the ultimate harm of betrayal, Rusbult has shown.

It is a willingness—stemming in part from an understanding that your well-being and your partner's are linked over the long term—to depart from direct self-interest, such as erecting a grudge when you feel hurt.

The Michelangelo phenomenon gives the lie to the soul mate search. You can't find the perfect person; there is no such thing. And even if you think you could, the person he or she is today is, hopefully, not quite the person he or she wants to be 10 years down the road. You and your partner help each other become a more perfect person—perfect, that is, according to your own inner ideals. You are both, with mutual help, constantly evolving.

On-Again, Off-Again

What drives couples to repeatedly break up and then make up?

ELIZABETH SVOBODA

For Laura, a 35-year-old corporate recruiter from New York City, dating had always felt like a Ferris wheel ride. When a relationship started to feel wrong, she'd leave to get a new vantage point on things, but as the pain of singleness set in, she retreated to her former partner for comfort, ending up back where she started. She'd repeat the cycle several times before breaking things off permanently. "It became this crazy pattern," she says. "They weren't good guys at all, but whenever something in my life was difficult, I would go back."

Laura's longtime boomeranging habit puts her in good company. The dynamic is quite common. University of Texas communications professor René Dailey found that 60 percent of adults have ended a romantic relationship and then gotten back together, and that three-quarters of those respondents had been through the breakup, makeup cycle at least twice. But embarking on this bumpy relational road takes an emotional toll: On-off couples have more relational stress than non-cyclical couples, she found.

Given the obvious costs, why do couples keep dancing the on-and-off tango? Many who seesaw from freeze-outs to fervent proclamations of love know deep down that the relationship probably isn't right, says psychologist Steven Stosny. But when couples are faced with the loneliness and low self-esteem that accompany a breakup, they continually fall back on the temporary relief of reconciliation.

It's often the fleeting high points of a fundamentally rocky relationship that convince embattled partners to keep coming back for more, spurring a tortuous dynamic with no end in sight. "Often there is something that works very well for you about this person," says Gail Saltz, a Manhattan-based psychiatrist and author of *Becoming Real*. But when your mate's dreamy qualities are accompanied by deal-breaker ones like dishonesty or irresponsibility, it can be difficult to make a clear-headed assessment of whether to stay or leave.

Many couples with a boomeranging habit know deep down that the relationship probably isn't right.

While problem behaviors may prompt a periodic hiatus, on-again, off-again couples continue to reunite out of a persistent hope that the moments of happiness and fulfillment they've known will someday constitute the entire relationship. "People say, 'I can fix this other part of my partner,'" Saltz says, even though efforts at "remodeling" a mate are typically useless. The self-deprecating internal monologues that serial on-off artists conduct after a breakup—"What was I thinking? I'll never meet

Breaking the Breakup Cycle

On-again, off-again couples often find themselves caught between their desire for freedom and their fear of regret. Here's how to decide whether to sign on for the long haul or get out for good.

- **Adopt a worst-case-scenario** mindset. Many perpetual boomerangers keep returning because they assume they can change their partner's worst habits. But that's wishful thinking, psychotherapist Toni Coleman says. "You have to assume that the behaviors you see will get *more* entrenched and worse over time. Ask yourself, 'If that turns out to be the case, would I still want to be in this relationship?'"
- **Seek advice from** a trusted third party. Therapists fill the bill nicely, but family and friends can be just as helpful. Because they don't have as much invested in your partner as you do, they can provide unbiased opinions as to whether smooth sailing is in your relationship's future.
- **Take a time-out.** In an on-again, off-again pairing, hiatuses are par for the course. But resolve to make this one different. Use the emotional distance to think clearly about what you want from a long-term relationship. Make a list if it helps you organize your thoughts. If your partner doesn't measure up, make the hiatus permanent.

someone as funny, smart, and attractive ever again!"—can also lead to repeated reconciliations.

While periodic estrangement is painful, some couples see a silver lining. By experiencing life without their significant others for a while, they come away with a deeper understanding of the value of their bond, even if the romance doesn't always have storybook qualities.

But this kind of "pruning" is no panacea. Virginia psychotherapist Toni Coleman warns couples to steer clear of the false epiphanies making up and breaking up can encourage. After an emotion-filled reunion, it's tempting to assume your partner has permanently changed for the better. But underlying conflicts that simmered before the breakup will resurface—just ask consummate on-off artists Pamela Anderson and Tommy Lee, who married and divorced twice before breaking up for good. "Things will change only if both people commit to working on the big issues," says Coleman.

Saltz recommends veterans of the breakup, makeup carousel take time to think about why they've been there so long in the first place. "The key is in recognizing that there is a pattern," she says. "You need to elucidate what the draw of this relationship really is for you." Some on-off cyclists, she explains, repeatedly return to partnerships with flaws that mirror those in their own parents' marriage, which they've unconsciously internalized as fundamental to any relationship. If your mother took her cheating partner back over and over again, you maybe inclined to do the same. "Just the awareness of that can help you step out: 'Oh, my gosh, this is really me being my mother, and I don't want to recapitulate her love story,'" says Saltz.

Another way to decide whether to fish or cut bait for good, Coleman says, is to take as long a view as possible. By forcing partners to consider the implications of "forever," so-called fast-forwarding scenarios may make them less likely to acquiesce to the temporary high of being "on" again with a problematic mate.

Since casting aside her most recent drama-ridden relationship, Laura has decided to steer clear of the dating world for a while. She sees her new freedom as a chance to step back and contemplate how to avoid the trap in the future. "The whole love industry makes you feel like you have to be in a relationship all the time, but right now I'm just taking some time to figure things out," she says. "I truly am happy on my own."

ELIZABETH SVOBODA is a freelance writer in San Jose, California.

Fats, Carbs and the Science of Conception

In a groundbreaking new book, Harvard researchers look at the role of diet, exercise and weight control in fertility. Guarantee: you will be surprised.

JORGE E. CHAVARRO, MD, WALTER C. WILLETT, MD, AND PATRICK J. SKERRETT

Every new life starts with two seemingly simple events. First, an active sperm burrows into a perfectly mature egg. Then the resulting fertilized egg nestles into the specially prepared lining of the uterus and begins to grow. The key phrase in that description is "seemingly simple." Dozens of steps influenced by a cascade of carefully timed hormones are needed to make and mature eggs and sperm. Their union is both a mad dash and a complex dance, choreographed by hormones, physiology and environmental cues.

A constellation of other factors can come into play. Many couples delay having a baby until they are financially ready or have established themselves in their professions. Waiting, though, decreases the odds of conceiving and increases the chances of having a miscarriage. Fewer than 10 percent of women in their early 20s have issues with infertility, compared with nearly 30 percent of those in their early 40s. Sexually transmitted diseases such as chlamydia and gonorrhea, which are on the upswing, can cause or contribute to infertility. The linked epidemics of obesity and diabetes sweeping the country have reproductive repercussions. Environmental contaminants known as endocrine disruptors, such as some pesticides and emissions from burning plastics, appear to affect fertility in women and men. Stress and anxiety, both in general and about fertility, can also interfere with getting pregnant. Add all these to the complexity of conception and it's no wonder that infertility is a common problem, besetting an estimated 6 million American couples.

It's almost become a cliché that diet, exercise and lifestyle choices affect how long you'll live, the health of your heart, the odds you'll develop cancer and a host of other health-related issues. Is fertility on this list? The answer to that question has long been a qualified "maybe," based on old wives' tales, conventional wisdom—and almost no science. Farmers, ranchers and animal scientists know more about how nutrition affects fertility in cows, pigs and other commercially important animals than fertility experts know about how it affects reproduc-

tion in humans. There are small hints scattered across medical journals, but few systematic studies of this crucial connection in people.

We set out to change this critical information gap with the help of more than 18,000 women taking part in the Nurses' Health Study, a long-term research project looking at the effects of diet and other factors on the development of chronic conditions such as heart disease, cancer and other diseases. Each of these women said she was trying to have a baby. Over eight years of follow-up, most of them did. About one in six women, though, had some trouble getting pregnant, including hundreds who experienced ovulatory infertility—a problem related to the maturation or release of a mature egg each month. When we compared their diets, exercise habits and other lifestyle choices with those of women who readily got pregnant, several key differences emerged. We have translated these differences into fertility-boosting strategies.

At least for now, these recommendations are aimed at preventing and reversing ovulatory infertility, which accounts for one quarter or more of all cases of infertility. They won't work for infertility due to physical impediments like blocked fallopian tubes. They may work for other types of infertility, but we don't yet have enough data to explore connections between nutrition and infertility due to other causes. And since the Nurses' Health Study doesn't include information on the participants' partners, we weren't able to explore how nutrition affects male infertility. From what we have gleaned from the limited research in this area, some of our strategies might improve fertility in men, too. The plan described in The Fertility Diet doesn't guarantee a pregnancy any more than do in vitro fertilization or other forms of assisted reproduction. But it's virtually free, available to everyone, has no side effects, sets the stage for a healthy pregnancy, and forms the foundation of a healthy eating strategy for motherhood and beyond. That's a winning combination no matter how you look at it.

Slow Carbs, Not No Carbs

Once upon a time, and not that long ago, carbohydrates were the go-to gang for taste, comfort, convenience and energy. Bread, pasta, rice, potatoes—these were the highly recommended, base-of-the-food-pyramid foods that supplied us with half or more of our calories. Then in rumbled the Atkins and South Beach diets. In a scene out of George Orwell's "1984," good became bad almost overnight as the two weight-loss juggernauts turned carbohydrates into dietary demons, vilifying them as the source of big bellies and jiggling thighs. Following the no-carb gospel, millions of Americans spurned carbohydrates in hopes of shedding pounds. Then, like all diet fads great and small, the no-carb craze lost its luster and faded from prominence.

It had a silver lining, though, and not just for those selling low-carb advice and products. All the attention made scientists and the rest of us more aware of carbohydrates and their role in a healthy diet. It spurred several solid head-to-head comparisons of low-carb and low-fat diets that have given us a better understanding of how carbohydrates affect weight and weight loss. The new work supports the growing realization that carbohydrate choices have a major impact—for better and for worse—on the risk for heart disease, stroke, type 2 diabetes and digestive health.

New research from the Nurses' Health Study shows that carbohydrate choices also influence fertility. Eating lots of easily digested carbohydrates (fast carbs), such as white bread, potatoes and sugared sodas, increases the odds that you'll find yourself struggling with ovulatory infertility. Choosing slowly digested carbohydrates that are rich in fiber can improve fertility. This lines up nicely with work showing that a diet rich in these slow carbs and fiber before pregnancy helps prevent gestational diabetes, a common and worrisome problem for pregnant women and their babies. What do carbohydrates have to do with ovulation and pregnancy?

More than any other nutrient, carbohydrates determine your blood-sugar and insulin levels. When these rise too high, as they do in millions of individuals with insulin resistance, they disrupt the finely tuned balance of hormones needed for reproduction. The ensuing hormonal changes throw ovulation off-kilter.

Knowing that diet can strongly influence blood sugar and insulin, we wondered if carbohydrate choices could influence fertility in average, relatively healthy women. The answer from the Nurses' Health Study was yes. We started by grouping the study participants from low daily carbohydrate intake to high. One of the first things we noticed was a connection between high carbohydrate intake and healthy lifestyles.

Women in the high-carb group, who got nearly 60 percent of their calories from carbs, ate less fat and animal protein, drank less alcohol and coffee, and consumed more plant protein and fiber than those in the low-carb group, who got 42 percent of calories from carbohydrates. Women in the top group also weighed less, weren't as likely to smoke and were more physically active. This is a good sign that carbohydrates can be just fine for health, especially if you choose good ones.

The *total* amount of carbohydrate in the diet wasn't connected with ovulatory infertility. Women in the low-carb and high-carb groups were equally likely to have had fertility problems. That wasn't a complete surprise. As we described earlier, different carbohydrate sources can have different effects on blood sugar, insulin and long-term health.

Evaluating total carbohydrate intake can hide some important differences. So we looked at something called the glycemic load. This relatively new measure conveys information about both the amount of carbohydrate in the diet and how quickly it is turned to blood sugar. The more fast carbs in the diet, the higher the glycemic load. (For more on glycemic load, go to health. harvard.edu/newsweek.) Women in the highest glycemic-load category were 92 percent more likely to have had ovulatory infertility than women in the lowest category, after accounting for age, smoking, how much animal and vegetable protein they ate, and other factors that can also influence fertility. In other words, eating a lot of easily digested carbohydrates increases the odds of ovulatory infertility, while eating more slow carbs decreases the odds.

Because the participants of the Nurses' Health Study complete reports every few years detailing their average daily diets, we were able to see if certain foods contributed to ovulatory infertility more than others. In general, cold breakfast cereals, white rice and potatoes were linked with a higher risk of ovulatory infertility. Slow carbs, such as brown rice, pasta and dark bread, were linked with greater success getting pregnant.

Computer models of the nurses' diets were also revealing. We electronically replaced different nutrients with carbohydrates. Most of these substitutions didn't make a difference. One, though, did. Adding more carbohydrates at the expense of naturally occurring fats predicted a decrease in fertility. This could very well mean that natural fats, especially unsaturated fats, improve ovulation when they replace easily digested carbohydrates.

In a nutshell, results from the Nurses' Health Study indicate that the *amount* of carbohydrates in the diet doesn't affect fertility, but the *quality* of those carbohydrates does. Eating a lot of rapidly digested carbohydrates that continually boost your blood-sugar and insulin levels higher can lower your chances of getting pregnant. This is especially true if you are eating carbohydrates in place of healthful unsaturated fats. On the other hand, eating whole grains, beans, vegetables and whole fruits—all of which are good sources of slowly digested carbohydrates—can improve ovulation and your chances of getting pregnant.

Eating whole grains, beans, vegetables and whole fruits—all sources of 'slow carbs'— can improve ovulation and chances of pregnancy.

Balancing Fats

In 2003, the government of Denmark made a bold decision that is helping protect its citizens from heart disease: it essentially banned trans fats in fast food, baked goods and other commercially prepared foods. That move may have an unexpected effect—more little Danes. Exciting findings from the Nurses' Health Study indicate that trans fats are a powerful deterrent to ovulation and conception. Eating less of this artificial fat can improve fertility, and simultaneously adding in healthful unsaturated fats whenever possible can boost it even further.

Women, their midwives and doctors, and fertility researchers have known for ages that body fat and energy stores affect reproduction. Women who don't have enough stored energy to sustain a pregnancy often have trouble ovulating or stop menstruating altogether. Women who have too much stored energy often have difficulty conceiving for other reasons, many of which affect ovulation. These include insensitivity to the hormone insulin, an excess of male sex hormones and overproduction of leptin, a hormone that helps the body keep tabs on body fat.

A related issue is whether *dietary* fats influence ovulation and reproduction. We were shocked to discover that this was largely uncharted territory. Until now, only a few studies have explored this connection. They focused mainly on the relationship between fat intake and characteristics of the menstrual cycle, such as cycle length and the duration of different phases of the cycle. In general, these studies suggest that more fat in the diet, and in some cases more saturated fat, improves the menstrual cycle. Most of these studies were very small and didn't account for total calories, physical activity or other factors that also influence reproduction. None of them examined the effect of dietary fat on fertility.

The dearth of research in this area has been a gaping hole in nutrition research. If there is a link between fats in the diet and reproduction, then simple changes in food choices could offer delicious, easy and inexpensive ways to improve fertility. The Nurses' Health Study research team looked for connections between dietary fats and fertility from a number of different angles. Among the 18,555 women in the study, the total amount of fat in the diet wasn't connected with ovulatory infertility once weight, exercise, smoking and other factors that can influence reproduction had been accounted for. The same was true for cholesterol, saturated fat and monounsaturated fat—none were linked with fertility or infertility. A high intake of polyunsaturated fat appeared to provide some protection against ovulatory infertility in women who also had high intakes of iron, but the effect wasn't strong enough to be sure exactly what role this healthy fat plays in fertility and infertility.

Trans fats were a different story. Across the board, the more trans fat in the diet, the greater the likelihood of developing ovulatory infertility. We saw an effect even at daily trans fat intakes of about four grams a day. That's less than the amount the average American gets each day.

Eating more trans fat usually means eating less of another type of fat or carbohydrates. Computer models of the nurses' diet patterns indicated that eating a modest amount of trans fat (2 percent of calories) in place of other, more healthful nutrients like polyunsaturated fat, monounsaturated fat or carbohydrate would dramatically increase the risk of infertility. To put this into perspective, for someone who eats 2,000 calories a day, 2 percent of calories translates into about four grams of trans fat.

That's the amount in two tablespoons of stick margarine, one medium order of fast-food french fries or one doughnut.

Fats aren't merely inert carriers of calories or building blocks for hormones or cellular machinery. They sometimes have powerful biological effects, such as turning genes on or off, revving up or calming inflammation and influencing cell function. Unsaturated fats do things to improve fertility—increase insulin sensitivity and cool inflammation—that are the opposite of what trans fats do. That is probably why the largest decline in fertility among the nurses was seen when trans fats were eaten instead of monounsaturated fats.

The Protein Factor

At the center of most dinner plates sits, to put it bluntly, a hunk of protein. Beef, chicken and pork are Americans' favorites, trailed by fish. Beans lag far, far behind. That's too bad. Beans are an excellent source of protein and other needed nutrients, like fiber and many minerals. And by promoting the lowly bean from side dish to center stage and becoming more inventive with protein-rich nuts, you might find yourself eating for two. Findings from the Nurses' Health Study indicate that getting more protein from plants and less from animals is another big step toward walking away from ovulatory infertility.

Scattered hints in the medical literature that protein in the diet may influence blood sugar, sensitivity to insulin and the production of insulin-like growth factor-1—all of which play important roles in ovulation—prompted us to look at protein's impact on ovulatory infertility in the Nurses' Health Study.

We grouped the participants by their average daily protein intake. The lowest-protein group took in an average of 77 grams a day; the highest, an average of 115 grams. After factoring in smoking, fat intake, weight and other things that can affect fertility, we found that women in the highest-protein group were 41 percent more likely to have reported problems with ovulatory infertility than women in the lowest-protein group.

When we looked at animal protein intake separately from plant protein, an interesting distinction appeared. Ovulatory infertility was 39 percent more likely in women with the highest intake of animal protein than in those with the lowest. The reverse was true for women with the highest intake of plant protein, who were substantially less likely to have had ovulatory infertility than women with the lowest plant protein intake.

That's the big picture. Computer models helped refine these relationships and put them in perspective. When total calories were kept constant, adding one serving a day of red meat, chicken or turkey predicted nearly a one-third increase in the risk of ovulatory infertility. And while adding one serving a day of fish or eggs didn't influence ovulatory infertility, adding one serving a day of beans, peas, tofu or soybeans, peanuts or other nuts predicted modest protection against ovulatory infertility.

Eating more of one thing means eating less of another, if you want to keep your weight stable. We modeled the effect that juggling the proportions of protein and carbohydrate would have on fertility. Adding animal protein instead of carbohydrate was related to a greater risk of ovulatory infertility. Swapping 25 grams of animal protein for 25 grams of carbohydrates upped the risk by nearly 20 percent. Adding plant protein instead of carbohydrates was related to a lower risk of ovulatory infertility. Swapping 25 grams of plant protein for 25 grams of carbohydrates shrank the risk by 43 percent. Adding plant protein instead of animal protein was even more effective. Replacing 25 grams of animal protein with 25 grams of plant protein was related to a 50 percent lower risk of ovulatory infertility.

These results point the way to another strategy for overcoming ovulatory infertility—eating more protein from plants and less from animals. They also add to the small but growing body of evidence that plant protein is somehow different from animal protein.

Milk and Ice Cream

Consider the classic sundae: a scoop of creamy vanilla ice cream crisscrossed by rivulets of chocolate sauce, sprinkled with walnuts and topped with a spritz of whipped cream. If you are having trouble getting pregnant, and ovulatory infertility is suspected, think of it as temporary health food. OK, maybe that's going a bit too far. But a fascinating finding from the Nurses' Health Study is that a daily serving or two of whole milk and foods made from whole milk—full-fat yogurt, cottage cheese, and, yes, even ice cream—seem to offer some protection against ovulatory infertility, while skim and low-fat milk do the opposite.

The results fly in the face of current standard nutrition advice. But they make sense when you consider what skim and low-fat milk do, and don't, contain. Removing fat from milk radically changes its balance of sex hormones in a way that could tip the scales against ovulation and conception. Proteins added to make skim and low-fat milk look and taste "creamier" push it even farther away.

It would be an overstatement to say that there is a handful of research into possible links between consumption of dairy products and fertility. The vanishingly small body of work in this area is interesting, to say the least, given our fondness for milk, ice cream and other dairy foods. The average American woman has about two servings of dairy products a day, short of the three servings a day the government's dietary guidelines would like her to have.

The depth and detail of the Nurses' Health Study database allowed us to see which foods had the biggest effects. The most potent fertility food from the dairy case was, by far, whole milk, followed by ice cream. Sherbet and frozen yogurt, followed by low-fat yogurt, topped the list as the biggest contributors to ovulatory infertility. The more low-fat dairy products in a woman's diet, the more likely she was to have had trouble getting pregnant. The more full-fat dairy products in a woman's diet, the less likely she was to have had problems getting pregnant.

Our advice on milk and dairy products might be criticized as breaking the rules. The "rules," though, aren't based on solid science and may even conflict with the evidence. And for solving the problem of ovulatory infertility, the rules may need tweaking. Think about switching to full-fat milk or dairy products as a temporary nutrition therapy designed to improve your chances of becoming pregnant. If your efforts pay off, or if you stop trying to have a baby, then you may want to rethink dairy—especially whole milk and other full-fat dairy foods—altogether. Over the long haul, eating a lot of these isn't great for your heart, your blood vessels or the rest of your body.

Before you sit down to a nightly carton of Häagen-Dazs ("*The Fertility Diet* said I needed ice cream, honey"), keep in mind that it doesn't take much in the way of full-fat dairy foods to measurably affect fertility. Among the women in the Nurses' Health Study, having just one serving a day of a full-fat dairy food, particularly milk, decreased the chances of having ovulatory infertility. The impact of ice cream was seen at two half-cup servings a week. If you eat ice cream at that rate, a pint should last about two weeks.

Equally important, you'll need to do some dietary readjusting to keep your calorie count and your waistline from expanding. Whole milk has nearly double the calories of skim milk. If you have been following the U.S. government's poorly-thought-out recommendation and are drinking three glasses of milk a day, trading skim milk for whole means an extra 189 calories a day. That could translate into a weight gain of 15 to 20 pounds over a year if you don't cut back somewhere else. Those extra pounds can edge aside any fertility benefits you might get from dairy foods. There's also the saturated fat to consider, an extra 13 grams in three glasses of whole milk compared with skim, which would put you close to the healthy daily limit.

Aim for one to two servings of dairy products a day, both of them full fat. This can be as easy as having your breakfast cereal with whole milk and a slice of cheese at lunch or a cup of whole-milk yogurt for lunch and a half-cup of ice cream for dessert. Easy targets for cutting back on calories and saturated fat are red and processed meats, along with foods made with fully or partially hydrogenated vegetable oils.

Once you become pregnant, or if you decide to stop trying, going back to low-fat dairy products makes sense as a way to keep a lid on your intake of saturated fat and calories. You could also try some of the nondairy strategies for getting calcium and protecting your bones. If you don't like milk or other dairy products, or they don't agree with your digestive system, don't force yourself to have them. There are many other things you can do to fight ovulatory infertility. This one is like dessert—enjoyable but optional.

The Role of Body Weight

Weighing too much or too little can interrupt normal menstrual cycles, throw off ovulation or stop it altogether. Excess weight lowers the odds that in vitro fertilization or other assisted reproductive technologies will succeed. It increases the chances of miscarriage, puts a mother at risk during pregnancy of developing high blood pressure (pre-eclampsia) or diabetes, and elevates her chances of needing a Cesarean section. The dangers of being overweight or underweight extend to a woman's baby as well.

Weight is one bit of information that the participants of the Nurses' Health Study report every other year. By linking this information with their accounts of pregnancy, birth, miscarriage and difficulty getting pregnant, we were able to see a strong connection between weight and fertility. Women with the lowest and highest Body Mass Indexes (BMI) were more likely to have had trouble with ovulatory infertility than women in the middle. Infertility was least common among women with BMIs of 20 to 24, with an ideal around 21.

Keep in mind that this is a statistical model of probabilities that links weight and fertility. It doesn't mean you'll get pregnant only if you have a BMI between 20 and 24. Women with higher and lower BMIs than this get pregnant all the time without delay or any medical help. But it supports the idea that weighing too much or too little for your frame can get in the way of having a baby.

We call the range of BMIs from 20 to 24 the fertility zone. It isn't magic—nothing is for fertility—but having a weight in that range seems to be best for getting pregnant. If you aren't in or near the zone, don't despair. Working to move your BMI in that direction by gaining or losing some weight is almost as good. Relatively small changes are often enough to have the desired effects of healthy ovulation and improved fertility. If you are too lean, gaining five or 10 pounds can sometimes be enough to restart ovulation and menstrual periods. If you are overweight, losing 5 percent to 10 percent of your current weight is often enough to improve ovulation.

Being at a healthy weight or aiming toward one is great for ovulatory function and your chances of getting pregnant. The "side effects" aren't so bad, either. Working to achieve a healthy weight can improve your sensitivity to insulin, your cholesterol, your blood pressure and your kidney function. It can give you more energy and make you look and feel better.

While dietary and lifestyle contributions to fertility and infertility in men have received short shrift, weight is one area in which there has been some research. A few small studies indicate that overweight men aren't as fertile as their healthy-weight counterparts. Excess weight can lower testosterone levels, throw off the ratio of testosterone to estrogen (men make some estrogen, just as women make some testosterone) and hinder the production of sperm cells that are good swimmers. A study published in 2006 of more than 2,000 American farmers and their wives showed that as BMI went up, fertility declined. In men, the connection between increasing weight and decreasing fertility can't yet be classified as rock solid. But it is good enough to warrant action, mainly because from a health perspective there aren't any downsides to losing weight if you are overweight. We can't define a fertility zone for weight in men, nor can anyone else. In lieu of that, we can say to men who are carrying too many pounds that shedding some could be good for fertility and will be good for overall health.

The Importance of Exercise

Baby, we were born to run. That isn't just the tagline of Bruce Springsteen's anthem to young love and leavin' town. It's also a perfect motto for getting pregnant and for living a long, healthy life. Inactivity deprives muscles of the constant push and pull they need to stay healthy. It also saps their ability to respond to insulin and to efficiently absorb blood sugar. When that leads to too much blood sugar and insulin in the bloodstream, it endangers ovulation, conception and pregnancy. Physical activity and exercise are recommended and even prescribed for almost everyone—except women who are having trouble getting pregnant. Forty-year-old findings that too much exercise can turn off menstruation and ovulation make some women shy away from exercise and nudge some doctors to recommend avoiding exercise altogether, at least temporarily. That's clearly the right approach for women who exercise hard for many hours a week and who are extremely lean. But taking it easy isn't likely to help women who aren't active or those whose weights are normal or above where they should be. In other words, the vast majority of women.

Some exciting results from the Nurses' Health Study and a handful of small studies show that exercise can be a boon for fertility. These important findings are establishing a vital link between activity and getting pregnant. Much as we would like to offer a single prescription for conception-boosting exercise, however, we can't. Some women need more exercise than others, for their weight or moods, and others are active just because they enjoy it. Some who need to be active aren't, while a small number of others may be too active.

Instead of focusing on an absolute number, try aiming for the fertility zone. This is a range of exercise that offers the biggest window of opportunity for fertility. Being in the fertility zone means you aren't overdoing or underdoing exercise. For most women, this means getting at least 30 minutes of exercise every day. But if you are carrying more pounds than is considered healthy for your frame (i.e., a BMI above 25), you may need to exercise for an hour or more. If you are quite lean (i.e., your BMI is 19 or below), aim for the middle of the exercise window for a few months. Keep in mind that the fertility zone is an ideal, not an absolute. Hospital delivery rooms are full of women who rarely, or never, exercise. Not everyone is so lucky. If you are having trouble getting pregnant, then maybe the zone is the right place for you.

Whether you classify yourself as a couch potato or an exercise aficionado, your fertility zone should include four types of activity: aerobic exercise, strength training, stretching and the activities of daily living. This quartet works together to control weight, guard against high blood sugar and insulin, and keep your muscles limber and strong. They are also natural stress relievers, something almost everyone coping with or worrying about infertility can use.

Exercise has gotten a bad rap when it comes to fertility. While the pioneering studies of Dr. Rose Frisch and her colleagues convincingly show that too much exercise coupled with too little stored energy can throw off or turn off ovulation in elite athletes, their work says nothing about the impact of usual exercise in normal-weight or overweight women. Common sense says that it can't be a big deterrent to conception. If it were, many of us wouldn't be here. Our ancestors worked hard to hunt, forage, clear fields and travel from place to place. Early *Homo sapiens* burned twice as many calories each day as the average American does today and were fertile despite it—or because of it.

Results from the Nurses' Health Study support this evolutionary perspective and show that exercise, particularly vigorous exercise, actually improves fertility. Exercising for at least 30 minutes on most days of the week is a great place to start.

It doesn't really matter how you exercise, as long as you find something other than your true love that moves you and gets your heart beating faster.

JORGE E. CHAVARRO and **WALTER C. WILLETT** are in the Department of Nutrition at the Harvard School of Public Health. **PATRICK J. SKERRETT** is editor of the Harvard Heart Letter. For more information, go to health.harvard.edu/newsweek or thefertilitydiet.com.

Acknowledgements—Adapted from *The Fertility Diet* by Forge E. Chavarro, MD, ScD, Walter C. Willett, MD, Dr. P.H., and Patrick F. Skerrett. Adapted by permission from The McGraw-Hill Companies, Inc. Copyright © 2008 by the President and Fellows of Harvard College.

Originally from chapter 4 of *The Fertility Diet* (McGraw-Hill 2007) by Jorge E. Chavarro, Walter C. Willett, and Patrick J. Skerrett, pp. 54–62 excerpt. Copyright © 2007 by Jorge E. Chavarro, Walter C. Willett, and Patrick J. Skerrett. Reprinted by permission of the McGraw-Hill Companies.

Not Always 'the Happiest Time'

Pregnancy and depression: a new understanding of a difficult—and often hidden—problem.

LISA MILLER AND ANNE UNDERWOOD

L et's just say that you are among the millions of women for whom pregnancy was not bliss. You may have felt cranky or anxious, exhausted or fat, moody, stressed, nauseated, overwhelmed, isolated or lonely. You may even have felt bad about feeling bad. Now let's say that you, like Marlo Johnson, are a veteran of depression, someone who has battled the illness on and off for years. Then pregnancy can feel like the worst thing that ever happened to you. Johnson, 35 years old and from Brentwood, Calif., felt her mood plummet almost as soon as she conceived. But she put a brave face on it at work, with her family—even with her own therapist. The only time she cried was when she visited her obstetrician. Every time. Johnson's doctor encouraged her to look on the bright side. " 'Just think, at the end you're going to have this beautiful baby, the most beautiful gift'," Johnson recalls her saying, "and I said, 'I don't care. I don't want it. It doesn't matter to me'."

Contrary to conventional wisdom and medical lore, pregnancy does not necessarily equal happiness, and its hormones are not protective against depression. Doctors estimate that up to 20 percent of women experience symptoms of depression at some point during their pregnancy—about the same as women who are not pregnant. Even as postpartum depression has become morning-television fodder, the problem of depression during pregnancy has remained hidden—largely because most people still assume that pregnancy is or should be the realization of every woman's dream. When she was training as a psychiatric resident in the 1980s, Katherine Wisner, now a professor of psychiatry and Ob-Gyn at the University of Pittsburgh, remembers being told not to worry about pregnant patients who were, in her view, "very ill." Pregnant women, her teachers said, are "psychologically fulfilled."

Finally, pregnancy-linked depression is coming into the open. A series of studies, published this year in medical journals, is looking at all aspects of the problem—with special focus on the effects of anti-depressants on the health of pregnant women and newborn babies. These studies have launched, for the first time, a serious debate among doctors on the risks and benefits of treating pregnant women with medication. "There are still unanswered questions" about SSRIs and pregnancy, says Lee Cohen, a psychiatrist at Mass General Hospital in Boston and author of one of the recent studies. "But the doctors—the psychiatrists, the OBs—can't be cavalier, and can't presume that [without treatment] things are going to be fine."

Pregnancy probably doesn't cause depression, per se, but just like a divorce or a death in the family, it can trigger it in women who may already be genetically predisposed. And the hormones don't help. The relationship between estrogen, progesterone and mood is not well understood, but scientists believe it is the *changes* in hormonal levels, rather than the levels themselves, that affect people's moods. In a series of experiments published in *The New England Journal of Medicine* in 1998, psychiatrists Peter Schmidt and David Rubinow found that women who were prone to mild depression associated with premenstrual syndrome felt better only when their hormonal cycles were artificially shut down. They guess that the same is probably true with pregnancy: massive hormonal changes affect mood, but only in susceptible women. "In some women it may be the dramatic drop in hormones at childbirth that is the trigger," says Rubinow. "In others, it may be the elevated levels at the end of pregnancy."

It's difficult to detect depression in a pregnant woman, doctors say, because so few of them admit they're depressed—and because so many of the symptoms, such as sluggishness and sleeplessness, look alike. But Linda Worley, a psychiatrist at the University of Arkansas, who has a $250,000 federal grant to raise awareness about pregnancy and depression, says too many doctors don't ask pregnant patients about their mood or administer routine screening tests; some are too busy, some assume it isn't a problem and a few—not knowing where to refer such a patient—are afraid to hear the answer. According to preliminary results of a survey Worley received from 145 obstetrical providers, more than 80 percent rely on patients to self-report depression.

Treating a pregnant woman for depression is a delicate balancing act, a constant weighing of risks and benefits to the mother and to the fetus. But intervention is critical: a recent study by Columbia's Myrna Weissman shows that a mother's mental health directly affects the mental health of her children. Without aggressive treatment, "the whole family will suffer," Weissman says. Cohen's study, in *The Journal of the American Medical Association,* showed without a doubt that depressed mothers-to-be do better on SSRIs. Women who continued taking medication while pregnant were five times less likely to have a relapse of their illness than women who didn't. This is important—and not only because it improves the mother's health. Depressed women are far likelier to smoke, drink and miss doctors' appointments; depressed mothers give birth more often to under-weight babies. Faced with these facts, Claudia Crain of Newburyport, Mass., decided to continue taking her antidepressants: "The more research I did, the better I felt about what, in the end, was my personal decision." Her twins are due this month.

Most people assume that pregnancy is the realization of every woman's dream.

At the same time, no one would argue that antidepressants are good for growing fetuses. Two new studies help people assess the risks for themselves. In one, published in *The New England Journal of Medicine,* researchers found that newborns whose mothers took Prozac, Paxil or Zoloft in the third trimester had six times the risk of persistent pulmonary hypertension,

a rare blood-pressure condition that is potentially fatal. In another, smaller study, 30 percent of infants whose mothers took SSRIs showed symptoms of neonatal abstinence syndrome, a kind of supercrankiness linked to withdrawal. Most got better within days.

Therapy is a good alternative, especially for women with mild or moderate symptoms. In today's world, where families live far apart and everyone works all the time, many pregnant women say they feel isolated. This can be alleviated by talking. Margaret Spinelli, a psychiatrist at Columbia University, was surprised to find in a 2003 study that depressed pregnant women had a 60 percent recovery rate with interpersonal psychotherapy, a short-term, focused treatment—about the same rate as with antidepressants. "We just don't have the networks of close-by girlfriends and sisters and neighbors and moms that provide support," adds Pittsburgh's Wisner.

One of the reasons Marlo Johnson kept her depression hidden was that she didn't want to take antidepressants during her second pregnancy, as she had during her first. "I don't like being on medication; I kept telling myself I could handle it," she says. But finally Johnson's doctor took action. She ordered her to take a leave from work and to come clean with her therapist; Johnson's husband, who was working hundreds of miles away, came home. On March 20, Carter Patrick Johnson was born, weighing more than eight pounds. Mom says she loves the baby, "but I'm still depressed," and is back on medication. Sometimes even happy stories have bittersweet endings.

With Joan Raymond.

Truth and Consequences at Pregnancy High

The education of a teenage mother.

ALEX MORRIS

Before the sun has risen over the Bronx River, an alarm chimes in 17-year-old Grace Padilla's bedroom. Sliding from the lower bunk, she pads to the bathroom, flips on the light, brushes her teeth, then gathers up her hair into a short ponytail, which she wraps with a long row of black extensions and knots into a tight bun. She's quick and efficient, with none of the preening one might expect of a high-school junior. At 6:30 A.M., she goes back into the bedroom to wake her 2-year-old daughter.

Along with her grandparents, her mother, her sister, and her child, Grace lives in a small two-bedroom apartment on the second floor of a nondescript brick building in Hunts Point, where nearly half the residents live below the poverty line and roughly 15 percent of girls ages 15 to 19 become pregnant each year. It's the highest teen-pregnancy rate in the city, more than twice the national average.

"Lilah, wake up," Grace whispers, leaning in close. Lilah bats her mother away with a tiny hand and nestles up closer to Grace's own mother, Mayra, who had moments before returned home from her night shift as a cashier at a local food-distribution center and slipped, exhausted, into Grace's place in the bed.

"Come on, let's go get dressed," Grace pleads, pulling her daughter from under the covers as Lilah begins crying, flailing her arms and legs.

"Come *on*," Grace begs. She fights to keep her mounting frustration in check and then counts down the seconds before she'll make Lilah go stand against the wall, her usual form of punishment. "Five . . . four . . . three . . . two . . . one."

The threat is enough. Lilah's body goes slack, her screaming dissipates to a whimper. Grace is able to wrestle her into the clothes she'd laid out beforehand. But the child's screams have woken Grace's grandparents, who are now in the galley kitchen, arguing in Spanish. Her grandfather has Alzheimer's. He accidentally makes decaffeinated coffee, which infuriates his wife.

At 7:20, Grace smoothes a tiny hat over Lilah's curls, bundles her into a coat, then jostles schoolbooks into a bag. In the empty lot across the street, a rooster starts to crow.

When Grace arrives at Jane Addams High School for Academics and Careers, she joins the daily parade of mothers— pushing strollers, grasping the chubby fists of toddlers, perching bundled babies on cocked hips—making their way to basement room B17, the headquarters of the school's Living for the Young Family Through Education (LYFE) center. Run by the Department of Education, the LYFE program operates in 38 schools in the five boroughs, teaching parenting skills and providing on-site day care to teen parents who are full-time students in New York City's public schools. Jane Addams hosts one of the most active branches in the city, with sixteen mothers currently in the program.

While the students sign in on a clipboard, social worker Ana C. Martínez flits among them with her checklist of concerns. Is this baby eating enough? (Yes.) Does that one still have a cough? (No.) When will the heat be turned back on in one young mother's apartment? (Uncertain.) If it isn't soon, has she considered going to a shelter? (She has.)

"How's the baby?" Martínez asks Grace.

"She's fine," Grace answers.

Satisfied, Martínez turns her attention to Lilah. "Can I get a hug?"

"No," the child replies coyly, pretending to hide behind her mother's legs.

"Pretty please?"

Lilah finally concedes, jumping into the woman's arms.

Martínez laughs. "We have to play that game every morning, don't we?"

The girls cluster around a table laid out with bagels and jam, which Martínez serves every morning, both to entice her charges to be at school on time and also to make sure they get enough to eat ("Some don't at home," she clucks). She admits that the LYFE program, which serves 500 families and costs taxpayers about $13 million a year, has its naysayers, people who think that it makes life too easy for the mothers and diverts money from students who've made more-responsible choices.

"But the reality is, teens are having kids, and we've got to work with them," she says. "They're entitled to an education."

Grace greets Jasmine Reyes—a soft-spoken senior whose 2-year-old daughter, Jayleen, is Lilah's best friend in day care—before going over to peer at Nelsy Valerio's infant. When Iruma Moré enters the room with her 8-month-old daughter, Dymia, Grace beelines for the baby, unwrapping her from a pile of blankets.

"Dymia, Dymia, *Dy-mi-a*," she chants, bouncing the child on her lap. "She's so little," Grace marvels wistfully.

Iruma giggles. "I try to feed her all the time," she says, as she drops into a chair next to a locker crammed full of diapers. Though all four of Iruma's older sisters were teen mothers, she didn't know her school had day care until her sophomore year. "I started seeing the mothers coming in with their babies and stuff, and I always used to wonder where they take them," she says. One day, she looked through a doorway and it was like peering into a magic cupboard—a roomful of babies with soft skin and fine hair. Iruma thought she might like to have one of her own. By her junior year, she was pregnant. "I wasn't using nothing, no protection, so I mean, I knew it was gonna come sooner or later."

The nursery is a clown's paradise, brightly painted and well outfitted with funds donated by makeup artist Bobbi Brown. (In addition to the traditional high-school curriculum, Jane Addams teaches a number of vocations, including cosmetology, which Grace is studying.) Grace and Iruma each commandeer a crib and begin to strip down their daughters to their underwear, so that a caretaker can check the children for marks. Then the mothers fill out a form about when their child last ate, the child's mood, how the baby has been sleeping. Just before the bell rings for second period, they leave the nursery and head upstairs to school. For the next seven hours, they'll get to be kids again themselves.

Grace got pregnant in January 2006, less than a month after her 14th birthday and soon after she lost her virginity to a 15-year-old boy from the neighborhood named Nikko Vega. He was the only person she'd slept with, or even wanted to. After he broke up with a girlfriend ("A ho," Grace sniffs), she began cutting her eighth-grade classes to meet him at his apartment. Even then, she had full curves and a round and inviting face. She was normally sweet, but if pressed, she could fire off a string of expletives so fast the words blurred together. Nikko liked that about her. One day, the two of them found themselves playing more than Nintendo, and they just let it happen.

"It was heat-of-the-moment stuff," Grace says of having sex for the first time. Getting pregnant wasn't even on her mind. But it was on Nikko's: "A couple of hours after, I was thinking, like, *Damn*." He eventually asked Grace if she should go on birth control, but they knew that would make her mom suspicious. They decided to take their chances, though it bothered Nikko to be so reckless. "A lot of people I knew had kids young, and I didn't want to be one of them," he admits. He had hoped to go to college on a football scholarship, had even made a pact with his friends to put off fatherhood.

"Like, ever since we were younger, we all spoke about, 'No kids.' All of us."

Grace got pregnant at 14. She told Nikko that she wanted to keep the baby and that she was happy, "in a sad sort of way."

"It didn't work," Grace says archly. "Everybody he grew up with has a kid now."

Grace didn't know she was pregnant for months. She didn't get morning sickness, headaches, or cramps. She still did step dancing, played football after school, rode roller coasters when her mom took her to a theme park, fit into her regular clothes. She hadn't been having her period long enough for its absence to be a major cause for concern. When she went to a neighborhood clinic to get tested, just in case, and the results came back positive, she was shocked. "I didn't really know what to do," she says. "I didn't know what to ask. I was just like, 'What?' "

When she told Nikko, he walked away without saying a word, but a couple of hours later, he returned, driven back by the hangdog devotion he has for Grace and by fear of her disapproval. She told him that she wanted to keep the baby and that she was happy about the decision, "in a sad sort of way." She loved babies, but she wasn't sure what she was getting into. To the extent that he could be there for her, an extent that even he understood to be meager, Nikko said he was onboard.

It took Grace a month to work up the nerve to tell her mother. When Mayra came home from work one day, Grace, her older sister, Samantha, and her cousin were sitting in front of the building waiting for her "like there was a funeral." In the elevator ride up to the apartment, Mayra looked from one girl to the next. "Which one of you is pregnant?" she asked. She thought Samantha would answer, but when she didn't, the realization set in that it was her younger daughter who was in trouble.

"How could you?" Mayra screamed, standing in their living room, shaking with anger. "How could you? You see our situation, you see what I have on my plate. How could you be so selfish?"

Grace ran to her bedroom, sobbing. Mayra stayed in the living room, sobbing. Mayra's own mother walked in the door and demanded to know what was going on.

"Your granddaughter," Mayra wailed, "your *14-year-old* granddaughter decided you needed to see a great-grandkid."

"Oh my God," the old woman said. "*¡Ay, Dios mío! ¡Ay, Dios mío, ayúdenos!*"

For a month, Mayra cried every day. Having gotten married at 16 and had Samantha at 17, she was loath to become a grandmother at 36. She had asked Grace repeatedly if she had started having sex, and the girl had always denied it. Between her parents and her own children, the apartment was already overcrowded, and money stretched thin. She threatened to send Grace to live with her father, who had left the family a decade ago. For years, they hadn't been able to track him down. Now he had a new family in Philadelphia, and Grace had been in cautious contact. But when they called to tell him about the pregnancy, he made it clear that she wasn't welcome. Grace hasn't spoken to him since.

Mayra was surprised to find herself seriously considering abortion as an option. The South Bronx has a high birthrate in part because in this largely Hispanic and Catholic community, the idea of terminating a pregnancy meets with such intense disapproval. Her mother told her that she would not be able to live under the same roof if they went through with it, but Mayra didn't see how Grace could manage to raise a child, nor did she want to put her daughter through the difficulty of labor only to give the baby away. Grace guessed that she was about four months along and agreed to visit an abortion clinic. The sonogram showed that the baby was due in ten weeks.

"Ten weeks?" Mayra asked. "This is a 14-year-old who's been to theme parks, eaten junk food the whole time, had no prenatal care. Ten weeks? I don't know what this baby's gonna be like."

The nurse nodded sympathetically, but there was nothing to be done. "There's nowhere in this country where they'll do that abortion at seven months."

Mayra set about preparing for the baby. She arranged for Grace to be enrolled in Jane Addams, the closest school that had a LYFE program. She put a call out to friends and family for a crib, a stroller, secondhand baby clothes. She started making doctors appointments, pleading her daughter's way into clinics that didn't have openings until after the baby was due. Grace looked so young when she brought her in, no one could believe she was the one who was pregnant.

Grace's water broke in the hallway of Jane Addams the second week of her freshman year, a full month before her due date. Thinking she had wet her pants, she called her mother from a bathroom stall.

"Um, I want to go home," she said when Mayra picked up.

"Why? What happened?"

"My pants are all wet."

"What do you mean your pants are all wet? Did a car splash you or something?"

"No. Like, they're all wet. Like, I went into the bathroom, and they're all wet."

"Oh my God," Mayra cut in. "Your water broke. Oh my God! You're gonna have this baby in that school!"

When Grace arrived at Albert Einstein hospital, she was having contractions. Her mother stepped outside to calm her nerves with a cigarette, and Grace took the moment alone to ask her doctor if it was possible that she might die in childbirth. He reassured her that the chances were infinitesimally slim. "He sugarcoated it," she says. "He was a nice guy."

By the time Nikko arrived the following afternoon, Grace was in the throes of "the worst pain I ever felt in my life," she says, gasping just at the thought. She refused to allow him in the room. "I was in so much pain I really just wanted to kill him. I said, 'I advise security, doctors, nurses, everybody on this floor, if that man reaches this room, it's gonna be chaos, because this is all his fault.'"

On Sunday, September 17, 2006, at 2:55 A.M., Delilah Joli Vega was born, alert and healthy.

At the McDonald's on Prospect Avenue, teenagers crowd the counter, munching fries and competing for attention, the boys with their hooded sweatshirts pulled down low over their eyes, the girls in tight jeans and baby tees, nameplate jewelry shimmering, hair ruthlessly slicked back into high ponytails. As Iruma orders a pile of cheeseburgers and two Happy Meals, Grace and Jasmine drag high chairs up to the table and settle in with Nikko. The conversation is no different from that at any other table in the place, except for the constant interruption. There's drama going down on Grace's block—"Dumbass Samantha was talking about, 'Oh, if Sasha did punch A. J. in the face, it wasn't' cause A. J. hit her, it was over Killah . . .'"—but she can't focus on the story with Lilah sending golden arcs of boxed apple juice into the air.

"Lilah, you're spilling the juice," Grace points out. "You're. Spilling. The. Juice."

Jayleen, Jasmine's daughter, looks over at Lilah, then squeezes her own juice box with vigor.

"You must want to get smacked," Grace tells her, raising her eyebrows before turning to the girl's mother. "I been telling you about that, Jasmine."

"Later, later," Jasmine pleads, not in the mood for a parenting lesson. But the fact is the mothers often act as a check on one another, imparting what parenting wisdom they have, holding one another to a certain standard. Grace, particularly, prides herself on her parenting skills. She's observant. She's strict. Her mother, Mayra, taught her how to take care of Lilah but refused to do the tasks for her. Grace was the one who changed Lilah's diapers, fed her, got up in the middle of the night when she cried. "She's not Baby Alive, is she?" Mayra would ask. "There's no off-button on her."

Having teenage parents does mean that Lilah is prone to mimic teenage behavior. "Her attitude is serious," says Grace. "She'll be like, 'Mind your business.' Mind *my* business? You better be talking to the milkman! I love her, but sometimes I just want to bop her on her head." But the good manners Lilah displays in front of company—if not always at home—testify to Grace's efforts.

Even now, as Lilah eyes the chicken nuggets that Iruma has been tearing into bite-size chunks for Dymia, she doesn't reach out and take one. "Hee dat icken, Mommy?" she asks politely.

"I see that chicken," Grace answers. "But you asked for a burger, so now you're gonna eat a burger."

"She didn't ask for a burger. You said she wanted a burger," Jasmine points out. "You're mad mean."

Grace shrugs off the comment, as a girl from their school pauses on her way past their table.

"Hey! What's up, baby?" she coos at Dymia before turning to Iruma. "She's getting so big. Oh my God!"

Iruma pushes her glasses up on her nose and smiles contentedly. "Yeah, she getting big."

"Oh my God, you're so cute!" The girl stares at Dymia, shaking her head in amazement.

In the South Bronx, the stigma of having a child at a young age is remarkably absent, not just because teen parenthood has long been pervasive but also because the family structure is such that children often grow up raising younger siblings, nieces, and nephews. Adding a child of their own into the mix doesn't seem like it will change much in terms of daily routine, but it does feel like a rite of passage, a one-way ticket to adulthood. Motherhood cements a girl's fertility, her femininity. Louder than any clingy top or painted lip, it broadcasts that now she's a woman. And for some girls, that's appealing. When *The Tyra Banks Show* did an online survey of 10,000 girls across the country, one-fifth of them said they wanted to become teen moms. The latest Centers for Disease Control report shows a 3 percent increase in teen pregnancy in 2006 after more than a decade of decline. At Jane Addams, round bellies orbit the hallways like planets. The school doesn't keep track of pregnancies, but according to the attendance officer, one week this spring, seven girls out of a student body of about 1,500 were out of school to give birth.

The mothers watch as the girl from school continues on her way, joining a booth where a group of teenagers have piled in together, plopping on each other's laps, laughing loudly at each other's jokes. None of them have children. They seem not to have a single care. The chasm between being a parent and being a kid was difficult to intuit until it was crossed. Now Grace knows it well. When Nikko once teased her about all the fun she would have without him if she went to college, she leveled a cold stare at him and asked, "How am I gonna have fun in college with a child?"

Iruma fishes her cell phone out of a bag and presses a few buttons. Hip-hop starts to blare from the little speakers, setting a more festive mood. The moms relax. Jayleen and Lilah bounce in time to the music.

"Jayleen, you want to dance for everybody?" Jasmine asks. "You want to get on the table and dance?"

Jayleen tries to climb out of her high chair, and Jasmine lifts her up onto the bench, where she plants her feet and shakes her little bottom back and forth.

"Oh, she gotta donk, she gotta donk," Jasmine chants, as Jayleen's dance grows increasingly outrageous. The moms laugh.

Sometimes it's hard not to act their age. "You need to be adult and mature, but you're still young," says Grace. "Adults have fun all the time. They still joke, they still laugh. They can't take your kid away just because of that."

When grace gets home from school one afternoon, her grandparents have two eyes of the gas stove burning to drive away the apartment's chill. She steers Lilah away from the flame and to the refrigerator, where she allows her to choose a snack. Lilah points at a pitcher of red liquid, and Grace fixes her a bottle, waiting for Nikko to get home from the GED program he started the week before. When he does, he waves a sheet of loose-leaf paper in front of her. It's his first assignment, a short essay on why he should be a candidate for the program.

"I need to finish school for my 2-year-old daughter," he starts off in an even hand. "I need to finish school for her because she follows everything that I do, and I feel that it is time for me to step up to the plate." At the bottom of the page, his teacher has written "good ideas, good motivation" and given him a B-plus. Grace seems pleased. "Oh snap, babe. Now what are you gonna do to get an A-minus?"

She's only half-joking. Even if it is sometimes misplaced, Grace has a highly evolved sense of propriety. She expects to be treated a certain way, expects Nikko to embrace his responsibilities as a father. Her loyalties now are to Lilah, and her world is delineated: There are the players and hustlers and birds, people best avoided; then there are the "cousins" and *títís* and "brothers," people she may not be related to by blood but who do well by her and her daughter. She's not quite sure yet where Nikko falls. "He be all right," she says.

It took a long time for Mayra to accept Nikko as a de facto member of the family. It wasn't just his role in the pregnancy—she understood that Grace was equally at fault—it was his own neglectful upbringing that gave her pause. She refused to have his name listed on Lilah's birth certificate until her own mother interjected. "You're gonna leave her birth certificate just blank under father, like she doesn't know who her child's father is?" the older woman asked, horrified.

Since Lilah was born, Nikko has spent a smattering of nights in jail, mostly for getting in neighborhood fights or, as he says, "being in the wrong place at the wrong time." Because his mother did not force him to go to school, he has not a single high-school credit. When Mayra took him to family court for child support (a requirement of the LYFE program), Mayra told the judge that she didn't expect any money from Nikko, that she would prefer he get an education rather than a job now, so that he could support his child later; but the judge still awarded them $25 a month—less than the cost of a box of diapers—which Nikko's mother agreed to pay until her son turned 18. Grace and Mayra have still not seen a cent.

In the end, though, it was hard to keep blaming Nikko, a child, for what Mayra saw as his mother's failings. When he didn't have a winter coat, she bought him one. When he was hungry, she fed him. When his mother kicked him out after a fight with her boyfriend, Mayra temporarily let him stay with them. Over time, he grew on her. "I basically showed her a lot of respect," says Nikko. "A lot of butt kissing," corrects Grace. Mayra realizes that, in his capacity, he is a good father: He's present. Though other girls are still dating the fathers of their children, Nikko is the only boy who visits the LYFE center. A certificate stating that he completed LYFE's fatherhood-training program hangs in a frame over Grace's bed. "The only reason I don't press it is because this baby knows who her daddy is," says Mayra. "And she loves her daddy."

Still, both Mayra and Grace find their patience sputtering. In the three years since Grace got pregnant, Nikko hadn't held a single job or completed a single class. Mayra sees the writing on the wall. She knows that the statistics are not in Nikko and Grace's favor: Only 40 percent of teenagers who have children get their high-school diplomas, and 64 percent of children born to unmarried high-school dropouts live in poverty.

"Life isn't about you anymore," Mayra is quick to inform him. "You brought someone else into this world that you have to care for. If you're gonna be that type of person that's gonna just not do nothing—and because of that, statistics is gonna land you back in jail—you may as well say bye to them now while Lilah's small and can get over you fast. Because this baby's not visiting nobody in jail." At the beginning of this year, to make good on her word, she gave him one month to prove to her that he was in school or had landed a job. Right at the deadline, he signed up for his GED.

Sometimes Grace feels that she's leaving Nikko behind. She talks of going to college, studying business, opening her own beauty salon, getting her child out of Hunts Point, away from the "hustlers and divas." She expects that there will come a day when she alone is responsible for providing for Lilah. "You can hope, we can all hope that Nikko's gonna do something to better himself and want to be there and provide for his family," Mayra tells her. "But the fact remains, if he doesn't, he wouldn't be the first boy. You wouldn't be the first single mother."

One evening early this spring, the young family has the Padilla apartment to themselves. Mayra sleeps soundly behind the closed door of the bedroom, resting up for her night shift at eleven. Grace's grandparents are at church, her sister out with friends. At times like these, Grace likes to pretend the apartment belongs to her and Nikko, that she doesn't live with her mother and he doesn't crash at a friend's place, that they've managed to make a life for themselves and Lilah on their own.

Nikko prepares a bowl of popcorn, while Grace flips through channels on the TV, stopping at a music video she knows Lilah likes. The little girl follows along with the dance in the best rendition a 2-year-old could possibly muster, stroking her hips as they wiggle furiously and then flapping her wrists like a drag queen. When she looks behind her to make sure her parents are watching, Nikko and Grace laugh at her presumption. As parents, they share an easy rapport. She teases and prods him gently; he defers to her with a good-natured grin.

Later, there's homework to be done. Grace has a field trip tomorrow, so her load is light, but Nikko struggles to write an essay on the three branches of government. Once he finishes his GED, he's hoping to enroll in junior college. Grace pulls out her U.S. history folder, shows him a few photocopied papers, then goes into the kitchen to heat up frozen chicken patties.

After they eat, she gives Lilah a bath, crouching by the bathtub and allowing her daughter to splash around as long as she likes. "You a monkey," she says, laughing as Lilah dunks her head under the water and then shakes out her curls. "When she was a baby, the funnest part was the bath because her faces were just priceless." While Nikko heats up a bottle of chocolate milk, Grace towels Lilah off, rubs her down with lotion as the child tries to squirm out of her grasp—"She likes running around naked"—and dresses her in a diaper and footed fleece pajamas. Nikko puts his homework aside to give Lilah her bottle, stretching her out across his lap and rocking her gently. He waits until she's asleep to kiss Grace good-bye.

"Love you, babe," he says.

"Love you too."

Baby Survival Guide
7 Truths That'll Keep You Sane

MAURA RHODES

A week or so after I had my first baby, my friend Susan stopped by—just in the nick of time: Will had been crying for what felt like hours and nothing I did helped. Susan, who'd just had her second daughter, calmly scooped up my inconsolable newborn and did a sort of combo side-to-side swaying and up-and-down jostling that magically lulled him out of Waa-Waa Land.

I've had three kids since then, and Susan's "mommy jig" has been a lifesaver with every one of them. But I never would have known it if I hadn't let her help me out—and that's exactly why she, and I, and other moms who've been there want you to remember these seven rules:

1 Asking for Help Does Not Make You Incompetent

Precisely the opposite, in fact. Sometimes, there's no other way to get from point A to point B. Even if there is, getting there alone can take twice as long and make you crazy.

Kim Ganier of Huntington Beach, California, was always a self-sufficient person—until her first baby, Laci (now 3), was a week old and Ganier found herself doing laundry while "someone else was sitting in my glider and cuddling my baby. The lightbulb went on," she says. After that, visitors were put to work so Ganier could enjoy Laci. Her advice now: Speak up, be specific about what you need, and say yes when offered help of any kind. "You'll feel guilty at first, but you'll get over it," she says.

It'll be easier if you remember that someday you will reciprocate—if not to the particular mom who helped you out, then to another. Several months ago, I was having dinner out with my kids when the mom at the next table asked if I had an extra diaper. I happily handed one over. Sure enough, not long after that, I discovered I'd forgotten to bring a clean swim diaper to the pool and had to go begging from lounge chair to lounge chair for a spare. A better-prepared mom than I saved the day.

So never let guilt or embarrassment or even your ego get in the way of accepting help. Improvising a diaper is a lot harder than returning a favor.

2 Babies Don't Need as Much New Stuff as You Think

They seem to outgrow everything from stretchies to bassinets overnight, so why stock up? "I wish someone had told me not to buy cutesy, expensive clothes for my newborn," says Kristine Shuler, mom of 3-year-old Kaylee in Baroda, Michigan. "Little did I know she would spend most of the time in T-shirts from Target. She didn't wear half the clothes I bought!"

There are two lessons here: First, take your time when deciding what you'll really need. Do a little research, make a list, and stick with it. (*Parenting Magazine's Baby Must-Haves* book is a great resource for teasing out what to buy and what to skip, by the way.) Second, as tempting as it is to buy everything fresh and new and adorable for your first baby—resist. Some items, like swings and bouncy seats, are used for such short periods of time that they never see much wear and tear. Can you borrow from a friend? If not, check out Craigslist.org or Freecycle.org.

Marilyn Sklar swears by a children's resale store in her town. "When my daughter, Raquel, was born, I started buying gently used clothes from there. Later, I brought in some of Raquel's clothing and took an in-store credit to purchase more," says the mom of two in Phoenix. "Now I recycle that way whenever possible. We're saving money and being green!"

3 Getting a Baby to Sleep Is Worth the Trouble

This is a matter of basic maternal math: baby zzz's = mommy zzz's. Veteran moms will tell you that figuring out, early on, how to get your baby to go to sleep, stay asleep, and take regular naps is key to getting through that entire first year. "Being sleep-deprived is a fact of life, but the sooner you get sleep figured out, the better," says Michelle Wilkins, a mom of three in Blacksburg, Virginia.

For Theresa Cole, mom of Ethan, 5, and Jordan, 1, in Kansas City, Missouri, the trick is to get your newborn used to falling asleep on his own: "Think twice about feeding your baby to put him to sleep. He's a clean slate, waiting to learn how to do things. If you teach him he can only drift off with a boob or bottle in his mouth, that's the only way he will—even at two in the morning. And, seriously, who wants to deal with that every night for the next couple of years?"

I'm a firm believer in consistency. When my third baby was 9 months old and not taking decent naps during the day, I came up with some new routines. I stopped letting him catnap in the car while I ran errands, and planned outings around his naptime, to make sure he could go down in his crib. I also turned his room into a sleep haven (blackout shades, white-noise machine). Pretty soon he was napping twice a day, and snoozing better at night, too. To keep daytime noise to a minimum, Jamie Pearson, mom of Avery, 7, and Max, 5, in Palo Alto, California, adds this tip: "Make a diplomatic front-door sign that says, 'Baby napping. Please visit us another time.'"

4 Competitive Parenting: Not Cool

Of course you already know that babies develop at their own pace. And of course you know there's more to your baby than when he hits milestones. But when it seems like every kid in the playgroup except yours is sitting up or saying "Mama," it can take all your willpower to act like you just don't care.

It's totally understandable to compare. But for the sake of your sanity, it's worth trying to stop. "I made the conscious decision to believe the experts who said that the spectrum of normalcy was wide," says Susie Sonneborn Blim, a mom of three in Montclair, New Jersey. "I also stopped hanging out with moms who were constantly boasting about or obsessing over their babies' milestones, because that played a huge part in how caught up I got with comparing my baby to other babies."

Pearson had a similar tactic: "When Avery wasn't the first—or second, or third—baby in my mothers' group to crawl, I told myself that the impatient, intense, irritable babies were always the early crawlers and walkers," she says. "I kept these theories to myself, of course!"

If you're truly worried that your baby is falling behind, bring it up with your pediatrician. She should be your go-to expert when it comes to your child's health and development—not the bragging, pitying other moms.

5 You and Your Baby Don't Have to Be Joined at the Hip

Experts say: Being touched, held, carried, and cuddled is vital to a baby's development. Moms answer back: There's nothing more delicious than touching, holding, carrying, and cuddling a baby—to a point. When it's clear that you and/or your baby need a break from each other, take it. This is especially true when your infant's wailing or your pre-toddler's whining is about to push you over the edge. Hand her to Daddy or send out an SOS to a friend or relative.

There's nothing more delicious than cuddling a baby—to a point. So take a break.

If there's no one you can call on for help, take a tip from Christine Klepacz, a mom of two in Bethesda, Maryland. "When your baby is crying and you could burst into tears yourself, or when you're just overwhelmed, it's okay to put her in her crib for a while and sit by yourself. She's safe, and sometimes she needs time away from you, too. It's okay. We all do it!"

It's equally important to carve out time for yourself regularly—not just when you're about to go off the deep end. If there's one thing Jennifer Geddes, a *Parenting* staffer and mom of two girls, learned during the first year, it's that "you have to take a few minutes for yourself here and there. It's essential to being a happy and healthy mom. I was so concerned with attending to my daughter's needs that I neglected my own. I barely ate, slept, or left the house," she says.

If you're thinking, "Yeah, right—I can barely get a shower," wait: It's doable. You just have to plan ahead, be creative, and adjust your definition of what constitutes a relaxing break. Where, prebaby, you were used to spur-of-the-moment shopping sprees or on-a-whim workouts, you might find, like Marilyn Sklar, that your idea of a good time now is "a glass of wine and a good book after the children are in bed." Or a brisk walk in the morning before they get up. Me, I swear by weekend matinees. I can get a lot of regenerative mileage out of two hours by myself in a cozy, dark theater with a bag of popcorn, lost in a great story onscreen.

6 The Best Baby Stage Is the One You're In

"They grow up so fast." The reason you'll hear this from everyone and her grandmother: It's true. Kim Lavergne of Nashville, mom of 2-year-old Justin, remembers feeling like time was crawling after he was born. "In reality, the days go by so fast that the next thing you know, your child is no longer a baby," she says. "I've learned to cherish and enjoy the time I spend with Justin."

Charlene Kochensparger of Centerville, Ohio, who has a daughter and a son, seconds that. "First-time parents tend to wish the time away—'I can't wait for her to crawl, walk, talk'—and not enjoy the moment," she says.

The time slipped away from Loretta Sehlmeyer of Dix Hills, New York, because she was so focused on being a perfect parent to her son, Christian, now 4. "I fretted so much over caring for him that I missed the entire experience. I honestly didn't notice that my baby was growing and changing a little bit each day. I spent a lot of time looking at him, but I was way too distracted to actually see him," she says. "So take some time each day, real time, to hold your baby and do nothing else but use your senses to connect with him. Smell his sweetness, and look at those tiny fingers and toes and amazing little nose."

7 There's No One Else Like You

Only a handful of babycare rules are written in stone (specifically, those having to do with health and safety—like, you really should always put a baby to sleep on his back). Most everything else is up for interpretation. "It's great to read up, solicit opinions, and listen respectfully to advice you haven't asked for," says Michelle Wilkins. "But you know your baby and yourself best. You'll know when an idea resonates."

Adds Chantel Fry, mom of Dylan, 3, and Madalyn, 7 months, in Pittsburgh: "You're going to be different than the next mom. Not better, not worse—because you do the best you can, and if at the end of the day your child has laughed, and is clean and fed, you can go to sleep knowing that you did what is expected of you." No matter how you did those things, exactly, you can be proud that you're inventing your own special way of being a mom.

***

MAURA RHODES, a mom of four, is a contributing editor at *Parenting*.

UNIT 3
Family Relationships

Unit Selections

14. **Contributing to the Debate over Same-Sex Marriage,** Gwendolyn Puryear Keita
15. **Can Marriage Be Saved?,** Frank Furstenberg
16. **The Polygamists,** Scott Anderson
17. **Good Parents, Bad Results,** Nancy Shute
18. **Do We Need a Law to Prohibit Spanking?,** Murray Straus
19. **Children of Lesbian and Gay Parents,** Charlotte J. Patterson
20. **Minding the Kids,** Meg Caddoux Hirschberg
21. **Mother Damnedest,** Terri Apter
22. **The Forgotten Siblings,** Sally Young
23. **Four Myths About Older Adults in America's Immigrant Families,** Judith Teas

Key Points to Consider

- Is marriage necessary for a happy, fulfilling life? What are your expectations of your (future) spouse? What are your expectations of yourself? What are the attributes of marriage variants (e.g, same sex marriage or plural marriage?)

- What are the attributes of good parents? Of bad parents? What are your thoughts on spanking?

- What do you think is the appropriate adult–adult relationship between parents and children? At what point should parents back away to let their children "fly"?

Student Website
www.mhhe.com/cls

Internet References

Child Welfare League of America
   www.cwla.org
Coalition for Marriage, Family, and Couples Education
   www.smartmarriages.com
The National Academy for Child Development
   www.nacd.org
National Council on Family Relations
   www.ncfr.com
Positive Parenting
   www.positiveparenting.com
SocioSite
   www.pscw.uva.nl/sociosite/TOPICS/Women.html

And they lived happily ever after. . . . The romantic image conjured up by this well-known final line from fairy tales is not reflective of the reality of family life and relationship maintenance. The belief that somehow love alone should carry us through is pervasive. In reality, maintaining a relationship takes dedication, hard work, and commitment.

We come into relationships, regardless of their nature, with fantasies about how things ought to be. Partners, spouses, parents, children, siblings, and others—all family members have at least some unrealistic expectations about each other. It is through the negotiation of their lives together that they come to work through these expectations and replace them with other, it is hoped, more realistic ones. By recognizing and acting on their own contribution to the family, members can set and attain realistic family goals. Tolerance and acceptance of differences can facilitate this process as can competent communication skills. Along the way, family members need to learn new skills and develop new habits of relating to each other. This will not be easy, and, try as they may, not everything will be controllable. Factors both inside and outside the family may impede their progress. Even before we enter a marriage or other committed relationship, attitudes, standards, and beliefs influence our choices. Increasingly, choices include whether we should commit to such a relationship. From the start of a committed relationship, the expectations both partners have of their relationship have an impact, and the need to negotiate differences is a constant factor. Adding a child to the family affects the lives of parents in ways that they could previously only imagine. Feeling under siege, many parents struggle to know the right way to rear their children. These factors can all combine to make child rearing more difficult than it might otherwise have been. Other family relationships also evolve, and in our nuclear-family focused culture, it is possible to forget that family relationships extend beyond those between spouses and parents and children.

The initial subsection presents a number of articles regarding marital and other committed relationships, decisions about whether one wants to enter such a relationship, and ways of balancing multiple and often competing roles played by today's couples, who hope to fulfill individual as well as relationship needs. It is a difficult balancing act to cope with the expectations and pressures of work, home, children, and relational intimacy. The first article, "Contributing to the Debate over Same-Sex Marriage," provides the position of the American Psychological Association on same-sex marriage. The article that follows looks at the institution of marriage from an economic standpoint, where the author argues that marriages are in trouble primarily among lower income families, and not across the board, as some argue. The final article in this section addresses plural marriage. "The Polygamists" examines a conservative community in which plural marriage is the norm.

The next subsection examines the parent/child relationship. In the first article, "Good Parents, Bad Results," looks at

eight errors that well-meaning parents make and ways to avoid them. The next article, "Do We Need a Law to Prohibit Spanking?" addresses the fact that, although research strongly supports the drawbacks of corporal punishment, legislation may be necessary to end a practice that is commonly seen as relatively benign. "Children of Lesbian and Gay Parents" comes to the conclusion that sexual orientation of parents has no effect on the development and well-being of their children The next reading, "Minding the Kids," addresses a common struggle in today's economic climate: How to be a good parent while also achieving one's professional goals. The final article, "Mother Damnedest" concerns the vexing problem of deciding what one's responsibilities are toward an abusive parent.

The third and final subsection looks at other family relationships. "The Forgotten Siblings" draws attention to the fact that, in research on family, siblings often are forgotten. The other article in this section address issues of concern among aged family members. "Four Myths about Older Adults in America's Immigrant Families" discusses four common myths about older adults in immigrant families and counters these with facts.

Contributing to the Debate over Same-Sex Marriage

DR. GWENDOLYN PURYEAR KEITA

Among APA's primary roles is increasing and disseminating knowledge about human behavior and applying what we know about psychology to address human concerns. A recent example of our work in these areas was our filing an *amicus curie* brief, along with the California Psychological Association, the American Psychiatric Association and the National Association of Social Workers, in the California case that challenged the decision to deny marriage licenses to same-sex couples.

The court found that restricting marriage to same-sex couples violates the state constitution. In its decision, the court cited only APA's brief—one out of the 45 submitted. APA offered rigorous psychological evidence emphasizing the major impact stigma has on well-being, the benefits of marriage, and the lack of difference between lesbian and gay parents and heterosexual parents.

According to the brief:

1. Homosexuality is neither a disorder nor a disease, but rather a normal variant of human sexual orientation. The vast majority of social prejudice, discrimination and violence against lesbians, gay men and bisexuals takes a cumulative toll on the well-being of members in each of these groups. "Minority stress" is the term used by researchers to refer to the negative effects associated with the adverse social conditions experienced by those belonging to a stigmatized social group.

   As a product of sociopolitical forces, structural stigma "represents the policies of private and governmental institutions that restrict the opportunities of stigmatized groups." By legitimating and reinforcing the undesired differences of sexual minorities and by according them inferior status relative to heterosexuals, structural stigma gives rise to individual acts against them, subsequently increasing levels of stress as a result.

2. Substantial numbers of gay and lesbian couples are successful in forming stable, long-lasting, committed relationships. Empirical studies using nonrepresentative samples of gay men and lesbians show that the vast majority of participants have been involved in a committed relationship at some point in their lives. Data from the 2000 U.S. Census indicate that of the 5.5 million couples who were living together but not married, about one in nine had a same-sex partner.

3. Being married affords individuals a variety of benefits that have important implications for physical and mental health and for the quality of the relationship itself. These health benefits do not appear to result from simply being in an intimate relationship because most studies have found that married men and women generally experience better physical and mental health than their cohabiting unmarried counterparts.

4. Empirical research has consistently shown that lesbian and gay parents do not differ from heterosexuals in their parenting skills, and their children do not show any deficits compared with children raised by heterosexual parents.

In addition, if their parents are allowed to marry, the children of same-sex couples will benefit not only from the legal stability and other familial benefits that marriage provides, but also from elimination of state-sponsored stigmatization of their families.

In 2004, APA's Council of Representatives adopted two resolutions relevant to this issue, which can be found on APA's Public Interest Directorate Web pages. In the Resolution on Sexual Orientation and Marriage, it was resolved, based on empirical research concerning sexual orientation and marriage, "that the APA believes that it is unfair and discriminatory to deny same-sex couples legal access to civil marriage and to all its attendant benefits, rights, and privileges." In the Resolution on Sexual Orientation, Parents, and Children, the association recognized that "There is no scientific evidence that parenting effectiveness is related to parental sexual orientation."

Adopting these and similar resolutions and filing *amicus* briefs are but two of the many ways that APA demonstrates its steadfast commitment to providing scientific and educational resources and support to inform public discussion and a clear and objective understanding of these issues.

The full text of the California *amicus* brief can be found at www.apa.org/psyclaw/marriage.

Can Marriage Be Saved?

FRANK FURSTENBERG

A growing number of social scientists fear that marriage may be on the rocks and few doubt that matrimony, as we have known it, has undergone a wrenching period of change in the past several decades. Andrew Cherlin, a leading sociologist of the family, speaks of "the de-institutionalization of marriage," conceding a point to conservative commentators who have argued that marriage and the family have been in a state of free-fall since the 1960s.

Western Europe has experienced many of the same trends—declining rates of marriage, widespread cohabitation, and rising levels of nonmarital childbearing—but has largely shrugged them off. By contrast, concern about the state of marriage in the United States has touched a raw, political nerve. What ails marriage and what, if anything, can be done to restore this time-honored social arrangement to its former status as a cultural invention for assigning the rights and responsibilities of reproduction, including sponsorship and inheritance?

On the left side of the political spectrum, observers believe that the institutional breakdown of marriage has its roots in economic and social changes brought about by shifts in home-based production, structural changes in the economy, and the breakdown of the gender-based division of labor—trends unlikely to be reversed. The other position, championed by most conservatives, is that people have lost faith in marriage because of changes in cultural values that could be reversed or restored through shifts in the law, changes in administrative policies and practices, and public rhetoric to alter beliefs and expectations.

The Bush administration is trying to put into place a set of policies aimed at reversing the symptoms of retreat from marriage: high rates of premarital sex, nonmarital childbearing, cohabitation, and divorce. Do their policies make sense and do they have a reasonable prospect of success? To answer this question, I want to begin with the trends that Americans, including many social scientists, have found so alarming and then turn to the question of how much public policy and what kinds of policies could help to strengthen marriage.

Demographic Changes and Political Interpretations

When compared to the 1950s, the institution of marriage seems to be profoundly changed, but is the middle of the twentieth century an appropriate point of comparison? It has been widely known since the baby boom era that the period after the Second World War was unusual demographically: the very early onset of adult transitions; unprecedented rates of marriage; high fertility; an economy that permitted a single wage earner to support a family reasonably well; and the flow of federal funding for education, housing, and jobs distinguished the 1950s and early 1960s as a particular historical moment different from any previous period and certainly different from the decades after the Vietnam War era. For a brief time, the nuclear family in the United States and throughout much of Europe reigned supreme.

If we use the middle of the twentieth century as a comparison point, it might appear that we have been witnessing a deconstruction of the two-parent biological family en masse. But such a view is historically shortsighted and simplistic. The nuclear family, though long the bourgeois ideal, had never been universally practiced, at least as it was in the middle of the last century. Only in the 1950s—and then for a very brief time—did it become the gold standard for what constitutes a healthy family. Indeed, sociologists at that time fiercely debated whether this family model represented a decline from the "traditional" extended family. Even those who argued against this proposition could not agree whether this family form was desirable ("functional" in the language of the day) or contained fatal flaws that would be its undoing.

During the 1960s and 1970s, anthropological evidence indicated that family diversity is universal, and findings from the new field of historical demography revealed that families in both the East and the West had always been changing in response to economic, political, demographic, and social conditions. In short, the nuclear family was cross-culturally and historically not "the natural unit," that many wrongly presume today.

Although it was widely known that the family had undergone considerable changes from ancient times and during the industrial revolution, that family systems varied across culture, and that social-class differences created varied forms of the family within the same society, it was not until the 1960s, when historians began to use computers to analyze census data, that the extent of this variation came into clearer focus. For the first time, family scholars from several disciplines could see the broad outlines of a new picture of how family forms and functions are intimately related to the social, cultural, and perhaps especially the economic contexts in which household and kinship systems are embedded.

From this evidence, students of the family can assert three points. First, no universal form of the family constitutes the appropriate or normative arrangement for reproduction, nurturance, socialization, and economic support. Both across and within societies, family forms, patterns, and practices vary enormously. Second, change is endemic to all family systems, and at least in the West, where we have the best evidence to date, family systems have always been in flux. Typically, these changes create tensions and often ignite public concern. Since colonial times, the family has been changing and provoking public reaction from moralists, scientists, and, of course, public authorities. Finally, family systems do not evolve in a linear fashion but become more or less complex and more elemental in different eras or among different strata of society depending on the economic and social conditions to which families must adapt.

Does this mean that we are seeing a continuation of what has always been or something different than has ever occurred in human history—the withering of kinship as an organizing feature of human society? The decline of marriage suggests to some that this round of change is unique in human history or that its consequences for children will be uniquely unsettling to society.

Many scholars weighed in on these questions. It is fair to say that there are two main camps: (1) those who have decided that the family is imperiled as a result of changes in the marriage system, a position held by such respectable social scientists as Linda Waite, Norvel Glenn, and Judith Wallerstein; and (2) those who remain skeptical and critical of those sounding the alarm, a position held by the majority of social scientists. Many in this second camp take seriously the concerns of the "alarmists" that children's welfare may be at risk if the current family regime continues. Still, they doubt that the family can be coaxed back into its 1950s form and favor adaptations in government policy to assist new forms of the family—an approach followed by most European nations.

Some portion of those skeptics are not so alarmed by changes in the family, believing that children's circumstances have not been seriously compromised by family change. They contend that children's well-being has less to do with the family form in which they reside than the resources possessed to form viable family arrangements. Lacking these resources (material and cultural), it matters little whether the children are born into a marriage, cohabitation, or a single-parent household, because they are likely not to fare as well as those whose parents possess the capacity to realize their goals.

I place myself in this latter group. Of course, children will fare better when they have two well-functioning, collaborative parents than one on average, but one well-functioning parent with resources is better than two married parents who lack the resources or skills to manage parenthood. Moreover, parents with limited cultural and material resources are unlikely to remain together in a stable marriage. Because the possession of such psychological, human, and material capital is highly related to marital stability, it is easy to confuse the effects of stable marriage with the effects of competent parenting. Finally, I believe that the best way to foster marriage stability is to support children with an array of services

that assist parents and children, regardless of the family form in which they reside.

Marriage and Good Outcomes for Children

A huge number of studies have shown that children fare better in two-biological-parent families than they do in single-biological-parent families, leading most family researchers to conclude that the nuclear family is a more effective unit for reproduction and socialization. Yet this literature reveals some troubling features that have not been adequately examined by social scientists. The most obvious of these is that such findings rule out social selection.

If parents with limited resources and low skills are less likely to enter marriage with a biological parent and remain wed when they do (which we know to be true), then it follows that children will do worse in such single-parent households than in stable marriages. We have known about this problem for decades, but researchers have not been equipped adequately to rule out selection. The standard method for doing so is by statistically controlling for prior differences, but this method is inadequate for ruling out differences because it leaves so many sources of selection unmeasured, such as sexual compatibility, substance abuse, and so on. Newer statistical methods have been employed to correct for unmeasured differences, but strong evidence exists that none of these techniques is up to the challenge. Nevertheless, it is *theoretically* possible to examine social experiments such as those being mounted in the marriage-promotion campaign and assess their long-term effects on children.

Another useful approach is to examine macro-level differences at the state or national level that would be less correlated with social selection and hence more revealing of the impact of marriage arrangements on children's well-being. To date, there is little evidence supporting a correlation between family form and children's welfare at the national level. Consider first the historical data showing that children who grew up in the 1950s (baby boomers) were not notably free of problem behavior. After all, they were the cohort who raised such hell in the 1960s and 1970s. From 1955 to 1975, indicators of social problems among children (test scores, suicide, homicide, controlled-substance use, crime) that can be tracked by vital statistics all rose. These indicators accompanied, and in some cases preceded rather than followed, change in the rates of divorce, the decline of marriage, and the rise of nonmarital childbearing during this period. Conversely, there is no evidence that the cohort of children who came of age in the 1990s and early part of this century is doing worse than previous cohorts because these children are more likely to have grown up in single-parent families. Of course, compensatory public policies or other demographic changes such as small family size, higher parental education, or lower rates of poverty may have offset the deleterious effects of family form, but such an explanation concedes that family form is not as potent a source of children's well-being as many observers seem to believe.

We might also gain some purchase on this issue by comparing the success of children under different family regimes. Do the countries with high rates of cohabitation, low marriage, high divorce, and high nonmarital fertility have the worst outcomes for children? We don't know the answer to this question, but we do know that various indicators of child well-being—health, mental health, educational attainment—do show higher scores in Northern than in Southern Europe. They appear to be linked to the level of investment in children, not the family form (which is certainly more intact in Southern Europe). Still, this question deserves more attention than it has received.

Significantly, many of the countries that continue to adhere to the nuclear model have some of the world's lowest rates of fertility—a problem that seems worse in countries with very low rates of nonmarital childbearing. I am not claiming that nonmarital childbearing is necessarily desirable as a social arrangement for propping up fertility, but it is a plausible hypothesis that nonmarital childbearing helps to keep the birth rate up in countries that would otherwise be experiencing a dangerously low level of reproduction.

Finally, it is important to recognize that family change in the United States (and in most Western countries, it appears) has not occurred evenly among all educational groups. In this country, marriage, divorce, and nonmarital childbearing have jumped since the 1960s among the bottom two-thirds of the educational distribution but have not changed much at all among the top third, consisting, today, of college graduates and postgraduates. Though marriage comes later to this group, they are barely more likely to have children out of wedlock, have high levels of marriage, and, if anything, lower levels of divorce than were experienced several decades ago. In other words, almost all the change has occurred among the segment of the population that has either not gained economically or has lost ground over the past several decades. Among the most socially disadvantaged and most marginalized segments of American society, marriage has become imperiled and family conditions have generally deteriorated, resulting in extremely high rates of union instability. The growing inequality in the United States may provide some clues for why the family, and marriage in particular, is not faring well and what to do about it.

Marriage and Public Policy

The logic of the Bush administration's approach to welfare is that by promoting and strengthening marriage, children's well-being, particularly in lower-income families will be enhanced. At first blush, this approach seems to make good sense. Economies of scale are produced when two adults live together. Two parents create healthy redundancies and perhaps help build social capital both within the household and by creating more connections to the community. The prevalence of marriage and marital stability is substantially higher among well-educated and more stably employed individuals than among those with less than a college education and lower incomes. Wouldn't it be reasonable to help the less educated enjoy the benefits of the nuclear family?

There are several reasons to be skeptical of this policy direction. First, we have the experience of the 1950s, when marriages did occur in abundance among low-income families. Divorce rates were extremely high during this era, and many of these families dissolved their unions when they had an opportunity to divorce because of chronic problems of conflict, disenchantment, and scarcity. In my own study of marriages of teen parents in the 1960s, I discovered that four out of every five women who married the father of their children got divorced before the child reached age eighteen; the rate of marital instability among those who married a stepfather was even higher. Certainly, encouraging marriage among young couples facing a choice of nonmarital childbearing or wedlock is not an easy choice when we know the outcome of the union is so precarious. If divorce is a likely outcome, it is not clear whether children are better off if their parents marry and divorce than remain unmarried, knowing as we do that family conflict and flux have adverse effects on children's welfare.

What about offering help to such couples before or after they enter marriage? This is a good idea, but don't expect any miracles from the current policies. Strong opposition exists to funding sustained and intensive premarital and postmarital counseling among many proponents of marriage-promotion programs. Conservative constituencies largely believe that education, especially under the aegis of religious or quasi-religious sponsorship is the best prescription for shoring up marriage. Yet, the evidence overwhelmingly shows that short-term programs that are largely didactic will not be effective in preserving marriages. Instead, many couples need repeated bouts of help both before and during marriage when they run into difficult straits. Most of these couples have little or no access to professional counseling.

The federal government has funded several large-scale experiments combining into a single program marital education or counseling *and* social services including job training or placement. These experiments, being conducted by the Manpower Research Demonstration Corporation, will use random assignment and have the best hope of producing some demonstrable outcomes. Yet, it is not clear at this point that even comprehensive programs with sustained services will be effective in increasing partner collaboration and reducing union instability.

There is another approach that I believe has a better prospect of improving both children's chances and probably at least an equal chance of increasing the viability of marriages or marriage-like arrangements. By directing more resources to low-income children regardless of the family form they live in, through such mechanisms as access to quality child care, health care, schooling, and income in the form of tax credits, it may be possible to increase the level of human, social, and psychological capital that children receive. And, by increasing services, work support, and especially tuition aid for adolescents and young adults to attend higher education, Americans may be able to protect children from the limitations imposed by low parental resources. Lending this type of assistance means that young adults are more likely to move into higher paying jobs and acquire through education the kinds of communication and problem-solving skills that are so useful to making marriage-like relationships last.

When we invest in children, we are not only likely to reap the direct benefits of increasing human capital but also the indirect benefits that will help preserve union stability in the next generation. This approach is more likely to increase the odds of success for children when they grow up. If I am correct, it probably follows that direct investment in children and youth has a better prospect of strengthening marriage and marriage-like relationships in the next generation by improving the skills and providing the resources to make parental relationships more rewarding and enduring.

So it comes down to a choice in strategy: invest in strengthening marriage and hope that children will benefit or invest in children and hope that marriages will benefit. I place my bet on the second approach.

FRANK FURSTENBERG, Zellerbach Family Professor of Sociology at the University of Pennsylvania, has written extensively on children, families, and public policy. His most recent book is *On the Frontier of Adulthood* (co-edited with Rick Settersten and Ruban Rumbaut), University of Chicago Press, 2005.

Originally published in *Dissent Magazine*, Summer 2005, pp. 76–80. Copyright © 2005 by Foundation for Study of Independent Ideas, Inc. Reprinted by permission. www.dissentmagazine.org

The Polygamists

A sect that split from the Mormons allows multiple wives, expels "lost boys," and heeds a jailed prophet.

SCOTT ANDERSON

The first church members arrive at the Leroy S. Johnson Meeting House in Colorado City, Arizona, at about 6 P.M. Within a half hour the line extends out the front doors, down the side of the building, and out into the parking lot. By seven, it stretches hundreds of yards and has grown to several thousand people—the men and boys dressed in suits, the women and girls in Easter egg–hued prairie dresses.

The mourners have come for a viewing of 68-year-old Foneta Jessop, who died of a heart attack a few days ago. In the cavernous hall Foneta's sons form a receiving line at the foot of her open casket, while her husband, Merril, stands directly alongside. To the other side stand Merril's numerous other wives, all wearing matching white dresses.

Foneta was the first wife.

Colorado City is a town with special significance for those of Foneta's faith. Together with its sister community of Hildale, Utah, it is the birthplace of the Fundamentalist Church of Jesus Christ of Latter-Day Saints (FLDS), a polygamous offshoot of the Mormon Church, or LDS. Here in the 1920s and '30s, a handful of polygamous families settled astride the Utah-Arizona border after the leadership of the Mormon Church became increasingly determined to shed its polygamous past and be accepted by the American mainstream. In 1935 the church gave settlement residents an ultimatum: renounce plural marriage or be excommunicated. Practically everyone refused and was cast out of the LDS.

At the memorial service for Foneta, her husband and three sons give testimonials praising her commitment to the covenant of plural marriage, but there is an undertone of family disharmony, with vague references by Merril Jessop to his troubled relationship with Foneta. No one need mention that one of Merril's wives is missing. Carolyn Jessop, his fourth wife, left the household in 2003 with her eight children and went on to write a best-selling book on her life as an FLDS member. She describes a cloistered environment and tells of a deeply unhappy Foneta, an overweight recluse who fell out of favor with her husband and slept her days away, coming out of her room only at night to eat, do laundry, and watch old Shirley Temple movies on television.

At the conclusion of the service, most of the congregation walk over to the Isaac Carling cemetery for a graveside observance. I assume the enormous turnout—mourners have come in from FLDS communities in Texas, Colorado, and British Columbia—stems from the prominent position Foneta's husband holds: Merril Jessop is an FLDS leader and the bishop of the large chapter in West Texas. But Sam Steed, a soft-spoken, 37-year-old accountant acting as my guide, explains that elaborate funerals are a regular occurrence. "Probably between 15 and 20 times a year," he says. "This one is maybe a little bigger than most, but even when a young child dies, you can expect three or four thousand people to attend. It's part of what keeps us together. It reminds us we're members of this larger community. We draw strength from each other."

Few Americans had heard of the FLDS before April 2008, when law enforcement officials conducted a raid on a remote compound in West Texas known as the Yearning for Zion Ranch. For days after, television viewers witnessed the bizarre spectacle of hundreds of children and women—all dressed in old-fashioned prairie dresses, with elaborately coiffed hair—being herded onto school buses by social workers and police officers.

That raid had been spurred by phone calls to a domestic violence shelter, purportedly from a 16-year-old girl who claimed she was being sexually and physically abused on the ranch by her middle-aged husband. What lent credibility to the calls was that the residents of YFZ Ranch were disciples of the FLDS and its "prophet," Warren Jeffs, who had been convicted in a Utah court in 2007 for officiating at the marriage of a 14-year-old girl to a church member.

The raid made for gripping television, but it soon became clear that the phone calls were a hoax. And although authorities had evidently anticipated a violent confrontation like the 1993 shoot-out at the Branch Davidian compound in Waco—SWAT teams were brought in, along with an armored personnel carrier—the arsenal at the YFZ Ranch consisted of only 33 legal firearms. A Texas appeals court later found that authorities had not met the burden of proof for the removal of the more than 400 children, and most were returned to their families within two months.

Yet after interviewing teenagers who were pregnant or had children, Texas authorities began investigating how many underage girls might have been "sealed" to older men. (Plural marriages are performed within the church and are not legal.) The result: Twelve church members, including Warren Jeffs, were indicted on charges ranging from bigamy to having sex with a minor. The first defendant to stand trial, Raymond Jessop, was convicted of one charge last November. Trials of the other defendants are scheduled to take place over the coming year.

From the Bluff behind his Hildale home, Joe Jessop has a commanding view of the Arizona Strip, an undulating expanse of sagebrush and piñon-juniper woodland that stretches south of the Utah border all the way to the northern rim of the Grand Canyon, some 50 miles away. Below are the farm fields and walled compounds of Hildale and Colorado City, which Joe refers to collectively by their old name, Short Creek. "When I first came to Short Creek as a boy, there were just seven homes down there," says Joe, 88. "It was like the frontier."

Today, Short Creek is home to an estimated 6,000 FLDS members—the largest FLDS community. Joe Jessop, a brother of Merril, has contributed to that explosive growth in two very different ways. With the weathered features and spindly gait of a man who has spent his life outdoors and worked his body hard, he is the community's undisputed "water guy," a self-taught engineer who helped with the piping of water out of Maxwell Canyon back in the 1940s. He's had a hand in building the intricate network of waterlines, canals, and reservoirs that has irrigated the arid plateau in the decades since.

A highly respected member of the FLDS, Joe is also the patriarch of a family of 46 children and—at last count—239 grandchildren. "My family came to Short Creek for the same reason as everyone else," he says, "to obey the law of plural marriage, to build up the Kingdom of God. Despite everything that's been thrown our way, I'd say we've done a pretty good job."

Members of the faith describe the life that the Jessops and other founding families have built as idyllic, one in which old-fashioned devotion and neighborly cooperation are emphasized and children are raised in a wholesome environment free of television and junk food and social pressures. Critics, on the other hand, see the FLDS as an isolated cult whose members, worn down by rigid social control, display a disturbing fealty to one man, the prophet Warren Jeffs—who has claimed to be God's mouthpiece on Earth.

To spend time in Hildale and Colorado City is to come away with a more nuanced view. That view is revealed gradually, however, due to the insular nature of the community. Many of the oversize homes are tucked behind high walls, both to give children a safe place to play and to shield families from gawking Gentiles, as non-Mormons are known. Most residents avoid contact with strangers. *National Geographic* was given access to the community only on the approval of the church leadership, in consultation with the imprisoned Warren Jeffs.

In keeping with original Mormon teachings, much of the property in Hildale and Colorado City is held in trust for the church. Striving to be as self-sufficient as possible, the community grows a wide variety of fruits and vegetables, and everyone, including children, is expected to help bring in the yield. Church members also own and operate a number of large businesses, from hotels to tool and machine manufacturers. Each Saturday, men gather at the meetinghouse to go over a roster of building and maintenance projects around town in need of volunteers. In one display of solidarity, the men built a four-bedroom home, from foundation to roof shingles, in a single day.

This communal spirit continues inside the polygamous home. Although living arrangements vary—wives may occupy different wings of a house or have their own granny cottages—the women tend to carve out spheres of influence according to preference or aptitude. Although each has primary responsibility for her own children, one wife might manage the kitchen, a second act as schoolteacher (virtually all FLDS children in Hildale and Colorado City are homeschooled), and a third see to the sewing. Along with instilling a sense of sorority, this division of labor appears to mitigate jealousy.

"I know it must seem strange to outsiders," says Joyce Broadbent, a friendly woman of 44, "but from my experience, sister wives usually get along very well. Oh sure, you might be closer to one than another, or someone might get on your nerves occasionally, but that's true in any family. I've never felt any rivalry or jealousy at all."

Joyce is a rather remarkable example of this harmony. She not only accepted another wife, Marcia, into the family, but was thrilled by the addition. Marcia, who left an unhappy marriage in the 1980s, is also Joyce's biological sister. "I knew my husband was a good man," Joyce explains with a smile as she sits with Marcia and their husband, Heber. "I wanted my sister to have a chance at the same kind of happiness I had."

Not all FLDS women are quite so sanguine about plural marriage. Dorothy Emma Jessop is a spry, effervescent octogenarian who operates a naturopathic dispensary in Hildale. Sitting in her tiny shop surrounded by jars of herbal tinctures she ground and mixed herself, Dorothy admits she struggled when her husband began taking on other wives. "To be honest," she says, "I think a lot of women have a hard time with it, because it's not an easy thing to share the man you love. But I came to realize this is another test that God places before you—the sin of jealousy, of pride—and that to be a godly woman, I needed to overcome it."

What seems to help overcome it is an awareness that a woman's primary role in the FLDS is to bear and raise as many children as possible, to build up the "celestial family" that will remain together for eternity. It is not uncommon to meet FLDS women who have given birth to 10, 12, 16 children. (Joyce Broadbent is the mother of 11, and Dorothy Emma Jessop of 13.) As a result, it's easy to see why this corner of the American West is experiencing a population explosion. The 400 or so babies delivered in the Hildale health clinic every year have resulted in a median age of just under 14, in contrast with 36.6 for the entire U.S. With so many in the community tracing their lineage to a handful of the pioneering families, the same few names crop up over and over in Hildale and Colorado City, suggesting a murkier side to this fecundity: Doctors in Arizona say a severe form of a debilitating disease called fumarase deficiency, caused by a recessive gene, has become more prevalent in the community due to intermarriage.

The collision of tradition and modernity in the community can be disorienting. Despite their old-fashioned dress, most FLDS adults have cell phones and favor late-model SUVs. Although televisions are now banished, church members tend to be highly computer literate and sell a range of products, from soaps to dresses, via the Internet. When I noticed how few congregants wore glasses, I wondered aloud if perhaps a genetic predisposition for good eyesight was at work. Sam Steed laughed lightly. "No. People here are just really into laser surgery."

The principle of plural marriage was revealed to the Mormons amid much secrecy. Dark clouds hovered over the church in the early 1840s, after rumors spread that its founder, Joseph Smith, had taken up the practice of polygamy. While denying the charge in public, by 1843 Smith had shared a revelation with his closest disciples. In this "new and everlasting covenant" with God, plural wives were to be taken so that the faithful might "multiply and replenish the earth."

After Smith was assassinated by an anti-Mormon mob in Illinois, Brigham Young led believers on an epic 1,300-mile journey west to the Salt Lake Basin of present-day Utah. There the covenant was at last publicly revealed and with it, the notion that a man's righteousness before God would be measured by the size of his family; Brigham Young himself took 55 wives, who bore him 57 children.

But in 1890, faced with the seizure of church property under a federal antipolygamy law, the LDS leadership issued a manifesto announcing an end to plural marriage. That certainly didn't end the practice, and the LDS's tortured handling of the issue—some church leaders remained in plural marriages or even took on new wives after the manifesto's release—contributed to the schism between the LDS and the fundamentalists.

"The LDS issued that manifesto for political purposes, then later claimed it was a revelation," says Willie Jessop, the FLDS spokesman. "We in the fundamentalist community believe covenants are made with God and are not to be manipulated for political reasons, so that presents an enormous obstacle between us and those in the LDS mainstream."

Upholding the covenant has come at a high price. The 2008 raid on the YFZ Ranch was only the latest in a long list of official actions against polygamists—persecutions for simply adhering to their religious principles, in the eyes of church members—that are integral to the FLDS story. At various times both Utah and Arizona authorities attempted to crack down on the Short Creek community: in 1935, in 1944, and most famously, in 1953. In that raid some 200 women and children were hauled to detention centers, while 26 men were brought up on polygamy charges. In 1956 Utah authorities seized seven children of Vera Black, a Hildale plural wife, on grounds that her polygamous beliefs made her an unfit mother. Black was reunited with her children only after agreeing to renounce polygamy.

Melinda Fischer Jeffs is an articulate, outgoing woman of 37, and she gives an incredulous laugh when describing what she's read about the FLDS. "Honestly, I can't even recognize it!" the mother of three exclaims. "Most all of what appears in the media, it makes us sound like we're somehow being kept against our will."

Melinda is in a unique position to understand the conflicting views of this community. She is a plural wife to Jim Jeffs, one of the prophet's nephews and an elder in the FLDS. But she is also the daughter of Dan Fischer, a former FLDS member who has emerged as one of the church leadership's most vociferous critics. In 2008 Fischer testified before a U.S. Senate committee about alleged improprieties within the FLDS, and he now heads an organization that works with people who have been kicked out of the church or who have "escaped." When Fischer broke with the church in the 1990s, his family split apart too; today 13 of his children have left the FLDS, while Melinda and two of her half siblings have renounced their father.

"And that is not an easy thing," Melinda says softly, "obviously, because I still love my father. I pray all the time that he will see his errors—or at least, stop his attacks on us."

If there is one point on which FLDS defenders and detractors might agree, it is that most of the current troubles can be traced to when its leadership passed to the Jeffs family, in 1986. Until then, the FLDS had been a fairly loosely run group led by an avuncular man named Leroy Johnson, who relied on a group of high priests to guide the church. That ended when Rulon Jeffs took over following Johnson's death. After being declared the prophet by the community, Rulon solidified the policy of one-man rule.

Charges that a theocratic dictatorship was taking root in the Arizona Strip grew louder when, after Rulon's death in 2002, the FLDS was taken over by his 46-year-old son, Warren. Assuming the role of the prophet, Warren first married several of his father's wives—and then proceeded to wed many more women, including, according to Carolyn Jessop, eight of Merril Jessop's daughters. Although many FLDS men have multiple wives, the number of wives of those closest to the prophet can reach into the double digits. A church document called the Bishop's Record, seized during the Texas raid, shows that one of Jeffs's lieutenants, Wendell Nielsen, claims 21 wives. And although the FLDS would not disclose how many plural wives Warren Jeffs has taken (some estimate more than 80), at least one was an underage girl, according to a Texas indictment.

Although the issue of underage marriage within the church has garnered the greatest negative media attention, Dan Fischer has championed another cause, the so-called Lost Boys, who have left or been forced from the community and wound up fending for themselves on the streets of Las Vegas, Salt Lake City, and St. George, Utah. Fischer's foundation has worked with 300 such young men, a few as young as 13, over the past seven years. Fischer concedes that most of these boys were simply "discouraged out," but he cites cases where they were officially expelled, a practice he says increased under Jeffs.

Fischer attributes the exodus partly to a cold-blooded calculation by church leaders to limit male competition for the pool of marriageable young women. "If you have men marrying 20, 30, up to 80 or more women," he says, "then it comes down to biology and simple math that there will be a lot of other men who aren't going to get wives. The church says it's kicking these boys out for being disruptive influences, but if you'll notice, they rarely kick out girls."

Equally contentious has been the FLDS restoration of an early Mormon policy of transferring the wives and children of a church member to another man. Traditionally, this was done upon the death of a patriarch so that his widows might be cared for, or to rescue a woman from an abusive relationship. But critics argue that under Jeffs this "reassignment" became one more weapon to hold over the heads of those who dared step out of line.

Determining who is unworthy has been the exclusive province of the prophet. When in January 2004 Jeffs publicly ordered the expulsion of 21 men and the reassignment of their families, the community acquiesced. Jeffs's diary, also seized during the Texas raid, reveals a man who micromanaged the community's every decision, from chore assignments and housing arrangements to who married whom and which men were ousted—all directed by revelations Jeffs received as he slept. He claimed that God guided his every action, no matter how small. One diary entry reads: "The Lord directed that I go to the sun tanning salon and get sun tanned more evenly on their suntanning beds."

In 2005 a Utah court transferred control of the trust that oversees much of the land in Hildale and Colorado City from the FLDS leadership to a state-appointed fiduciary; the church is currently waging a campaign to recover control of the trust. As for Jeffs, after spending over a year on the lam avoiding legal issues in Utah—and earning a spot on the FBI's Ten Most Wanted list—he was caught and is currently serving a ten-year-to-life sentence as an accomplice to rape. He awaits trial on multiple indictments in Arizona and Texas. The 11 other church members awaiting trial in Texas include Merril Jessop, who was indicted for performing the marriage of Jeffs to an underage girl.

Yet Jeffs's smiling portrait continues to adorn the living room of almost every FLDS home. In his absence, his lieutenants have launched a fierce defense of his leadership. While conceding that underage marriages did occur in the past, Donald Richter, contributor to one of the official FLDS websites, says the practice has now been stopped. As for the Lost Boys, he argues that both the numbers involved and the reasons for the expulsions have been greatly exaggerated by the church's enemies. "This is only done in the most extreme cases," Richter says, "and never for the trivial causes they're claiming. And anyway, all religious groups have the right to expel people who won't accept their rules."

Certainly Melinda Fischer Jeffs hasn't been swayed by the ongoing controversy. "Warren is just the kindest, most loving man," she says. "The image that has been built up about him by the media and his enemies is just unrecognizable to who he really is." Like other church members, Melinda has ready answers for most of the accusations leveled against Jeffs and is especially spirited in defending the policy of reassignment.

According to her, it is almost always initiated at the request of a wife who has been abandoned or abused. This is debatable. In his diary Jeffs recounts reassigning the wives of three men, including his brother David, because God had shown him that they "couldn't exalt their ladies, had lost the confidence of God." One of his brother's wives had difficulty accepting the news and could barely bring herself to kiss her new husband. "She showed a great spirit of resistance, yet she went through with it," Jeffs records. "She needs to learn to submit to Priesthood."

Yet Melinda's defense of Jeffs underscores one of the most curious aspects of the polygamous faith: the central role of women in defending it. This is not new. In Brigham Young's day a charity rushed to Utah to establish a safe house for polygamous women seeking to escape this "white slavery"; that house sat virtually empty. Today FLDS women in the Hildale–Colorado City area have ample opportunity to "escape"—they have cell phones, they drive cars, there are no armed guards keeping them in—yet they don't.

Undoubtedly one reason is that, having been raised in this culture, they know little else. Walking away means leaving behind everything: the community, one's sense of security, even one's own family. Carolyn Jessop, the plural wife of Merril Jessop who did leave the FLDS, likens entering the outside world to "stepping out onto another planet. I was completely unprepared, because I had absolutely no life skills. Most women in the FLDS don't even know how to balance a checkbook, let alone apply for a job, so contemplating how you're going to navigate in the outside world is extremely daunting."

It would seem there's another lure for women to stay: power. The FLDS women I spoke with tended to be far more articulate and confident than the men, most of whom seemed paralyzed by bashfulness. It makes sense when one begins to grasp that women are coveted to "multiply and replenish the earth," while men are in extraordinary competition to be deemed worthy of marriage by the prophet. One way to be deemed worthy, of course, is to not rock the boat, to keep a low profile. As a result, what has all the trappings of a patriarchal culture, actually has many elements of a matriarchal one.

There are limits to that power, of course, for it is subject to the dictates of the prophet. After hearing Melinda's stout defense of Jeffs, I ask what she would do if she were reassigned.

"I'm confident that wouldn't happen," she replies uneasily.

"But what if it did?" I ask. "Would you obey?"

For the only time during our interview, Melinda grows wary. Sitting back in her chair, she gives her head a quarter turn to stare at me out of the corner of one eye.

On a sunny afternoon in March 2009, Bob Barlow, a friendly, middle-aged member of the FLDS, gives me a tour of the YFZ Ranch in West Texas. The compound consists of about 25 two-story log-cabin-style homes, and a number of workshops and factories are scattered over 1,700 acres. At the center sits a gleaming white stone temple. It is remarkable what the residents have created from the hardscrabble plain. With heavy machinery, they literally made earth out of the rocky terrain, crushing stone and mixing it with the thin topsoil. They planted orchards and gardens and lawns and were on their way to creating a self-sufficient community amid the barren landscape. All that ground to a halt after the 2008 raid.

"The families are slowly coming back now," Barlow says. "We'll come out the other side of this better and stronger than before."

I suspect he's right. So many times in the history of Mormon polygamy the outside world thought it had the movement on the ropes only to see it flourish anew. I'm reminded of this one afternoon in Colorado City when I speak with Vera Black. Now 92 and in failing health, Vera is the woman whose children were taken from her by Utah authorities in 1956 and returned only after she agreed to renounce polygamy. Within days of making that promise, she was back in Short Creek with her children and had renewed her commitment to the everlasting covenant.

Now living with her daughter Lillian, Vera lies in a daybed as her children gather around. Those children are now in their 50s and 60s, and as they recount the story of their long-ago separation—both from their mother and their faith—several weep, as if the pain were fresh.

"I had to make that promise," Vera says, with a smile, "but I crossed my fingers while I did it."

From *National Geographic*, February 2010, Vol. 217, No. 2, pp. 34–57. Copyright © 2010 by National Geographic Society. Reprinted by permission.

Good Parents, Bad Results

Science is providing proof of where Mom and Dad go wrong.

Nancy Shute

Does your 3-year-old throw a five-alarm tantrum every time you drop him off at day care? Does "you're so smart!" fail to inspire your 8-year-old to turn off *Grand Theft Auto IV* and tackle his math homework? Do the clothes remain glued to your teenager's bedroom floor, along with your antisocial teenager, no matter how much you nag or cajole? Being a parent has never been easy—just ask your own. But in this day of two-earner couples and single parents, when 9-year-olds have cellphones, 12-year-olds are binge drinking and having oral sex, and there is evidence that teens are more fearful and depressed than ever, the challenges of rearing competent and loving human beings are enough to make a parent seek help from Supernanny. Actually, there is something better: science.

Researchers have spent decades studying what motivates children to behave and can now say exactly what discipline methods work and what don't: Call it "evidence-based parenting." Alas, many of parents' favorite strategies are scientifically proven to fail. "It's intuitive to scream at your child to change their behavior, even though the research is unequivocal that it won't work," says Alan Kazdin, a psychologist who directs the Yale Parenting Center and Child Conduct Clinic. Other examples:

- Yelling and reasoning are equally ineffective; kids tune out both.
- Praise doesn't spoil a child; it's one of the most powerful tools that parents can use to influence a child's actions. But most parents squander praise by using it generically—"you're so smart" or "good job!"—or skimping.
- Spanking and other harsh punishments ("You're grounded for a month!") do stop bad behavior but only temporarily. Punishment works only if it's mild, and it is far outweighed by positive reinforcement of good behavior.

As yet, few of the bestselling books and videos that promise to turn surly brats into little buttercups make use of this knowledge. That may be because the research goes on in academia—at Yale, at Vermont's Behavior Therapy and Psychotherapy Center, and at the University of Washington's Parenting Clinic, for example. Surprisingly, many family therapists and parenting educators aren't up to speed on the research, either, so that parents who seek professional help won't necessarily get the most proven advice. Case in point: Just 16 programs designed for treating kids with disruptive behavior have been proven "well established" in randomized clinical trials, according to a review led by Sheila Eyberg at the University of Florida and published in the January *Journal of Clinical Child and Adolescent Psychology*. Kazdin, who for years has pushed clinical psychologists to adopt evidence-based methods, published a book for parents earlier this year: *The Kazdin Method for Parenting the Defiant Child*. Other lab-tested tomes include *Parenting the Strong-Willed Child* by Rex Forehand and Nicholas Long and *The Incredible Years* by Carolyn Webster-Stratton.

These discipline programs are grounded in classical behavioral psychology—the positive reinforcement taught in Psych 101. Researchers have run randomized controlled trials on all the nuances of typical parent-child interactions and thus can say just how long a timeout should last to be effective or how to praise a 13-year-old so that he beams when he takes out the trash. Who knew that effectively praising a child in order to motivate her has three essential steps? They are: 1) Praise effusively, with the enthusiasm of a Powerball winner. 2) Say exactly what the child did right. 3) Finish with a touch or hug.

What else can parents learn from the science? Researchers say these are the biggest common boo-boos:

1. Parents Fail at Setting Limits

It would be hard to find a parent who doesn't agree that setting and enforcing rules are an essential part of the job description. Yet faced with whining, pouting, and tantrums, many parents cave. "The limited time you have with your kids, you want to make it ideal for them," says Forehand, a professor of psychology at the University of Vermont whose evidence-based program is outlined in his book. "As a result, we end up overindulging our kids."

Faced with whining and pouting, many parents cave, Result: domestic inferno.

A Good Parent's Dilemma: Is It Bad to Spank?

Plenty of people argue for an occasional swat

Last year, the California Legislature considered criminalizing the spanking of toddlers. But at least half of parents, and according to some surveys as many as 94 percent, consider a swat on the bottom to be an appropriate form of discipline. "spanking has worked very well for us," says Tim Holt, a 45-year-old insurance agent and the father of four children, ages 4 to 13, in Simpsonville, S.C., who notes that he and his wife spank very rarely. He recalls spanking his 7-year-old son, Scott, after Scott hit his brother in the head with a shoe and then lied to his father about it. "I pulled Scott aside. We discussed what he had done: Why is it wrong? What does God's law say? That we don't take our anger out on others." Then Holt put Scott over his knee and smacked him on his pants with a plastic glue stick. "It's something that gets his attention and provides a little bit of pain to his bottom."

Proponents include James Dobson, a psychologist and founder of Focus on the Family, who likens squeezing a child's shoulder or spanking his behind to discomfort that "works to shape behavior in the physical world." He writes in *The New Dare to Discipline:* "The minor pain that is associated with this deliberate misbehavior tends to inhibit it. . . . A boy or girl who knows love abounds at home will not resent a well-deserved spanking." But the subject generates more heat than just about any other child-rearing issue. Sweden banned spanking in 1979. The United Nations Committee on the Rights of the Child has been seeking a ban on corporal punishment worldwide since 1996.

The evidence. The debate roils academia, too. Murray Straus, a professor of sociology at the University of New Hampshire, says 110 studies have linked spanking to increased misbehavior in childhood as well as adult problems such as increased spousal abuse and depression. In February, Straus published research linking being spanked in childhood with an adult preference for sadomasochistic sex. Straus acknowledges that most of today's parents were themselves spanked as children but says that since spanking is no more effective than other discipline methods and can cause harm it's not worth the misery. Other researchers, including Diana Baumrind, a psychologist at the University of California-Berkeley, have found that children who were spanked occasionally had no more behavior problems than children who were never spanked. But Baumrind says regular reliance on physical punishment, as well as "impulsive and reactive spanking," causes harm to a child. The bottom line: Proponents of either position can come up with enough evidence to support their belief-but not enough to convince the other side.

Demonizing spanking may leave some parents feeling they must avoid *any* discipline that makes a child feel bad, says Lawrence Diller, a developmental pediatrician in Walnut Creek, Calif., who works with children with attention deficit hyperactivity disorder. He speculates that a more coherent disciplinary approach that includes an occasional well-timed swat can make the overall system more effective and could "make the difference in whether your child will be on Ritalin or not. You don't have to spank. But if you're using spanking as one of array of tools to get control of your kid, you're not hurting them in the long term."

—N.S.

But, paradoxically, not having limits has been proven to make children *more* defiant and rebellious, because they feel unsafe and push to see if parents will respond. Research since the 1960s on parenting styles has found that a child whose mom and dad are permissive is more likely to have problems in school and abuse drugs and alcohol as teenagers. "Parents ask their 1-year-olds what they want for dinner now," says Jean Twenge, an associate professor of psychology at San Diego State University and author of *Generation Me.* "No one ever said that a generation or two ago." Using surveys dating back to the 1930s, Twenge has found significant increases in reported symptoms of depression and anxiety among today's children and teenagers, compared with earlier generations. Suniya Luthar, a psychologist at Columbia University Teachers College, reported in 2003 that children who are showered with advantages are more likely to be depressed and anxious and to abuse drugs and alcohol than the norm. Luthar says that's probably because those children are under a lot of pressure to achieve at school and think that their parents value their achievements more than themselves. They also feel isolated from their parents.

Rule-setting works best when parents give simple, clear commands and discuss the family rules with kids well in advance of a conflict, according to Robert Hendren, a professor of psychiatry at the Medical Investigation of Neurodevelopmental Disorders Institute at the University of California-Davis and president of the American Academy of Child and Adolescent Psychiatry. A common recommendation for parents who fear coming off as a meanie: Let the child choose between two options when either choice is acceptable to the parent. A half-hour of Nintendo right after school, then homework? All homework before game time?

Consistency is also key. "I have to be very strict with myself and go over and tell him the rules and walk away," says Lauren Jordan, a stay-at-home mom in Essex Junction, Vt., whose 4-year-old son, Peter, would scream and hit Jordan and her husband, Sean, then kick the wall during timeout. "It felt out of control." Jordan signed up with Vermont's Behavior Therapy and Psychotherapy Center to learn Forehand's five-week process.

The first week was spent just "attending" to Peter, watching him play and commenting without telling the preschooler what to do. "He *loved* it," says Jordan, whose older son has autism and has required an outsize share of her energy. "I realized at that point that he needs this one-on-one attention." Jordan then had to learn to ignore Peter's minor bad behavior (such as screaming for attention while Mom is on the phone) and to not rush in to scold him during a timeout. "Consistency is the key. It's not easy," Jordan says. "But it's made our home a much happier place."

2. They're Overprotective

Teachers, coaches, and psychotherapists alike have noticed that parents today can't stand to see their children struggle or suffer a setback. So they're stepping in to micromanage everything from playground quarrels to baseball team positions to grades. Even bosses aren't immune. One owner of a New York public relations firm says he has gotten E-mails from parents telling him that's he's making their child work too much. The child in question is in his 20s.

"Many well-meaning parents jump in too quickly," says Robert Brooks, a clinical psychologist in Needham, Mass., and coauthor of *Raising Resilient Children.* "Resilient children realize that sometimes they will fail, make mistakes, have setbacks. They will attempt to learn from them." When parents intercede, Brooks says, "it communicates to the kid that 'I don't think you're capable of dealing with it.' We have to let kids experience the consequences of their behavior."

Otherwise, they may grow afraid to try. "I see a lot of kids who seem really unmotivated," says Kristen Gloff, 36, a clinical and school social worker in the Chicago area. "It's not that they're lazy. They don't want to fail."

3. They Nag. Lecture. Repeat. Then Yell.

If one verbal nudge won't get a kid to come to dinner, 20 surely will. Right? In fact, there's abundant evidence that humans tune out repeated commands. "So many parents think they have to get very emotionally upset, yell, threaten, use sarcasm," says Lynn Clark, a professor emeritus of psychology at Western Kentucky University and author of *SOS Help for Parents.* "The child imitates that behavior, and you get sassy talk."

Nagging also gives children "negative reinforcement," or an incentive—parental attention—to keep misbehaving. "I was kind of ignoring the good behavior, and every time he did something wrong, I would step in and give him attention," says Nancy Ailes, a 46-year-old stay-at-home mom in East Haven, Conn. She was frustrated with her 9-year-old son, Nick, who would melt down and throw things if the day's schedule changed, drag his feet about cleaning his room or doing homework, and call her "bad Mommy" if she complained.

Parent management training this spring at the Yale Child Conduct Center taught Ailes and her husband how to use positive reinforcement instead—to praise Nick immediately and enthusiastically. Now, when Nick is picking up his toys in the family room, she sits down, watches, and says: "Wow, that looks really nice!"

Ailes and her husband, David, also learned how to set up a reward system with points that Nick can cash in for Yu-Gi-Oh cards and Game Boy time and to back up the system with timeouts

for bad behavior. Within three weeks, Ailes says, Nick had made a complete turnaround. "Instead of doing things that make people unhappy," she says, "you do things that make them happy!"

4. They Praise Too Much— and Badly

It seems like a truism that praising children would make them feel good about themselves and motivate them to do better. But parents don't give children attaboys as often as they think, Kazdin says. And when they do, it's all too often either generic ("good job!") or centered on the person, not the task ("you're so smart!"). This kind of praise actually makes children less motivated and self-confident. In one experiment by Carol Dweck, a psychologist now at Stanford University, fifth graders who were praised for being intelligent, rather than making a good effort, actually made less of an effort on tests and had a harder time dealing with failure.

"It's so common now for parents to tell children that they're special," says Twenge. That fosters narcissism, she says, not self-esteem. Twenge thinks parents tell a child "You're special" when they really mean "You're special to me." Much better in every way, she says, to just say: "I love you."

5. They Punish Too Harshly

Although spanking has been deplored by child-development experts since the days of Dr. Spock in the 1940s, as many as 90 percent of parents think it's OK to spank young children, according to research by Murray Straus, a professor of sociology at the University of New Hampshire (more on the spanking controversy in the box). Kazdin and other behavioral researchers say parents commonly punish far more harshly than they need to.

After all, it's not supposed to be about payback, though that's often what's going on, says Jamila Reid, codirector of the Parenting Clinic at the University of Washington. The clinic's "The Incredible Years" program has been found in seven studies to improve children's behavior. "Often parents come looking for bigger sticks. We tell parents the word discipline means 'teach.' It's something to teach a child that there's a better way to respond."

Consider the fine art of the timeout. Parents often sabotage timeouts by lecturing or by giving hugs, according to Sheila Eyberg, a professor of psychology at the University of Florida. Her Parent-Child Interaction Therapy is used in many mental health clinics. Forehand and other researchers have spent many hours observing the use of timeout as a disciplinary strategy to determine exactly what makes it effective. The key finding: Discipline works best when it's immediate, mild, and brief, because it's then associated with the transgression and doesn't breed more anger and resentment. A timeout should last for just a few minutes, usually one minute for each year of age of the child.

Teenagers who have outgrown timeouts shouldn't lose a privilege for more than a day. Beyond that, the child's attitude shifts from regretting bad behavior to resenting the parent. "The punishment business isn't just ineffective," Kazdin says. "It leads to avoidance and escape. It puts a little wedge in the relationship between parent and child." Long groundings also make it more likely that the parents will relent after a few days. Better, Kazdin says, to ask the child to practice good behavior, such as fixing something he damaged, in order to win privileges back.

6. They Tell Their Child How to Feel

Most parenting books focus on eradicating bad behavior. But in study after study, empathy for other people leads the list of qualities that people need to successfully handle relationships at school, at work, and in the family. Children need to think about how their own feelings will be affected by what they do, as well as the feelings of others, says Myrna Shure, a developmental psychologist at Drexel University and author of *Raising a Thinking Child.* "That is what will inhibit a child from hurting others, either physically or emotionally."

And parents, by telling children "you're fine" or "don't cry," deny children the chance to learn those lessons. "The child learns empathy through being empathized with," says Stanley Greenspan, a child psychiatrist in Chevy Chase, MD, whose most recent book, *Great Kids,* tells parents how to help their child develop 10 essential qualities for a happy life. Empathy, creativity, and logical thinking top the list. A simple "We're so sorry, we know how it feels" is enough.

"Modeling empathic behavior is really very important," says James Windell, a counselor with the juvenile court system in Oakland County, Mich., and author of *8 Weeks to a Well-Behaved Child.* "How you respond to your children's needs sets the stage. It's really easy to be a supportive parent when they bring home a straight-A report card. When they get a bad grade, that's when they really need our support."

7. They Put Grades and Sats Ahead of Creativity

An overemphasis on good grades can also distort the message about how and what children should learn. "We like kids to learn rules, and we want them to learn facts," says Greenspan. "We're impressed when they can read early or identify their shapes. It's much harder for us to inspire them to come up with a creative idea." Children who can think creatively are more likely to be able to bounce back if their first idea doesn't work. They also know it can take time and patience to come up with a good solution. The goal, says Greenspan, is not to have a child who knows how to answer questions but one who will grow up to ask the important questions.

Parents can help their children become independent thinkers by asking open-ended questions like: Can you think of another way to solve the problem with your teammate? Or ask a whining preschooler: Can you think of a different way to tell me what you want?

8. They Forget to Have Fun

"When I talk to families that aren't functioning so well, and I ask, how often do you laugh together, they say: We haven't laughed together for a long time," says Hendren. Those little signs of love and connection—a laugh, a song shared in the car—are, he says, signs of health.

Do We Need a Law to Prohibit Spanking?

Murray Straus, PhD

The proposal by a member of the California legislature to prohibit spanking and other corporal punishment of children age three and younger has attracted nationwide interest—and outrage. Newspapers around the country published editorials about it. I read many of them, and all opposed the proposal. The two main objections are that spanking children is sometimes necessary and that it is an unprecedented and horrible example of government interference in the lives of families. The editorials usually also say or imply that "moderate" spanking does not harm children. These objections accurately represent the beliefs of most Americans, but they are not accurate representations of the scientific evidence on the effectiveness and side effects of spanking. They are also historically inaccurate about government interference in the family.

The research on the effectiveness of spanking shows that it does work to correct misbehavior. But the research also shows that spanking does not work better than other modes of correction and control, such as time out, explaining, and depriving a child of privileges. Moreover, the research clearly shows that the gains from spanking come at a big cost. These include weakening the tie between children and parents, and increasing the probability that the child will hit other children, hit their parents, and as adults hit a dating or marital partner. Spanking also slows down mental development and lowers the probability of a child doing well in school and in college. There have been more than a hundred studies of these side effects of spanking, and there is over 90% agreement between them. There is probably no other aspect of parenting and child behavior where the results are so consistent.

Despite this overwhelming evidence, few believe that "moderate" spanking harms children, including few psychologists. It seems to contradict their own experience and that of their children. They say "I was spanked and I was not a violent kid and I did well in school." That is correct, but the implication that spanking is harmless is not correct. Like smoking, spanking is a "risk factor"—not a one-to-one cause of problems. About a third of heavy smokers die of a smoking related disease. That is gruesome, but it also means that two thirds can say "I smoked all my life and I am OK." Does that mean smoking is OK? No, it just means that they are one of the lucky two thirds. Similarly, when someone says "I was spanked and I am OK," that is

correct. However, the implication that spanking is harmless is not correct. The correct implication is that they are one of the lucky majority, rather than one of those harmed by spanking.

The large and consistent body of evidence on the harmful side effects of spanking is also not believed because because so few get to know about it.

Another reason the evidence is not believed is because the harm from spanking occurs down the road. Parents can see that the spanked child stopped what they were doing wrong. They cannot see the harmful effects that occur months or years later.

The large and consistent body of evidence on the harmful side effects of spanking is also not believed because so few get to know about it. I analyzed the content of ten child psychology textbooks published in the 1980's, ten in the 1990's, and ten published since 2000. These giant textbooks averaged only half a page on spanking, despite the fact that almost all American toddlers are spanked. None reported the fact that over 90% of the studies found harmful side-effects. Or putting it the other way around, none let their readers know that children who are not spanked, rather than being out of control brats, are more likely than spanked children to be well behaved and to have fewer psychological problems. This may be the best kept secret of American child psychology.

What about no-spanking legislation being an unprecedented interference in the family? Until the 1870's husbands had the right to use corporal punishment to correct an "errant wife." When the courts started to rule that this aspect of the common law was no longer valid, it was regarded by many as an outrageous interference in what should be a private family matter. Government now prohibits "physically chastisting an errant wife" and prohibits many other things to protect family members and to enhance the stability of the family, starting with prohibiting marriage at an early age.

The proposed California law, however, has two major problems. First, it applies only to children age three and younger. Therefore it has the ironic implication of endorsing the hitting of older children. A second irony is that this law would be doing the very thing it wants parents not to do—use harsh punishment to correct misbehavior. A better model is the 1979 Swedish no-spanking law. It has no criminal penalty. The purpose of that type of law is to set a standard for how children should be treated, and to make money available to educate the public about these standards and to provide services to help parents who are having enough difficulty with their children that they spank. The Swedish law has proven to be very effective. Spanking children has declined tremendously. Opponents of the law feared that Swedish children would be "running wild." The opposite has happened. Youth crime rates, drug use, and suicide have all decreased.

Fifteen nations now prohibit spanking by parents. There is an emerging consensus that this is a fundamental human right for children. The United Nations committee charged with implementing the Charter of Children's Rights is asking all nations to prohibit spanking. Never spanking will not only reduce the risk of delinquency and mental health problems, it will also bring to children the right to be free of physical attacks in the name of discipline, just as wives gained that human right a century and a quarter ago.

MURRAY A. STRAUS, PhD has studied spanking by large and representative samples of American parents for thirty years. He is the author of *Beating the Devil out of Them: Corporal Punishment in American Families and Its Effects on Children* (Transaction Press, 2001). He has been president of three scientific societies including the National Council On Family Relations, and an advisor to the National Institutes of Health and the National Science Foundation. He can be reached at 603 862-2594 or by email at murray.straus@unh.edu. Much of his research on spanking can be downloaded from http://pubpages.unh.edu/~mas2.

NCFR Report, *Family Focus* Section, volume FF34, June 2007. Used by permission. Copyright 2007.

Children of Lesbian and Gay Parents

Does parental sexual orientation affect child development, and if so, how? Studies using convenience samples, studies using samples drawn from known populations, and studies based on samples that are representative of larger populations all converge on similar conclusions. More than two decades of research has failed to reveal important differences in the adjustment or development of children or adolescents reared by same-sex couples compared to those reared by other-sex couples. Results of the research suggest that qualities of family relationships are more tightly linked with child outcomes than is parental sexual orientation.

CHARLOTTE J. PATTERSON

Does parental sexual orientation affect child development, and if so, how? This question has often been raised in the context of legal and policy proceedings relevant to children, such as those involving adoption, child custody, or visitation. Divergent views have been offered by professionals from the fields of psychology, sociology, medicine, and law (Patterson, Fulcher, & Wainright, 2002). While this question has most often been raised in legal and policy contexts, it is also relevant to theoretical issues. For example, does healthy human development require that a child grow up with parents of each gender? And if not, what would that mean for our theoretical understanding of parent–child relations? (Patterson & Hastings, in press) In this article, I describe some research designed to address these questions.

Early Research

Research on children with lesbian and gay parents began with studies focused on cases in which children had been born in the context of a heterosexual marriage. After parental separation and divorce, many children in these families lived with divorced lesbian mothers. A number of researchers compared development among children of divorced lesbian mothers with that among children of divorced heterosexual mothers and found few significant differences (Patterson, 1997; Stacey & Biblarz, 2001).

These studies were valuable in addressing concerns of judges who were required to decide divorce and child custody cases, but they left many questions unanswered. In particular, because the children who participated in this research had been born into homes with married mothers and fathers, it was not obvious how to understand the reasons for their healthy development. The possibility that children's early exposure to apparently heterosexual male and female role models had contributed to healthy development could not be ruled out.

When lesbian or gay parents rear infants and children from birth, do their offspring grow up in typical ways and show healthy development? To address this question, it was important to study children who had never lived with heterosexual parents. In the 1990s, a number of investigators began research of this kind.

An early example was the Bay Area Families Study, in which I studied a group of 4- to 9-year-old children who had been born to or adopted early in life by lesbian mothers (Patterson, 1996, 1997). Data were collected during home visits. Results from in-home interviews and also from questionnaires showed that children had regular contact with a wide range of adults of both genders, both within and outside of their families. The children's self-concepts and preferences for same-gender playmates and activities were much like those of other children their ages. Moreover, standardized measures of social competence and of behavior problems, such as those from the Child Behavior Checklist (CBCL), showed that they scored within the range of normal variation for a representative sample of same-aged American children. It was clear from this study and others like it that it was quite possible for lesbian mothers to rear healthy children.

Studies Based on Samples Drawn from Known Populations

Interpretation of the results from the Bay Area Families Study was, however, affected by its sampling procedures. The study had been based on a convenience sample that had been assembled by word of mouth. It was therefore impossible to rule out the possibility that families who participated in the research were especially well adjusted. Would a more representative sample yield different results?

To find out, Ray Chan, Barbara Raboy, and I conducted research in collaboration with the Sperm Bank of California

(Chan, Raboy, & Patterson, 1998; Fulcher, Sutfin, Chan, Scheib, & Patterson, 2005). Over the more than 15 years of its existence, the Sperm Bank of California's clientele had included many lesbian as well as heterosexual women. For research purposes, this clientele was a finite population from which our sample could be drawn. The Sperm Bank of California also allowed a sample in which, both for lesbian and for heterosexual groups, one parent was biologically related to the child and one was not.

We invited all clients who had conceived children using the resources of the Sperm Bank of California and who had children 5 years old or older to participate in our research. The resulting sample was composed of 80 families, 55 headed by lesbian and 25 headed by heterosexual parents. Materials were mailed to participating families, with instructions to complete them privately and return them in self-addressed stamped envelopes we provided.

Results replicated and expanded upon those from earlier research. Children of lesbian and heterosexual parents showed similar, relatively high levels of social competence, as well as similar, relatively low levels of behavior problems on the parent form of the CBCL. We also asked the children's teachers to provide evaluations of children's adjustment on the Teacher Report Form of the CBCL, and their reports agreed with those of parents. Parental sexual orientation was not related to children's adaptation. Quite apart from parental sexual orientation, however, and consistent with findings from years of research on children of heterosexual parents, when parent–child relationships were marked by warmth and affection, children were more likely to be developing well. Thus, in this sample drawn from a known population, measures of children's adjustment were unrelated to parental sexual orientation (Chan et al., 1998; Fulcher et al., 2005).

Even as they provided information about children born to lesbian mothers, however, these new results also raised additional questions. Women who conceive children at sperm banks are generally both well educated and financially comfortable. It was possible that these relatively privileged women were able to protect children from many forms of discrimination. What if a more diverse group of families were to be studied? In addition, the children in this sample averaged 7 years of age, and some concerns focus on older children and adolescents. What if an older group of youngsters were to be studied? Would problems masked by youth and privilege in earlier studies emerge in an older, more diverse sample?

Studies Based on Representative Samples

An opportunity to address these questions was presented by the availability of data from the National Longitudinal Study of Adolescent Health (Add Health). The Add Health study involved a large, ethnically diverse, and essentially representative sample of American adolescents and their parents. Data for our research were drawn from surveys and interviews completed by more than 12,000 adolescents and their parents at home and from surveys completed by adolescents at school.

Parents were not queried directly about their sexual orientation but were asked if they were involved in a "marriage, or marriage-like relationship." If parents acknowledged such a relationship, they were also asked the gender of their partner. Thus, we identified a group of 44 12- to 18-year-olds who lived with parents involved in marriage or marriage-like relationships with same-sex partners. We compared them with a matched group of adolescents living with other-sex couples. Data from the archives of the Add Health study allowed us to address many questions about adolescent development.

Consistent with earlier findings, results of this work revealed few differences in adjustment between adolescents living with same-sex parents and those living with opposite-sex parents (Wainright, Russell, & Patterson, 2004; Wainright & Patterson, 2006). There were no significant differences between teenagers living with same-sex parents and those living with other-sex parents on self-reported assessments of psychological well-being, such as self-esteem and anxiety; measures of school outcomes, such as grade point averages and trouble in school; or measures of family relationships, such as parental warmth and care from adults and peers. Adolescents in the two groups were equally likely to say that they had been involved in a romantic relationship in the last 18 months, and they were equally likely to report having engaged in sexual intercourse. The only statistically reliable difference between the two groups—that those with same-sex parents felt a greater sense of connection to people at school—favored the youngsters living with same-sex couples. There were no significant differences in self-reported substance use, delinquency, or peer victimization between those reared by same- or other-sex couples (Wainright & Patterson, 2006).

Although the gender of parents' partners was not an important predictor of adolescent well-being, other aspects of family relationships were significantly associated with teenagers' adjustment. Consistent with other findings about adolescent development, the qualities of family relationships rather than the gender of parents' partners were consistently related to adolescent outcomes. Parents who reported having close relationships with their offspring had adolescents who reported more favorable adjustment. Not only is it possible for children and adolescents who are parented by same-sex couples to develop in healthy directions, but—even when studied in an extremely diverse, representative sample of American adolescents—they generally do.

These findings have been supported by results from many other studies, both in the United States and abroad. Susan Golombok and her colleagues have reported similar results with a near-representative sample of children in the United Kingdom (Golombok et al., 2003). Others, both in Europe and in the United States, have described similar findings (e.g., Brewaeys, Ponjaert, Van Hall, & Golombok, 1997).

The fact that children of lesbian mothers generally develop in healthy ways should not be taken to suggest that they encounter no challenges. Many investigators have remarked upon the fact that children of lesbian and gay parents may encounter anti-gay sentiments in their daily lives. For example, in a study of 10-year-old children born to lesbian mothers, Gartrell, Deck, Rodas, Peyser, and Banks (2005) reported that a substantial minority had encountered anti-gay sentiments among their peers. Those who had had such encounters were likely to report having felt angry, upset, or sad about these experiences. Children of lesbian and gay parents may be exposed to prejudice against their parents in some settings, and this may be painful for them, but evidence for the idea that such encounters affect children's overall adjustment is lacking.

Conclusions

Does parental sexual orientation have an important impact on child or adolescent development? Results of recent research provide no evidence that it does. In fact, the findings suggest that parental sexual orientation is less important than the qualities of family relationships. More important to youth than the gender of their parent's partner is the quality of daily interaction and the strength of relationships with the parents they have.

One possible approach to findings like the ones described above might be to shrug them off by reiterating the familiar adage that "one cannot prove the null hypothesis." To respond in this way, however, is to miss the central point of these studies. Whether or not any measurable impact of parental sexual orientation on children's development is ever demonstrated, the main conclusions from research to date remain clear: Whatever correlations between child outcomes and parental sexual orientation may exist, they are less important than those between child outcomes and the qualities of family relationships.

Although research to date has made important contributions, many issues relevant to children of lesbian and gay parents remain in need of study. Relatively few studies have examined the development of children adopted by lesbian or gay parents or of children born to gay fathers; further research in both areas would be welcome (Patterson, 2004). Some notable longitudinal studies have been reported, and they have found children of same-sex couples to be in good mental health. Greater understanding of family relationships and transitions over time would, however, be helpful, and longitudinal studies would be valuable. Future research could also benefit from the use of a variety of methodologies.

Meanwhile, the clarity of findings in this area has been acknowledged by a number of major professional organizations. For instance, the governing body of the American Psychological Association (APA) voted unanimously in favor of a statement that said, "Research has shown that the adjustment, development, and psychological well-being of children is unrelated to parental sexual orientation and that children of lesbian and gay parents are as likely as those of heterosexual parents to flourish" (APA, 2004). The American Bar Association, the American Medical Association, the American Academy of Pediatrics, the American Psychiatric Association, and other mainstream professional groups have issued similar statements.

The findings from research on children of lesbian and gay parents have been used to inform legal and public policy debates across the country (Patterson et al., 2002). The research literature on this subject has been cited in amicus briefs filed by the APA in cases dealing with adoption, child custody, and also in cases related to the legality of marriages between same-sex partners. Psychologists serving as expert witnesses have presented findings on these issues in many different courts (Patterson et al., 2002). Through these and other avenues, results of research on lesbian and gay parents and their children are finding their way into public discourse.

The findings are also beginning to address theoretical questions about critical issues in parenting. The importance of gender in parenting is one such issue. When children fare well in two-parent lesbian-mother or gay-father families, this suggests that the gender of one's parents cannot be a critical factor in child development. Results of research on children of lesbian and gay parents cast doubt upon the traditional assumption that gender is important in parenting. Our data suggest that it is the quality of parenting rather than the gender of parents that is significant for youngsters' development.

Research on children of lesbian and gay parents is thus located at the intersection of a number of classic and contemporary concerns. Studies of lesbian- and gay-parented families allow researchers to address theoretical questions that had previously remained difficult or impossible to answer. They also address oft-debated legal questions of fact about development of children with lesbian and gay parents. Thus, research on children of lesbian and gay parents contributes to public debate and legal decision making, as well as to theoretical understanding of human development.

References

American Psychological Association (2004). Resolution on sexual orientation, parents, and children. Retrieved September 25, 2006, from www.apa.org/pi/lgbc/policy/parentschildren.pdf

Brewaeys, A., Ponjaert, I., Van Hall, E.V., & Golombok, S. (1997). Donor insemination: Child development and family functioning in lesbian mother families. *Human Reproduction, 12,* 1349–1359.

Chan, R.W., Raboy, B., & Patterson, C.J. (1998). Psychosocial adjustment among children conceived via donor insemination by lesbian and heterosexual mothers. *Child Development, 69,* 443–457.

Fulcher, M., Sutfin, E.L., Chan, R.W., Scheib, J.E., & Patterson, C.J. (2005). Lesbian mothers and their children: Findings from the Contemporary Families Study. In A. Omoto & H. Kurtzman (Eds.), *Recent research on sexual orientation, mental health, and substance abuse* (pp. 281–299). Washington, DC: American Psychological Association.

Gartrell, N., Deck., A., Rodas, C., Peyser, H., & Banks, A. (2005). The National Lesbian Family Study: 4. Interviews with the 10-year-old children. *American Journal of Orthopsychiatry, 75,* 518–524.

Golombok, S., Perry, B., Burston, A., Murray, C., Mooney-Somers, J., Stevens, M., & Golding, J. (2003). Children with lesbian parents: A community study. *Developmental Psychology, 39,* 20–33.

Patterson, C.J. (1996). Lesbian mothers and their children: Findings from the Bay Area Families Study. In J. Laird & R.J. Green (Eds.), *Lesbians and gays in couples and families: A handbook for therapists* (pp. 420–437). San Francisco: Jossey-Bass.

Patterson, C.J. (1997). Children of lesbian and gay parents. In T. Ollendick & R. Prinz (Eds.), *Advances in clinical child psychology* (Vol. 19, pp. 235–282). New York: Plenum Press.

Patterson, C.J. (2004). Gay fathers. In M.E. Lamb (Ed.), *The role of the father in child development* (4th ed., pp. 397–416). New York: Wiley.

Patterson, C.J., Fulcher, M., & Wainright, J. (2002). Children of lesbian and gay parents: Research, law, and policy. In B.L. Bottoms, M.B. Kovera, & B.D. McAuliff (Eds.), *Children, social science and the law* (pp. 176–199). New York: Cambridge University Press.

Patterson, C.J., & Hastings, P. (in press). Socialization in context of family diversity. In J. Grusec & P. Hastings (Eds.), *Handbook of socialization.* New York: Guilford Press.

Stacey, J., & Biblarz, T.J. (2001). (How) Does sexual orientation of parents matter? *American Sociological Review, 65,* 159–183.

Wainright, J.L., Russell, S.T., & Patterson, C.J. (2004). Psychosocial adjustment and school outcomes of adolescents with same-sex parents. *Child Development, 75,* 1886–1898.

Wainright, J.L., & Patterson, C.J. (2006). Delinquency, victimization, and substance use among adolescents with female same-sex parents. *Journal of Family Psychology, 20,* 526–530.

Address correspondence to **CHARLOTTE J. PATTERSON,** Department of Psychology, P.O. Box 400400, University of Virginia, Charlottesville, VA 22904; e-mail: cjp@virginia.edu.

Minding the Kids

For better or for worse—and that's mostly up to you—your children are deeply involved in your business.

MEG CADDOUX HIRSCHBERG

Now that our youngest is about to graduate from high school, my husband, Gary, and I have been reflecting on how we raised our three kids. Curiously, it had never occurred to us to ask our children how they felt about our company, Stonyfield Yogurt, and its endless claims on Gary's time, presence, and attention. Gary always worked hard to make up for his frequent absences. If he couldn't be there consistently, he wanted at least to be consistent about some things that were meaningful to the kids. When he was home, he would rise with them, make yogurt smoothies for breakfast, and drive them to school. He coached their soccer teams. When he was away, he constructed crossword puzzles, which he faxed to them from the road.

We both hoped it was enough. But we didn't really know. So I posed the question to each of my children: What was this like for you?

Part of my inspiration to ask this simple question came from a conversation I had at last year's Inc. 500 conference with Salem Samhoud, founder of &Samhoud, a consulting firm in the Netherlands. Stealing a trick from the manager's tool kit, Salem holds quarterly "360 degree reviews" with his wife and three children, ages 20, 13, and 9. The reviews show him where he's falling down as a parent and also where he doesn't need to sweat it. "Last September, they told me I spend too much time on my iPhone," he told me. "They were right. Now I switch it off on weekends. Because of their feedback, I already feel more relaxed and focused. They asked me to do it for them, but it's also better for me." Every six months, each child spends a day with Salem at the office. "They get to see not just the negative—my absence—but the positive—what I do all day, how I work, how my work is valued," he says.

The subject of children is fraught for many working parents, but company owners experience extra dimensions of guilt. It's one thing to expose yourself and your spouse to financial risk and instability, another to expose kids who have no voice in the matter. Work follows the entrepreneur wherever he or she goes—into the family room, onto the beach—providing an ever-present reminder that Mom or Dad has competing priorities. Frequent travel is usually unavoidable. And even when you're there, you're often not *there*. Your body is at the Girl Scout meeting with your daughter, but your mind is mulling over margins.

When children are affected by a parent's absence or preoccupation, they often have ways of letting the parent know. At the same conference last fall, I met Susan Edwards, who told me that her entrepreneur-husband, Barry Edwards, got a wake-up call when their youngest child was about 2 years old. Susan had just pulled up to her husband's office with their son Cody. The boy excitedly pointed at the building and exclaimed, "Daddy's house!" "That comment changed my husband," Susan said. Across from his desk, Barry hung a poster of a little boy who looked like Cody. Printed in bold at the bottom was the word *Priorities*. "It's been his daily reminder of the need to shut down and go home," Susan said.

The competing pressures of business and children can be hardest on female entrepreneurs. Entrepreneurship is attractive to mothers, because it promises flexible hours, but how flexible can hours be when you're working 16 of them? Recently I met Amy Cueva, co-founder of a technology-design firm called Mad*Pow and the mother of three children, ages 5, 11, and 12. "Sometimes I don't even feel like a woman," she told me. "I don't have time to nurture and be there the way my mom was. Recently my daughter e-mailed me with a detailed plan for her 11th-birthday party. I didn't know whether to be proud of her organization and tech savvy or be depressed that she knows that e-mail is the best way to get in touch with me.

"People tell me how amazing it is that I accomplish all that I do," Amy said. "But I feel like I'm screwing up every day."

Still, there are upsides to being the progeny of an entrepreneur. Many company owners have extraordinary latitude to involve their kids in their work, spending time together while providing an early education in business. Packing boxes after school or counting inventory on weekends is often a terrific first job. Laboring alongside a parent, children feel proud of the family business—this is ours! We are making this! And they watch their parents acting as leaders, taking responsibility both for their own lives and for the lives of others.

The intimate observation of entrepreneurship also helps shape children's future decisions. Some find their own horizons expanding as they realize they can choose to build something themselves rather than become part of something built by others. I was surprised to learn that my son Ethan, 19, is now interested in business. "Dad has a cool life," he told me. "It's really busy and demanding, but he has a personal attachment to what he does." Some children see the labor, the stress, and the sacrifice and decide the entrepreneur's life is not for them. My 17-year-old daughter, Danielle, for instance. "When I was a kid, I thought it would be cool to have Dad's job, but as I got exposed to what it's really like, I'm just like, ugh."

My children also had differing reactions to Gary's absences, mental and physical. The boys weren't much bothered by them. "Dad was there for things I cared about, like my soccer games and teaching me to ride a bike," said Alex, who is now 21. "All I remember now are the things that he was able to do." "I think Dad's absences put a lot more pressure on you than they did on us," said Ethan.

Danielle had another view. "It was great that he coached my soccer team. But during those times he was my coach, not my dad," she said. "Our games and practices were just part of his busy schedule. Sometimes I felt bad when he came to soccer games, because I knew there were more 'important' things he should be doing.

"At this point in my life, I appreciate his mission and what he's doing to support organic farmers," Danielle continued.

"But sometimes I think, Why does my dad have to be the guy who saves the world? Sometimes you need to be the guy who chills out. Let somebody else save the world for a while."

A business sucks the entire family into its vortex. Marinating in guilt is an opportunity lost.

An entrepreneurial business sucks the entire family into its vortex. Marinating in guilt is an opportunity lost. So invite your kids into your work life. Let them see how things are made or marketed, how problems are tackled and solved. They will gain more appreciation for what you do. "Daddy's (or Mommy's) house" will feel more like their house, too.

My "interviews" with our children let Gary and me understand them better and deepened our relationship as a result. Your kids' feedback may change the way you run your business and live your life. As I write this, Gary is downstairs in the den with Danielle, watching her latest favorite show (*United States of Tara*) and, to all appearances, completely chilling out.

Of course, it's possible he's mulling over margins.

MEG CADDOUX HIRSCHBERG (mhirshberg@inc.com) writes a regular column about the impact of entrepreneurial businesses on families. She is married to Gary Hirshberg, president and CEO of Stonyfield Yogurt.

Mother, Damnedest

Sure, everyone thinks he has a difficult mother; it's a measure of our desire for her approval.
But a truly difficult mother imposes a bind that forces offspring to develop costly ways of coping.

Terri Apter

Who has a difficult mother? I pose the question to a group of teenage girls, who raise their hands high. Grown women, too, nod knowingly, while adding, "I hope I don't turn out to be like her."

Teenage boys and men are, of course, less absorbed with wondering how to be different from Mom. Nonetheless, their highly charged love and empathy with her can make them uneasy about regulating closeness and distance.

In a sense, difficult mothers are the norm. Our need for a mother's attention, appreciation, and understanding is great; our expectations are high. We tend to be critical of responses that are not precisely what we hope for. Her shortcomings—the endless reminders to be careful; her compulsive checking-up whether you have your keys as you head out the door, when you forgot them only once, two years ago; her inability to read an instruction manual—irritate and embarrass us, because we retain our idealization of the powerful nurturer of infancy.

But psychologically speaking, a difficult mother is a great deal more than a person with whom we have difficulties from time to time. A truly difficult mother is one who presents her child with a profound dilemma: "Either develop complex and constricting coping mechanisms to maintain a relationship with me, at great cost to your own outlook, imagination, and values, or suffer ridicule, disapproval, or rejection."

A difficult mother presents challenges that a difficult father or other relative does not. That's because, starting in the earliest days of life, a child's relationship with her or his mother is the foundation of a sense of self. Through maternal attachment, we begin to learn who we are and what we feel and to acquire the ability to interact with others. The process continues with a mother's ongoing ability to acknowledge her developing child as a person with independent thoughts and feelings.

A truly difficult mother uses a son's or daughter's ongoing need for responsiveness to control or manipulate the child.

A difficult mother, however, uses a son's or daughter's continuing need for responsiveness to control or manipulate the child. The repeated threat of ridicule, disapproval, or rejection is experienced as a choice between life and death. Children of difficult mothers, like others who experience difficulties growing up, can show great resilience. But such a child will face extra tasks in establishing a comfortable sense of self-worth and in trusting others.

Patty Mooney, *54*, woke up one Mother's Day, opened the *Detroit Free Press,* and found that her mother had phoned a reporter at the newspaper and announced she was resigning from motherhood: "I don't think I ever really wanted to be in this position. In retrospect, it was stupid, making carbon copies of yourself."

- Mooney was the oldest of six "carbon copies," so when her mother told the paper, "Let them wash their own damn socks," that job, along with the cooking and cleaning, fell to Mooney—until she happily left for college. "I felt so independent at age 18," she says.

  A successful video producer in San Diego with a supportive husband, Mooney contends she is thankful her mom retired. "Thus,I learned what mothering was all about. And I was able to make the decision to not have any children of my own because I believe in the Peter Pan way of life—if you have a child, it is very difficult or impossible to be a child. I'm a happy adult, able to do whatever I want whenever I want without having to give my life up to serve children."

- Unlike some of her siblings, Mooney holds no grudge, although in her teens she had a hard time. "I felt I didn't ask to be born." Over the years she has come to see that her mother, who grew up scrubbing floors in a devout Polish Catholic household, "had been the victim of her own mom."

Difficult mothers are capable of engaging with a child—but they set fixed conditions on their love and approval and appreciation.

Difficult mothers should be distinguished from abusive mothers, whose children exhibit abnormalities in brain development that can impair the ability to regulate emotions, engage in social interaction, and organize memories. Difficult mothers are capable of engaging with a child—but they set fixed conditions on their love and approval and appreciation.

My own research on mothers and teenagers, and on midlife development, shows that many children of difficult mothers become generally high-functioning adults. Difficult mothers may be good-enough mothers, able to support normal development within a wide range. Yet in all stages of life, children of difficult mothers struggle with self-doubt, on the one hand, and close relationships, on the other, or project dissatisfaction and doubt onto people who love them.

The difficult mother imposes her dilemma harshly—with unpredictable and ferocious anger, punitive inflexibility, rigid expectations, and expressions of neediness that take priority over a child's needs. Envy may compound the mix. Sure, many mothers show anger, inflexibility, neediness, and elements of envy from time to time. But it's the routine use of such behaviors that distinguishes difficult mothers and sets up a coercive relationship.

A child does not have the option to say to a mother, I don't care whether you think I'm bad, or, I am not frightened by the prospect of your leaving me. A primitive panic at rejection lasts long after the infant's physical helplessness comes to an end.

Children are therefore likely to work hard to adopt special strategies to protect themselves from a mother's rejection. The particular strategies a difficult mother imposes on a child are ruled by fear, anxiety, and confusion. And each mother's particular brand of difficult shapes the strategies that a child develops.

Unpredictable and Ferocious Anger

"Everyone Shouts," Lois protests when 17-year-old Margot reveals to me that she has to "take a deep breath before I face Mom." Margot's eyes are bright with alarm at her own courage. "She complains I never eat breakfast. Well, I can't because I come downstairs and she's there and that puts a knot in my stomach. I can't feel hungry till I'm two blocks from the house."

"So I have a short fuse," Lois cedes. "Since when does shouting kill you? Besides, if she respected my wishes, I wouldn't shout. She makes life difficult for herself, but she knows I love her."

Difficult mothers may love their children, but inability to control the inevitable frustrations of day-to-day life or long-term disappointments can create a disorganized volatility and obliviousness to a child's experience that overpower the love a child can take in. Margot, at 17, is hollow-eyed and anxious, her nails bitten to the quick. Her social and academic interests are limited; she craves a simple world, safe from her mother's tantrums.

In my research, I found that even independent adults in their 40s are haunted by memories of maternal anger. Those who as children experience chaotic storms imagine endless scenarios involving threatening circumstances. "When I walk home from school, I open the door and think what to say if she's mad because my room isn't clean enough," Margot explains. "Or maybe she'll be mad because I was supposed to be home five minutes ago. Or maybe some friend I'm not supposed to be seeing phoned the landline. Or maybe, she'll be in a good mood and I can just relax."

Children like Margot inhabit an exhausting emotional world, hedged with dangers that make them anxious and cautious. Others acquire a set of routines to placate a mother with signs of affection or a constant stream of compliments, or by always being available to do her bidding. Sometimes they assume a sweet or ingratiating persona, trying to waylay the rage they fear may be lurking beneath every greeting and smile.

Their aim in personal interactions is to please and placate, rather than to genuinely engage. They may be primed to respond with compliance to outbursts or even hints of anger in others; they may assume that others are behaving appropriately in expressing anger towards them. In some cases, they may even be attracted to people whose anger is easily aroused—because they associate that behavior with attachment and authority.

Teri Ross, *56*, grew up not knowing whether she lived in a family of means or not. "We had a beautiful house," she says, and her mother spent lavishly, but her father would come home and yell about lights left on. "If I listened to my mother, we were rich. If I listened to my father, we were poor." That was the least of her confusion. "From as young as I can remember, I never knew if what came out of my mother's mouth was the truth or not. She was highly manipulative and said yes when she meant no, no when she meant yes. I had to learn to read between the lines and develop my own intuition."

- What she was not confused about was her mother's complete indifference to her and her sister. Today a successful Minneapolis-based Internet marketing consultant, Ross as a child loved coming home from school to play the piano. With her own allowance she bought sheet music and taught herself show tunes. "One day I came home and the piano was gone. When I asked, my mother said she was redecorating that room. It was a demonstration that nothing about me mattered; everything was always her agenda. There were many other places to put a piano in that huge house.

- Ross can recall no hugs, no stories read. "we had live-in help, and they became my surrogate mothers. They cushioned me, may be saved me. I found how to get the mothering I needed." It's no accident, she say that "today I have no less than 10 older women in my life whose daughters are jealous of my relationships with their mothers."

Inflexibility and Rigid Expectations

"My Mom always sets a gold standard," 25-year-old Craig explains. "My dad said that's what drove him to leave. So I always knew this gold standard had a dark side—like, would I have to leave, too? I see pictures of myself as a boy, doing ordinary boy things, but what I remember is wondering whether I could figure out what I needed to be for her, and whether I could be that. She said I was her golden boy, with stars in his eyes, and that she knew I would always be loyal and brave. I'm not any of those things, not now, not ever. 'Stars in my eyes'—what a load of bull."

A recently discharged marine, Craig is trying to make sense of having pursued a career for which he never felt anything but dread. Any other career possibilities were silenced by his mother's pride. Even as he seeks support from the person he still loves most, he finds her inflexible. "She'll wave her hands and jump like a flea and say, 'You can't stay in my house and say things like that' whenever I try to say what I'm feeling. It's pretty clear I have a choice: Be her brave golden boy or get my butt out of here."

Inflexibility is destructive when incorporated into the structure of mother-child interaction so that the mother is the sole authority on the legitimacy of the child's experiences. It usually arises from a mother's narcissistic investment in a child's trajectory, a need to have a high-achieving child or one with a particular set of skills. A child's independent interests seem a betrayal.

To accommodate maternal inflexibility, a daughter (or son) may suppress her real thoughts, real feelings, even her own sense of self as a person with independent desires and needs. Choices are irrelevant because

Shayne Hughes, *39*, dodged plates, pans, even a carving fork hurled by his underachieving and overwhelmed mother, who was "prone to flipping out. Then she would run out of the house screaming that she wasn't coming back, that she'd kill herself, leaving me shattered and with a screaming infant, my little half brother."

Life outside the house reinforced the negativity within. Hughes attended three kindergartens and eight schools by eighth grade, dragged between New England and California by a divorced mother who was "constantly running to someplace better." He always felt like an outsider, "never good enough or integrated," even when settled into a Rhode Island high school as cocaptain of the varsity basketball team and president of the National Honor Society.

He coped by becoming overly responsible financially, working throughout—and by binge-drinking and smoking dope, fueled by rage and suicidal despair. "When I drank, I felt connected to other people." His love life brought more pain and fear. "Because I concluded I'm not lovable, I was constantly withdrawing from relationships or getting judgmental."

After a DUI arrest put him in jail for a night, Hughes accepted a suggestion from his stepmother to attend a workshop that wound up being the beginning of insight and forgiveness. The day his mother told him, "I just couldn't nurture you the way you needed to be nurtured" was the day he understood that "I wasn't a hateful kid; my mother had her own stuff." Now married, a leadership trainer, and a father of two, Hughes enjoys a comfortable relationship with his mother, who "is able to give love as a grandmother that she couldn't as a mother."

---

acting on her own preferences threatens the maternal relationship. Why even identify one's own desires?

Lying is a common strategy children invoke to resist maternal inflexibility. It's a way of preserving their "real" self.

Lying is a common strategy children invoke to resist maternal inflexibility. They see it as a way of preserving their real self, without engaging in useless fights. They construct false stories about themselves to retain some control over their lives.

But all too often lying then becomes a general coping strategy. Teachers and even peers identify such children as flaky or unreliable. Still, they may come to believe that lying is necessary to any relationship. The underlying assumption is, "To be accepted or loved, or just to get by, I have to disguise myself."

While some offspring suppress their thoughts and feelings or retreat into silence in the face of a mother's inflexibility, some find other listeners—a father, sibling, friend, or lover—and develop self-reflection and expression through such close connections. But there remains a profound betrayal: "Why does my mother, whose responses mean so much, refuse to listen to me?" For some, the answer is to aim to meet a mother's ideal, propelled by the assumption that "I will be loved only if I am perfect." But like Craig, others relinquish the goal of perfection—and with it all goals, and all hope of being loved.

Need, Seduction, and Resentment

Just as devastating as chaotic anger and inflexibility is inability to engage with a child as someone with highly charged needs of her own. A mother may use unhappiness or incapacity to pose the following dilemma: "Either develop strategies to meet my needs or I'll be utterly disappointed in you." Children commonly respond by achieving early-maturing competence to compensate for a mother's demanding helplessness.

Sarah Ann, at 15, took over the care of her younger sister and half sisters and brothers while her mother, likely suffering from depression, came to respond to every child's request with, "This is just too much for me." Her mother loaded Sarah Ann with praise that was more coercive than appreciative: "You're so reliable. You're my angel. Everyone can always depend on you."

Children who take on adult roles may appear mature and controlled, but they feel helpless and frightened. Their competence is achieved at the cost of youthful curiosity and exploration. I first met Sarah Ann in my study of midlife women, when she was working to overcome the fear that she would lose everything she had and destroy everyone she loved if she gave into her urge to travel. She remembered being the mini-mother, checking that her brother did his homework and her mother was settled, while "the person I could have been was dying inside. I had to let that reckless teenage girl die; otherwise, my mom would despise the daughter she called her angel."

Some mothers, like Sarah Ann's, use praise to coerce a child into meeting her needs; others use seduction. As a child, Jon saw his mother as confident and compelling. "I thought everyone who met her loved her. She'd say, 'See how he looked at me? He couldn't take his eyes off me.' I picked up that that's what she needed to believe. And I learned to tell her everyone loved her, and that I was the luckiest guy because I had her as my mom."

When he started dating and spent time away from home, she engaged in pitiful self-abuse: "I'm just an old, useless woman. I look in the mirror and I don't know how you can bear to see me. I hope my organs are aging as quickly as my face, so I won't live to get much older." The implicit message—"Show me you adore me and put me first or I'll die"—overwhelmed Jon. "The idea of her being sad was like falling into a pit. I just decided I would prop her up." Now 37, Jon is watching his second marriage fall apart. "I can't get my wife to see that when Mom needs me, I have to see her."

Envy

Envy is one of the most confusing and disturbing maternal emotions a child can face. Sometimes a child's joy or delight can spark a mother's resentment. Or a child's success is greeted with cold suspicion. Since envy is usually directed toward someone with whom we (negatively) compare ourselves, daughters are more likely to be the object of a mother's envy than are sons, more likely to elicit an invidious, "Why didn't I have what she has?"

Tess, age 14, tries to measure up by getting great grades, although her 11-year-old sister is Mom's favorite. Doing well is not enough; she has to be a prominent prizewinner. Tess recognizes the bind her mother imposes: "You must shine for me in your achievements at school, and put aside all your other interests, or you will not be worthy of my love." Yet, when Tess succeeds, her mother's envy kicks in. "If you think you're better than everyone else in this house, you can leave" and "You need to learn some humility if you're going to sit at this table," her mother taunts her.

It's no surprise that Tess is ambivalent about achievement, which promises approval but delivers rejection. A likely outcome is that she will be driven to achieve throughout adulthood—but obtain more anxiety than pleasure from her achievements.

Adult Survival Strategies

Reposition the Fear

A mother's anger is likely to have controlled and frightened you at many stages of your life, particularly in childhood, but you can reshape your response. Instead of reacting to her anger by thinking, "What can I do to placate her?", understand that the anger is *her* problem. You may offer to help her understand her problem and deal with it, but it is not up to you to manage her emotions.

Silence Self-Doubt

When you understand the possible consequences of a difficult mother—such as self-doubt and anxious expectations that others will disapprove of you—catch hold of the "shadow voices" telling you that you don't measure up. Notice them and identify them as legacies of a difficult mother; then you can challenge them and put them to rest.

Particularize her Power

Children of a difficult mother often come to expect that others will also try to coerce them. Value those people who listen as you speak your mind and who encourage you to identify your own preferences and desires. This will remind you that close relationships can be different from your first primary relationship with your mother. Remember, some people fall into the pattern of forging difficult relationships because these feel familiar and "comfortable."

Call the Bluff

Dealing with a difficult mother is exhausting, but it can make you strong. You value the ability to negotiate within a relationship—and know the danger of a refusal to negotiate. A difficult mother tries to give you no choice. But in fact you always do have a choice. Understand your point of no return, the point at which you will not give in, and call her bluff. You may find that the relationship continues after all.

Phil Petree, *52*, Internet entrepreneur, was 1 of but 2 of 12 siblings to attend his mother's funeral. "It's a joke among us that no one ever says 'Mom'; it's always 'your mother.' She was very manipulative and I can't remember one thing she ever said that was honest. She would tell five brothers five different stories to draw them into whatever drama she was constructing in her head." By the time he was six or seven, Petree was avoiding going home after school. "You don't understand why, you just realize it's stressful and painful."

As a high school freshman, he was tall, gangly, "covered in acne," and had red hair down to his shoulders. New to another school after many family moves, befriended by none, he was feeling "extremely vulnerable" when his mother told him that a girl across the street liked him but wouldn't date him unless he cut his hair—which he did. Then he saw the girl, approached her, and said, "'My mom told me you like me and wanted me to get my hair cut.' She looked at me and said, 'Who are you?'" Humiliated and hurt, he returned home only to hear his mother say, "No girl would ever like you with all that acne."

Petree's teen years were filled with anger. "The one place where a child should be able to get encouragement and love was fraught with danger." Although a wise sergeant in the Army helped him overcome his anger, the legacy of his maternal experience was a hypervigilance in relationships: "You're always trying to figure out what's real, what's not."

There is no single template for a difficult mother. Sometimes one sibling finds a mother difficult and another does not. One sibling can trigger a mother's inflexibility or anger or dependence, while another evokes protectiveness and empathy. A mother may demand subservience from a daughter but not from a son; she may pressure one child to conform to her ambitious expectations, but allow another to go her own way. Gender, personality, birth order all moderate the complex, interactive maternal bond.

To add to the complexity, mothers themselves undergo change and growth. A woman may be high functioning as mother to a 4-year-old who remains compliant and eager to please, but difficult to a 14-year-old exercising a teen's capacity for criticism and opposition—and yet mellow to a 40-year-old, when her anxieties about a child's independence or difference may have finally been resolved. Even so, a mother's evolution does not necessarily release her child from debilitating strategies developed to cope with her. Even a mother's death cannot abolish the history of a child's self.

Most children, as they grow, engage in a healthy resistance to the covert terms imposed by a difficult mother. Resistance comes in many forms. There's persuasion, sometimes expressed in arguments aimed to make a mother "see me and accept me as I am." But by definition, a difficult mother does not engage with her child's perspective or modify expectations in line with a child's changing needs. She will usually punish resistance.

Sometimes understanding a mother's perspective eases a child's anger and confusion. But the effort to understand is itself exhausting and debilitating.

Another path to resistance is containment, involving efforts to understand that the difficulties a mother poses will not always be posed by others. Even with clinical help, it can take a great deal of work for a grown child to separate experiences with a difficult mother from expectations about interactions with others.

Clinical help may also prevent the child from seeking out friends, lovers, and mentors who share her mother's difficult traits. Such associates may feel comfortable in the sense of being familiar, or present the opportunity to try again to tame the difficult mother. Nevertheless, they keep a child bound to a toxic legacy.

Complete release from the habits of thought and response patterns comes only from understanding ourselves and our history, how being forced to placate a difficult mother has shaped our fears, self-doubt, and dissatisfaction. Then we can begin to cope with our fears and dissatisfactions on their own terms.

TERRI APTER is senior tutor at Newnham College, Cambridge, and author most recently of *The Sister Knot*. Her *PT* blog is *Domestic Intelligence*.

The Forgotten Siblings

In this article I wish to argue that the qualities and dynamics of sibling relationships may have been overlooked in family therapy. In overlooking them, we have also overlooked a significant feature in the emotional life of children. I would like to suggest that sibling relationships are where children practise identity. In these relationships we can learn how to be one in a group. Family Therapy treatment may not make enough use of the dynamic of the sibling relationship.

SALLY YOUNG

Family therapists have prided themselves on their peripheral vision. Part of the claim of systemic therapy is to see the 'big picture.' In terms of families, this often means seeing the whole family. At the very least, it means that the therapist must take into account the existence and importance of family viewpoints other than those represented in the therapy room. However, it could he contended that our primary focus has been on the parent-child relationship and that the sibling relationship is on the periphery. At worst these relationships may have been taken for granted rather than analysed.

In the course of writing this article I opened many relationship and psychology books and looked up 'sibling' in the index. What was interesting was how few references there were, and that usually the word 'sibling' was coupled with 'rivalry.' That in itself was disquieting, in that it suggests that the rivalry in sibling relationships has been emphasised above other emotional dynamics.

Siblings engage in multiple, complex interactions over many years, and in the process they learn much, and could be said to 'practise' many positions they will later take in adult life and relationships. From a lifespan perspective, sibling relationships are often the longest-lasting relationships we have—outlasting relationships with parents, partners, and our own offspring. Here are some key 'sibling learnings':

- That love and hate can quickly follow each other; this is the precursor to ambivalence, where a mixture of feelings can be tolerated together.
- That we can *feel* 'murderous,' but also come to know that we would not *act* on this: an important experience in differentiating thought and action.
- That there is a thin line between a tight hug and a strangle, that we can come to know about our desire to hurt, that in this way we become aware of our own potential for cruelty and our own potential to manage this.
- That we get to be alone together (Winnicott, 1958).
- That we can hate a sibling at home but defend him/her outside the home. That loyalty and honour involve the ability to manage our own ambivalence.
- That being a parent's favourite can ultimately be as burdensome as not being the favourite.
- That we can never overtake our older siblings—a challenge to our magical thinking.
- That we can imitate, anticipate, or dread, the developmental stages that we see our older siblings go through.
- That our sibling relationships offer an invisible continuity throughout our lives, although the grievances, the jealousy, and the competitiveness may be lifelong as well.

In the past couple of years, I have noticed a resurgence of interest in sibling relationships in the systemic and psychodynamic literature. *The Journal of Family Psychology* devoted a special edition to sibling relation-ships in 2005. This special edition emphasises the need for further research in this complex area, but looks at the state of the evidence for sibling relationships in the development of psychopathology. Juliet Mitchell's book. *Siblings* (2003) and *The Importance of Sibling Relationships in Psychoanalysis* (2003) by Prophecy Coles are another two examples. All in different ways suggest that our culture emphasises 'vertical relationships' and marginalises horizontal relationships such as those with our siblings. Sibling relationships are the prototype of peer and later collegial relationships. This idea attracted me as I have long felt that families, classrooms and workplaces survive on the capacity of individuals to find peers, as well protectors, in the face of the inevitable predators. Judy Dunn writes:

> There are powerful arguments for viewing siblings as potentially developmentally important: Their daily contact and familiarity, their emotionally uninhibited relationship, and the impact of sharing parents all suggest that the relationship may have a developmental influence (2005: 654).

Some scenarios come to mind.

Scenario 1

Sharon is a 17-year-old girl, who has a turbulent history. Her brother Mark is a source of great suffering for her. She feels tormented and intimidated by him. The intensity of their arguments has the quality of lovers' tiffs but without the love. One night, Sharon falls back on the familiar solution of cutting herself, as if in search of the lifeblood of her pain. Mark uncharacteristically tries to stop her. Sharon uncharacteristically does stop. Later in a session she says 'I stopped, as it was such a shock that he cared whether I lived'.

Scenario 2

Kathleen is in her forties. Suddenly and unexpectedly her eldest brother dies of a coronary. She awakes in the night anxious about her own mortality. The thought that she is one step closer to death strikes her: a rung has been removed in the ladder of mortality. Somewhere it reflects how deep the sense of sibling order is in her mind. As if some unconscious law dictates we must all die in timely order? Instead, reality declares an untimely disorder

I would now like to look at theoretical constructions of sibling relationships.

As suggested earlier, 'sibling rivalry' is often the only aspect of sibling relationships to receive attention, and has become somewhat clichéd. Perhaps it is worth revisiting. Rivalry is often seen as negative and destructive, yet it can be a positive spur to development. Circular questioning in family therapy often illustrates that there is more than rivalry in sibling relationships, and that siblings can understand each other well, particularly when it comes to issues of the familiar war between parents and children.

Nonetheless it is important not to deny the power and at times the secession between siblings. I think aggressive

feelings between siblings are much less repressed than those between parents and children. Juliet Mitchell writes:

> I believe we have minimized or overlooked entirely the threat to our existence as small children that is posed by the new baby who stands in our place or the older child who was there before us (2003: xv).

She suggests there is little difference between the tantrumming two-year-old who feels left out by the attention given to the baby, and the hysteria of adult life. In both, she argues the demand is 'Look at me, I am unique, there is only room for me!'

Perhaps all of us in family work have come across individuals who cannot bear the sharing of emotional space that is needed in families, and in family therapy. Juliet argues that beneath this is something that may have its roots in traumatic sibling rivalry; that is, the threat of annihilation by the other, even if that annihilation is figurative rather than actual—a child feels obliterated just by the fact of its sibling's existence. Mitchell goes on to speak about the triumph which psychopaths feel in obliterating the other.

Both Mitchell and Coles argue that theoretically we have overemphasised the Oedipal complex, and as a result have looked vertically (at child—parent relationships) rather than horizontally (at the child—child level). The equivalent of this could be most graphically seen in the structural school of family therapy (Minuchin, 1974). Also the strategic school (Haley, 1976) places enormous emphasis on parental—child relationship. In family therapy perhaps this goes with the understandable stress on parents being parents, taking on their parental authority and functioning in an aware manner. All this I agree with completely, yet is it the complete story?

The danger of the parentified child is something we are all alert to. Yet many of us see single-parent families under stress, where it is necessary for the family's survival that a child carries some parental functions. I wonder if one aspect that may test the difference between functional and dysfunctional parentification is how the parent manages the differences in roles between the siblings. For instance, is it still clear that the child is a child carrying some parental functions, as opposed to being mother's partner, which can only promote aggression and rivalry between the siblings?

Psychodynamic authors suggest that siblings who are very rivalrous may reflect unresolved sibling conflict in the parent's family of origin. In my work in CYMHS, I am struck with how often a parent will, on exploration, reflect a concern that a child will be like a troublesome uncle or aunt. The parent's childhood experiences of their sibling are echoed in the child's behaviour. The child is seen like a sibling, and the parent often attempts to be like or very unlike their own parents, in the management of the sibling ghost. Byng-Hall calls this the replicative or corrective script (Byng-Hall, 1995).

The Development of Group Psychology

I think one of the most powerful areas that have been overlooked in sibling relationships is the power of identification. In childhood, it is an important experience to feel part of a group and be able to step inside the shoes of another. Mary Target (2002) refers to research that suggests that younger siblings are slightly better at reading the intentions of older siblings than their older siblings are, given that they are born into a sibling order with big sister or big brother predecessors. Peter Fonagy and Mary Target's work's (2003) highlights the concept of 'mentalisation' in emotional development. This is really the capacity to think about thinking and feeling, in ourselves and others. They suggest this capacity is vital for us in digesting the realities of our internal and external lives. The people we have the most practice in interpreting/thinking about in childhood are our siblings. After all, we often spend the most time with them, in the timeless world of childhood.

It is worth reflecting on how powerfully siblings 'wind each other up,' so equally, they bear witness to each other's emotional worlds. Sibling can bring each other alive. In theory, circular questioning may access these understandings. However, this depends on a level of verbalisation that may be beyond many children, and perhaps we need to find a 'play equivalent' of this technique to access these understandings between siblings. These sibling insights may be accessed through projective games such as the Bear Cards (St Lukes Innovative Resources) and family drawings.

Michael Rutter's studies of children from Romanian orphanages who had been adopted in England indicated that these traumatised children, from horrific institutional situations, like to be with babies—as though the baby gives them back their lost baby selves (Mitchell: 227). Similarly, one can see in many families the way in which a new baby can regenerate a capacity for feelings in siblings and in parents.

Juliet Mitchell writes of having the experience of being part of a group and not feeling annihilated by it (Mitchell, 2003: 52). Sibling relationships give us an early but important experience of being the same but different, which is an experience we have whenever we are in a group. Clearly, our parents are central in managing this experience. The capacity to be in a group is something that we have psychologically undervalued.

Stuart Twemlow (2001), in his research on bullying in schools, stresses the significance of the group, comparing schools with high and low rates of bullying. What he discovered to be the significant factor is what is called the bystander affect. If, when a victim was being bullied, the rest of the group acted as passive bystanders, this was oxygen for the bullying—it inflamed it; if the others were not prepared to be passive, but expressed a point of view, the bullying diminished. Our preparedness to participate in group life is vital, in personal life and in a democracy. In families, whether a troubled sibling is left isolated, or feels some connectedness with a sibling, is often predictive of how likely the family is to respond positively to treatment. Perhaps all family work on some level is looking for the capacity to imaginatively identify with the other.

Prophecy Coles writes:

> Emde, surveying research on infant development to date . . . suggests we need a new concept of the 'we' ego. That is children by the age of three had developed an executive sense of 'we', of the other being with them which gave them increased sense of power and control (Coles, 2003: 76).

Emde says:

> It is perhaps ironic that in our age, so preoccupied with narcissism and self, we are beginning to see a different aspect of psychology, a 'we' psychology in addition to a self psychology . . . This represents a pro-found change in our world view (Coles, 2003: 76).

The Significance of Birth Order

From Adler to the more recent work by Sulloway in his book *Born to Rebel,* theorists have asserted the determinative effects of birth order, though others have argued that these effects are exaggerated, or non-existent. Sulloway hypothesises that the eldest is more authoritarian, having lost something by his displacement by his younger siblings, and the youngest is more likely to rebel, having the security of being the baby of the family. This strikes me as over-deterministic.

However, each individual will experience and interpret family dynamics differently. Siblings growing up in the same family may report very different experiences. Research has indicated that inter-family experiences may be almost as diverse as between-family experiences (Richardson & Richardson, 1990). The differences in family experiences might partly be due to parental expectations, which vary depending on birth order. In their seminal book *Separate Lives: Why Sibling Are So Different,* Robert Plomin and Judy Dunn argue that despite siblings being brought up in the same environment, the environment only *seems* the same. Each sibling perceives their family environment differently, which explains why they turn out so different. I also wonder if a factor in identity formation is the experience of feeling individual through differentiation from one's sibling.

Michael Duffy's joint biography of politicians Mark Latham and Tony Abbott points out that

> ... each is the eldest child of four children, the others being three girls, each had parents who were enormously ambitious for their only son, and each was as highly competitive and aggressive in sport as they were to be in Federal parliament (Fitzgerald, 2004: 11).

Whether it is completely accurate or not, this description gives a sense of the complex mixture of personality, sibling order, parental expectations and gender mix in families.

In fact, I wonder if one of the many insufficiently understood dynamics in sibling relationships is gender. Being a child with siblings of the other gender is a primary experience of a gendered relationship. Perhaps a test of this is the difference in associations in the public mind between brotherly love, sisterly love and love between a brother and a sister. I recall seeing a mother who had three sons, but who described having only sisters in her family of origin. Despite having a good relationship with her husband, she says 'I just don't understand boys.' I thought that she felt that without brothers, she had missed out on an imaginative understanding of boys, an understanding 'from the inside out,' in the way a sibling might.

Birth order can have determinative effects; take, for example, the case of the eldest child, accorded a special place with a grandparent, as the first grandchild. Yet many other factors can mitigate these effects. For instance, school gives children another chance with their peers. A youngest child who is the 'baby' at home may find herself being able to take a leadership role at school, in this way finding a possibility of being taken seriously by others and by herself.

It is important not to leave out the single child, frequently called the only child. For myself this has associations of 'only an only' child, as if the very description raises an idea of a disappointment that there aren't more children. Miriam Cosic, in her book *Only Child*, argues that culturally the drawbacks of being an only child have been overstated. Perhaps we may potentially envy the only child for not having to share! Single children frequently imagine what happened to the possibility of other children. Family therapists will be increasingly challenged to adapt when the single child family becomes more common. I think one particular difficulty is that the child then has no potential child witnesses or allies in the therapy room. Perhaps when the family has only one child, the onus on the therapist is increased, to join with the child and allow him/her to remain a child, not a pseudo-adult in the sessions.

Single children frequently imagine what happened to the possibility of other children.

It is not unusual for children to carry the fantasy of a twin as a comforting solution to isolation. For example, Mary is complaining with great intensity about her troublesome little brother. He is indeed troublesome but something in her complaints makes me feel there is more. 'Do you wish you had a sister?' I ask. What then emerges is a very full imagining of a twin sister with whom she could play soccer. Later in the session it was possible for her to have some more hopeful imaginings of when her *brother* could manage to play soccer with her.

The Ghosts in the Nursery

We are generally alert to the influence of the parent's childhood lying like a shadow over their parenting. However, many children, too, carry ghosts—the ghosts of their sibling experiences, which can sometimes include a sibling's mental disturbance. The most poetic description I have found has been in the Oliver Sacks' autobiography, in which he describes the psychotic breakdown of his brother Michael, when Oliver was 12.

> Michael could no longer sleep or rest, but agitatedly strode to and fro in the house, stamping his feet, glaring, hallucinating, shouting. I became terrified of him, for him, of the nightmare which was becoming reality for him, the more so as I could recognize similar thoughts and feelings in myself, even though they were hidden locked up in my own depths. What would happen to Michael, and would something similar happen to me, too? It was at this time that I set up my own lab in the house, and closed the doors, closed my ears against Michael's madness. It was at this time that I sought for (and sometimes achieved) an intense concentration, a complete absorption in the worlds of mineralogy and chemistry and physics, in science—focusing on them, holding myself together in the chaos. It was not that I was indifferent to Michael; I felt a passionate sympathy for him, I half-knew what he was going through, but I had to keep a distance also, create my own world from the neutrality and beauty of nature, so that I would not be swept into the chaos, the madness, the seduction, of his (Sacks, 2001: 186).

It is not easy to deal with a child's trauma about a disturbed sibling. I have sometimes seen siblings who have such a fear of madness or emotionality, that it can be difficult to find a therapeutic engagement to support them. However, a timely family session can provide a forum for siblings to speak of their distress, and this can help rescue the parents from focusing only on the disturbed sibling.

> Rose is 13 years old. Her elder sister. Sara, has early symptoms of anorexia nervosa. Both parents are understandably preoccupied with Sara's mental and physical health. When asked in a family session how this affects her, Rose says, 'I just come home from school and go to my room. The talk is always about Sara'. Her parents are initially shocked, and mother says she feels the same as Rose, unheard above the worry about Sara. A few minutes later we are again talking about Sara, but Mother and Rose have noticeably faded into the background. It seems important to draw attention that what happens in the family's daily life is happening in the session.

I am very fond of the idea, borrowed from physics, that in a family system, every action has an opposite and equal reaction. I have been struck many times over the years by how siblings tend towards either identifying with each other or individuating by being opposite. Often a conduct-disordered teenager who takes inadequate responsibility, somewhere has a sibling who takes too much responsibility. I think it often happens that the reactions to each other can be seen on the internalising–externalising spectrum. By this I mean that one child may 'internalise' his/her emotional life, perhaps by being withdrawn and depressive, and the other sibling may 'externalise' by being actively disobedient, showing aggression, doing drugs, and the like. Perhaps this 'equal and opposite' phenomenon could be a worthy area of further research, as if proven it would give further support to the systemic model of intervention.

> Harry is part of a large single-parent family. They are a poor family, struggling to keep their heads above water. Harry has an explosive temper that is frightening to everyone in the family. Harry is seen as following in the footsteps of his father's violence. When Harry explodes it reminds everyone in the family of the terrors of the past. Jean, the eldest girl in the family, stands up to Harry, trying to support her mother. Harry hates this, saying to Jean 'You are not my mother'. One day Jean unexpectedly runs away, perhaps in search of a childhood. Later she returns, wanting to live with the family. The family work is about helping Harry free himself from his identification with his father, but also to allow Jean

to be a big sister, not to replay a mother fighting with a father.

The siblings of children with special needs themselves have particular needs. Kate Strohm's book. *Siblings: Brothers and Sisters of Children with Special Needs,* vividly describes her own experience of growing up with a sister who had cerebral palsy. This work assisted in the development of a website www.siblingsaustralia.org.au, which provides information and Internet support to siblings. On this site, children whose siblings have special needs can talk about the dangers of lack of information about the disability, and their feelings of isolation, resentment and grief. The Internet chat room functions as a cyberspace sibling group for these young people. Anecdotal evidence suggests that siblings of special needs children sometimes become health professionals, so this may be pertinent to the professional reader.

Family Sessions as 'Commissions for Truth, Justice and Reconciliation'

I have long been struck by how significant the concept of fairness is in psychological life. An article by the British analyst Eric Rayner (Rayner, 2000: 153) drew my attention the preoccupation with fairness, in both therapy and everyday life. For instance, in writing this article, my wish to create case examples that would suit my argument might conflict with my wish to do justice to those involved, even if only in my imagination. It strikes me that the original arena for this fight for justice is the sibling group, and subsequently the playground. The oft-heard retort of childhood, 'S'not fair', echoes this preoccupation.

I think family therapy has a forgotten but useful sibling, anthropology. The anthropological attitude is very valuable in its enquiry into meaning, rituals and events. Sometimes we will be dealing with hostile 'warring tribes.' And in certain situations the anthropological attitude allows us not to feel compelled to be the agents of change, and can allow a more respectful attitude towards the family, so that they can create solutions within their own culture.

This idea of justice for multiple voices is exemplified by Helen Garner:

> I went to visit my four sisters, carrying a tape recorder and my imagined map of my family. It was unsettling to learn that each sister has her own quite individual map of that territory: the mountains and rivers are in different places, the borders are differently constituted and guarded, the history and politics and justice system of the country are different according to who's talking (Garner, 1997: vi).

In a very poetic way, Garner is alerting us to the trauma of growing up and dealing with competing claims within the same psychological territory. Since I decided to write this article I have been much more consciously asking children about their relationship about their siblings. This list is my attempt at the top 10 complaints:

1. *She gets into my things and sometimes breaks them.* This seems to be the precursor to:
2. *She gets under my skin.*
3. *It's not fair, he gets away with murder.*
4. *She is such a goody-goody.*
5. *Mum and Dad don't know what she gets up to.*
6. *He's the favourite.*
7. *I wish they were dead* [and they are not].
8. *They get all the attention.*
9. *He stinks.*
10. *She spends all her time in front of the mirror.*

I have found that surprisingly often, *the acknowledgement of some feeling of unfairness* seems to take the heat out of the anger, as if the child has felt that no one sees his or her point of view, that a sense of internal justice has been lost. This fight for justice happens in families and between couples as well. I think we do not do it psychological justice if we only call it a 'power struggle.' The apparent tussle for 'power' conceals a deeper concern with fairness.

Couples

Perhaps as a part of my recent focus on siblings, it is has been striking me that over time a sibling-type dynamic can develop in couple relationships. This has positive features, such as companionship and knowing each other very well. But it can also embody negative aspects, such as knowing each other too well, and being able to get under each other's skin. From this point of view, I wonder if the wish for space within a couple is sometimes the wish *to feel less like siblings* and hence to recapture some desire. I think sometimes the ghost of sibling relationships is enacted within these couples.

> Mr X was the eldest child in his family. He has been married to Mrs X for 30 years, and she was the youngest child in her family. In the early stages of their relationship, some of his protective capacities were attractive to Mrs X. Gradually, however, she has come to feel restricted in the relationship as though she can never grow up, as though she always remains the little sister. Of course this description of their relationship would not do justice to its other dynamics. Yet to ignore this aspect would mean one

might never uncover what their sibling roles had meant in their identity formation, leaving them feeling stuck forever in an unfair childhood.

Conclusion

Throughout this paper, I have tried to argue that our sibling relationships have a power and dynamism of their own, not to be tidied away as a shadow of the parent–child relationship. Family therapy may not have paid enough attention to this dynamic, both theoretically and technically. Perhaps the question of 'Where are the siblings?' is an extension of Catherine Sanders' comment that has there been 'a recurrent failure to embrace children as clients' (2003: 177). A recent family therapy book by Robert Sanders (2004), *Sibling Relationships: Theory and Issues for Practice* may be testimony to a growing interest within family therapy. Sanders raises many dilemmas for practice such as the question of siblings in care being kept together and of course the danger of assuming we know what is best without assessing the uniqueness of any sibling relationship.

One area ripe for investigation is the actual history of this neglect of conceptualisation of sibling relationships, across all therapies. I wonder if unspoken assumptions that siblings are rivalrous and destructive has meant we potentially neglect the value of these early 'we' relationships. Ironically as systemic therapists, have we neglected the group experience of siblings as a subsystem? Has there been a therapeutic reenactment of the saying, 'Two's company, three is a crowd'?

References

Byng-Hall, J., 1995. *Rewriting Family Scripts,* NY, Guilford.

Coles, P., 2003. *The Importance of Sibling Relationships in Psychoanalysis,* London, Karnac.

Cosic, M., 1999. *Only Child; A Provocative Analysis of the Impact of being an Only Child,* Sydney, Lansdowne.

Dunn, J., 2005. Commentary: Siblings in their Families, *Journal of Family Psychology,* 19, 4: 654–657.

Dunn. J. & Plomin, R., 1990. *Separate Lives: Why Siblings Are So Different.* NY, Basic.

Fitzgerald, R., 2004. Review of Michael Duffy, *Abbott and Latham: The Lives and Rivalry of Two of the Finest Politicians of their Generation,* Sydney, Random House, 2004, *Sydney Morning Herald,* Spectrum Section: 11, August 14–15, 2004.

Fonagy, P. & Target, M., 2003. *Psychoanalytic Theories, Perspectives from Developmental Psychopathology,* London, Whurr.

Garner, H., 1997. A Scrapbook, An Album. In J. Sauers (Ed.), *Brothers and Sisters: Intimate Portraits of Sibling Relationships,* Melbourne, Random House.

Minuchin, S., 1974. *Families and Family Therapy,* London, Tavistock.

Mitchell, Juliet, 2003. *Siblings,* Cambridge, Polity Press.

Rayner, E., 2000. In M. Whelan (Ed.), *Mistress of Her Own Thoughts: Ella Freeman Sharpe and the Practice of Psychoanalysis,* London, Rebus Press.

Richardson, R. W. & Richardson, L. A., 1990. *Birth Order and You,* North Vancouver, British Columbia, Self-Counsel Press.

Sacks, O., 2001. *Uncle Tungsten,* NY, Picador.

Sanders, C., 2003. Living up to our Theory: Inviting Children to Family Sessions, *ANZJFT,* 24, 4: 177–182.

Sanders, R., 2004. *Sibling Relationships: Theory and Issues for Practice,* NY, Macmillan.

Sauers, J., 1997. *Brothers and Sisters: Intimate Portraits of Sibling Relationships,* Melbourne, Random House.

Sulloway, F., 1996. *Born to Rebel: Birth Order, Family Dynamics and Creative Lives,* NY, Random House.

Target, M., 2002. Adolescent Breakdown, A Developmental Perspective [Videotape of Lecture], Sydney. NSW Institute of Psychoanalytic Psychotherapy.

Twemlow. S., 2001. An Innovative Psychodynamically Influenced Approach to Reduce School Violence, *Journal of American Academy of Child and Adolescent Psychiatry,* 40, 3 (March): 741–785.

Winnicott, D., 1958. The Capacity to be Alone, *International Journal of Psychoanalysis,* 39, 5: Sept–Oct: 416–420.

SALLY YOUNG is a Senior Social Worker at Greenslopes Child and Youth Mental Health Clinic, 34 Curd St. Brisbane 4120: yngs@bigpond.com. An earlier version of this paper was presented at the Australian Family Therapy Conference in Brisbane in 2004.

Four Myths about Older Adults in America's Immigrant Families

JUDITH TREAS

Elderly newcomers who follow their adult children to the United States are valuable members of many immigrant households. Little known outside their families and ethnic communities, they never win spelling bees. They do not join criminal gangs. Nobody worries about Americans losing jobs to Korean grandmothers. Arriving too late in life for the Americanizing influences of school and workplace, they remain invisible to the broader society and dependent on kin for support, companionship, and help in navigating U.S. society. Being focused on the economic and cultural incorporation of working-age immigrants and their children, researchers have neglected older newcomers. As shadowy figures on the American landscape, older newcomers succumb to easy stereotyping.

Invisible to the broader society, they are easily stereotyped.

Most of the older immigrants in the U.S. are not newcomers, but rather have lived in the country for many years. Having immigrated as children or young adults, they are usually well incorporated into our society. However, one in eight older foreign-born persons now in the U.S. is a newcomer—a late-life immigrant who arrived in the U.S. during the last decade (Treas and Batalova, 2007). Almost 50,000 adults age 65 and older were admitted to permanent residence in the U.S. in 2005. Another 2.3 million older adults come and go as "temporary visitors" each year. Most of the older people who immigrate permanently are the aging parents of naturalized U.S. citizens. Middle-aged and older parents make up 7.5 percent of all legal immigrants annually (Treas and Batalova, 2007).

U.S. immigration law places a premium on reuniting families, instead of focusing solely on serving the labor needs of the economy. The appropriate balance between family reunification and labor immigration is in fact a point of contention. Higher levels of immigration have led to a growing population of naturalized citizens who are able to sponsor the immigration of aging parents. There is no immediate economic advantage to bringing an older adult to the U.S. Ever since welfare and immigration reform of the mid 1990s, newcomers have been largely barred from receiving federal benefits (Estes et al., 2006). Family sponsors are legally responsible for the support of aging newcomers.

My research focuses on older newcomers who have relocated, often reluctantly, over long distances. They have moved at a time in their lives when most older adults are content to do what gerontologists call "aging in place"—growing old in the communities where they have lived most of their lives. Whatever their places of origin, these immigrants to the U.S. have much in common simply by virtue of age and immigrant experience. They share concerns about the upbringing of their grandchildren, about who will care for them (the elders) when they can no longer care for themselves, and about learning English when you struggle with poor memory or bad dentures. Their common experience refutes many stereotypes. In particular, findings about older newcomers challenge four myths about the lives of the older people in immigrant families.

The Older Newcomers

The study on which this article is based examined the results of intensive interviews with older, foreign-born adults who were either residing permanently in the U.S. or visiting from their residence elsewhere. Advanced sociology students (whom I trained and supervised) recruited and interviewed the older adults. Informants were usually the interviewers' family members, family friends, or friends' family members. Scientific sampling was ruled out by the difficulty of locating transient visitors and securing the reluctant cooperation of non-English speakers protected by family gate-keepers. Interviewers' personal relationships overcame these barriers. Besides speaking the same language as the informants, interviewers were able to interpret interviews in light of their own knowledge of the informant's culture and personal history. The study included fifty-five persons in their sixties, seventies, and eighties. Reflecting gender differences in mortality, three-quarters were women, half of whom were widowed, while all the men were married. They came from fifteen countries: The Philippines, Korea, Mexico, Pakistan, Iran, Taiwan, Vietnam, Bangladesh, Egypt, Spain, Cambodia, Belize, Jordan, Cuba, and Japan. (For more on the sample and methodology, see Treas, 2008; Treas and Mazumdar, 2002.) Results of the study defied a number of common myths about older immigrants, as described below.

Myth 1: Immigrant Families Are Traditional

We often think of immigrants as traditional. They often think of themselves as traditional. Criticizing "American" families, an undergraduate student from an immigrant household pronounced, "My family is very traditional. We take care of *our* grandmother." This South Asian family was not really traditional. In the U.S., the grandmother lived with the family of her married daughter. In India, she would have been expected to live with her son.

Many immigrant families were untraditional. In a manner unthinkable in earlier generations, some older adults shuttled between continents on a routine schedule. A Pakistani widow lived near her sons in England, but she traveled for most of the year to spend time with each of three daughters. During autumn in Canada, winter in Southern California, and spring in Australia, she pitched in to help around the house and teach religion to her grandchildren.

Other older adults moved between the homes of children who cared for them, perhaps spending the workweek with one family and the week-end with another. In another Indian household, an elderly couple lived apart from one another for several years. With their daughter in medical school, they took turns babysitting her children. When one grandparent arrived on a six-month visit, the other returned home to apply for another short-term visa. Maintaining traditions is difficult. Indian parents of the Brahman caste in prosperous families were sometimes rumored to be doing such shocking activities as toilet scrubbing, because Mexican immigrant housekeepers could not be trusted to follow hygienic Hindu rituals correctly.

Circumstances call for innovative adaptations, expedient compromises, and sacrifices in order to honor important cultural values. These adaptive practices are hardly traditional, even if they are recast as "tradition" by immigrants themselves. In such ways, immigrants themselves often participate directly in the making of the "traditional" myth, but they are not alone. Noting the immigrant propensity to live in multi-generational households or to receive family care rather than formal care (Moon, Lubben, and Villa, 1998; Wilmoth, 2001), we often point to cultural differences as characterizing immigrant families. Although culture plays a role, it takes a fine eye to distinguish what is "traditional" as opposed to a practical adaptation to poverty, ineligibility for public programs, or the need for trusted household help.

Myth 2: Immigrant Older Adults Are Family Dependents

Older newcomers do depend on family members. Because they lack incomes and are unfamiliar with American society, these elders rely on kin for support, housing, companionship, transportation, and help understanding English and navigating American society. It is easy to imagine that dutiful adult children bring their parents to the U.S. just so they can look after the older generation. Older people, however, give as well as they get. Immigrant family life emphasizes interdependence over dependence. Grown children invite parents to join them in the U.S. in part because they know that the older generation will help them out.

What do older family members do? They do the cooking and cleaning that permit the dual-earner couple or the single mother to get an economic toehold in American society. The older family members free older children from household responsibilities so they can go to school. Elders are babysitters, sometimes moving between households as each new grandchild is born (Treas and Mazumdar, 2004). Even if they themselves have little schooling or knowledge of English, they monitor study time at the kitchen table. They offer encouragement to despondent college students who call home. They care for the sick. They teach family traditions, native customs, and their own language. They keep in touch with relatives separated by great distances. In households where others are too busy to follow strict religious traditions, they are the designated performers of prayer and other rituals. In their spare time, they help to make ends meet by recycling aluminum cans, growing vegetables, and shopping at thrift stores.

Take one example. An 84-year-old Filipina described her day looking after her son's five-year-old twin boys:

> If I am caring for the kids, I wake up early and give them food and drink. I cook for the kids because the parents work. I care and bathe them. I make lunch and rest when they go to school. But I don't rest much because I clean, wash clothes, and then fold laundry. Then they come home and I change their clothes and give them food. Then I cook again for dinner, wash dishes, and then I sleep. . . . I sleep with the twins on either side.

Studies of American grandparents report that most of us are either "distant" (largely uninvolved) or perhaps "fun-loving" (enjoying the good times but leaving the hard work of child-rearing to the parents) (Cherlin and Furstenberg, 1986). Older immigrants are hands-on caregivers. While grandchildren eventually grow up and grandparents grow too old to help out, older immigrants are important to the well-being of the younger generation.

Myth 3: Immigrant Elders Are Authority Figures

Despite everyday household responsibilities, despite the affection of kin, older immigrants do not call the shots. Respect for the aged is the hallmark of many countries, especially Asian societies with a Confucian heritage of filial piety. This situation suggests that older kin are respected people whose counsel is sought and whose wishes are catered to. Whatever the culture, the authority of older immigrants is undermined by their limited resources and their lack of familiarity with American society.

First, older newcomers lack money. They are neither employed nor eligible for U.S. pensions. They are reluctant to cash out a family homestead when it can support kin who stay behind or provide a place to live should they decide to return. Because they depend on their children for support here, older adults subordinate their preferences to the needs of the young. A grandmother living with grown children may feel at home in an ethnic neighborhood where others speak her language. Still, she has to go along if younger kin decide to move to a distant suburb with better schools for the kids.

Second, older newcomers are seldom conversant with the English language or American ways. They rely on family members to navigate American society—translating at the doctor's office or driving to church. Aware that their children are more incorporated into the culture, older adults defer to their greater knowledge of American society. A 61-year-old Mexican woman laughingly insisted that her kids were smarter than she was, because they had learned modern ways while parents only knew the old ways.

Or, consider the wisdom of a 54-year-old Taiwanese woman who frequently makes extended visits to be with her daughter in Los Angeles:

> I only come to stay for a very short period of time, so I respect my daughter's way of living. . . . It is like taking a taxi. If I don't like the music a taxi driver plays, I won't interrupt his . . . choice. I only take the taxi for a very short period of time, but the taxi driver has to drive the car for the whole day.

Older relations may offer gentle advice, but only in rare cases (when an older parent is very rich or an adult child very dependent) do parents call the shots. Grandparents defer to parents in the upbringing of grandchildren. And, the elders' lives go on according to the younger generation's terms, usually reflecting the demands of their work and school schedules. Older people's visits to friends wait until some family member is available to drive. Even immigrating may reflect not so much the older person's desires as the needs of younger family members. This situation is not unique to older immigrants. Euro-American older adults, too, give up some autonomy if they are dependent on younger family members (Pyke, 1999).

Myth 4: Immigrant Family Life Guarantees Happiness and Security

Many immigrant families are what sociologists refer to as "familistic"—characterized by high levels of interpersonal solidarity and kin togetherness. One downside of immigrant family life is the limited control that older immigrants have over their own lives. The strength of family ties should not blind us to their limitations.

The warm embrace of family life would seem to insulate older immigrants from the problems facing other older Americans. This myth persists despite research that finds high rates of depression among older immigrants, specifically newcomers (Lee, Crittenden, and Yu, 1996; Mui, 1996). My research finds that boredom and loneliness are big problems, even for those who live with their kin (Treas and Mazumdar, 2002).

High cultural expectations for family togetherness are difficult to achieve in American society. Other family members are too busy going to school or earning a living to provide companionship. Those who immigrate at older ages have fewer opportunities to forge new relationships outside the family. The upshot is often older adults who are isolated by old age and circumstances.

Lamenting the absence of household servants and visiting neighbors, a Filipina in her 80s poignantly describes the loneliness that can confront older immigrants, even in multigenerational households:

> I get lonely because my husband died. Especially when I am left home alone. . . . I do nothing sometimes, just staring out the window or pray. . . . I pray the novena, and when it's time to sleep, I pray the rosary three times. . . . I don't like it when it's nighttime and I'm alone. I get scared. Maybe there will be a burglar or ghost or something. (laughs). . .

Social isolation occurs when older immigrants are too busy caring for younger kin to build any life outside the family. Learning English, mastering public transportation, and making friends with people their own age can get put off until the grandchildren are launched. By then, older immigrants may be too frail to get out much. They are also too old to go home. As time passes, hometowns change, kin move away, friends die, and there is little left to return to. Sadly, the U.S.—once seen as just a temporary detour in response to the needs of the younger generation—becomes the end of the line (Becker, 2002).

If family cannot guard against loneliness, neither can it guarantee a secure old age. With her small Supplemental Security Income (S.S.I.) benefit, an 82-year-old Vietnamese refugee demonstrates both the resilience and the limitations of immigrant family life. After immigrating to live with a daughter in New York, she moved to California to live with her granddaughter, Lucy. She says the following:

> I lived there for a while until she had money problems and went bankrupt. Lucy asked me to move out because she could no longer afford the house. I don't know what's wrong with that girl. I help her out in paying for rent, but she's always investing into new businesses . . . .

> I then move in with my other granddaughter, Stacy. I live with Stacy for a while up until the day she got married. Everywhere I live I pay rent, even if they don't accept it, I make them take it. After she got married, her parents, my son and his wife, decided to move in. So they took over my room and basically kick me out, telling me "go somewhere else." I was hurt but I couldn't do anything.

> At that time Lucy had started another business and was doing okay, so she asks me to move back in with her. But this didn't last long either. She and her husband started to drift apart from one another to the point where divorce is the only answer. I know, my family is messy, and I can't do anything about it.

> During this time, my son from Oregon had moved to California, and I was hoping to stay with him, but he

didn't want me to live there with him because his wife didn't like me. His house had an extra room, too!

You'll probably think I am homeless by then, right? You guess wrong. At that time, my fourth son had divorced his wife, and was traveling like me, too. So I couldn't stay with him, because I can't even find him. So I moved to Houston, Texas, to live with my third son for a while, but he had lung cancer and passed away.

Ever since then, I have been flying back and forth between D.C. and Orlando living with only my two daughters.

Indeed, despite mutual support, there are holes in the safety net provided even by a large immigrant family. Although welfare and immigration reforms of the 1990s heightened family members' dependence on one another, family cannot guarantee happiness and economic security for elderly newcomers.

Conclusion

At an age when other elders are aging in place, older immigrants sally forth to distant corners of the globe. These journeys are often made with great trepidation by older people whose heart is still in their homeland. At an age when many older Americans retire, older newcomers are keeping house for busy two-earner couples. While other Americans think about downsizing, they are caring for large, multigenerational households. While the usual American grandparent is an intermittent playmate, the immigrant grandparent is a hands-on caregiver for small children. Foreign-born older adults instill family values, teach religious rituals, promote ethnic traditions, conserve family history and genealogies, pass on native languages, and foster transnational commitments to kin in other countries.

Their emphasis on tradition does not necessarily mean that they are traditional. They must adapt to new circumstances in American society. The grandmother mopping the kitchen floor may well have had maids to do all the work in the Philippines. Nor does being embedded in an immigrant family assure companionship. Older immigrants reported feeling lonely and bored despite living with kin. Whatever authority they might have in their homeland is eroded by their diminished resources in the U.S. Older newcomers defer to the needs of the younger generation on whom they depend.

Newcomers of all ages face new opportunities and new constraints in the U.S. that demand novel adaptations, some welcome and some not. A Taiwanese woman worried about what would become of her if her Americanized son got married. However, she was delighted that her husband had adopted the American custom of helping to wash the dishes. Asked about maintaining Chinese customs in the U.S., she said, "Keep the good one and throw away the bad one!"

Challenging myths about older adults in America's immigrant families can inform policy. Elderly parents of naturalized citizens are at high risk of becoming casualties of any reforms that shift legal priorities from family reunification to labor immigration. The failed 1997 immigration proposals offered these parents immigration capped at half the numbers currently admitted and a point system favoring occupational credentials that older adults rarely possess. Whatever the merits of these proposals, older informants give voice to those who would be affected by changes in U.S. immigration law.

References

Becker, G. 2002. "Dying Away from Home: Quandaries of Migration for Elders in Two Ethnic Groups." *Journal of Gerontology B: Social Sciences* 57: s79–95.

Cherlin, A. J., and Furstenberg, F. F., Jr. 1986. *The New American Grandparent: A Place in the Family, A Life Apart.* New York: Basic Books.

Estes, C. L., et al. 2006. "Implications of Welfare Reform on the Elderly: A Case Study of Provider, Advocate, and Consumer Perspectives." *Journal of Aging and Social Policy* 18: 41–63.

Lee, M. S., Crittenden, K. S., and Yu, E. 1996. "Social Support and Depression Among Elderly Korean Immigrants in the United States." *International Journal of Aging and Human Development* 42: 313–27.

Moon, A., Lubben, J. E., and Villa, V. 1998. "Awareness and Utilization of Community Long-Term Care Services by Elderly Korean and Non-Hispanic White Americans." *The Gerontologist* 38: 309–16.

Mui, A. C. 1996. "Depression Among Elderly Chinese Immigrants: An Exploratory Study." *Social Work* 41: 633–45.

Pyke, K. 1999. "The Micropolitics of Care in Relationships Between Aging Parents and Adult Children: Individualism, Collectivism, and Power." *Journal of Marriage and Family* 61: 661–72.

Treas, J. 2008. "Transnational Older Adults and Their Families." *Family Relations* 57.

Treas, J., and Batalova, J. 2007. "Older Immigrants." In K. Warner Schaie and P. Uhlenberg, eds., *Social Structures: The Impact of Demographic Changes on the Well-Being of Older Persons,* pp. 1–24. New York: Springer.

Treas, J., and Mazumdar, S. 2002. "Older People in America's Immigrant Families: Dilemmas of Dependence, Integration, and Isolation." *Journal of Aging Studies* 16: 243–58.

Treas, J., and Mazumdar, S. 2004. "Caregiving and Kinkeeping: Contributions of Older People to America's Immigrant Families." *Journal of Comparative Family Studies* 35: 105–22.

Wilmoth, J. M. 2001. "Living Arrangements Among Older Immigrants in the United States." *The Gerontologist* 41: 228–38.

Judith Treas, PhD, is professor of sociology and director, Center for Demographic and Social Analysis, University of California, Irvine.

From *Generations*, Vol. xxxii, No. 4, 2009, pp. 40–45. Copyright © 2009 by American Society on Aging. Reprinted by permission.

UNIT 4

Challenges and Opportunities

Unit Selections

24. **Recognizing Domestic Partner Abuse,** *Harvard Women's Health Watch*
25. **Domestic Abuse Myths,** Raina Kelley
26. **The Fatal Distraction: Forgetting a Child in the Backseat of a Car Is a Horrifying Mistake. Is It a Crime?,** Gene Weingarten
27. **Children of Alcoholics,** Cara E. Rice et al.
28. **Impact of Family Recovery and Pre-Teens and Adolescents,** Virginia Lewis and Lois Allen-Byrd
29. **Love but Don't Touch,** Mark Teich
30. **Is This Man Cheating on His Wife?,** Alexandra Alter
31. **The Opt-Out Myth,** E. J. Graff
32. **Making Time for Family Time,** Tori DeAngelis
33. **Mother (and Father) Can You Spare a Dime?** Dan Kadlec
34. **Rise of the Desperate House Husband,** Gaby Hinsliff
35. **Trust and Betrayal in the Golden Years,** Kyle G. Brown
36. **Dealing** *Day-to-Day with* **Diabetes: A Whole Family Experience,** Karen Giles-Smith
37. **The Positives of Caregiving: Mothers' Experiences Caregiving for a Child with Autism,** Michael K. Corman
38. **Bereavement after Caregiving,** Richard Schulz, Randy Herbert, and Kathrin Boerner
39. **Love, Loss—and Love,** Karen Springen
40. **A Family Undertaking,** Holly Stevens
41. **Stressors Afflicting Families during Military Deployment,** Gina M. Di Nola
42. **Children of the Wars,** Lawrence Hardy
43. **A Divided House,** Mark Teich
44. **Civil Wars,** Christopher Munsey
45. **Estranged Spouses Increasingly Waiting out Downturn to Divorce,** Donna St. George

Key Points to Consider

- How does an abusive relationship develop? What, if anything, can be done to prevent it?
- What is forgotten baby syndrome? What can you do to prevent its happening to you?
- What are the particular risks for children of alcoholics? What contributes to resilience for them?
- If you felt your intimate relationship was troubled, how would you act? Would you discuss it with your partner? Would you hope that it would correct itself without your doing anything?
- What is the best way to work out the competing demands of work and family?
- How do you think you would respond if your child or partner was diagnosed with a life-threatening disease? What is the relationship among loss, grief, and care?
- How can you go about helping a family cope when a member is deployed?
- Discuss how the breakup of a relationship or a divorce affects the people involved. Is it possible to have a "good" divorce? What would that good divorce look like?

Student Website

www.mhhe.com/cls

Internet References

Alzheimer's Association
www.alz.org

Caregiver's Handbook
www.acsu.buffalo.edu/~drstall/hndbk0.html

National Crime Prevention Council
www.ncpc.org

Widow Net
www.widownet.org

Stress is life and life is stress. Sometimes stress in families gives new meaning to this statement. When a stressful event occurs in families, many processes occur simultaneously as families and their members cope with the stressor and its effects. One thing that can result is a reduction of the family members' ability to act as resources for each other. Indeed, a stressor can overwhelm the family system, and family members may be among the least effective people in coping with each other's behavior.

In this unit, we consider a wide variety of crises. Family violence is the focus of the first articles. "Recognizing Domestic Partner Abuse" presents warning signs and resources for those who experience or those who hope to help those experiencing domestic partner abuse. "Domestic Abuse Myths" addresses common myths about partner violence—even when the victim is a popular celebrity, teens appear to believe that she must have "done something to deserve it." Each year, children die needlessly because they are left in overheated vehicles. Gene Weigarten discusses the lasting effects when this is the result of "Forgotten Baby Syndrome." Substance abuse is next addressed in "Children of Alcoholics" and "Impact of Family Recovery and Pre-Teens and Adolescents." The first article looks at ways in which children of alcoholics (COA) are put at risk by substance abuse in their families, while it also presents surprising resilience factors that may serve to protect these children from their family dysfunction. The second looks at the nature of family recovery, the traumatic effect of family recovery on the young, and potential treatments. Next, emotional infidelity is addressed in "Love but Don't Touch." This is a form of unfaithfulness that many see as less serious than sexual infidelity, but others view as just a damaging to a couple's relationship. In this article, Mark Teich addresses a variety of ways of spotting emotional cheating as well as ways of strengthening a relationship after or in anticipation of its happening. A new phenomenon, "Is This Man Cheating on His Wife?," is explored in the final article in this subsection.

The subsection that follows, Economic Concerns, looks at the work/family connection with interesting results. The "Opt-Out Myth" questions a common belief that women are leaving the workforce to focus on their home life. The view that family and work life must arrive at some form of appropriate balance is the focus of "Making Time for Family Time." The struggle of coping with the financial needs of one's adult child is addressed in "Mother (and Father), Can you Spare a Dime?" The author, Dan Kadlec, suggests a number of issues related to financially helping an adult child, and ways in which it can be done to financially protect the often aging parents. This is followed by the "Rise of the Desperate House Husband," a relatively new phenomenon in which men, who have less capacity to earn a decent living than their wives, become the stay-at-home parent. The final article in this subsection, "Trust and Betrayal in the Golden Years," addresses a serious concern faced by too many elderly—the exploitation and abuse of the elderly by their children.

© Charlie Schuck/Alamy

The nature of stress resulting from a life-threatening illness as well as loss and grief are the subject of the next subsection. Life-threatening illnesses can place tremendous strain on couples' relationships. "Dealing Day-to-Day with Diabetes" documents the ways in which families adapt to live with a serious chronic illness. The next article, "The Positives of Caregiving," addresses ways in which mothers are able to respond to the needs of their autistic child in a positive way. The next article, "Bereavement after Caregiving," shows that the stress of caregiving does not end with death. The struggle faced by bereaved parents, addressed in "Love, Loss–and Love," is how and when to open one's heart to the thought of having another child after losing a child. "A Family Undertaking" discusses the final act of love and respect for a loved one in the form of a home funeral.

In the next subsection, the many crises of war are portrayed. "Stressors Affecting Families during Military Deployment" catalogues stressors faced by military families when a member is deployed to a war zone. "Children and the Wars" looks specifically at the issues of the children of those deployed. Divorce and remarriage are the subjects of the final subsection. The first articles in this subsection, "A Divided House" and "Civil Wars," both address ways in which the divorcing (and then divorced) couple may use their children as pawns in their battles with each other. The needs of the children must be paramount when a couple divorces—this is too often not the case. Finally, "Estranged Spouses Increasingly Waiting out Downturn to Divorce" describes a new phenomenon, that of couples waiting to divorce because of strained finances, or living together after their divorce for the same reason.

Recognizing Domestic Partner Abuse

With its daunting complexities, the path to change takes courage and support.

Domestic abuse. Battering. Intimate partner violence. These are terms that make us wince. And they should: The phenomenon is widespread in the United States, and its effects can be long-lasting and life-threatening. Breaking the pattern of domestic violence can be extremely difficult and may take a long time. It requires courage, planning, and a support network.

The U.S. Department of Health and Human Services defines domestic violence as "a pattern of assaultive and/or coercive behaviors . . . that adults use against their intimate partners to gain power and control in that relationship." It includes not only physical and sexual abuse but also emotional abuse. All can have serious health consequences.

Domestic violence affects people of all ethnic backgrounds; it occurs among the poor and the rich and among the well educated and the poorly educated. Men are usually (though not always) the abusers, and women are usually on the receiving end. In the United States, a woman's lifetime risk of being a victim of such violence is 25%. Women who were abused as children are at an increased risk for being in an abusive relationship as an adult.

First Signs

Women don't consciously choose to have an abusive partner. In fact, the abuser may be charming and well liked by most of the people who know him, but at home he shows a different side. Friends, family, and colleagues are often shocked when his abusive behavior becomes known. In the beginning, it may also be a shock to the abused woman. She may have regarded her relationship with this man as the most

---

Selected Resources

National Domestic Violence Hotline
800-799-7233 (toll free)
800-787-3224 (for the hearing impaired; toll free)

National Sexual Assault Hotline
800-656-4673 (toll free)

National Women's Health Information Center, "Violence against Women"
womenshealth.gov/violence/domestic/
800-994-9662 (toll free)

United Way First Call for Help
800-231-4377 (toll free)

---

wonderful, romantic, fairy tale–like experience imaginable, says Susan Neis, executive director of Cornerstone, a shelter that serves five suburbs of Minneapolis.

Changes in the relationship can be difficult to see at first. The abuser's need for control often begins to show itself in little things he says and does. He may criticize the way his partner acts or looks. He may say deeply hurtful things, such as accusing her of being a bad mother. "When somebody says this to you, somebody you're in love with, it's devastating," says Neis, who is herself a survivor of domestic abuse.

Over time, the abuser's words can chip away at a woman's sense of herself. She starts to doubt her perceptions and may even come to believe the horrible things he says about her. She feels isolated, ashamed, and helpless, but at the same time may feel an obligation to keep herself convinced of the fairy tale because "there's nothing else to hold onto," says one 35-year-old woman who received help from Cornerstone.

Control and Power

At the center of domestic violence is the issue of control. The abuser is intent on gaining and maintaining power over his partner through fear and intimidation. Abuse doesn't necessarily involve physical harm. Threats can also be highly effective and should not be minimized, suggests Dr. Judith Herman, clinical professor of psychiatry at Harvard Medical School and training director of the Victims of Violence Program at Cambridge Health Alliance in Cambridge, Mass. A man who says "If you leave me, I'll track you down and kill you and anyone who helps you" can instill as much (or more) fear as one who strikes his partner.

The abusive partner uses various tactics to achieve control. He may intimidate and demean his partner by constantly criticizing her, monopolizing household finances, or telling her what she can wear, where she can go, and whom she can see. He may play "mind games," such as suggesting that she's hypersensitive, hysterical, or mentally unbalanced. Often he isolates the woman from family, friends, and colleagues, either by removing her from them physically or by limiting her employment options and social contacts. Abuse may also take the form of pathological jealousy, such as false accusations of adultery. Soon, the woman may find that she's cut off from all outside connections, no longer in touch with the people and services that could help her.

Isolation may also disconnect her from a sense of what's normal. She may not even think of herself as a victim of domestic violence, says Dr. Megan Gerber, an internist at Cambridge Health Alliance who specializes in women's health and an instructor of medicine at Harvard Medical School. After an incident, the abuser often apologizes and tries to placate his victim. There may be periods of relative calm. It may take a victim a long time to recognize that her partner's behaviors aren't random but form a pattern of abuse.

Intimate Partner Abuse Is a Health Issue

Intimate partner abuse can have profound effects on a woman's health, both physical and mental. Physical harm, including fractures, lacerations, and soft tissue trauma, is one obvious effect. Intimate partner abuse is also linked to chronic health problems and even death—from either suicide because of depression or murder (or manslaughter) by the partner.

The intense, ongoing stress may result in chronic pain or gastrointestinal symptoms. Victims of domestic abuse are more likely to have arthritis, neck pain, pelvic pain, and migraine headaches. They also have an increased risk of menstrual problems and difficulties during pregnancy, including bleeding, low birth weight, and anemia.

Domestic abuse is closely linked with mental illness and substance abuse. A recent study found that 47.6% of battered women were depressed and 63.8% had post-traumatic stress disorder; 18.5% used alcohol excessively; 8.9% used drugs; and 7.9% committed suicide.

Because women in abusive relationships often need emergency room and primary care services, physicians, nurses, and other clinicians are often the first outsiders to learn about the emotional or physical abuse. Women are often reluctant to mention the subject on a patient history form, but if asked by a clinician, they may be relieved to acknowledge it.

Getting Out

Walking away from an abusive relationship is a process more than a single action. Women usually make several attempts—five, on average—before they leave the partner for good. Isolation and fear may prevent a woman from leaving, even when she knows it is probably for the best. She may still love her partner or worry about what will happen to her children if she leaves. She may be unsure how to escape or how to survive financially and care for her children.

Community support can be crucial (see "Selected Resources"), although a woman in an abusive relationship often has difficulty taking advantage of that support. The abuser may track her computer use, looking for visits to websites and evidence of keyword searches. If that's a concern, says Rita Smith, executive director of the National Coalition Against Domestic Violence in Boulder, Colo., she should use a computer outside the home—for example at a library or a friend's home or work place. As a safeguard, the coalition's own site (www.ncadv.org) features a red "Escape" button that immediately switches the user to an Internet search engine.

Care for the Children

Each year, up to 10 million children witness the abuse of a parent or caregiver. Many women stay in an abusive relationship because they think it's best not to disrupt the children's lives so long as they're not being abused themselves. But children who live with domestic violence are at serious risk for behavioral and cognitive problems. In later life, they may suffer depression and trauma symptoms, and they may tolerate or use violence in their own relationships.

Experts say that women leaving an abusive relationship should take their children with them. Otherwise, it can be difficult to get the children later, because police may not want to remove them from the home if the abusive partner is their biological father. Also, the abuser may later try to get custody by arguing that the woman abandoned her children.

What Can I Do to Help?

You suspect that your friend is in an abusive relationship. For example, she seems anxious and fearful when she recounts arguments with her husband. Or she may mention having to ask him each time she needs money. (While by itself not a sign of abuse, controlling finances can be part of a pattern of abuse.)

Part of you wants to rescue her and take her to a safe place where her husband can't find her. Yet you worry that any action you take could make things worse, increasing the danger she's already in. You know the decision is hers to make, not yours. But you can do a lot to help. Here are some things to consider:

- Think about your relationship with your friend. When and where might you talk with her safely, and what could you say? Does she trust you? Does she feel that she can confide in you without fearing that you'd judge her harshly or dismiss her concerns?
- Ask questions that let her know of your suspicions and concern. One question might be: Are you afraid of your husband? Understand that she might be hesitant to talk about this directly—or might deny or minimize what's happening. Assure her that you'll keep what she says strictly confidential.
- When she talks about the situation, believe what she says and validate her concerns. Let her know you don't think she's crazy or it's all in her head. And let her know that she's not to blame, despite what her partner may have told her.
- Help your friend make use of local resources—public health services, a hospital or clinic, a women's shelter, or a legal assistance program. If she thinks the abuser is monitoring her phone calls, offer her the use of your home phone or cell phone to make these contacts.
- Work with your friend to develop a personal safety plan. One resource for this step is the National Coalition Against Domestic Violence, www.ncadv.org/protectyourself/MyPersonalSafetyPlan_131.html.
- Help her prepare to leave if the danger and abuse escalate. Your friend should have coins with her at all times for phone calls, or a phone card. She should prepare a small bag with clothes, cash, and copies of important documents (birth certificate and passport, for example) and keep it in a safe place. Would you be willing to keep the bag for her in case of need?
- Knowing that someone believes her and is ready to help can be crucial to your friend's safety and eventual escape from the abusive relationship. Be patient, listen, and offer her hope. Recognize that it may take a long time, and often several attempts at leaving, for the relationship to end.

From *Harvard Women's Health Watch*, September 2006, pp. 6–7. Copyright © 2006 by Harvard Health Publications Group. Reprinted by permission via the Copyright Clearance Center.

Domestic Abuse Myths

Five mistakes we make when we talk about Rihanna and Chris Brown's relationship.

RAINA KELLEY

Last week, R&B singer Chris Brown was formally charged with two felonies, assault and making criminal threats, in connection with the alleged beating of his pop-star girlfriend Rihanna on Feb. 8. Though we will never know exactly what happened that night, many of us have seen Rihanna's bruised and bloodied face on the front pages and read horrific details of the alleged attack from the affidavit of a LAPD detective in which he describes contusions on the singer's body. At same time, rumors are that the 21-year-old singer is back in a relationship with Brown, whom she has accused, according to the affidavit, of biting, choking and punching her until her mouth filled with blood.

While we can argue about how much of all that is true, it really doesn't matter. This sad story doesn't have to be verifiable for it to potentially warp how Rihanna's hundreds of thousands of tween fans think about intimate relationships. We've all heard that this should be a "teachable moment"—a chance to talk about domestic violence with our kids. But children and teens aren't just listening to your lectures, they're listening to the way you speculate about the case with other adults; they're absorbing how the media describes it; they're reading gossip websites. When you tune into to all the talk about Rihanna and Chris Brown, it's scary how the same persistent domestic-violence myths continue to be perpetuated. Celebrity scandals may have a short shelf life, but what we teach kids about domestic violence will last forever. So rather than "raise awareness," here are five myths that anyone with a child should take time to debunk:

Myth No. 1: It Was a Domestic Argument, and She Provoked Him

We need to remember that any discussion of domestic violence should not revolve around what the couple may have been arguing about, or as one CNN anchor put it: "the incident that sparked

the fight." Nor should we be using the word "provoked" when describing this case, as in the Associated Press account that said the "argument" was "provoked" by Rihanna's "discovery of a text message from another woman." Domestic violence has to do with, well, physical violence, not arguments. There isn't a verbal argument that should "spark" or "provoke" an attack of the kind that leaves one person with wounds that require medical attention.

Cable news has to stop referring to this incident as a "violent fight." A "fight" involves two people hitting each other, not—as is alleged in this case—a woman cowering in a car while a man punches and bites her. If Rihanna had called the police beaten and bloodied and alleging an attack of this nature by a stranger, no one would be calling it a "fight." They'd say that a man was being accused of severely beating and choking a young woman half his size.

Myth No. 2: Evolution Makes Us Do It

Steven Stosny, a counselor and founder of an organization that treats anger-management issues believes that the tragic tendency of women to return to the men who hurt them (battered-woman syndrome) is a product of evolution. Stosny was quoted on CNN.com as saying "To leave an attachment relationship—a relationship where there's an emotional bond—meant certain death by starvation or saber-tooth tiger."

Apologies to Mr. Stosny, but that is the most ridiculous thing I have ever heard. This is the kind of argument that really boils my blood because it seems to naturalize the torture of women. Very little is known about the emotional attachments of early humans. And trust me, after 50,000 years, our fear of saber-tooth tigers has abated. In most domestic-abuse cases, we're talking about a situation where one person is wielding power over an individual through pain, fear, and domination. It's not about being scared to leave because of the dangers that await you in the world, it's about being too scared of what's at home to leave.

Myth No. 3: People Make Mistakes. Give the Guy a Break

When singer Kanye West talked about the Rihanna-Brown case with his VH1 audience recently, he asked: "Can't we give Chris a break? . . . I know I make mistakes in life." Kanye's not the only one saying this kind of thing, so let's get something straight: People leave the oven on or fry turkeys in the garage and burn their house down. One may even accidentally step on the gas instead of the brake and run over the family cat. Mistakes resulting in tragic consequences happen all the time. But one cannot mistakenly beat someone up. You do not accidentally give someone black eyes, a broken nose, and a split lip.

Myth No. 4: Brown Said He Was Sorry and They're Working It Out

Experts will tell you that domestic violence is an escalating series of attacks (not fights) designed to increase a victim's dependence on her abuser. According to the police documents released last week, Rihanna told police that Brown had hit her before and it was getting worse. Sorry means you don't do it again. In discussions about abuse, we need to make it clear that sorry is not enough.

Myth No. 5: She's Young, Rich and Beautiful. If It Was Really as Bad as the Media Says, She'd Leave

The secret to the abuser's power is not only making his victim dependent on him, but convincing her that she is to blame for the attack. No amount of money or fame can protect someone from the terrible cycle of emotional dependence, shame and fear that keeps them with abusive partners. Women who are abused look for ways they may have "provoked" an attack, finding fault with their own behavior to explain the unexplainable—why would someone they love hurt them? And it doesn't help when people outside the relationship blame the victim. In this case, Phylicia Thompson, a cousin of Brown's, told "Extra TV" that, *"Chris was not brought up to beat on a woman. So it had to be something to provoke him for Chris to do it."* As the rumors swirl about whether Rihanna is back with Brown, understand that those who are abused do not stay with their abusers because they want to be beaten again, or because they are really at fault; it's usually because they feel trapped and guilty.

You may have noticed that the words *power, control,* and *domination* running through my rant. That was purposeful. What we need to remember, and what we need to teach our children, is that yes, you should never hit anybody and you should never let anybody hit you. But, we also need to tell them that love does not guarantee respect and that any relationship they find themselves involved in should be based on both equally.

The Fatal Distraction: Forgetting a Child in the Backseat of a Car Is a Horrifying Mistake. Is It a Crime?

Every year, at least a dozen children die in overheated cars in the U.S. because parents forgot they were there. Don't assume, says The Washington Post's Gene Weingarten, that it couldn't happen to you.

GENE WEINGARTEN

The defendant was an immense man, well over 300 pounds, but in the gravity of his sorrow and shame he seemed larger still. He hunched forward in his wooden chair, sobbing softly into tissue after tissue, a leg bouncing nervously under the table. The room was a sepulcher. Witnesses spoke softly of events so painful that many lost their composure. When a hospital emergency room nurse described how the defendant had behaved after the police first brought him in, she wept. He was virtually catatonic, she remembered, his eyes shut tight, rocking back and forth, locked away in some unfathomable private torment. He would not speak at all for the longest time, not until the nurse sank down beside him and held his hand. It was only then that the patient began to open up, and what he said was that he didn't want any sedation, that he didn't deserve a respite from pain, that he wanted to feel it all, and then to die.

The charge in the courtroom was manslaughter, brought by the Commonwealth of Virginia. No significant facts were in dispute. Miles Harrison, 49, had been a diligent businessman and a doting, conscientious father until the day last summer—beset by problems at work, making call after call on his cell phone—he forgot to drop his son, Chase, at day care. The toddler slowly sweltered to death, strapped into a car seat for nearly nine hours in an office parking lot in the blistering heat of July.

It was an inexplicable, inexcusable mistake, but was it a crime? That was the question for a judge to decide.

"Death by hyperthermia" is the official designation. When it happens to young children, the facts are often the same: An otherwise attentive parent one day gets busy, or distracted, or confused by a change in his or her daily routine, and just . . . forgets a child is in the car. It happens that way somewhere in the United States 15 to 25 times a year, parceled out through the spring, summer, and early fall. The season is almost upon us.

Two decades ago, this was relatively rare. But in the early 1990s, car-safety experts declared that passenger-side front airbags could kill children, and they recommended that child seats be moved to the back of the car; then, for even more safety for the very young, that the baby seats be pivoted to face the rear. If few foresaw the tragic consequence of the lessened visibility of the child . . . well, who can blame them? What kind of person forgets a baby?

The wealthy do, it turns out. And the poor, and the middle class. Parents of all ages and ethnicities do it. Mothers are just as likely to do it as fathers. It happens to the chronically absent-minded and to the fanatically organized, to the college-educated and to the marginally literate. Last year it happened three times in one day, the worst day so far in the worst year so far in a phenomenon that gives no sign of abating.

The facts in each case differ a little, but always there is the terrible moment when the parent realizes what he or she has done, often through a phone call from a spouse or caregiver. This is followed by a frantic sprint to the car. What awaits there is the worst thing in the world.

In Miles Harrison's case, the judge ultimately decided there was no crime because there was no intent. Prosecutors, judges, and juries reach similar conclusions in many of these cases. But if Harrison's failing is not manslaughter, what is it? An accident?

"That's an imperfect word."

This is Mark Warschauer, an expert in language learning. "The word 'accident' makes it sound like it can't be prevented, but 'incident' makes it sound trivial. And it is not trivial."

Warschauer is a professor at the University of California at Irvine. In the summer of 2003, he returned to his office from lunch to find a crowd surrounding a car in the parking lot. Police had smashed the window open with a crowbar. Only as he got closer did Warschauer realize it was his car. That was his first clue that he'd forgotten to drop his 10-month-old son, Mikey, at day care that morning. Mikey was dead.

Warschauer wasn't charged with a crime, but for months afterward he contemplated suicide. Gradually, he says, the urge subsided, if not the grief and guilt.

"We lack a term for what this is," Warschauer says. And also, he says, we need an understanding of why it happens to the people it happens to.

David Diamond is picking at his breakfast at a Washington, D.C., hotel, trying to explain.

"Memory is a machine," he says, "and it is not flawless. If you're capable of forgetting your cell phone, you are potentially capable of forgetting your child."

Diamond is a professor of molecular physiology at the University of South Florida. He's in D.C. to give a conference speech about his research, which involves the intersection of emotion, stress, and memory. What he's found is that under some circumstances, the most sophisticated part of our thought-processing center can be held hostage to a competing memory system, a primitive portion of the brain that is—by a design as old as the dinosaur's—pigheaded, nonanalytical, stupid.

Diamond recently forgot, while driving to a mall, that his infant granddaughter was asleep in the back of his car. He remembered, he said, only because his wife mentioned the baby. So he understands what could have happened had he been alone with the child. Almost worse, he understands exactly why.

The human brain, he says, is a jury-rigged device in which newer and more sophisticated structures sit atop a junk heap of prototype brains still used by lower species. At the top are the most nimble parts: the prefrontal cortex, which thinks and analyzes, and the hippocampus, which makes and holds on to our immediate memories. At the bottom is the basal ganglia, nearly identical to the brains of lizards, controlling voluntary but barely conscious actions.

Diamond says that in situations involving familiar, routine motor skills, the human animal presses the basal ganglia into service as a sort of autopilot. When our prefrontal cortex and hippocampus are planning our day on the way to work, the ignorant basal ganglia is operating the car; that's why you'll sometimes find yourself having driven from point A to point B without a clear recollection of the route you took, the turns you made, or the scenery you saw.

Ordinarily, says Diamond, this delegation of duty "works beautifully, like a symphony." But sudden or chronic stress can weaken the brain's higher-functioning centers, making them more susceptible to bullying from the basal ganglia. He's seen that pattern in cases he's followed involving infant deaths in cars.

"The quality of prior parental care seems to be irrelevant," he said. "The important factors that keep showing up involve a combination of stress, emotion, lack of sleep, and change in routine, where the basal ganglia is trying to do what it's supposed to do, and the conscious mind is too weakened to resist. What happens is that the memory circuits in a vulnerable hippocampus literally get overwritten, like with a computer program. Unless the memory circuit is rebooted—such as if the child cries, or, you know, if the wife mentions the child in the back—it can entirely disappear."

Diamond stops. "There is a case in Virginia where this is exactly what happened, the whole set of stress factors. I was consulted on it a couple of years ago. It was a woman named, ah . . . "

He puts down his fork and shakes his head. He's been stressing over his conference speech, he says, and his memory retrieval is shot. He can't summon the name.

Lyn Balfour?

"Yeah, Lyn Balfour! The perfect storm."

Raelyn Balfour is what is commonly called a type-A personality. The 37-year-old Army reservist is the first to admit that her inclination to take on multiple challenges at once contributed to the death of her son, Bryce, two years ago. It happened on March 30, 2007, the day she accidentally left the 9-month-old in the parking lot of the Charlottesville, Va., judge advocate general's office, where she worked as a transportation administrator. The temperature that day was only in the 60s, but heat builds quickly in a closed vehicle in the sun. The temperature inside Balfour's car that day topped 110 degrees.

Circumstances had conspired against Balfour. She had been up much of the night, first baby-sitting for a friend with a pet emergency, then caring for Bryce, who was cranky with a cold. Because the baby was still tired, he uncharacteristically dozed in the car, so he made no noise. Because Balfour was planning to bring Bryce's usual car seat to the fire station to be professionally installed, Bryce was positioned in a different car seat that day, directly behind the driver, and thus less visible. Because of a phone conversation with a young relative in trouble, and another with her boss about a crisis at work, Balfour spent most of the trip on her cell, stressed, solving other people's problems.

One more thing: Because the baby sitter had a new phone, it didn't yet contain Balfour's office phone number, only her cell number—so when the sitter phoned to wonder why Balfour hadn't dropped Bryce off that morning, it rang unheard in Balfour's pocketbook.

Balfour was charged with second-degree murder in Bryce's death but was eventually acquitted. The key moment in her trial was when the defense attorney played for the jury a recording of a 911 call made by a passer-by in the first few seconds after Balfour discovered Bryce's body. That tape is unendurable. Mostly, you hear the passer-by's voice, tense but precise, explaining to a police dispatcher what she is seeing. Initially, there's nothing in the background. Then Balfour howls at the top of her lungs, "OH, MY GOD, NOOOO!"

For a few seconds, there's nothing. Then another deafening shriek: "NO, NO, PLEASE, NO!!!"

Unlike most parents who have suffered similar tragedies, Balfour now is willing to talk to the media, anytime. She works with a group called Kids and Cars, telling her story repeatedly. In public, she seldom seems in particular anguish. No one sees her cry. She has, she says, consciously crafted the face she shows. "People say I'm a strong woman, but I'm not. I would like to disappear, to move someplace where no one knows who I am and what I did. But I can't. I'm the lady who killed her child, and I have to be that lady because I promised Bryce."

Balfour has kept her promise in a way suited to her personality: She has become a modern, maternal version of the Ancient Mariner. When speaking to the media, her consistent message is that cars need safety devices to prevent similar tragedies. From time to time, though, she will simply belly up to strangers in, say, a Sam's Club, and start a conversation about children, so she can tell them what she did to one of hers. Her message: *This can happen to anyone.*

Children of Alcoholics
Risk and Resilience

CARA E. RICE, MPH, ET AL.

In 2002, over 17 million people in the United States were estimated to suffer from alcohol abuse or alcohol dependence (NIAAA, 2006). These alcohol disorders have devastating effects on the individuals, their families, and society. It has been reported that one in four children in the United States has been exposed to alcohol abuse or dependence in the family (Grant, 2000). A 1992 survey revealed that over 28 million children in the United States lived in households with one or more adults who had an alcohol disorder at some time in their lives, while nearly 10 million children lived with adults who reported alcohol disorders in the past year (Grant, 2000). Children of alcoholics (COAs) are at increased risk for a variety of negative outcomes, including fetal alcohol syndrome, substance use disorders, conduct problems, restlessness and inattention, poor academic performance, anxiety, and depression (West & Prinz, 1987). Furthermore, children of alcoholics are more likely to be exposed to family stressors such as divorce, family conflict, parental psychopathology, and poverty, which, in turn, may contribute to their negative outcomes.

In particular, COAs show increased risk of alcoholism and other substance use disorders. Genetic factors have been identified as increasing the risk of developing substance use problems among COAs (Schuckit, 2000). However, the risk faced by COAs is best understood as resulting from the interplay of both genetic and environmental factors (McGue, Elkins, & Iacano, 2000). We will discuss the factors that influence the development of substance abuse and other negative outcomes in COAs. We will also review three models in the development of substance disorders for COAs. These models are not mutually exclusive, and all three may influence a child. We will also discuss protective factors that may decrease COAs' risk for the development of future negative outcomes.

Prenatal Risk

One pathway for increased risk among COAs is through prenatal exposure to alcohol. Fetal alcohol syndrome (FAS), which can occur if a woman drinks alcohol during pregnancy, is a condition characterized by abnormal facial features, growth retardation, and central nervous system problems. Children with FAS may have physical disabilities and problems with learning, memory, attention, problem solving, and social/behavioral problems (Bertrand et al., 2004).

Pathways of Risk for the Development of Substance Disorders

Multiple pathways have been studied in the development of substance use disorders. Three important ones are the deviance proneness model, the stress/negative affect model, and the substance use effects model (Sher, 1991). Although these models were originally proposed to explain the development of alcohol disorders among COAs, they can also be extended to a consideration of other negative outcomes.

Deviance Proneness Pathway

The deviance proneness pathway theorizes that parental substance abuse produces poor parenting, family conflict, difficult child temperament and cognitive dysfunction. Poor parenting along with conflicted family environment are thought to interact with a child's difficult temperament and cognitive dysfunctions, which raises the child's risk for school failure and for associating with peers who themselves have high levels of conduct problems. Affiliation with these antisocial peers then increases the likelihood of antisocial behavior by COAs, including substance use (Dishion, Capaldi, Spracklen, & Li, 1995). Conduct problems in childhood and later adolescence predict the development of substance use disorders in young adulthood (Chassin et al., 1999; Molina, Bukstein, & Lynch, 2002).

One component of the deviance proneness model is difficult temperament or personality. The temperament and personality traits that are associated with adolescent substance use include sensation seeking, aggression, impulsivity, and an inability to delay gratification (Gerra et al., 2004; Wills,

Windle, & Cleary, 1998). For example, 3-year-old boys observed to be distractible, restless, and impulsive were more likely to be diagnosed with alcohol dependence at the age of 21 (Caspi, Moffitt, Newman, & Silva, 1996). Importantly, these characteristics, which are associated with adolescent substance use, have also been shown to be more common among COAs and children of drug users. (e.g., Carbonneau et al., 1998). This suggests that COAs may be at risk for substance use, in part, because of their personality traits.

One in four children in the United States has been exposed to alcohol abuse or dependence in the family.

Another component of the deviance proneness model is a deficit in cognitive function. Children of alcoholics may also be at risk for substance abuse because of deficits in cognitive functioning that have been called "executive" functions. Executive functioning refers to the ability to adjust behavior to fit the demands of individual situations and executive functioning includes planning, working memory and the ability to inhibit responses (Nigg et al., 2004). COAs have demonstrated poor response inhibition (Nigg et al., 2004), and impairments in executive functioning have found to predict drinking among young adult COAs (Atyaclar, Tarter, Kirisci, & Lu, 1999).

The deviance proneness pathway also suggests that COAs may be at risk because of the poor parenting that they receive. Decreased parental monitoring of the child's behavior, inconsistent discipline, and low levels of social support from parents are associated with increased levels of adolescent substance use and conduct problems (Brody, Ge, Conger, Gibbons, Murry, Gerrard, & Simons, 2001; Wills, McNamara, Vaccaro, & Hirky, 1996). These negative parenting behaviors have been found in substance-abusing families (Chassin, Curran, Hussong, & Colder, 1996; Curran & Chassin, 1996), suggesting that alcoholic parents may engage in poor parenting practices, which may in turn place their children at risk for substance use and/or conduct problems.

Most researchers have assumed that poor parenting leads to behavior problems in children, making it the basis for many prevention and intervention programs. However, developmental researchers have suggested that child behavior also affects parenting (Bell & Chapman, 1986). For example, Stice and Barrera (1995) found that low levels of parental control and support predicted adolescent substance use. However, adolescent substance use, in turn, predicted decreases in parental control and support. Therefore, the link between parenting and adolescent conduct problems and substance use may best be thought of as a system in which parents affect children, and children affect parents.

Stress and Negative Affect Pathway

The stress and negative affect pathway suggests that parental substance abuse increases children's exposure to stressful life events such as parental job instability, familial financial difficulty, parental legal problems, etc. (Chassin et al., 1993; Sher, 1991). These potentially chronic stressors may lead to emotional distress in COAs such as depression and/or anxiety. Substance use may then be used to control this distress.

Research has shown a link between negative affect and substance use in adolescence (see Zucker, 2006, for a review). For example, depression has been found to co-occur with adolescent substance abuse (Deykin, Buka, & Zeena, 1992) and heavy alcohol use (Rohde, Lewinson, & Seely, 1996). Moreover, negative life events have been associated with adolescent substance use (Wills, Vaccaro, & McNamara, 1992). However, not all findings support a negative affect pathway to adolescent substance use problems.

One explanation for the conflicting findings is that not all adolescents with negative affect will be at risk for substance use. Rather, adolescents who suffer from negative affect may only use alcohol and drugs if they also lack good strategies to cope with their negative moods and/or if they believe that alcohol or drugs will help them cope. Therefore, helping COAs to develop coping strategies can potentially serve as an intervention. There may also be gender differences in the extent to which COAs use substance use to cope with stress and negative mood (Chassin et al., 1999).

Substance Use Effects Model

The substance use effects model focuses on individual differences in the pharmacological effects of substances. It is hypothesized that some individuals are more sensitive to the pleasurable effects of alcohol and substance use and/or less sensitive to the adverse effects. For example, Schuckit and Smith (1996) found that male COAs with extremely low levels of negative responses to alcohol were more likely be to diagnosed with alcohol abuse/dependence almost a decade later. It is possible that individuals who do not experience negative effects from drinking may lack the "natural brakes" that limit drinking behavior. Some researchers have also suggested that COAs receive greater stress reduction effects from drinking alcohol (Finn, Zeitouni, & Pihl, 1990). Thus, COAs would be expected to engage in more stress-induced drinking than non-COAs because they derive greater physiological benefit from it. It is important to note, however, that not all studies have supported this finding and more research is needed to draw concrete conclusions concerning COAs' physiological response to alcohol (see Sher, 1991, for a review).

Resilience/Protective Factors

Despite the risks presented by genetic, social, and psychological variables, not all COAs experience negative outcomes. These individuals who, despite high-risk status, manage to defeat the odds, are labeled resilient (Garmezy & Neuchterlein, 1972). Resilience has been extensively studied in a variety of populations, but resilience among COAs remains an area that needs further research (Carle & Chassin, 2004). Sher (1991) hypothesized that factors that can help protect COAs from developing alcoholism include social class, preservation of family rituals, amount of attention received from primary caregivers, family harmony during infancy, parental support, personality, self-awareness, cognitive-intellectual functioning, and coping skills.

COAs show increased risk of alcoholism and other substance use disorders.

Carle and Chassin (2004) examined competence and resilience of COAs and found a significant difference between COAs and non-COAs in competence with regards to rule-abiding and academic behaviors, but no differences in social competence. A small subset of resilient COAs demonstrated at or above average levels of academic and rule-abiding competence. These resilient COAs also had fewer internalizing symptoms and reported increased levels of positive affect than did the general COA population (Carle & Chassin, 2004). This suggests that COAs with average or above average academic and rule-abiding competence as well as low levels of internalizing symptoms and high positive affect may be resilient to the risk associated with having an alcoholic parent.

Another potential source of resilience for COAs may be the recovery of the alcoholic parent. Hussong and colleagues (2005) found support for this idea in a study of social competence in COAs. Results from this study indicated that children of recovered alcoholics demonstrated comparable levels of social competence when compared to children of nonalcoholic parents, suggesting again that not all COAs are at equivalent levels of risk.

Along with recovery of parental alcohol symptoms, previous research has also demonstrated the importance of a number of familial factors in buffering the risk associated with parental alcoholism. For example, parental social support, consistency of parental discipline, family harmony, and stability of family rituals have all been shown to protect COAs from the development of alcohol and drug use and abuse (King & Chassin, 2004; Marshal & Chassin, 2000; Stice, Barrera, & Chassin, 1993).

Although there is evidence to suggest that family factors play a protective role in children's risk for substance use and substance use disorders, there is evidence to suggest that this protection may not be equal for all children (Luthar, Cicchetti, & Becker, 2000). In other words, the protective family factor may reduce the negative effect of parental alcoholism for some children, but may lose its effectiveness at the highest levels of risk. For example, King and Chassin (2004) found that parental support reduced the negative effect of family alcoholism for children with low and average levels of impulsivity and sensation seeking, but not for children with high levels of impulsivity and sensation seeking. In other words, parental support was protective for most children, but not for those with the highest levels of risk. Similarly, Zhou, King, and Chassin (2006) found that the protective effect of family harmony was lost for those children with high levels of family alcoholism. Together these studies provide evidence that consistent and supportive parenting and family harmony are protective for many children of alcoholics, but those children at especially high risk may not benefit from these familial protective factors.

Family relationships, though clearly an important aspect of resilience in COAs, are not the only relationships that appear to contribute to positive outcomes in children of alcoholics. There is also evidence to suggest that, for older children, peer relationships may be as influential as family relationships on adolescents' decision to use substances (Mayes & Suchman, 2006). Therefore, peer relationships may also provide protection against the risk associated with having an alcoholic parent. For example, Ohannessian and Hesselbrock (1993) found that COAs with high levels of social support from friends drank at levels similar to non-COAs, indicating that friendships may also work to reduce the negative effects of parent alcoholism.

Conclusion

Although much work remains to be done in understanding both risk and resilience among COAs, the work that has been done provides important implications for preventive interventions. For example, family factors appear to protect many COAs from negative outcomes. This knowledge supports the need for family-based preventive interventions, which seek to improve both parenting practices and family relationships among families of alcoholics. As research in this area continues to uncover the complex interplay of both the genetic and environmental factors that contribute to COA risk and resilience, prevention researchers will be afforded the opportunity to design and implement interventions to assist this prevalent and heterogeneous population of children.

References

Atyaclar, S., Tarter, R.E., Kirisci, L., & Lu, S. (1999). Association between hyperactivity and executive cognitive functioning in childhood and substance use in childhood and substance use in early adolescence. *Journal of the American Academy of Child and Adolescent Psychiatry, 38,* 172–178.

Bell, R.Q., & Chapman, M. (1986). Child effects in studies using experimental or brief longitudinal approaches to socialization. *Developmental Psychology, 22,* 595–603.

Bertrand, J., Floyd, R.L., Weber, M.K., O'Connor, M., Riley, E.P., Johnson, K.A., Cohen, D.E., National Task Force on FAS/FAE.

(2004). *Fetal Alcohol Syndrome: Guidelines for Referral and Diagnosis.* Atlanta, GA: Centers for Disease Control and Prevention. Available online at http://www.cdc.gov/ncbddd/fas/documents/FAS_guidelines_accessible.pdf

Brody, G.H., Ge, X., Conger, R., Gibbons, F.X., Murry, V.M., Gerrard, M., & Simons, R.L. (2001). The influence of neighborhood disadvantage, collective socialization, and parenting on African American children's affiliation with deviant peers. *Child Development, 72*(4), 1,231–1,246.

Carbonneau, R., Tremblay, R.E., Vitaro, F., Dobkin, P.L., Saucier, J.F., & Pihl, R.O. (1998). Paternal alcoholism, paternal absence, and the development of problem behaviors in boys from age 6 to 12 years. *Journal of Studies on Alcohol, 59,* 387–398.

Carle, A.C., & Chassin, L. (2004) Resilience in a community sample of children of alcoholics: Its prevalence and relation to internalizing symptomatology and positive affect. *Applied Developmental Psychology, 25,* 577–595.

Caspi, A., Moffitt, T., Newman, D., & Silva, P. (1996). Behavioral observations at age 3 years predict adult psychiatric disorders. *Archives of General Psychiatry, 53,* 1,033–1,039.

Chassin, L., Curran, P., Hussong, A., & Colder, C. (1996). The relation of parent alcoholism to adolescent substance use: A longitudinal follow-up study. *Journal of Abnormal Psychology, 105,* 70–80.

Chassin, L., Pillow, D., Curran, P., Molina, B., & Barrera, M. (1993). The relation between parent alcoholism and adolescent substance use: A test of three mediating mechanisms. *Journal of Abnormal Psychology, 102,* 1–17.

Chassin, L., Pitts, S.C., DeLucia, C., & Todd, M. (1999). A longitudinal study of children of alcoholics: Predicting young adult substance use disorders, anxiety, and depression. *Journal of Abnormal Psychology, 108,* 106–118.

Curran, P.J., & Chassin, L. (1996). Longitudinal study of parenting as a protective factor for children of alcoholics. *Journal of Studies on Alcohol, 57,* 305–313.

Deykin, E.Y., Buka, S.L., & Zeena, T.H. (1992). Depressive illness among chemically dependent adolescents. *American Journal of Psychiatry, 149,* 1,341–1,347.

Dishion, T.J., Capaldi, D., Spracklen, K.M., & Li, F. (1995). Peer ecology of male adolescent drug use. *Development and Psychopathology. Special Issue: Developmental Processes in Peer Relations and Psychopathology, 7*(4), 803–824.

Finn, P., Zeitouni, N., & Pihl, R.O. (1990). Effects of alcohol on psychophysiological hyperreactivity to nonaversive and aversive stimuli in men at high risk for alcoholism. *Journal of Abnormal Psychology, 99,* 79–85.

Garmezy, N., & Neuchterlein, K. (1972). Invulnerable children: The fact and fiction of competence and disadvantage. *American Journal of Orthopsychiatry, 42,* 328–329.

Gerra, G., Angioni, L., Zaimovic, A., Moi, G., Bussandri, M., Bertacca, S., Santoro, G., Gardini, S., Caccavari, R., & Nicoli, M.A. (2004). Substance use among high-school students: Relationships with temperament, personality traits, and personal care perception. *Substance Use & Misuse, 39,* 345–367.

Grant, B.F. (2000). Estimates of U.S. children exposed to alcohol use and dependence in the family. *American Journal of Public Health, 90,* 112–115.

Hussong, A.M., Zucker, R.A., Wong, M.M., Fitzgerald, H.E., & Puttler, L.I. (2005). Social competence in children on alcoholic parents over time. *Developmental Psychology, 41,* 747–759.

King, K.M., & Chassin, L. (2004). Mediating and moderated effects of adolescent behavioral under control and parenting in the prediction of drug use disorders in emerging adulthood. *Psychology of Addictive Behaviors, 18,* 239–249.

Luthar, S.S., Cicchetti D., & Becker, B. (2000). The construct of resilience: A critical evaluation and guidelines for future work. *Child Development, 71*(3), 543–562.

Marshal, M.P., & Chassin, L. (2000). Peer influence on adolescent alcohol use: The moderating role of parental support and discipline. *Applied Developmental Science, 4,* 80–88.

Mayes, L.C., & Suchman, N.E. (2006). Developmental pathways to substance use. In D. Cicchetti & D.J. Cohen (Eds.), *Developmental Psychopathology: Vol. 3. Risk, Disorder, and Adaptation* (2nd ed., pp. 599–619). New Jersey: John Wiley & Sons.

McGue, M., Elkins, I., Iacono, W.G. (2000). Genetic and environmental influences on adolescent substance use and abuse. *American Journal of Medical Genetics, 96,* 671–677.

Molina, B.S.G., Bukstein, O.G., & Lynch, K.G. (2002). Attention-deficit/hyperactivity disorder and conduct disorder symptomatology in adolescents with alcohol use disorder. *Psychology of Addictive Behaviors, 16,* 161–164.

National Institute on Alcohol Abuse and Alcoholism. (2006). NIAAA 2001–2002 NESARC [Data File]. Accessed August 1, 2006. from http://niaaa.census. gov/index.html.

Nigg, J.T., Glass, J.M., Wong, M.M., Poon, E., Jester, J.M., Fitzgerald, H.E., Puttler, L.I., Adams, K.A., & Zucker, R.A., (2004). Neuropsychological executive functioning in children at elevated risk for alcoholism: Findings in early adolescence. *Journal of Abnormal Psychology, 113,* 302–314.

Ohannessian, C.M., & Hesselbrock, V.M. (1993). The influence of perceived social support on the relationship between family history of alcoholism and drinking behaviors. *Addiction, 88,* 1,651–1,658.

Rohde, P., Lewinson, P.M., & Seeley, J.R. (1996). Psychiatric comorbidity with problematic alcohol use in high school students. *Journal of the American Academy of Child and Adolescent Psychiatry, 35,* 101–109.

Schuckit, M.A. (2000). Genetics of the risk for alcoholism. *The American Journal on Addictions 9,* 103–112.

Schuckit, M.A., & Smith, T.L. (1996). An 8-year follow-up of 450 sons of alcoholic and control subjects. *Archives of General Psychiatry, 53*(3), 202–210.

Sher, K.J. (1991). *Children of Alcoholics: A Critical Appraisal of Theory and Research.* Chicago: University of Chicago Press.

Stice, E., & Barrera, M. (1995). A longitudinal examination of the reciprocal relations between perceived parenting and adolescents' substance use and externalizing behaviors. *Developmental Psychology, 31*(2), 322–334.

Stice, E., Barrera, M., & Chassin, L. (1993). Relation of parental support and control to adolescents' externalizing symptomatology and substance use: A longitudinal examination of curvilinear effects. *Journal of Abnormal Child Psychology, 21,* 609–629.

West, M.O., & Prinz, R.J. (1987). Parental alcoholism and childhood psychopathology. *Psychological Bulletin, 102*(2), 204–218.

Wills, T.A., McNamara, G., Vaccaro, D., & Hirky, A.E. (1996). Escalated substance use: A longitudinal grouping analysis from early to middle adolescence. *Journal of Abnormal Psychology, 105,* 166–180.

Wills, T.A., Vaccaro, D., & McNamara, G. (1992). The role of life events, family support, and competence in adolescent substance use: A test of vulnerability and protective factors. *American Journal of Community Psychology, 20,* 349–374.

Wills, T.A., Windle, M., & Cleary, S.D. (1998). Temperament and novelty seeking in adolescent substance use: Convergence of dimensions of temperament with constructs from Cloninger's theory. *Journal of Personality and Social Psychology, 74*(2), 387–406.

Zhou, Q., King, K.M., & Chassin, L. (2006). The roles of familial alcoholism and adolescent family harmony in young adults' substance dependence disorders: mediated and moderated relations. *Journal of Abnormal Psychology, 115,* 320–331.

Zucker, R.A. (2006). Alcohol use and the alcohol use disorders: A developmental-biopsychosocial systems formulation covering the life course. In D. Cicchetti & D.J. Cohen (Eds.), *Developmental Psychopathology: Vol 3. Risk, Disorder, and Adaptation* (2nd ed., pp. 620–656). New Jersey: John Wiley & Sons.

CARA E. RICE, MPH, is Project Director of the Adult and Family Development Project at Arizona State University. DANIELLE DANDREAUX, MS, is a doctoral student in applied developmental psychology at the University of New Orleans and is currently employed by the Department of Psychology at Arizona State University. ELIZABETH D. HANDLEY, MA, is a doctoral student in clinical psychology at Arizona State University. Her research and clinical training are focused on at-risk children and families. LAURIE CHASSIN, PhD, is Professor of Psychology at Arizona State University. Her research focuses on longitudinal, multigenerational studies of risk for substance use disorders and intergenerational transmission of that risk.

Preparation of this article was supported by grant AA16213 from the National Institute of Alcohol Abuse and Alcoholism to Laurie Chassin.

Impact of Family Recovery on Pre-Teens and Adolescents

VIRGINIA LEWIS, PhD AND LOIS ALLEN-BYRD, PhD

When discussing parental alcoholism, it is often assumed that the parent's entry into recovery will resolve all problems. However, our research, which examined the impact of family recovery from alcoholism, shows that rather than being a unifying force for all family members, this process is traumatic, with pre-teens and adolescents frequently becoming the "forgotten" members of the family. The effects upon these forgotten members can be explained and understood in the context of recovery stages and family types. The purpose of this article is threefold: (1) to present a very complex process called family recovery, (2) to describe its traumatic impact on pre-teens and adolescents, and (3) to provide treatment suggestions for supporting young people.

The Family Recovery Project

In 1989, Drs. Stephanie Brown and Virginia Lewis were the first researchers to study the processes of family recovery from alcoholism. This research marked a dramatic shift from understanding how alcoholism affects all family members, to identifying the dynamics of family recovery and its influence on all aspects of family and individual functioning.

There were three questions of interest to this project: 1) What happens to the family when one or both parents stop drinking? 2) Is there a normal developmental process of recovery? and 3) What allows some alcoholic families to maintain recovery while others relapse (often repeatedly)?

Methodology

The research methodology was a cross-sectional design, studying 54 volunteer families who ranged in sobriety from a few months to 18 years. The study was multi-perspective (participants' data and researchers' observations) and multi-level (tests that measured individual, dyad, and family dynamics) in order to obtain a comprehensive picture of family recovery dynamics. In addition, two types of data analysis were used—qualitative (research team analyzing video tapes to determine individual and family functioning) and quantitative (a battery of paper/pencil measures administered to each family member). (Specific information on research methodology and results can be found in Brown & Lewis, 1995, 1999; Brown, Lewis, & Liotta, 2000;

Petroni, Allen-Byrd, & Lewis, 2003; Rouhbakhsh, Lewis, & Allen-Byrd, 2004.)

Due to the focus of this research, the drinking stage and its impact upon family members were studied retrospectively. Families were asked to describe the drinking years which, when combined with the data collected, provided a before and after sobriety perspective. Although painful for many, this journey into the past was necessary as family recovery cannot be fully understood without knowing what life was like, individually and systemically, during the drinking years.

Important Findings

Information from this research revealed that: a) there are normal developmental stages of recovery, b) there are different types of recovering families, and c) the early years of recovery are very traumatic. These latter two findings were surprising and clinically significant. For example, we found that the type of recovering family impacts stage development and requires different treatment approaches for both type of family and stage of recovery. The concept that the early years of recovery were traumatic came from the families' descriptions that this time was very disruptive, frightening, and dynamic. However, rather than being a negative, this "trauma" was normal, allowing for the disequilibrium and collapse of the addictive processes at the individual and system levels. In its place was a void without a map of how to navigate this necessary state. In time, the void was replaced with new knowledge, coping skills, and real-time functioning, providing the parents stayed in recovery through participation in 12-step programs, remained abstinent, and used various treatment modalities (individual, marital, familial) at different times during the recovery journey.

The early years of recovery are very traumatic.

These findings led to the emergence of two theoretical models: The Family Recovery Model and The Family Recovery Typology Model. Both models are briefly discussed below.

The Family Recovery Model

The Family Recovery Model captures the complex nature of family recovery. This complexity is critical for clinicians to understand because *rather than being the end point, abstinence is the beginning of a long and arduous journey that affects all functioning within a family.*

The Family Recovery Model has two dimensions: time and domain. Time is noted by four developmental stages: (1) drinking, (2) transition, (3) early recovery period, and (4) ongoing recovery period. Each domain is examined at three levels: the environment (family atmosphere); the system (family functioning—roles, rules, routines, communication patterns); and the individual (all family members, their emotions, cognitions, behaviors). The three domains are described in detail in *The Alcoholic Family in Recovery* (Brown & Lewis, 1999).

Developmental Recovery Stages

The following is a brief discussion of the three developmental recovery stages. See Box 1 for a summary of this information.

Transition Stage. This stage, which is characterized by the individual moving from drinking to abstinence, can last for several years during which there may be frequent shifts by the alcoholic between drinking and sobriety. The alcoholic feels completely out of control and the family system is in total chaos. The abstinence sub-stage is referred to as the "trauma of recovery"— there is the relief of sobriety and the utter terror of relapse. For example, although the adults in the family are feeling confused, frightened, and out of control, they are attempting to attend meetings and learning that recovery is possible. Their children, however, typically have no one available to them for support, information, or guidance, leaving them also feeling frightened and confused.

Early Recovery Stage. In this stage, the learning curve is steep for the parents as they are learning self-responsibility and self-care, and are slowly acquiring non-addictive lifestyles. It is a time of tremendous acquisition and application of knowledge. The alcoholic and co-alcoholic (spouse) are breaking addictive interactive patterns and learning to "separate" in order to develop their own individuality. Children and adolescents may cope by withdrawing, acting-out, "adopting" a friend's family, or attending 12-step meetings.

Ongoing Recovery Stage. In this stage, the process of recovery is becoming internalized. Recovery has become a central organizing principle (main force of focus) for the alcoholic and co-alcoholic. Life feels manageable and healthy. Problems, when they do occur, are addressed and resolved whenever possible. Parents can tolerate hearing about their children's pain and anger during the drinking and early recovery years. There is a process of healing between the parents and their now late adolescent or adult children.

Family Recovery Typology Model

The second theoretical model with significant implications for understanding recovery emerged from the finding that there were three types of families who differed dramatically from one another in terms of their recovery process. There were families who, regardless of time in recovery, seemed successful in their recovery processes while others appeared trapped in their dysfunctional patterns despite abstinence by the alcoholic.

The "successful" family style was the Type I family— both spouses were in recovery attending 12-step programs, accepting responsibility for change, and participating in therapy at different points in time. They practiced their sobriety, and recovery was a central organizing principle. The more rigid, stuck, and dysfunctional styles were found in the Type II and Type III families. In the Type II family, only one spouse was in recovery (typically the alcoholic who attended AA meetings), and the family environment and system retained the alcoholic dynamics, influences, and tensions. The alcoholic straddled two worlds: individual recovery and marital/family non-recovery. In the Type III family (of which there were only a few and the alcoholics were all males with short-term recovery), the alcoholics just quit drinking without participation in any 12-step program. Although they "looked" the best on the tests

---

Box 1
Family Recovery Model: Three Developmental Recovery Stages

	Drinking	Transition	Early Recovery	Ongoing Recovery
Alcoholic/Spouse:		Alcoholic moves from drinking to abstinence; may involve frequent shifts between drinking and sobriety, lasting several years.	Alcoholic and spouse are breaking addictive interactive patterns.	The family recovery process is becoming internalized.
Children:		Alcoholics' children typically have no supports, information, or guidance available at this time. They are left feeling frightened and confused.	Alcoholics' children may be left to cope by withdrawing, "acting out," "adopting" a friend's family, or attending 12-step meetings.	By this point, most children are now adult age. A possible healing process between the parents and children may begin.

(probably due to denial of any problems), they were the most rigid and stilted in the interviews.

Effects of Recovery on Pre-Teens and Adolescents

Recovery is a life-long process for families that is very complex, traumatic, and utterly confusing in the early years. One major and disheartening discovery in our research was that pre-teens and adolescents were generally ignored in recovery (similar to their experiences during the drinking years). When one or both spouses became sober and began participating in 12-step programs, they became immersed in working at staying sober. For example, they attended meetings, spoke a new language (recovery terms), and developed new relationships. They were told that their number one focus was to stay abstinent. The result was that their children lacked much-needed effective and active parenting.

For pre-teens and adolescents, the early years of recovery were often worse than the drinking years. For example, they had learned how to "function" in the alcoholic system while the alcoholic was drinking; but with recovery, everything changed with no understanding of what was happening to their family. According to several adult children in the study, they "preferred" the drinking period to early recovery for a variety of reasons. For example, they had learned how to read some of the "signs" associated with drinking, (such as the alcoholic going on a binge, the first drink of the day), and, consequently, knew how to affect damage control. Initial recovery, on the other hand, was fraught with unpredictable, traumatic and out-of-control dynamics resulting in uncertainty on the part of the adolescent on how to deal with these new issues.

The following vignettes demonstrate the impact of alcoholism and recovery on adolescents.

Vignette 1

In one family, the oldest adolescent overdosed on over-the-counter medication (an attempt to break the denial that there was a problem). As she was going to the hospital, she handed her mother a note saying, "Please go to AA, you are an alcoholic." Initially her mother refused, but in time she became sober, both parents went into recovery, and they became a Type I family. For the first few months in the Transition Stage, the teens would come home, find no food on the table, and become angry. "Our parents got their own place (e.g., AA and AlAnon) and new 'parents' (sponsors), and we lost the parents we knew." Six months later, the youngest child left home as he found the changes and abandonment too painful. When this family was interviewed, they were in the Ongoing Recovery Stage and the parents had developed close relationships to their now adult children. This closeness and healing was hard-earned, requiring individual, couple, and family therapy at different times in the recovery years.

Vignette 2

A late adolescent child in the study became very anxious during the research interview. His parents had been in recovery for years and were a Type I family in the Ongoing Recovery Stage. While they were describing the drinking years, he became aware of how much he had denied that there was a problem in the family while growing up. His mother (who kept her alcohol stash in a closet in his room) would frequently drive him to school functions while drunk—behavior he would say was normal or not his problem. He began to frequently stay over at his friend's house thus "adopting" another set of parents in his early teens. Since no one commented, he thought it was normal. As the interview progressed, he said, "This is making me question my reality checks, my perceptions of life." What had been his constructed reality of himself and his family was being shattered. This is threatening for young people launching into adulthood as it questions their identity and their ability to understand reality and their place in the family system. His father said that there was one regret in recovery—that they had abandoned their son to meetings and new people (sponsors, AA members, etc.), and did not help him understand what was happening or how important he was to his parents. This was a common regret expressed by parents who had years of recovery and the ability to reflect on the past (Brown & Lewis, 1999).

Vignette 3

This last vignette is adapted from Lewis and Allen-Byrd (in press) as a brief portrayal of what an adolescent may experience in the transition/early periods of recovery.

Kayla, the oldest child, was the identified caregiver in the family and was gratefully supported by the non-alcoholic parent. She assisted in household decisions and duties, provided parental guidance to the younger children, and had special privileges because of her elevated role and status in the family system. When the parents/family went into recovery, Kayla was, in essence, demoted because as the recovering parent became more actively involved in the family, Kayla's role and functions were no longer needed. Her sense of worth and power, her identity and understanding of her family's reality were taken away when her parents went into recovery leaving Kayla feeling resentful, angry, and bewildered. Without appropriate intervention, adolescents in situations similar to Kayla's will typically act out and/or withdraw from the family.

Treatment Suggestions to Support Young People

With the awareness that family recovery is difficult for pre-teens and adolescents, positive and therapeutic action can be taken. Practitioners can play a vital role in helping children make the transition from drinking into early family sobriety. They can educate the parents, normalize the process of recovery, and provide a safe place for young people to express their fears and feelings. Box 2 provides a number of examples.

The family type will dictate how practitioners can approach parents and provide parenting guidelines. The Type I family will be open and receptive to new ideas and knowledge as both parents are in recovery and accept responsibility for change,

Box 2
Strategies for Facilitating Adolescents' Healthy Transition from Family Drinking to Early Family Sobriety

- Work with parents on basic parenting skills, inform them of the importance of these skills for abating turmoil within the pre-teen and/or adolescent.
- Explain alcoholism and recovery to the pre-teen and adolescent in age-appropriate terms.
- Educate parents on the needs of adolescents who are developmentally leaving the family and may not be interested in becoming involved in the new recovery family structure and dynamics.
- Provide safe parental substitutes for their children.
- Provide opportunities for children and adolescents to become involved in Alateen, Alakid, Alatot.
- Let children know they are not responsible for their parents' alcoholism, recovery, or relapse.
- Encourage parents to ask for help before parent-child problems become a crisis.
- Refer pre-teens and adolescents for individual therapy with a therapist who understands the recovery process and can help the young person navigate through the bewildering and newly emerging family system. The therapy focus should be on helping teens define their own individuality; work through new roles, rules, boundaries; and find their own voice.

(Adapted from Lewis & Allen-Byrd, in press)

growth, and the hope of a healthy family. In the early years, they will require a great deal of external support in the form of sponsors, 12-step members, and therapists.

The Type II and III families present additional issues. In the Type II family, one member is in recovery while the family system remains alcoholic. There is chronic marital and environmental tension that, while unnamed, is typically experienced by the children. For example, the recovering alcoholic becomes the scapegoat as a way to explain problems and tension in the family, or splitting may occur when the adolescent aligns with one parent against the other. Initially the therapist can effect change by working at the marital level and educating the adults on family recovery (e.g., the three domains of recovery, how every member in the family is impacted by alcoholism, and the danger for relapse when only one parent is in recovery).

Hopefully, with intervention, the Type II family will transition into a Type I family. If the "non-alcoholic" parent refuses marital treatment in order to change the alcoholic system into a recovery system, he/she could join a group that educates families about family recovery.

Pre-teens and adolescents may join another group to become educated about family recovery, to find alternative ways to cope with the tensions and changes, and to acquire healthy ways to begin the separation and individuation process. Frequently, without appropriate intervention, the adolescents in Type II and Type III families become involved in the rebellious, acting-out phase of life.

The Type III families (who were typically in therapy for parent-child issues because their children were identified as the "cause" of the family problems) presented unique challenges. Although the alcoholic stopped drinking, nothing else changed. The alcoholic may have cognitive rigidity (black and white thinking), emotional intolerance, and be on a collision course with the adolescent who is acting out and/or attempting to break away from a stifling, straight jacket, family dynamic. During our research Type III families remained the least clear because of their defensive stance in the interviews and paper-pencil measures. For them, the first step is to break individual and systemic denial. The least threatening approach is an educational format where the adults can attend a parent group to learn about the impact of alcoholism on family members, even though no one is currently drinking, and learn healthier parenting skills (e.g., learn what the developmental needs of the pre-teen and adolescent are). There could be a parallel education group for pre-teens and adolescents wherein they could learn the effect alcoholism had on their lives and the toll it took on their personality development, as well as help them become empowered to alter internalized alcoholic processes and develop healthy choices for their future.

Limitations

There were several limitations to the study, noted by the following: (1) the participants were all volunteers; (2) they were educated (high school graduates to all levels of college degrees); (3) they were predominantly Caucasians (multiple attempts were made to recruit a greater ethnic diversity) and, (4) small sample size. Further contribution to family recovery could be made by studying single-parent families, court-ordered families, and families from other cultures.

Summary

Family recovery from alcoholism is still an unfamiliar concept in the field of addictions and treatment (Lewis & Allen-Byrd, in press; Brown & Lewis, 1995, 1999). The more knowledgeable practitioners are in the dynamics of recovery, the more effective they will be in helping families and their children move through the normal developmental processes of recovery and launching young people into healthy adulthood.

Practitioners are on the front lines providing vital and appropriate treatment plans and referrals for recovering families with children. Their understanding of the normal processes in the stages of recovery and the knowledge of the different types of families can assist them in creating more successful interventions while minimizing family relapses and preventing adolescents from acting out or withdrawing. Pre-teens and adolescents need a voice and therapists can provide a safe and knowledgeable format for them to be heard and to help guide them through the bewildering times of adolescence in general, and in family systems of recovery, in particular.

References

Brown, S. (1985). *Treating the Alcoholic: A Developmental Model of Recovery*. New York: Wiley.

Brown, S., & Lewis, V. (1995). The alcoholic family: A developmental model of recovery. In S. Brown (Ed.), *Treating Alcoholism* (pp. 279–315). San Francisco: Jossey-Bass.

Brown, S., & Lewis, V. (1999). *The Alcoholic Family in Recovery: A Developmental Model*. New York: Guilford Press.

Brown, S., Lewis, V., & Liotta, A. (2000). *The Family Recovery Guide*. Oakland, CA: New Harbinger Publications.

Lewis, V., & Allen-Byrd, L. (2001). Family recovery typology: A new theoretical model. *Alcoholism Treatment Quarterly, 19*(3), 1–17.

Lewis, V., & Allen-Byrd, L. (in press). Coping strategies for the stages of family recovery. *Alcoholism Treatment Quarterly,* special edition.

Lewis, V., Allen-Byrd, L., & Rouhbakhsh, P. (2004). Understanding successful family recovery: Two models. *Journal of Systemic Therapies, 23*(4), 39–51.

Petroni, D., Allen-Byrd, L., & Lewis, V. M. (2003). Indicators of the alcohol recovery process: Critical items from Koss-Butcher and Lachan-Wrobel analysis of the MMPI-2. *Alcoholism Treatment Quarterly, 21*(2), 41–56.

Rouhbakhsh, P., Lewis, V., & Allen-Byrd, L. (2004). Recovering alcoholic families: When normal is not normal and when is not normal healthy. *Alcoholism Treatment Quarterly, 22*(2), 35–53.

VIRGINIA LEWIS, PhD, is co-founder and co-director of the Family Recovery Project and a Senior Research Fellow at the Mental Research Institute (MRI) in Palo Alto, California. **LOIS ALLEN-BYRD,** PhD, is a Research Associate at MRI. Dr. Lewis has co-authored two books on family recovery and both she and Dr. Allen-Byrd have published numerous articles on the subject.

From *The Prevention Researcher,* November 2006, pp. 14–17. Copyright © 2006 by Integrated Research Services, Inc. Reprinted by permission. www.tpronline.com

Love but Don't Touch

Emotional infidelity is intense but invisible, erotic but unconsummated. Such delicious paradoxes make it every bit as dangerous as adultery.

MARK TEICH

She was the first girl Brendan ever kissed, the first he made love with, the first he truly loved. They'd lost their virginity together on a magical trip to Amsterdam. He felt they were soul mates and believed that their bond would never be severed. But she had suddenly broken up with him after eight months, and they lost touch until 2000, when he paid her a visit. Their exchange was unremarkable, but they traded e-mail addresses. At first, they merely sent an occasional message, chatting superficially. But the correspondence became more frequent and personal. It was easy—she was sunnier and more passionate than Brendan's wife, Lauren, who was bleary-eyed from caring for their sick son while working full-time to pay the bills. Without the burden of these responsibilities, his old love divided her days between visits to the gym and e-mails to him. Yes, she had a husband: but while Brendan was "witty and creative," she said in her lustful notes, her husband was a drone. What a high it was for Brendan to see himself through this complimentary lens after Lauren's withering view of him: hypercritical, angry, money-obsessed.

At the same time, Lauren found herself drawn to a love interest with roots in *her* past: a man she met through a website devoted to the neighborhood she grew up in. In short order, Lauren was deeply involved in an Internet relationship that kept her mood aloft throughout the day. In every way, her new companion was superior: While Brendan had set out to be a novelist, he now worked for a little health newsletter. It was Lauren's online friend, a research biologist, who spent his free hours writing a novel, and what a gifted writer he was! While Brendan talked about bills past due and criticized everything from her clothes to her weight, her online partner was fascinated by her thoughts and the minutiae of her day. He abounded in the type of wit and imagination Brendan had lacked for years. Sure, her online partner was married, too; he described his wife as remote and inaccessible—a scientist like himself, but so involved with her work that she left the child-rearing to him and almost never came home.

The New Anatomy of Infidelity

Brendan and Lauren never slept with or even touched their affair partners. Yet their emotional involvements were so all-consuming, so blinding, that they almost blew off their marriage for the disembodied fantasies of online love. Infidelity, of course, is older than the Bible. And garden-variety cheating has been on the rise for 25 years, ever since women swelled the workforce. But now, infidelity has taken a dangerous—and often profoundly stirring—new turn that psychologists call the biggest threat marriage has ever faced. Characterized by deep emotional closeness, the secret, sexually charged (but unconsummated) friendships at issue build almost imperceptibly until they surpass in importance the relationship with a spouse. Emotional involvement outside of marriage has always been intoxicating, as fictional heroines such as Anna Karenina and Emma Bovary attest. But in the age of the Internet and the egalitarian office, these relationships have become far more accessible than ever before.

The late psychologist Shirley Glass identified the trend in her 2003 book, *Not Just Friends.* "The new infidelity is between people who unwittingly form deep, passionate connections before realizing they've crossed the line from platonic friendship into romantic love," Glass wrote. Eighty-two percent of the unfaithful partners she'd counseled, she said, had had an affair with someone who was at first "just a friend." What's more, she found 55 to 65 percent of men and women alike had participated in relationships she considered *emotionall*y unfaithful—secret, sexually energized and more emotionally open than the relationship with the spouse.

Glass cited the workplace as the new minefield for marriage; 50 percent of unfaithful women and 62 percent of unfaithful men she treated were involved with someone from work. And the office has only grown more tantalizing, with women now having affairs at virtually the same rate as men. Factor in the explosive power of the Internet, and it's clear that infidelity has become an omnipresent threat. No research exists on how many affairs are happening online, but experts say they're rampant—more common than work affairs and multiplying fast.

> You go on the Internet and ask, 'Whatever happened to so and so?' Then you find him. As soon as you do, all of those raw emotions flood back.

The Slippery Slope

An emotional affair can threaten any marriage—not just those already struggling or in disrepair.

"No one's immune," says Peggy Vaughan, author of *The Monogamy Myth* and creator of the website, DearPeggy.com, where surveys and discussion reflect the zeitgeist. Although those with troubled marriages are especially susceptible, a surprising number of people with solid relationships respond to the novelty and are swept away as well.

Because it is so insidious, its boundaries so fuzzy, the emotional affair's challenge to marriage is initially hard to detect. It might seem natural to discuss personal concerns with an Internet buddy or respond to an office mate having trouble with a spouse. But slowly, imperceptibly, there's an "emotional switch." The friends have built a bubble of secrecy around their relationship and shifted allegiance from their marriage partners to the affair.

Web of Deceit

The perfect petri dish for secret, sexually charged relationships is, of course, the Internet. The new American affair can take place right in the family room; within feet of children and an unsuspecting spouse, the unfaithful can swap sex talk and let emotions run amok.

Often, it's the anonymity of online encounters that invites emotional disclosure, says Israeli philosopher Aaron Ben-Ze'ev, president of the University of Haifa and author of *Love Online*. "Like strangers on a train who confess everything to an anonymous seatmate, people meeting online reveal what they might never tell a real-world partner. When people reveal so much, there is great intimacy." But the revelations are selective: Without chores to do or children to tend, the friends relate with less interference from practical constraints, allowing fantasy to take hold. Over the Internet, adds Ben-Ze'ev, the power of imagination is especially profound.

In fact, says MIT psychologist Sherry Turkle, author of *Life on the Screen: Identity in the Age of the Internet*, it's particularly what's *withheld*—the "low bandwidth" of the information online partners share—that makes these relationships so fantasy-rich and intense. She compares the phenomenon to that of transference in psychotherapy—where patients, knowing little about their therapists, invest them with the qualities they want and need. Similarly, the illicit partner is always partly a fantasy, inevitably seen as wittier, warmer and sexier than the spouse.

So is online love real? "It has all the elements of real love," says Ben-Ze'ev: obsessive thoughts of the lover, an urgent need to be together and the feeling that the new partner is the most

---

Are You an Emotional Cheat? 7 Telltale Signs

Ever since Scarlett O'Hara flirted in front of Rhett Butler, the jury has been out on extramarital friendships that are sensual, even intimate, yet don't cross the line to actual sex. With emotional affairs so prevalent, psychologists studying the issue have finally drawn some lines in the sand. You may be emotionally unfaithful, they say, if you:

- Have a special confidante at the office, someone receptive to feelings and fears you can't discuss with your partner or spouse.
- Share personal information and negative feelings about your primary relationship with a "special friend."
- Meet a friend of the opposite sex for dinner and go back to his or her place to discuss your primary relationship over a drink, never calling your partner and finally arriving home at 3 A.M.
- Humiliate your partner in front of others, suggesting he or she is a loser or inadequate sexually.
- Have the energy to tell your stories only once, and decide to save the juiciest for an office or Internet friend of the opposite sex.
- Hook up with an old boyfriend or girlfriend at a high school reunion and, feeling the old spark, decide to keep in contact by e-mail.
- Keep secret, password-protected Internet accounts, "just in case," or become incensed if your partner inadvertently glances at your "private things."

---

wonderful person on earth. You experience the same chemical rush that people get when they fall in love.

"But the chemicals don't last, and then we learn how difficult it is to remain attached to a partner in a meaningful way," points out Connecticut psychologist Janis Abrahams Spring, author of *After the Affair*.

Blasts from the Past

People may be exceptionally vulnerable to affairs when they reconnect with someone from their past, for whom they may have long harbored feelings. "It's very common online," says Vaughan. "You go on the Internet, and the first thing you say to yourself is, 'What happened to so and so?' Then you go find them."

Lorraine and Sam had been high school friends during the Sixties, and even camped out together at Woodstock in 1969. In love with Sam but "awed by his brilliance," Lorraine remained too shy to confess. Then he went off to the University of Chicago while she stayed in New Jersey. She married and had a family, but the idea of Sam still smoldered: If only she had admitted her love!

One day she Googled him and located him in Chicago—and they began to correspond by e-mail. He was a partner in a law firm, had a physician wife and coached his daughter's

Inoculating Your Relationship

The biggest mistake couples make is taking monogamy for granted. Instead, they should take affairs for granted and protect themselves by heading infidelity off at the pass.

As part of a proactive approach, psychologist Barry McCarthy suggests couples discuss the importance of fidelity from the outset, identifying the type of situation that would put each at greatest risk. Is drinking on a business trip your downfall, or the novelty of an exotic individual from a far-off locale? Whatever your weakness, work together to make sure you help each other walk past it.

As for Internet relationships, Peggy Vaughan says the safest way to protect the primary relationship is to "make sure that no online interactions are secret. This means having your partner agree that neither of you will say anything to someone online that you aren't willing for the other one to read. If they resist and invoke privacy rights," she adds, "it is probably because they already have something to hide."

Miami Beach psychologist M. Gary Neuman recommends that in addition to setting limits, you actively build the bond with your partner every day. Among the protective strategies he suggests are exchanging "five daily touch points," or emotional strokes, ranging from bringing your partner a cup of tea to a kiss and hug. He also suggests that partners talk for 40 minutes, uninterrupted, four times a week and go on a weekly date. "It's so easy," Neuman says, "to forget why we fell in love."

—MT

Little League team. "Originally I e-mailed just to say, 'hi,'" she explains. But after a few friendly notes, Sam sent a confession. He'd always been in love with her. But her beauty had daunted him, so he'd settled for a plain, practical woman—his wife—instead. E-mails and then phone calls between Lorraine and Sam soon became constant, whipping both of them into a frenzy of heat and remorse. "I can't stop thinking about you. I'm obsessed," one of Sam's e-mails said. But Sam could never get away, never meet face-to-face. "I feel so guilty," he confessed.

That's when Lorraine stopped sending e-mails or taking his calls. "He was a coward," she says, adding that he disappointed her even more by "begging to continue the affair over the phone."

What kind of person chooses to remain immersed in fantasy? It could be someone who "compartmentalizes the two relationships," psychologist Janis Abrahms Spring suggests. "The person may not want to replace the marriage partner, but may want that extra high."

A woman may languish for years in the throes of her "special friendship," while her male counterpart considers it a nice addition to his life.

Women in Love

Frank Pittman, author of *Private Lies,* says that Lorraine lucked out. If she's like most of those involved in Internet affairs, "the face-to-face meeting would have killed it." And if she'd run off with Sam, it probably would have been far worse. "In the history of these crazy romantic affairs, when people throw everything away for a fantasy, the success rate of the new relationship is very low," he explains.

But Lorraine was just acting true to her gender. It is the woman who typically pushes the relationship from friendship to love, from virtual to actual, says Pittman. It's the woman who gets so emotionally involved she sees the affair as a possible replacement for her marriage—even if her marriage is good—and wants to test that out.

American University professor of psychology and affair expert Barry McCarthy explains that for men, "most affairs are high opportunity and low involvement. For women, an affair is more emotional. President Clinton and Monica Lewinsky are the prototypes," he says.

How does this translate to emotional infidelity, where opportunity may be thwarted but emotion reigns supreme? Some men have begun following female patterns, placing more emphasis on emotion than in the past, while women are increasingly open to sex, especially as they achieve more financial independence and have less to fear from divorce.

Even so, says Peggy Vaughan, women are usually far more involved in these relationships than men. A woman may languish for years in the throes of her "special friendship," while her male counterpart considers it a nice addition to the life he already has. As a result, men and women involved in emotional dalliances often see the same affair in different ways. The woman will see her soul mate, and the man will be having fun. Sometimes, says Ben-Ze'ev, a woman will feel totally invested in an affair, but her partner will be conducting two or even four such affairs at once. (The pattern holds for consummated affairs, too.)

For women, the dangers are great. When an emotional affair results in sex, the man's interest usually cools instantly, says Pittman. Meanwhile, husbands are less forgiving than wives, making it more likely for a woman caught up in such an entanglement to be slammed with divorce.

Total Transparency?

With easy access to emotional relationships so powerful they pass for love, how can we keep our primary relationships intact? Psychotherapist M. Gary Neuman of Miami Beach, author of *Emotional Infidelity,* draws a hard line, advocating a rigorous affair-avoidance strategy that includes such strictures as refusing to dance or even eat lunch with a member of the opposite sex. Vaughan suggests we put transparency in our Web dealings—no secret e-mail accounts or correspondence a partner wouldn't be welcome to see.

Others say such prescriptives may be extreme. "Some Internet relationships are playful," Turkle comments. "People may take on different identities or express different aspects

After Infidelity: The Road Back

An emotional affair can deliver a body blow to a marriage, but it rarely results in divorce. Instead, couples can navigate recovery to make their union stronger than before.

The first step in recovery, says psychologist Barry McCarthy, is honesty. "It is secrecy that enables affairs to thrive. The cover-up, for most people, is worse than the actual infidelity," he says. "So it's only by putting everything on the table that you'll be able to move on."

"The involved partner must be honest about all aspects of the affair," says author Peggy Vaughan. Moving on too fast usually backfires, leaving the injured party reeling and the problem unresolved. "Many people believe that too much discussion just reopens the wound; but, in fact, the wound needs to be exposed to the light of day so that it can heal." The involved partner must answer questions and soothe the injured partner for as long as that person needs.

Psychologist Janis Abrahms Spring says the ultimate goal is restoring trust and suggests couples make a list of the trust-enhancing behaviors that will help them heal. Both partners may need compassion for their feelings, she says, but "the hurt partner shoulders a disproportionate share of the burden of recovery and may require some sacrificial gifts to redress the injury caused." These may range from a request that the unfaithful partner change jobs to avoid contact with the "special friend" to access to that partner's e-mail account.

McCarthy, meanwhile, emphasizes that sexual intimacy should resume as soon as possible, as part of the effort to restore closeness and trust.

"In the course of an emotional affair, you open the window to your affair partner and wall off your spouse," McCarthy says. "To repair the marriage, you must open your windows to your partner and wall off the affair."

—MT

"Someone may want just a chess partner, and the technology allows for that."

But if you're going to permit some leeway in the context of your marriage, where do you draw the line? "It's a slippery slope," says Ben-Ze'ev. "You may set limits with your spouse—no phone contact, don't take it off the screen. But people can break the deal. It is a profound human characteristic that sometimes we cross the line."

At best, notes Turkle, a serious emotional affair can alert you to problems in the primary relationship. The injured partner can view it as "a wake-up call" that needs are not being met.

It was perhaps no more than the glimmer of that alarm that enabled Brendan and Lauren to navigate back home. For both, that happened when fantasy clashed with reality—especially when they needed to pull together and care for their sick son. Brendan told Lauren he wanted to take some time to "visit his dad," when his intent was to see his old girlfriend. "I'm so exhausted. Please don't go," Lauren had said, finally asking for help. Using the excuse of a book deadline, she soon began answering e-mails from her online partner only sporadically, then hardly at all.

The illicit partner is always partly a fantasy, she or he is inevitably seen as wittier, warmer and sexier than the spouse.

What had caused them to pull back? On one level it was the need to care for their child, but on another, it was the realization that their online affairs had been a diversion from intimacy, not intimacy itself.

"The idea of actually meeting made me feel ill. I was relieved when Lauren asked me to help at home," Brendan confesses.

"There was so much about my life I never discussed in those e-mails," says Lauren. "In the end, all that witty, arch banter was just a persona, and another job."

of self; an introvert can play at extroversion, a man at being a woman." The experience may be transformative or casual.

MARK TEICH is publications manager of the Skin Cancer Foundation.

Is This Man Cheating on His Wife?

Alexandra Alter

On a scorching July afternoon, as the temperature creeps toward 118 degrees in a quiet suburb east of Phoenix, Ric Hoogestraat sits at his computer with the blinds drawn, smoking a cigarette. While his wife, Sue, watches television in the living room, Ric chats online with what appears on the screen to be a tall, slim redhead.

He's never met the woman outside of the computer world of *Second Life,* a well-chronicled digital fantasyland with more than 8 million registered "residents" who get jobs, attend concerts, and date other users. He's never so much as spoken to her on the telephone. But their relationship has taken on curiously real dimensions. They own two dogs, pay a mortgage together, and spend hours shopping at the mall and taking long motorcycle rides. This May, when Ric, 53, needed real-life surgery, the redhead cheered him up with a private island that cost her $120,000 in the virtual world's currency, or about $480 in real-world dollars. Their bond is so strong that three months ago, Ric asked Janet Spielman, the 38-year-old Canadian woman who controls the redhead, to become his virtual wife.

The woman to whom he's legally wed is not amused. "It's really devastating," says Sue Hoogestraat, a 58-year-old export agent who married Ric just seven months ago. "You try to talk to someone or bring them a drink, and they'll be having sex with a cartoon."

While many busy people can't fathom the idea of taking on another set of commitments, especially imaginary ones, *Second Life* and other multiplayer games are complicating many lives besides the Hoogestraats.' With some 30 million people now involved worldwide, there is mounting concern that some are squandering, even damaging their real lives by obsessing over their "second" ones. According to a recent survey of 30,000 gamers, nearly 40 percent of men and 53 percent of women who play online games said their virtual friends were equal to or better than their real-life friends. More than a quarter of gamers said the emotional highlight of the past week occurred in a computer world.

A burly man with a long gray ponytail and a handlebar mustache, Ric Hoogestraat looks like the cross between a techie and the Grateful Dead fan that he is. He drives a motorcycle and wears faded black Harley-Davidson T-shirts around the house. A former college computer graphics teacher, Ric was never much of a game enthusiast before he discovered *Second Life.* But since February, he's been spending six hours a night as Dutch Hoorenbeek, his 6-foot-9, muscular, motorcycle-riding cyberself.

In the virtual world, he's a successful entrepreneur with a net worth of about $1.5 million in the site's currency, the linden, which can be purchased through the site at a rate of about 250 lindens per U.S. dollar. He owns a mall, a private beach club, a dance club, and a strip club. He has 25 employees, online persons known as avatars who are operated by other players, including a security guard, a mall concierge, and the "exotic" dancers at his club. He designs bikinis and lingerie, and sells them through his chain store, Red Headed Lovers. "Here, you're in total control," he says, moving his avatar through the mall using the arrow keys on his keyboard.

Virtual worlds like *Second Life* have fast become a testing ground for the limits of relationships, both online and off. The site's audience of more than 8 million is up from 100,000 in January 2006, though the number of active users is closer to 450,000, according to the site's parent company, Linden Lab. A typical "gamer" spends 20 to 40 hours a week in a virtual world.

Though academics have only recently begun to intensively study the social dynamics of virtual worlds, some are saying that they are astonished by how closely virtual relationships mirror real life. On a neurological level, says Byron Reeves, a Stanford University professor, players may not be distinguishing between virtual and real-life relationships. "Our brains are not specialized for 21st-century media," he says. "There's no switch that says, 'Process this differently because it's on a screen.'"

On a Saturday afternoon in July, Ric Hoogestraat decides to go to the beach. So he lights a cigarette and enters *Second Life,* becoming one of 42,752 people logged on at the time. Immediately, he gets an instant message from Tenaj Jackalope, his *Second Life* wife, saying she'll be right there.

They meet at their home, a modern-looking building that overlooks the ocean, then head to his beach club. A full-blown dance party is under way. A dozen avatars, digital representations of other live players, gyrate on the sand, twisting their hips and waving their arms. Several dance topless and some are fully nude. Dutch gets pelted with instant messages.

"What took you so long, Dutch?" a dancer asks.

"Howdy, Boss Man," an avatar named Whiskey Girl says.

Before discovering *Second Life,* Hoogestraat had bounced between places and jobs, working as an elementary schoolteacher and a ski instructor, teaching computer graphics, and spending two years on the road selling herbs and essential oils at Renaissance fairs. Along the way, he picked up a bachelor's degree and took graduate courses at both the University of Wyoming and the University of Arizona. He currently works as a call-center operator for Vangent Inc., a corporation that outsources calls for the government and private companies. He makes $14 an hour.

Hoogestraat learned about *Second Life* in February, while watching a morning news segment. His mother had just been hospitalized with pancreatic cancer—she died two weeks later—and he wanted a distraction. He was fascinated by the virtual world's freewheeling atmosphere. With his computer graphics background, he quickly learned how to build furniture and design clothing. He upgraded his avatar, buying stomach muscles and special hair that sways when he walks. Before long, Hoogestraat was spending most nights and weekends acting out his avatar's life.

When Hoogestraat was diagnosed with diabetes and a failing gallbladder a few months ago, he was homebound for five weeks. Some days, he played from a quarter to 6 in the morning until 2 in the morning, eating in front of the computer and pausing only for bathroom breaks.

During one marathon session, Hoogestraat met Tenaj (Janet spelled backward) while shopping. They became fast friends, then partners. A week later, he asked her to move into his apartment. In May, they married in a small ceremony in a garden over-looking a pond. Thirty of their avatar friends attended. "There's a huge trust between us," says Spielman, who is a divorced mother of two living in Calgary, Alberta. "We'll tell each other everything."

That intimacy hasn't spilled into real life. They never speak and have no plans to meet.

Still, Hoogestraat's real-life wife is losing patience with her husband's second life. "Everybody has their hobbies," says Sue Hoogestraat, who is dark-haired and heavy-set. "But when it's from 6 in the morning until 2 in the morning, that's not a hobby, that's your life."

The real Mrs. Hoogestraat is no stranger to online communities—she met her husband in a computer chat room three years ago. Both were divorced and had adult children from previous marriages, and Sue says she was relieved to find someone educated and adventurous after years of failed relationships. Now, as she cooks, does laundry, takes care of

three dogs, and empties ash-trays around the house while her husband spends hours designing outfits for virtual strippers and creating labels for virtual coffee cups, she wonders what happened to the person she married.

One Saturday night in early June, she discovered his cyber wife. He called her over to the computer to show her an outfit he had designed. There, above the image of the redheaded model, it said "Mrs. Hoorenbeek." When she confronted him, he huffily replied that it was just a game.

Two weeks later, Sue joined an online support group for spouses of obsessive online gamers called EverQuest Widows, named after another popular online fantasy game that players call Evercrack.

"It's avalanched beyond repair," says Sharra Goddard, 30, Sue Hoogestraat's daughter. Goddard says she and her two brothers have offered to help their mother move out of the house.

Sue says she's not ready to separate though. "I'm not a monster; I can see how it fulfills parts of his life that he can no longer do because of physical limitations, because of his age. His avatar, it's him at 25," she says. "He's a good person. He's just fallen down this rabbit hole."

Ric, for his part, doesn't feel he's being unfaithful. "I tried to get her involved so we could play together," he says. "But she wasn't interested."

Early in the morning on the day after Dutch and Tanej's virtual beach party, Ric Hoogestraat is back at his computer, wearing the same Harley-Davidson T-shirt he had on the day before. Four hours after logging on, he manipulates his avatar, who is wearing cut-off denim shorts and renovating the lower level of his mall. "Sunday is my heavy-duty work day," he explains.

From the kitchen, Sue asks if he wants breakfast. Ric doesn't answer. She sets a plate of breakfast pockets on the computer console and goes into the living room to watch a dog competition on television. For two hours, he focuses intently on building a coffee shop for the mall. Two other avatars gather to watch as he builds a counter, using his cursor to resize wooden planks.

At 12:05, he's ready for a break. He changes his avatar into jeans and motorcycle chaps, and "teleports" to a place with a curvy mountain road. It's one of his favorite places for riding his Harley look-alike. The road is empty. He weaves his motorcycle across the lanes. Sunlight glints off the ocean in the distance.

Sue pauses on her way to the kitchen and glances at the screen.

"You didn't eat your breakfast," she says.

"I'm sorry, I didn't see it there," Ric responds.

Over the next five hours, he is barely aware of his physical surroundings. He adds potted palms to his cafe, goes swimming through a sunken castle off his water-front property, chats with friends at a biker clubhouse, meets a new store owner at the mall, counsels an avatar friend who had recently split up with her avatar boyfriend, and shows his wife, Tenaj, the coffee shop he's built.

By 4 P.M., he's been in *Second Life* for 10 hours, pausing only to go to the bathroom. His wrists and fingers ache from manipulating the mouse. His back hurts. Yet he feels it's worth the effort. "If I work a little harder and make it a little nicer, it's more rewarding," he says.

Sitting alone in the living room in front of the television, Sue says she worries it will be years before her husband realizes that he's traded his real life for a pixilated fantasy existence, one in which she's been replaced.

"This other life is so wonderful; it's better than real life," she says. "Nobody gets fat, nobody gets gray. The person that's left can't compete with that."

The Opt-Out Myth

E. J. GRAFF

On October 26, 2003, *The New York Times Magazine* jump-started a century-long debate about women who work. On the cover it featured "The Opt Out Revolution," Lisa Belkin's semipersonal essay, with this banner: Why don't more women get to the top? They choose not to. Inside, by telling stories about herself and eight other Princeton grads who no longer work full-time, Belkin concluded that women were just too smart to believe that ladder-climbing counted as real success.

But Belkin's "revolution"—the idea that well-educated women are fleeing their careers and choosing instead to stay home with their babies—has been touted many times before. As Joan C. Williams notes in her meticulously researched report, "Opt Out or Pushed Out? How the Press Covers Work/Family Conflict," released in October 2006 by the University of California Hastings Center for WorkLife Law, where she is the director, *The New York Times* alone has highlighted this "trend" repeatedly over the last fifty years: in 1953 (Case History of an Ex-Working Mother), 1961 (Career Women Discover Satisfactions in the Home), 1980 (Many Young Women Now Say They'd Pick Family over Career), 1998 (The Stay-at-Home Mother), and 2005 (Many Women at Elite Colleges Set Career Path to Motherhood).

And yet during the same years, the U.S. has seen steady upticks in the numbers and percentages of women, including mothers, who work for wages. Economists agree that the increase in what they dryly call "women's participation in the waged workforce" has been critical to American prosperity, demonstrably pushing up our GDP. The vast majority of contemporary families cannot get by without women's income—especially now, when upwards of 70 percent of American families with children have all adults in the work force, when 51 percent of American women live without a husband, and when many women can expect to live into their eighties and beyond.

The moms-go-home story keeps coming back, in part, because it's based on some kernels of truth. Women *do* feel forced to choose between work and family. Women *do* face a sharp conflict between cultural expectations and economic realities. The workplace is still demonstrably more hostile to mothers than to fathers. Faced with the "choice" of feeling that they've failed to be *either* good mothers or good workers, many women wish they could—or worry that they should—abandon the struggle and stay home with the kids.

The problem is that the moms-go-home storyline presents all those issues as personal rather than public—and does so in misleading ways. The stories' statistics are selective, their anecdotes about upper-echelon white women are misleading, and their "counterintuitive" narrative line parrots conventional ideas about gender roles. Thus they erase most American families' real experiences and the resulting social policy needs from view.

Here's why that matters: if journalism repeatedly frames the wrong problem, then the folks who make public policy may very well deliver the wrong solution. If women are happily choosing to stay home with their babies, that's a private decision. But it's a public policy issue if most women (and men) need to work to support their families, and if the economy needs women's skills to remain competitive. It's a public policy issue if schools, jobs, and other American institutions are structured in ways that make it frustratingly difficult, and sometimes impossible, for parents to manage both their jobs and family responsibilities.

So how can this story be killed off, once and for all? Joan Williams attempts to chloroform the moms-go-home storyline with facts. "Opt Out or Pushed Out?" should be on every news, business, and feature editor's desk. It analyzes 119 representative newspaper articles, published between 1980 and 2006, that use the opt-out storyline to discuss women leaving the workplace. While business sections regularly offer more informed coverage of workplace issues, the "opt out" trend stories get more prominent placement, becoming "the chain reaction story that flashes from the *Times* to the columnists to the evening news to the cable shows," says Caryl Rivers, a Boston University journalism professor and the author of *Selling Anxiety: How the News Media Scare Women* (April 2007).

There are a number of problems with the moms-go-home storyline. First, such articles focus excessively on a tiny proportion of American women—white, highly educated, in well-paying professional/managerial jobs. Just 8 percent of American working women fit this demographic, writes Williams. The percentage is smaller still if you're dealing only with white women who graduated from the Ivies and are married to high-earning men, as Belkin's article does. Furthermore, only 4 percent of women in their mid-to late thirties with children have advanced degrees and are in a privileged income bracket like that of Belkin's fellow Princeton grads, according to Heather Boushey, a senior economist with the Center for Economic and Policy Research. That group is far more likely than average women to be married when they give birth (91 percent, as opposed to 73 percent of all women), and thus to have a second income on which to survive. But because journalists and editors increasingly come from and socialize in this class, their anecdotes loom large in our personal rearview mirrors—and in our most influential publications. Such women are chastised for working by Caitlin Flanagan (a woman rich enough to stay home and have a nanny!) in *The Atlantic,* and for lacking ambition by Linda Hirshman in *The American Prospect.* But such "my-friends-and-me" coverage is an irresponsible approach to major issues being wrestled with by every American family and employer.

The stories are misleading in a second important way. Williams's report points out that "opt-out stories invariably focus on women in one particular situation: after they have 'opted out' but before any of them divorce." The women in those articles often say their skills can be taken right back onto the job. It's a sweetly optimistic notion, but studies show that, on average, professional women who come back after time away—or even after working part-time, since U.S. women working part-time earn 21 percent less per hour worked than those who work full-time—take a hefty and sustained pay cut, and a severe cut in responsibility level. Meanwhile, nearly 50 percent of American marriages end in divorce, according to the latest census figures. While numbers are lower for marriages in the professional class, divorce remains a real possibility. Williams points to Terry Martin Hekker, one of the opt-out mothers, who in 1977 published an op-ed in *The New York Times* entitled, "The Satisfactions of Housewifery and Motherhood in 'An Age of Do-Your-Own-Thing.'" In 2006, Hekker wrote—again in the *Times,* but demoted to the Sunday Style section—about having been divorced and financially abandoned: "He got to take his girlfriend to Cancun, while I got to sell my engagement ring to pay the roofer."

In other words, interview these opt-out women fifteen years later—or forty years later, when they're trying to live on skimpy retirement incomes—and you might hear a more jaundiced view of their "choices."

The opt-out stories have a more subtle, but equally serious, flaw: their premise is entirely ahistorical. Their opening lines often suggest that a generation of women is flouting feminist expectations and heading back home. At the simplest factual level, that's false. Census numbers show no increase in mothers exiting the work force, and according to Heather Boushey, the maternity leaves women do take have gotten shorter. Furthermore, college-educated women are having their children later, in their thirties—after they've established themselves on the job, rather than before. Those maternity leaves thus come in mid-career, rather than pre-career. Calling that "opting out" is misleading. As Alice Kessler-Harris, a labor historian at Columbia University, put it, "I define that as redistributing household labor to adequately take care of one's family." She adds that even while at home, most married women keep bringing in family income, as women traditionally have. Today, women with children are selling real estate, answering phone banks,

or doing office work at night when the kids are in bed. Early in the twentieth century, they might have done piecework, taken in laundry, or fed the boarders. Centuries earlier, they would have been the business partners who took goods to market, kept the shop's accounts, and oversaw the adolescent labor (once called housemaids and dairymaids, now called nannies and daycare workers).

Which brings us to an even deeper historical flaw: editors and reporters forget that Belkin's generation isn't post-feminism; it's mid-feminism. Women's entrance into the waged work force has been moving in fits and starts over the past century. Earlier generations of college-educated women picked either work *or* family, work *after* family, or family *after* work; those who graduated in the 1980s and 1990s—Belkin's cohort—are the first to expect to do both at the same time. And so these women are shocked to discover that, although 1970s feminists knocked down the barrier to entering the professions in large numbers, the workplace still isn't fixed. They are standing on today's feminist frontier: the bias against mothers that remains embedded on the job, in the culture, and at home.

Given that reality, here's the biggest problem with the moms-go-home storyline: it begins and ends with women saying they are *choosing* to go home, and ignores the contradictory data sandwiched in between.

Williams establishes that "choice" is emphasized in eighty-eight of the 119 articles she surveyed. But keep reading. Soon you find that staying home wasn't these women's first choice, or even their second. Rather, every other door slammed. For instance, Belkin's prime example of someone who "chose" to stay home, Katherine Brokaw, was a high-flying lawyer until she had a child. Soon after her maternity leave, she exhausted herself working around the clock to prepare for a trial—a trial that, at the last minute, was canceled so the judge could go fishing. After her firm refused even to consider giving her "part-time" hours—forty hours now being considered part-time for high-end lawyers—she "chose" to quit.

More than a third of the articles in Williams's report cite "workplace inflexibility" as a reason mothers leave their jobs. Nearly half mention how lonely and depressed those women get when they've been downgraded to full-time nannies. Never do such articles cite decades of social science research showing that women are happier when occupying several roles; that homemakers' well-being suffers compared to that of working women; or that young adults who grew up in dual-earner families would choose the same family model for their own kids. Rarely do such articles ask how husband and wife negotiated which one of them would sacrifice a career. Only by ignoring both the women's own stories and the larger context can the moms-go-home articles keep chirping on about choice and about how such women now have "the best job in the world."

Underlying all this is a genuinely new trend that the moms-go-home stories never mention: the all-or-nothing workplace. At every income level, Americans work longer hours today than fifty years ago. Mandatory overtime for blue- and pink-collar workers, and eighty-hour expectations for full-time professional workers, deprive everyone of a reasonable family life. Blue-collar and low-wage families increasingly work "tag-team" schedules so that someone's always home with the kids. In surveys done by the Boston College Sloan Work and Families Research Network and by the New York-based Families and Work Institute, among others, women and men increasingly say that they'd like to have more time with their families, and would give up money and advancement to do it—if doing so didn't mean sacrificing their careers entirely. Men, however, must face fierce cultural headwinds to choose such a path, while women are pushed in that direction at every turn.

Finally, the opt-out articles never acknowledge the widespread hostility toward working mothers. Researching the book I wrote for Evelyn Murphy in 2005, *Getting Even: Why Women Don't Get Paid Like Men—and What to Do About It,* I was startled by how many lawsuits were won because managers openly and publicly told women that they couldn't be hired because they were pregnant; or that having a child would hurt them; or that it was simply impossible for women to both work and raise kids. Many other women we talked with had the same experience, but chose not to ruin their lives by suing. One lawyer who'd been on the partner track told us that once she had her second child, her colleagues refused to give her work in her highly remunerative specialty, saying that she now had other priorities—even though she kept meeting her deadlines, albeit after the kids were asleep. She was denied partnership. A high-tech project manager told me that when she was pregnant in 2002, she was asked: Do you feel stupider? Her colleague wasn't being mean; he genuinely wanted to know if pregnancy's hormones had dumbed her down. Or consider the experience of Dr. Diane Fingold, an internist at Massachusetts General Hospital in Boston and an assistant professor at Harvard Medical School, where she won the 2002 Faculty Prize for Excellence in Teaching, the school's highest teaching award. Her credentials are outstanding, yet when she asked to work three-and-a-half fewer hours a week so that she could manage her family demands—"just a little flexibility for a short period in my life!"—her practice refused. She was enraged. "I thought hard about leaving medicine altogether," she said. Her husband is a successful venture capitalist whose "annual Christmas bonus is what I make in a year!"

Had Fingold left, in other words, she would have fit neatly with Belkin's hyperachievers. But she loves practicing and teaching medicine, and realized she couldn't reenter at the same level if she walked away entirely. So she moved to another practice that was willing to accommodate her part-time schedule until, in a few years, she can return to full-time. Had she chosen the Belkin course, would she have opted out—or been pushed out?

Experiences like Fingold's bear out what social scientists are finding: strong bias against mothers, especially white mothers, who work. (Recent research shows bias against African American mothers of any class who don't work, a subject that deserves an article of its own.) Consider the work being done by Shelley Correll, a Cornell sociology professor, described in an article in the March 2007 *American Journal of Sociology.* In one experiment, Correll and her colleagues asked participants to rate a management consultant. Everyone got a profile of an equally qualified consultant—except that the consultant was variously described as a woman with children, a woman without children, a man with children, and a man without children. When the consultant was a "mother," she was rated as less competent, less committed, less suitable for hiring, promotion, or training, and was offered a lower starting salary than the other three.

Here's what feminism hasn't yet changed: the American idea of mothering is left over from the 1950s, that odd moment in history when America's unrivaled economic power enabled a single breadwinner to support an entire family. Fifty years later we still have the idea that a mother, and not a father, should be available to her child at every moment. But if being a mom is a 24-hour-a-day job, and being a worker requires a similar commitment, then the two roles are mutually exclusive. A lawyer might be able to juggle the demands of many complex cases in various stages of research and negotiation, or a grocery manager might be able to juggle dozens of delivery deadlines and worker schedules—but should she have even a fleeting thought about a pediatrics appointment, she's treated as if her on-the-job reliability will evaporate. No one can escape that cultural idea, reinforced as it is by old sitcoms, movies, jokes—and by the moms-go-home storyline.

Still, if they were pushed out, why would smart, professional women insist that they chose to stay home? Because that's the most emotionally healthy course: wanting what you've got. "That's really one of the agreed-upon principles of human nature. People want their attitudes and behavior to be in sync," said Amy Cuddy, an assistant professor in the management and organizations department at Northwestern Kellogg School of Management. "People who've left promising careers to stay home with their kids aren't going to say, 'I was forced out. I really want to be there.' It gives people a sense of control that they may not actually have."

So yes, maybe some women "chose" to go home. But they didn't choose the restrictions and constrictions that made their work lives impossible. They didn't choose the cultural expectation that mothers, not fathers, are responsible for their children's doctor visits, birthday parties, piano lessons, and summer schedules. And they didn't choose the bias or earnings loss that they face if they work part-time or when they go back full time.

By offering a steady diet of common myths and ignoring the relevant facts, newspapers have helped maintain the cultural temperature for what Williams calls "the most family-hostile public policy in the Western world." On a variety of basic policies—including parental leave, family sick leave, early childhood education, national childcare standards, after school programs, and health care that's not tied to a single all-consuming job—the U.S. lags behind almost every developed nation. How far behind? Out of 168 countries surveyed by Jody Heymann, who teaches at both the Harvard School of Public Health and McGill University, the U.S. is one of only five without mandatory paid maternity leave—along with Lesotho, Liberia, Papua New Guinea, and Swaziland. And any parent could tell you that it makes no sense to keep running schools on nineteenth century agricultural schedules, taking kids in at 7 A.M. and letting them out at 3 P.M. to milk the cows, when their parents now work until 5 or 6 P.M. Why can't twenty-first century school schedules match the twenty-first century workday?

The moms-go-home story's personal focus makes as much sense, according to Caryl Rivers, as saying, "Okay, let's build a superhighway; everybody bring one paving stone. That's how we approach family policy. We don't look at systems, just at individuals. And that's ridiculous."

E. J. GRAFF is senior researcher at Brandeis University's Schuster Institute for Investigative Journalism. From "The opt-out myth: most moms have to work to make ends meet. So why does the press write only about the elite few who don't?" *Columbia Journalism Review* 45.6 (March-April 2007): 51(4).

Making Time for Family Time

Advice from early-career psychologists on how they juggle family and career.

TORI DEANGELIS

Starting your psychology career is one of the most exciting—and stressful—times of your life. It's also a period when many early-career psychologists take on new personal responsibilities, such as marrying, starting families and caring for aging parents.

Pulling this off is a lot like spinning plates, and the field's expectations don't make it any easier, says Carol Williams-Nickelson, PsyD, associate executive director of the American Psychological Association of Graduate Students (APAGS), herself working at APA and raising a family.

"There's still a pretty strong undercurrent, especially for women, that career needs to come first if you want to advance," she says.

Other factors make this scenario even more complex, other early-career experts say. For some women, it's the ticking biological clock; for many men, it's changing roles in relation to family and work.

Capt. Jason Prinster, PhD, whose internship led into his current job heading the mental health clinic at the Nellis Air Force Base in North Las Vegas, reflects this attitude.

"Three years from now, my wife could be the one making more money, and I could be the one taking the kids to work and working part time," Prinster says. "I don't think my dad ever had that thought 30 years ago."

Yet to some extent, work places still stigmatize men who openly say they value family as much as work, which puts such men in a bind, Williams-Nickelson adds.

Given these complexities, it helps to get advice from people on the front lines. Early-career experts recommend that you:

- **Communicate.** It's Psych 101, but it's true: Good communication greases the wheels of family sanity, other early-career experts say. A case in point is Jay Robertson-Howell, PsyD, a psychologist at Seattle University's counseling and psychological services center who is raising two young children with his partner, veterinarian Travis Robertson-Howell, DVM. He and Travis make sure to talk not only about each other's needs, but also the needs of the family and their professional concerns, Robertson-Howell says. As time

pressures mount, it's easier to avoid hard topics: "We constantly have to remind ourselves to keep at it," he says.

- **Negotiate.** A central tenet of good communication is agreeing on the particulars of duties and schedules, other early-career psychologists say. While couples arrange these basics in different ways, it's important for both people to discuss and agree on the arrangements and be willing to tweak them as necessary, Prinster says.

Balancing work and family is a lot like spinning plates, and psychology's expectations don't make it any easier.

For instance, Prinster and his wife, Colleen, had many discussions before deciding to split their duties along fairly traditional gender lines, with Colleen staying home with their two children and Prinster bringing home the paycheck. "We talked a lot about our respective roles and made peace with that, at least while the kids are young," Prinster says. "That's really helped. I don't feel guilty working all day, because I know we've already talked about what she expects and what I expect."

- **Schedule time for your family and yourself.** Make sure to ink in family time as an explicit part of your schedules, adds Kristi Sands Van Sickle, PsyD, who is starting her career as an assistant professor at the Florida Institute of Technology and is raising a young daughter with her husband, retired business executive Paul Van Sickle.

"We carve out family time so that even if I'm really busy, we have one day on the weekend when we're all together," says Van Sickle. The two also plan regular visits with Paul's two children from a previous marriage, who live about an hour away. "It's important to put in extra effort to make sure they feel included," she says.

Schedule time for yourself, too, for exercise, hobbies or just to regroup, advises Robertson-Howell. "Sometimes we get going so fast in this society that we forget about that."

- **Trim the excess.** Just as important as good communication is a strategy many of our parents advised us to use: Boil things down to the basics, Prinster says. He and Colleen went from being a couple that pursued many individual interests before they had children, to a team that pursued their family's interests, he says.

"I work to make money to support my family, and I spend time with my wife and kids," Prinster says. "Beyond that, only the things that are really, really important get the resources." That applies to money, too: Colleen works at their children's cooperative preschool in exchange for reduced tuition, and they cut out cable TV—a sensible move, because "we don't have time for TV!" Prinster says.

- **Pick a job that makes sense.** Some early-career psychologists consciously choose jobs that may lack outward razzle-dazzle but offer reasonable hours, decent pay and good boundaries. To spend more time with his partner, David, and their young twins, Seth Williams, PsyD, left a job that expected him to be on "24/7, 365" to one with more reasonable hours and expectations.

"If the kids are sick, I can leave any time if there's nothing life-or-death hanging on it," says Williams, associate director of clinical training at the online graduate school Capella University. He got lucky with his supervisor, too: She has a family and "walks the talk" of work-family balance, he notes.

- **Get more creative.** While there's nothing wrong with traditional job trajectories, other early-career experts

say it's worth thinking outside the typical career box to accommodate family needs.

Although her graduate program emphasized academic careers, Eileen Kennedy-Moore, PhD, chose to write books and have a small clinical practice instead. The combination allowed her to work and meet the needs of her four children.

"It gave me flexibility," Kennedy-Moore explains. "If a kid was sick one day, I could handle that and just work harder the next day." It also proved a smart career move: Her books have been published by major publishing houses, and she's garnered many therapy clients and speaking engagements as a result.

- **Find support.** Relying on trusted others is vital, whether it's fellow moms or dads to vent with, or relatives or babysitters who can give you breaks, Van Sickle says.

But your most important support may be your spouse, so nurture that relationship, she recommends. "Paul is my anxiety barometer," she says. "He's better at reading when I'm feeling anxious and overwhelmed than I am."

- **Put family first.** You only have one chance to raise your children, says Williams-Nickelson, who has two young daughters with her husband, psychologist and attorney David Nickelson, PsyD, JD. An avid careerist before she had children, she was overwhelmed by the strength of her feelings toward her girls and now knows they will be her top priority for a long time.

"I feel like I've given a lot to my career and to the profession, and now it's time to give to my kids," she says.

Williams-Nickelson adds that she now understands what mentors advised her in the years before she had children. "You can have it all," they told her. "Just not all at once."

Mother (and Father), Can You Spare a Dime?

Your adult child may need your financial help now more than ever. Be sure you consider these questions first.

DAN KADLEC

I could not have bought my first house long ago without borrowing the down payment from Mom and Dad. Their loan got me started down the home-equity path, and it's paid dividends ever since. Yet, at that young age, I had no idea how difficult it would be to repay them, and one Christmas they graciously wiped the slate clean as a gift. I was relieved. But I was also humbled by the weight of debt that no bank would accept—and now am thankful for that early lesson in the pitfalls of borrowing money from family.

As late-stage teens, my own kids are fast approaching the day when they'll need thousands of dollars for a car and, soon after, tens of thousands for their own down payment. Lately, I've been thinking about how I might handle such requests. Perhaps your grown children are already hitting you up. In the U.S., about $45 billion of parent-child loans are extended every year, and that borrowing—used for everything from paying down student loans and credit-card debt to funding a new business—is certain to grow given the tumultuous state of the economy. These are your kids. You want to help. But precautions are in order. Before you lend a dollar, ask yourself these questions:

Can You Really Afford It?

Your ability to lend to a grown child, or any family member for that matter, has likely taken a gut shot in the past six months. The stock market is down sharply. Home equity has eroded. Jobs are less secure. Many corporations have slashed their dividends—and your income if you are a shareholder. Short-term yields are falling (perhaps further cutting your income). Meanwhile, your taxes may be going up under the Obama administration. So reconsider your resources. Nine in 10 boomer parents have helped their adult children financially, according to a study by Ameriprise—even though to do so 40% of them had to draw down savings while 17% had to take a loan. But sacrificing your security to make things easier for your child is rarely a smart idea.

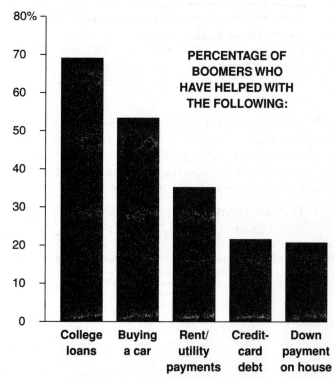

PERCENTAGE OF BOOMERS WHO HAVE HELPED WITH THE FOLLOWING:

Lending your kid a financial hand. Nine out of 10 boomer parents help their adult children with expenses, but some bills appear more pressing than others.

Source: Ameriprise Financial, Money Across Generations study.

What Could Go Wrong?

About 14% of loans between family and friends end up in default, far more than the under 3% of consumer bank loans that go bad. So understand that you may not get paid back. That may not bother you if the child who is borrowing is in your will anyway and you can afford the loss. But the IRS views loans that are forgiven as gifts, subject to a limit of $13,000 this year ($26,000 if you are married) per recipient before the gift tax kicks in. If the loan is small enough—and you really can afford to lose it—consider keeping things simple by making it a gift from the start.

Does Your Child Truly Need It?

Helping a son or daughter who's just been laid off cover the rent for a few months is a more compelling reason to lend money than helping said child pay for a winter getaway to a sunny locale with friends. Alarms should also go off if your offspring is asking for a third loan in your lifetime—maybe he or she has a larger, underlying financial problem that needs to be addressed, suggests Karen Ramsey, author of *Think Again: New Money Choices, Old Money Myths*. "Tell her you won't loan her the money but you will pay for credit counseling or a visit with a financial planner," Ramsey advises. "We love our kids but at some point the dependency has to stop." If saying an outright no is too difficult, blame your decision on forces outside your control—like the slumping stock market or a financial adviser who has warned you and your spouse that you're in danger of outliving your money.

What Terms Will You Set?

If you do decide to extend a loan, set it up for success. That means choosing a reasonable interest rate and repayment schedule. If you lend more than $10,000, the rate must be equal to or greater than what's called the applicable federal rate or you will run into gift-tax issues. You can find this rate, which fluctuates monthly, at irs.gov. Currently it ranges from 1.6% to 4.2%, depending on the length of the loan. If you charge less, or nothing, the IRS will treat the value of the forgone interest as income to you and a gift to your child.

Don't leave the repayment period open-ended. Such personal loans default nearly three times more often than those structured with monthly payments, says Asheesh Advani, CEO of Virgin Money USA, a peer-to-peer loan facilitator. "They cause all kinds of family stress," he says. "You end up wondering how the borrower can possibly take a nice vacation when he owes you all that money. But that doesn't come up if he's making regular payments."

Are Your Expectations Clear?

Put everything in writing, spelling out the loan amount, interest rate and payback schedule. It's also a good idea to tell your other kids about the loan so they're not surprised and possibly resentful if they find out about the arrangement. You can purchase a simple loan document from the website nolo.com for about $7.50. Fill in the terms and have all parties sign it.

You can also set up a personal loan through Virgin Money, which will handle details like billing and collection for a setup fee of $199 and a small monthly fee (for mortgages, the fees range from $649 to $2,299). Using a loan facilitator like Virgin probably doesn't make sense for a small sum but works well for larger amounts, especially a mortgage. Then too, in the case of a mortgage your child will be able to deduct the interest, and if things go really badly you'll have a tax-deductible loss. Sure, it's a bit formal for a loan between parent and child. But putting everything in writing is just part of keeping the peace—never easy when blood and money mix.

DAN KADLEC is co-author of *The Power Years,* a guide for boomers. You can e-mail him at boom_years@moneymail.com.

Rise of the Desperate House Husband

GABY HINSLIFF

There were two fathers this week at our tiny Oxfordshire playgroup. One dad among all the mothers, mumbling valiantly through the more obscure nursery songs in the manner of John Redwood tackling the Welsh anthem, is de rigueur for modern toddler gatherings. But two? Two means solidarity, a masculine presence subtly altering the chemistry in a roomful of women. They ended up happily talking football while washing up the Play-Doh cutters.

For both sexes, such blurred gender lines should be welcome. One of the biggest shocks of my maternity leave was navigating the overwhelmingly female world of those at home with small children: after a career spent in testosterone-soaked newsrooms, I found all that warm fuzziness confusing. Men used to living and working with women might equally find an all-male office weirdly retro now.

But suddenly these divides have started to crumble at great speed. A recession that has pummelled traditionally male industries—construction, finance, manufacturing—while sparing the female-dominated public sector (at least until the spending cuts start) is quietly redrawing family lives. This recession has driven men back home and some women into work.

In Canada, the number of women in employment recently overtook the number of men for the first time. Women in the US may pass the same milestone soon, having reached 49.9 percent of the workforce. Although such progress looks breathtaking, it is less a female surge than a case of men falling back. But it has profound implications: four in ten American working mothers are now their family's main breadwinner, while the number of US female professionals whose husbands don't work has risen by 28 per cent in the past five years.

After the Mancession

In Britain, the pace of change is slower—over 46 per cent of the workforce is now female, up from 45 per cent in 2007—but there are still a lot of men who suddenly have time for playgroup. In every quarter since last spring, redundancies hit men proportionally harder than women. Employers report part-time women asking for more hours because a partner's income is at risk. And a surprising 7 per cent of mothers with three children now have more than one (usually low-paid) job. Research from the Family Commission, a study of roughly 1,000 families, led by the charity 4 Children, has shown a rising trend for house husbands.

The rise of the female breadwinner/male homemaker model seems a logical outcome of a "mancession". It happened during the Great Depression, too—the percentage of working women in the US rose between 1930 and 1940, despite immense social disapproval of women "stealing" male jobs. Then, as now, need simply trumped other considerations for many couples: typically "female" clerical or sales jobs survived the slump better than "male" roles, and were thus easier to get. The trend continued into wartime as female employees replaced men away at the front.

Without a war, the gender power shift could quickly go into reverse when the recovery begins (or public-service jobs start being axed). But if it isn't a temporary blip, how might that affect both professional and domestic life? Does she who earns the pay cheque call the shots? Should he who changes nappies get custody of the children after a divorce? Some men, post-recovery, may not automatically pick up where they left off. Treasury officials predict a permanently smaller future economy, with some manufacturing jobs migrating overseas and a shrunken City. Many new jobs will be graduate-only, favouring girls, who now outnumber boys at university.

Other questions arise for fathers pushed into temporary part-time working as an alternative to redundancy. When recovery comes, might some who can afford it, having got used to seeing more of their children, seek permanently shorter hours? Similarly, some mothers forced into upshifting their careers will discover they don't want to stop when the crisis is over.

Status Anxiety

Office culture has already been greatly feminised over the past 40 years, both superficially—girlie calendars stripped from garage walls, tights machines installed in the House of Commons–and more profoundly, with a new emphasis on "soft" skills and parental rights. The critical mass of working women has started to change the culture, but has proved weaker on structural inequalities such as the pay gap. Canadian women still earn 74 cents on average for every man-dollar. A female-dominated workforce counts for little if most of those women remain stuck in low-status jobs.

And becoming the breadwinner in a crisis may be a bittersweet experience. Many working mothers will simply be relieved they can still support their family if a partner loses his job, others genuinely liberated by doing so. But some will be torn between suddenly needing to make more money and still wanting more time with their children. And while it may make financial sense for an unemployed father to mind the children, emotions are less easily directed. Where house husbands are reluctant, and working mothers guilty or jealous, resentment quickly follows. Evolution in family structure is a sensitive business and changes that are hard to debate calmly in public—as recent near-hysteria at Westminster over the future of marriage has shown—can be even harder to negotiate within a stressed home.

But we are entering a new year and, perhaps, a new decade characterised by uncertainty and change. It will bring opportunities as well as conflicts. Like it or not, the recession is reshaping our domestic landscape. Time to consider seriously how that should look.

GABY HINSLIFF is former political editor of the Observer, newstatesman.com/writers/gaby_hinsliff.

Trust and Betrayal in the Golden Years

Just when they're needed most, a growing number of children are turning on aging parents—taking away their nest eggs and their independence.

KYLE G. BROWN

Concerned about her mother's mental health, Sarah took decisive action. She helped 82-year-old Celia move to a retirement community, she set up accounts for her at a local health-food store and an upscale clothing boutique. She also took over her financial affairs.

But at the mention of her daughter, Celia says: "I swear to God, she should be in jail."

Since 2004, when an Alberta court granted her daughter guardianship of her mother and control of her $400,000 in savings and stocks, Celia claims Sarah has taken almost all of her possessions—and left her without a bank account, or even identification. (Both of their names have been changed to protect their privacy.) While her daughter claims to be acting in her best interests, Celia feels betrayed and helpless.

And she is hardly alone. Toronto lawyer Jan Goddard, who has worked on elder-abuse issues for 17 years, says financial exploitation of seniors is now "endemic across the country." This can range from snatching a few dollars from grandma's purse to transferring property.

Brenda Hill, the director of the Kerby Rotary House Shelter in Calgary, agrees. "We've had people who have had their homes sold, who have been virtually on the street with no food and no money because their children have taken all their assets," she says. "It happens quite often."

And the problem is likely to get worse before it gets better. People 65-plus are the fastest-growing segment of the Canadian population—but cuts to health services in the 1990s have meant that fewer seniors are living in public institutions.

This, in turn, has placed increased pressure on family members, which a Statistics Canada report in 2002 suggested could lead to a rise in the abuse of older adults.

South of the border, taking money from mom and dad is also seen as a serious issue. So much so, that the Elder Financial Protection Network predicts that it will become the "crime of the century."

Ageism is partly to blame. As is a culture of entitlement—where the money parents spend can be seen as a "waste" of the child's future inheritance.

Charmaine Spencer, a gerontologist at B.C.'s Simon Fraser University, says both are particularly prevalent in North America. Although she adds, "I have not seen a single culture in which abuse of the elderly does not take place—it's financial and psychological abuse, and when that doesn't work, it's physical."

But addressing such exploitation is anything but straightforward. How do legal and medical professionals determine when adult children are taking advantage of aging parents—and when they are enforcing necessary restrictions on those no longer able to care for themselves? How do they intervene, either to stop abuse or to help elderly parents cope with newly dependent roles, when seniors are enmeshed in painful power struggles with grown sons and daughters?

Take one of Ms. Goddard's eightysomething clients. The increasingly frail woman complained that she needed more support than her son—who lives in her house—was providing. She decided to revoke his power of attorney.

But, according to Ms. Goddard, when the woman told her son about the meeting, he was furious. The next day, she called Ms. Goddard to cancel everything. As she spoke nervously on the phone, Ms. Goddard could hear the woman's son in the background, telling her what to say.

Though lawyers like Ms. Goddard can call in the police in such situations, getting seniors to make formal complaints against their children can be difficult. Ultimately, she says, clients have to face the repercussions of confronting their families and "keep wavering whenever they go back home."

Seniors' own shame can also keep them from reporting that their children are taking advantage of them. Although abuse seems to cut across socio-economic lines (even New York socialite Brooke Astor made headlines recently because of her son's alleged neglect), older adults often feel guilty talking publicly about private matters.

As for those who do brave action against their children, many do not make it very far. While money is in their children's hands, victims of financial abuse cannot afford the fees to take a case to court—which can run at a minimum of $10,000. And legal aid is rarely awarded to seniors involved in civil cases.

Ms. Hill tells the story of a Calgary widow who sold her house and moved into her daughter's home. Her children transferred money from her account to theirs, borrowed her bank card and charged her for "services" such as rides and errands.

A few months later, the woman fled to the Kerby Rotary House Shelter with a small fraction of her savings. But at the age of 87 she could not face the idea of spending what little time and money she had left in the courts. Now, she resides in a seniors' lodge with just enough cash to live out her days—though her daughter will never be brought to justice.

Dr. Elizabeth Podnieks, the founder of the Ontario Network for the Prevention of Elder Abuse, conducted the first national survey on elder abuse in 1990. She says that even when lawyers do take seniors' cases, complainants have difficulty convincing the court that they are the victims of theft and exploitation. For example, their memory is often called into question, as they struggle to recall "giving" money to defendants.

Family members who question their parents' ability to look after their finances may consult a capacity assessor—a health professional with special training in assessing mental capacity.

Tests vary from province to province, but Larry Leach, a psychologist at Toronto's Baycrest centre for geriatric care, says they generally set out to answer the tricky question of whether elderly adults "appreciate all the risks of making an investment and giving gifts to people."

If a parent is deemed incapable, the government may then become the guardian of property until a family member applies to the courts to gain guardianship.

This is what soured the relationship between Celia and her daughter. In 2004, Celia was diagnosed with dementia and deemed "unable to care for herself." Her daughter then won guardianship over Celia's affairs.

Celia hotly disputes the doctor's findings—but now the onus is on her to prove that she is mentally fit or to appoint a new guardian.

Meanwhile, she is no longer speaking to Sarah. Once in charge of her own health-food store, she feels humiliated taking "handouts" from her daughter. "I can't do anything. Where can I go with no money?" she says.

As for more cut and dried cases, where neither dementia nor family dynamics is in play, Dr. Podnieks says: "Older people don't understand why the police can't just 'go in and get my money back.' They know it's a crime, you know it's a crime, the abuser knows it's a crime—so where is the law, where is the protection?"

Detective Tony Simioni, who is part of the Edmonton Police Force's Elder Abuse Intervention Team, says senior abuse is about 20 years behind child abuse, both in terms of public awareness and government and police resources. "Financial-abuse cases rarely see the top of the agenda," he says. "It's low on the totem pole of crimes."

Still, Judith Wahl, who has been working at the Advocacy Centre for the Elderly in Toronto for more than 20 years, remains optimistic. She believes that public education campaigns on elder abuse are making an impact. The rising number of reported incidents, she says, is partly due to a growing willingness to talk openly about abuse.

A 75-year-old Winnipeg woman is a case in point. She was coerced for years into paying her daughter's bills, rent and grocery tabs.

"I would come home and cry and sort of tear my hair, and think, 'Where do I turn to for help? Who do I go to?'" she says.

But eventually her friends encouraged her to contact a seniors support centre. With their help, she gained the confidence to confront her daughter—and to grant her son power of attorney.

These days, she gives gifts to her granddaughter, but when her daughter asks her for more, she tells her to talk to her "attorney."

KYLE G. BROWN is a freelance writer based in Calgary.

Dealing *Day-to-Day with* Diabetes
A Whole Family Experience

Karen Giles-Smith, MS, RD

When a child is diagnosed with diabetes, it's a time of upheaval for the entire family. Gayle Hood, a dietitian and mother of two young boys, was devastated when one of her sons was diagnosed with type 1 diabetes. Hood experienced myriad emotions: denial, fear, sadness, guilt, and anger. "I knew life would never be the same from that moment on," she says. "I was right. We have a new 'normal' now."

Unless they've experienced it themselves, most people don't realize how diabetes affects families. A basic understanding of what families of children with diabetes go through and a willingness to offer encouragement and support can help these families adjust to their "new life."

A Devastating Diagnosis

Life was relatively carefree for the Hood family—Gayle, her husband Mike, and their two sons, Matt and Jacob—until nearly one year ago when Matt, then aged 8, was diagnosed with diabetes. The diagnosis was unexpected; neither side of the family has a history of diabetes. When Matt began drinking large amounts of water and getting up several times during the night to use the bathroom, Gayle subconsciously recognized the symptoms. She took Matt to the doctor but didn't allow herself to seriously consider the possibility of diabetes until the pediatrician said, "Matt has glucose in his urine. I'm on the phone right now with the hospital. They're expecting him in the pediatrics unit." As Gayle gathered their belongings, she replied, "That's what I was afraid of," and began to cry.

Gayle called Mike at work. He heard the distress in her voice but didn't fully understand the implications of the diagnosis. When Mike arrived at the hospital and saw the physicians and nurses crowded around Matt's bed, he also realized life would never be the same. He likens it to the sobering feeling many men experience the moment their baby is born.

"This is something families live with 24 hours a day," says Gayle. "When I counseled diabetics, I saw them once, and as a clinical dietitian, that was the most important time to me. But health professionals have to see the bigger picture." The bigger picture is the family dynamics—the milieu of emotions and worries and the ways families deal with the initially overwhelming aspects of learning about and living with diabetes.

The Parents' Experience

Parents of children newly diagnosed with diabetes are given all the facts about managing diabetes from a clinical standpoint. However, according to Alicia McAuliffe-Fogarty (formerly Alicia McAuliffe), PhD, who has type 1 diabetes and is the founder and director of the Circle of Life Camp, Inc., a nonprofit camp for children and young adults with diabetes, the social and emotional aspects of diabetes are probably underemphasized.[1]

Denial, guilt, and fear are often the first feelings parents face. McAuliffe-Fogarty's mother explains her reaction when her daughter was diagnosed with diabetes at the age of 11: "Not my little girl! I had nursed her forever, three years to be exact. She ate all the right homemade food, had sun and fresh air. What could we have done differently? We wracked our brains as to how we could have done this to her. We feared the same for her sister. We feared for her future as well as ours. How could fate be so cruel?"[1]

Gayle had had a similar reaction. "All I could think about was why this was happening to our family," she says, "and I was worried about giving Matt the insulin shots." In fact, during the first few days at home, Gayle was terrified that she might harm Matt by giving him the wrong amount of insulin.

Mike worried about the future. He wondered how he and his family would cope. In the hospital, he watched a video of parents of children with diabetes explaining that life can be normal again. During the video, Mike wondered how they would ever reach that point.

According to McAuliffe-Fogarty, who wrote the book *Growing Up With Diabetes: What Children Want Their Parents to Know,* parents have more difficulty accepting and adjusting to diabetes than children. "It is more difficult to fit diabetes into an adult lifestyle and to relearn a new routine while unlearning old habits," she says. McAuliffe-Fogarty recalls one parent saying, "At first, you feel like your entire life has been taken away and you are a slave to diabetes."[1]

McAuliffe-Fogarty counsels parents to move past feelings of guilt and anger as soon as possible and focus on their children and managing their diabetes. An optimistic attitude about diabetes and making sure diabetes doesn't limit the child helps him or her live a normal life. McAuliffe-Fogarty tells parents,

Gayle's Recommended Readings

A First Book for Understanding Diabetes by H. Peter Chase, MD

Growing Up with Diabetes: What Children Want Their Parents to Know by Alicia McAuliffe

Helping the Student with Diabetes Succeed: A Guide for School Personnel, The National Diabetes Education Program (Available at: http://www.ndep.nih.gov/resources/school.htm)

Safe at School (information packet), American Diabetes Association, 1-800-DIABETES

Taking Diabetes to School by Kim Gosselin and Moss Freedman

A Typical School Day

- 6:30 AM: Matt gets up and tests his blood sugar level.
- 7 AM: Gayle gets up and the family eats breakfast. Gayle counts the carbs that Matt eats and inputs the data into his pump.
- 7:30 AM: Gayle packs school lunches and a snack for Matt. She writes the amount of carbs in the snack on the snack bag and the amount of carbs in Matt's lunch on a piece of paper for him to carry in his pocket.
- 8 AM: The boys go to school.
- 10 AM: In class, Matt tests his blood sugar, eats his snack, and enters the data into his pump.
- 12 PM: Matt tests his blood sugar, eats lunch, and walks to the school office. The secretary checks the note in Matt's pocket and makes sure Matt enters the correct data into the insulin pump. She may need to refigure the carbs if Matt didn't eat all of his lunch.
- 3 PM: Matt tests his blood sugar before he gets on the bus. If his blood sugar is low, he takes fast-acting glucose and the teacher calls Gayle to pick him up. If Matt feels "low" during the bus ride, the driver gives Matt a snack from the stash Gayle has supplied.
- 4 PM: Matt has a snack at home and enters the data into his pump.
- 6 PM: Matt tests his blood sugar, eats dinner, and inputs the data into his pump.
- 8 PM: Matt tests his blood sugar, eats a snack, and inputs the data into his pump.
- 9 PM: The boys go to bed.
- 3 AM: Gayle tests Matt's blood sugar while he sleeps if changes have been made to the pump settings during the day or if a high or low blood sugar is suspected.
- Every 72 hours: Change infusion set.
Additional glucose checks may be needed if Matt is feeling "high" or "low."
- Once per week: Data from the meter/pump is uploaded to the pump company's website where the pediatric endocrinologist's office can access the data and suggest any necessary changes to the care plan.

"Your child is able to do anything as long as she fits her diabetes regimen into her schedule."[1]

The Child's Experience

When some children are diagnosed with diabetes, they become angry and feel sorry for themselves or deny they have diabetes—and they should be allowed to feel this way. Deanne Kelleher, RD, a pediatric endocrinology dietitian with Sparrow Health System in Lansing, Mich., says children's feelings of self-pity come and go, but it's important not to give in to pity parties, especially with teens. "I allow the tears initially, then encourage them to move on," says Kelleher. "They'll say it's not fair that they have to manage their diabetes, and I say, 'No, it's not fair, but it's lifesaving therapy," Kelleher also stresses the importance of listening to the family and letting them lead the education. "It helps me get the family's perspective—how they're doing and how they're handling things," she says. "I just ask them to tell me about it. I've learned a lot from my patients."

Parents, too, must listen to their child's concerns, questions, and feelings. McAuliffe-Fogarty says, "Children lean on their parents for support and encouragement, and for a child living with diabetes, this is even more important." She tells parents, "You taught your child how to crawl, walk, and talk. Now you must teach her to live, to survive, and to thrive."[1]

The Hood Family: Surviving and Thriving

After becoming comfortable with the basics, such as insulin injections, calculating carbohydrates and exchanges, and interpreting food labels, Gayle says the most helpful part in managing Matt's diabetes was working with the endocrinology team to set up a flexible routine. "It's important to consider the family as a whole," says Gayle, "instead of only treating the clinical symptoms."

Together, the endocrinology team and the Hood family made accommodations in Matt's care plan for his activities and sports, family traditions, and the family's lifestyle, such as who would manage what (eg, grocery shopping, meal preparation, counting carbs). "At Christmastime, we put less candy and more fun stuff in their stockings," Gayle says. "And instead of giving the boys giant Easter baskets, we have a scavenger hunt." She explains that, especially with children, it's important to be lenient with what they're allowed to eat. "They shouldn't have to feel left out, deprived, or that they have to hoard candy bars."

When working with families, Kelleher gets a comprehensive idea of what goes on at home to customize the education: How is food viewed in the family? Are any foods considered a treat or a reward? What were mealtimes like before the diagnosis? "Parents' No. 1 concern," says Kelleher, "is that they're stuffing their child with food when the child doesn't want to eat." To make it possible for children to honor their feelings of hunger and fullness, Kelleher develops a more flexible insulin plan—based on what they're actually going to eat—as early as possible. She also teaches children how to manage insulin to enjoy a birthday treat or a snack at school. "Kids with diabetes don't need special snacks," Kelleher says. "With proper guidance, planning, and family support, we can help them feel not so different from other kids."

The ABCs of Diabetes

Even though Gayle has a background in nutrition and counseled type 2 diabetics as a clinical dietitian, she was floored by how much she had to learn about diabetes management after Matt was diagnosed. For many months, Gayle's full-time "job" was to educate herself and others to ensure Matt received proper care at home and school. "The most important thing you can do for your child is to educate the adults surrounding [him or] her, so your child is not excluded or treated differently," McAuliffe-Fogarty says. "Also, educate your child about diabetes and the misconceptions surrounding the condition so [he or] she is prepared . . . When schools, peers, and the general public are educated and understand diabetes, their misconceptions are dispelled, they are less afraid of it, and they will feel more comfortable around people with diabetes."[1]

Kelleher agrees: "Part of my responsibility is to make sure we educate as many people in the patients' lives as possible: the nanny or the day care provider, siblings, Grandpa and Grandma, and the schoolteacher."

To educate the school employees, Gayle did her homework and a lot of legwork. Armed with information about how to help the school staff and students feel comfortable caring for and being around Matt, Gayle visited the school several times to talk to school staff and Matt's classmates.

Gayle met with several staff members individually: the principal, secretary, Matt's third grade teacher, art teacher, music teacher, gym teacher, and bus driver. She had to start at square one since there hadn't been a student with newly diagnosed diabetes in need of insulin injections for as long as the principal could remember. To make matters more complicated, there wasn't a school nurse at the elementary school. Gayle explained Matt's needs and provided the staff with detailed verbal and written instructions for school days and field trips. She also added information about diabetes to the school's 504 (laws prohibiting discrimination against someone with a disability) and medical management plan. (Visit www.diabetes.org for more information.)

When Matt started third grade in the fall, Gayle visited the school every day at lunch to give Matt an injection until the special education teacher, the only staff member willing to wield a needle, took over. "I let the teacher practice on me," says Gayle.

How Parents Can Help Educate Schools

- Ask for the school district policy on medication administration, blood glucose testing, and injections.
- Meet with the teacher and principal one week or more before the school informs them that your child has diabetes. Explain daily management and effects of high and low blood glucose.
- Obtain the daily class schedule: recess, gym class, lunch time, snack time, etc.
- Establish a box of emergency snacks in locations such as the main office, homeroom, gym teacher's desk, and on the bus.
- Teach how to give injections to someone at the school, particularly if there is no school nurse. Even if your child has a pump, someone still needs to know how to administer glucagon in an emergency.
- Meet with any staff member at the school that your child has regular contact with: music teacher, art teacher, librarian, playground supervisors.
- Talk to the bus driver. Make sure he or she knows that your child must be able to eat on the bus, if necessary.
- Find out where blood glucose testing will occur (may be in the office or classroom).
- Get the menu from the school cafeteria to determine carbohydrates.
- Educate your child's classmates about diabetes.
- Prepare a 504 plan and a medical management plan.

"Practicing on an orange isn't the same, and I wanted to be sure she was comfortable." The special education teacher called Gayle every day to ask how many units Matt needed, which depended on his blood glucose before lunch and how many carbs he ate. In October, Matt switched from insulin shots to the pump, and Gayle visited the school twice every day—at 10 am and 12:30 pm—to help Matt enter data into the computerized pump until he felt confident doing it while supervised by the school secretary. Gayle says the school staff has been supportive and followed through responsibly several times, such as calling her when Matt's low blood sugar didn't improve after a snack. The school staff also makes sure substitute teachers receive information about Matt's condition, including the symptoms to watch for and what to do.

To make sure Matt's classmates didn't think something was "wrong" with him, Gayle read them the book *Taking Diabetes to School*. The book is written from the perspective of a child with diabetes in a way that's easy for children to understand: "Doctors and nurses don't know how or why I have diabetes. I didn't do anything wrong (like eat too many sweets), and it's nobody's fault! Doctors and nurses do know you can't catch diabetes from me. It's okay to play with me and be my friend."[2]

Education can prevent value judgments that may hurt a child's feelings and self-esteem. Word choices, for instance, make a big difference. Instead of calling a child "a diabetic," the child is "a person with diabetes." Instead of calling diabetes a "disease" (although technically, it is), it can be referred to as "a condition." And glucose readings should be called "low," "normal," or "high" instead of "good" or "bad." Without this type of age-appropriate education, children may believe Matt did something wrong to have diabetes, that he's sick and may die, or that he should be treated differently or avoided.

"I feel like I'm broadcasting [Matt's diabetes] to the world," says Gayle. "I communicate with everyone: all of Matt's coaches and the staff at all the summer day camps. But if I don't let everyone know, they might think he's just acting goofy when his blood sugar is low. It's a delicate balance. I want Matt to be treated normally, but the adults taking care of him need to know about his diabetes."

The New Normal

"I've been able to deal with everything pretty well," says Gayle, "because I have a type A personality. But to avoid getting overwhelmed, I have to think ahead and be very organized." Mike says he feels things are "pretty normal" now, but it's tough to be spontaneous. "You always have to remember to bring the meter, glucose tabs, and a cooler with you and eat on a fairly regular schedule," says Mike. "I'm not very organized, so I'm grateful that Gayle is."

Events that are fun and exciting for Matt are usually stressful for Gayle. "I still worry when there's a substitute teacher or when Matt goes on a field trip, to a birthday party, or stays at a friend's house overnight," she says. "But I let him go and have fun and be a kid." Something as simple as a trip to a nearby beach requires a lot of time planning and packing. Gayle developed a checklist of 18 items to pack. The list helps her remember everything, which gives her peace of mind.

Matt has learned to do some age-appropriate self-care, such as blood glucose monitoring, ketone testing, and entering his blood glucose levels into the computerized insulin pump. It took him more than three months to muster the courage to do his own finger sticks, but now it's as routine as brushing his teeth. Matt has a mind-over-matter approach to his diabetes management, recently telling his mom, "If you believe something won't hurt, it won't."

Gayle treats Matt the same as always and encourages others to do the same. "I don't allow diabetes to be used as an excuse or a crutch. I want him to be a normal kid," she says, "and to do all the things other kids can do. He's a kid with diabetes, but he's still a kid."

References

1. McAuliffe A. *Growing Up with Diabetes: What Children Want Their Parents to Know.* New York: John Wiley & Sons, Inc.; 1998.
2. Gosselin K, Freedman M. *Taking Diabetes to School.* Plainview, N.Y.: Jayjo Books; 1998.

KAREN GILES-SMITH, MS, RD, is the manager of nutrition communications for the Dairy Council of Michigan and a freelance writer.

The Positives of Caregiving: Mothers' Experiences Caregiving for a Child with Autism

Michael K. Corman

The documentation and representation of the experiences of caregivers of children with autism and other developmental disabilities has been one dimensional at best, with a pervasive focus on the stresses, burdens, and parental coping associated with caregiving (Grant, Ramcharan, McGrath, Nolan, & Keady, 1998). Much of this focus is warranted. For example, sources of stress (stressors) for caregivers of these children are numerous and might include the autistic traits themselves (DeMyer, 1979; Tomanik, Harris, & Hawkins, 2004), social stigmas from the general public and health practitioners (Gray, 1998, 2002a, 2002b), and the social support system that is intended to alleviate stress (Corman, 2007a; DeMyer, 1979; Gray, 1998).

This multitude of stressors can have an immense effect on individuals in the family, including parents and siblings (DeMyer, 1979; Kaminsky & Dewey, 2001; Schopler & Mesibov, 1994), extended family members (Gray, 1998), and, depending on how caregivers cope, the possible life gains that the individual with autism can make (Schopler & Mesibov, 1994). For example, parents often experience a combination of emotional problems (such as depression, isolation, and feelings of being a failure as a parent), physical problems (fatigue, ulcers, headaches, fluctuation in weight, dermatitis, and other physical health conditions), career problems (limited or no employment—specifically for mothers and career changes), and negative effects on the marriage (marital discord often ending in divorce; Gray, 1998, 2002a). Parents also report feelings of guilt, isolation, doubts of their ability to care for their child, anger toward the symptoms of autism, increased physical and psychological tensions, frustrations, lack of life satisfaction, and feelings of exhaustion and old age (DeMyer, 1979; Gray, 2002b). Last, because of the unique and often complex symptomatology associated with autism, such as a lack of verbal communication, variant cognitive functioning, and severe behaviors, comparative studies have reported that the burden of caregiving for children with autism is greater than that of parenting a child with other disabilities (Weiss, 2002), such

as mental retardation, Down's syndrome, cystic fibrosis, and chronic and fatal physical illness.

Caregiving for a child with autism is stressful! But what about the positive side of caregiving? The narrow focus on the stressful and negative aspects of the caregiving experience offers only partial insights into the experiences of caregiving for children with chronic conditions. There is a need for research to examine the other side of the spectrum, the positive and often joyous side of parenting children with disabilities. The purpose of this article is to provide insight into that positive side by exploring the experiences of mothers of children with autism through in-depth interviews. Although these mothers portrayed an experience that was often stressful, they also discussed many joys of caregiving. This article attempts to strike a balance with the majority of research that focuses on the negatives of caregiving; it will show that caregiving for children with autism is not solely stressful. These findings have theoretical and practical implications. First, this article provides a brief overview of the literature on the positives of caregiving for individuals with chronic conditions.

Literature Review

Most caregiving research focuses solely on the negative aspects of the experience (Chappell, Gee, McDonald, & Stones, 2003), which may be indebted to the pathological models of stress that guide such inquiries. For instance, Pearlin, Lieberman, Menaghan, and Mullan's (1981) framework of the stress process focuses on the stressors (antecedents to stress) associated with caregiving and pays specific attention to the many related relationships, and the developing and changing nature of these relationships over time, that eventually lead to stress (see also Pearlin, Mullan, Semple, & Skaff, 1990). Lazarus and Folkman (1984) offered a framework that focuses on the more individual and psychological components of what they called the *stress-coping process*. They suggested that it is how stressors are appraised, in addition to individual resources, that determines whether or not an event is stressful (Lazarus & Folkman, 1984). Although these conceptualizations are useful for exploring the stressful aspects of caregiving and how individuals cope, they are limited in that they fail to address any positives of caregiving in a systematic way; positives have been left by the wayside (Kelso, French, & Fernandez, 2005). As Grant et al. (1998) suggested, such a singular view fails to account for other important dimensions.

Research on caregiving has only recently considered gratification and the role of positives in the caregiving experience. For example, in Susan Folkman's (1997) seminal study of caregiving for men with HIV/AIDS, she discussed how positive states of mind can co-occur with negative states. She reported that "despite high levels of distress, people also experience positive psychological states during caregiving and bereavement" (p. 1207). Folkman described four psychological states associated with coping: (a) positive reappraisal, (b) goal-directed problem-focused coping, (c) spiritual beliefs and practices, and (d) the infusion of ordinary events with positive meaning. All four states have an underlying characteristic, that is, the appraisal of positive meanings occurring within a stressful event, which she referred to as *meaning-based coping*.

Grant et al. (1998) explored the positives of caregiving by interviewing 120 caregivers of individuals with intellectual disabilities. They described rewards and caregiver gratification as emerging from three sources: (a) the relationship between caregiver and care receiver, (b) intrapersonal characteristics of the caregiver, and (c) the desire for positive outcomes or the avoidance of negative affect. They also found that many of the gratifications expressed by caregivers were related to, or a product of, successful coping strategies, supporting Folkman's (1997) findings.

More recently, Chaya Schwartz (2003) defined caregiver gratification as "fulfilling parental duties, a better idea of 'what's important in life', learning about inner strengths, aware of personal limitations, learning to do new things, satisfaction from doing what's right, personal growth, [and] becoming more self-confident" (p. 580). In her study of 167 primary caregivers of individuals with mental, developmental, or physical disabilities, she found that caregivers who were younger, unemployed, and had poor health were more likely to experience caregiver gratification. In addition, she found the only characteristics of the child that factored into experiencing gratification were the age of the child (younger children) and the type of disability (having a physical rather than a mental disability). Last, subjective (perceived stress) rather than objective burden (the level of care required) was associated with less caregiver gratification (Schwartz, 2003). Schwartz speculated that the gratification parents experienced might be a product of how they perceived or created meaning in their caregiving role.

In the field of autism, research has only provided marginal insights into the more rewarding aspects of caregiving. For instance, in a study about narratives published on the Internet by parents, Amos Fleischmann (2004) found that in addition to the demanding aspects of caregiving, a majority of Web sites focused on the positive essence of individuals with autism and the caregiving experience, with an emphasis on parents'

positive relationship with their child and joyous experiences derived from caregiving. Fleischmann's study is supported by other research on the contributions people with disabilities make to their families: families might benefit in terms of strengthened family ties, compassion and fulfillment, and happiness (Pruchno, 2003).

Despite the shortcomings of Pearlin et al. (1981, 1990) and Lazarus and Folkman's (1984) models, they allow for a scope that looks beyond adjustment and toward positives (Kelso et al., 2005). This is apparent in Folkman's (1997) work on caregiving for individuals with HIV/AIDS (see also Folkman & Moskowitz, 2000a, 2000b). Using these insights, the positives of caregiving are defined in this article as experiences or events that caregivers appraise as positive and sometimes joyous. It is important to note that if this definition seems ambiguous, it is because the positives of caregiving remain relatively uncharted, lacking conceptual clarification (Grant et al., 1998). Based on mothers' reflections, this article explores the positives of caregiving for a child with autism. In doing so, a more complete understanding of these parents' lived experiences emerges, with important contributions to the broader constellation of caregivers of children with chronic conditions.

Method
Participants

Results reported in the next section were drawn from a larger study that explored mothers' experiences of caregiving for a child with autism, before and after their child was placed outside of the home (either in foster care, a group home setting, or a treatment-care facility, hereafter referred to as *placed* or *placement*). Interviews occurred between November 2005 and February 2006. Nine mothers participated in total; 6 lived in British Columbia, and 3 lived in Alberta, Canada. The average age of mothers was 46, with a range between 35 and 62 years old. For 7 out of the 9 mothers, family income ranged between $30,000 and more than $100,000. One mother responded "middle class," and another chose not to answer. As of the first interview, the children with autism were between the ages of 8 and 18, with the average being 14 years old. The age of these children at the time of placement was 6–15, with an average of 11 years old. Mothers were purposively chosen because they are usually the primary caregivers (Gray, 2003) and are therefore more likely to be involved in the day-to-day ups and downs of caregiving. Furthermore, a unique sample of mothers was chosen; their experiences were so stressful that their child was ultimately placed outside of the home (see Corman, 2007a). Although this study did not aim to be generalizable, it was assumed that if this sample experienced positives, caregivers in less stressful circumstances (e.g., caregivers of a child with less severe autistic characteristics and other disabilities) would also experience them. Therefore, these findings are potentially transferable to other constellations of caregivers.

A diagnosis of autism was reported by 7 out of the 9 mothers during the initial contact, with the remaining 2 mothers reporting a diagnosis of pervasive developmental disorder (PDD) and PDD not otherwise specific (PDD-NOS). Mothers also reported co-occurring conditions, including Landau-Kleffner syndrome, obsessive compulsive disorder, mental handicap, epilepsy (for three children), and Down's syndrome. Two of the mothers had a female child, and 7 had a male child. Although I refer to a generalized *autism,* it is important to note that there is no all-or-nothing form of autism but rather a continuum of severity, known as autism spectrum disorders (Wing, 1988). Based on mothers' descriptions, these children would most likely fall within the moderate to severe end of the spectrum.

Research Design

In-depth, semistructured interviews were conducted based on transcendental phenomenology (Moustakas, 1994), a qualitative research strategy and philosophy that allows researchers to identify the essence of experience as it relates to certain phenomena as described and understood by participants of a study (Creswell, 2002). Mothers were interviewed at their homes and asked to retrospectively talk about their caregiving experiences. Questions were geared toward exploring the positives and joys of caregiving, the demands of caregiving, and how mothers coped, focusing on the times before and after out-of-home placement. The portion of the interviews reported in the analysis below are based on the questions that explored the positives during the early years prior to placement (approximately 0–8 years of age, depending when the placement process was activated) and after their child left home. Interviews lasted on average 2.24 hours with a range of 1.5–3 hours. The interviews and the numbers of mothers interviewed continued until sufficiency and saturation of information were reached.

Interviews were transcribed in their entirety and analyzed based on a modified approach offered by Moustakas (1994), specifically intended for the analysis of qualitative data. Eight steps were followed: (1) identifying patterns in the data based on the lived experiences of participants, (2) reducing the data by identifying unique aspects of experience, (3) organizing the data into core themes that represent the experience of participants, (4) validating step 3 by reviewing the complete transcript of participants, (5) constructing an individual textural description of the experience presented by each participant, (6) based on step 5, constructing a clear account of the dynamics of the experience, (7) combining steps 5 and 6 to create a textural-structural description of each participant that incorporated the experiences of participants, and (8) combining individual textual descriptions of each participant into one that represents the experience presented by the group as a whole.

To assist in the process just described, insights offered by Moerer-Ur-dahl and Creswell (2004) were followed. Initially, significant statements within each participant's transcripts were identified, with a primary focus on understanding how individuals viewed different aspects of their experiences as they related to the positives and joys of caregiving. The goal here was to ground or contextualize the positives of caregiving to gain a better understanding of the distinct character of positives as described by mothers. The data were then broken down into themes based on the experiences of mothers. Once themes were developed, a detailed description of the experience of each mother as it related to the themes that emerged was provided. Conclusions were then drawn in accordance with the lived experiences expressed by participants. The product of this process was the grouping of statements into the themes discussed in the next section.

Results
Pockets of Child Development

All parents expressed the positives during the early years of their child's development as "pockets" because they were "kind of few and far between." Positives discussed by mothers included their child developing, seeing their child happy, times devoid of negative autistic traits or maladaptive behaviors (as perceived by the mother) that are often associated with autism, spending time with their child, unique and/or positive personality traits of their child, and knowing or discovering what was wrong with their child. I discuss each in the following paragraphs.

Developmental Gains

With a diagnosis on the autism spectrum, parents are often left in ambiguity because of the nature of the disability; they do not know how much their child will develop in the years to come. As a result, mothers described feelings of joy when their child started to make developmental gains. For example, one mother discussed how she was "very pleased" when her child progressed in developmental areas, such as "when he started to speak." Another mother commented on her child's success in learning new tasks; "Oh yeah, his success still makes me feel good, no matter what. Like I remember when he learned how to wave good-bye. That made me cry that day [laugh]." Another mentioned the "little milestones that parents take for granted, I think are tremendous."

Another mother discussed how watching her child was "hugely satisfying . . . it makes it all worth it when you start to see a little bit of language or a behavior, or a skill emerge." For some mothers, this gave them hope for their child's future. One mother explained, "I think . . . a little bit of joy with a child that's seriously handicapped goes a long way. It gives you a lot of hope."

Child being Happy

All mothers experienced positives derived from seeing their child happy. Although this might seem like a common experience of all parents, it is important to contextualize this side of caregiving in that many mothers viewed their child as being chronically unhappy. One mother put it best, "just to see him happy, because all through his life he's lived either withdrawn or anxious, or afraid of doing things." When mothers saw their child happy, they were especially happy. For example, joy arose for one mother when she watched her child enjoy his favorite activity. She explained:

> You see this bright-eyed little boy at the top of the slide, that was his favorite activity was going down the slides. So when you see him at the top of the slide with this big grin on his face, those kinds of times were really exciting for me . . . . I just knew that he enjoyed that.

Seeing her child happy made her feel "really good. . .That is sort of what we hope our kids are going to feel." Another mother described, "when he's happy and having a really good time, then I'm happy. It's like I'm just a normal parent."

Times Devoid of Negative Autistic Traits or Maladaptive Behaviors

Mothers also talked about times devoid of negative behaviors (negative autistic traits), which they thought of as "normal" times. For instance, one mother described how when her child "didn't throw his food . . . [or] didn't have any feces smearing in the bathroom," these were more positive times. Others experienced positives when their child "hadn't pinched another child or hit another child." One mother went on to explain, "So any time he was cooperating . . . times that he was being and not bothering anybody . . . . If I heard that he sat for five minutes in his desk, or he sat in circle time without poking the next person." During these times, some mothers expressed being "really happy."

Spending Time with Your Child

Despite many of the difficulties, all mothers described the positives of spending time with their child. For instance, one mother discussed how she and her child would go swimming together and go down to the beach to spend time together. Her child "loved it" and always "liked hanging off me." She described how there were so many "nice times" that they spent together. Another mother described how she felt "just connected" to her child because of the times they spent together, specifically "the caregiving part . . . being hands on, physically connected." She talked about how she "really enjoyed" the connection she had with her child: "We're connected on a different level." This mother concluded:

> I guess having a child with autism, you connect with them on a completely different level than I think you would with other children because you don't have language. He's also mostly nonverbal, so physical connections are really important; it's the way you communicate that's beyond words I guess, so I think that's part of it.

For this mother, what might be viewed as a demanding aspect of caregiving was in fact very joyous for her.

Unique And/Or Positive Personality Traits of Their Child

Individuals with autism often have a variety of challenges, including maladaptive behaviors, difficulty in communicating with others, difficulty listening and following directions, and other co-occurring medical conditions. However, individuals who have autism are heterogeneous; the severities of impairments vary from person to person (Gray, 2003; Seltzer, Shattuck, Abbeduto, & Greenberg, 2004). Nonetheless, the positive side of this uniqueness often goes unrecognized. All mothers in this study recognized the uniqueness of their child. In doing so, they expressed many positives derived from the unique personality traits of their child.

For example, mothers discussed how their child was "real sweet" and showed affection. Another mother talked about her child being a "very warm individual . . . . We were blessed that way, I guess; very cuddly, quite attached to your close family members." Other personality traits included being "very funny, like she's got a good sense [of humor] . . . she's quite a little monkey," and being "a very good-natured kid . . . he still has a happy disposition." Despite the negative traits mothers dealt with throughout their caregiving experience, which sometimes worsen or change as their child ages into adulthood (Gray, 2002a), mothers described the many unique personality traits of their child as a positive side of caregiving.

Knowing or Discovering What Was Wrong with Their Child

Common perceptions of receiving a diagnosis on the autism spectrum suggest that the experience is devastating, and often it is (Mansell & Morris, 2004). In fact, for many of the mothers in this study, the autism diagnosis represented the loss of the child that was or could have been. One mother explained how "the day that I found out [I was floored] because there's nothing like that in my family, and we've always been high achievers . . . and I don't know where that [diagnosis] came from."

Although some mothers described receiving the diagnosis of autism as very burdensome—"it was sad, it's pretty devastating, to have a child who's not typical"—for others, the receipt of the diagnosis was not a stressful experience but a positive one. With a diagnosis, mothers were relieved to finally know what was wrong with their child after having entered into multiple systems of care in search for answers and supports. For example, after receiving a diagnosis, one mother described how "all of a sudden you know . . . because up until this point everybody's been asking me 'Why is he doing this? What's he doing?' And I'd be going 'I don't know; I don't know'. I really had no answers for anybody." With a diagnosis, answers started "coming out." With these answers, mothers described a positive experience derived from knowing and understanding.

Furthermore, the receipt of a diagnosis allowed the mother to gain access to specialized services and supports for her child, such as intervention therapy, and herself, such as respite, and set out a pathway of care for her child.[1] The ability to take action was positive, and often a relief, because now the mother was able to help her child. One mother expanded upon this point:

> I'm very much a doer, and so when you have a diagnosis, then you can look at putting the pieces together to move forward and do something; especially I hear so much about early development and early intervention. It was right around the time that the money was being made available for early intervention, and I didn't want to waste a minute, especially knowing that that money would dissolve when he was 6.

The Impacts of Positives

Parents did not just describe the positive side of caregiving, they also discussed how the positives interacted with negative and stressful experiences (i.e., their stress-coping process). For example, the positives associated with their child developing gave mothers hope. One mother, like many parents of children with autism, worried about her child's future (Ivey, 2004). When her child started to make developmental milestones, she began to have a more positive outlook for her child's future. This hope impacted the concerns and worries she had for her child's future. She went on to explain how the positives "are the things that keep you going . . . a little bit of joyful experience gives you . . . the ability to go on."

On a more general note, one mother described how the positives of caregiving had an impact on her stress-coping process.

Well they (the positives) kept me going . . . it wasn't all negative. It kind of gave me hope to continue on, like every day is a new day kind of thing . . . . It gave me a reason to get up in the morning so I wouldn't be waking up going "oh no, I have to deal with another day" sort of thing . . . any time you have any kind of joy or positive feelings then that . . . just gives you a really good feeling that you can continue over the next period of time.

Another mother explained:

[The positives] just keep you going. Without the moments of comic relief, without the joys, without those moments of connection where he catches your eye directly for 1 minute and you actually have his gaze directly, without those things, you'd go stir crazy. Those are the things that feed you. I get a huge amount of strength from the tiniest little things.

Despite the demands of caregiving, mothers experienced a multitude of positives during their caregiving years, many of which brought joy to their lives.

Positive Reflections on Their Overall Caregiving Experience

All mothers spoke about personal transformation as a result of their caregiving years. This transformation included learning from their experience and growing as a person. It is important to note that these positive reflections are not linked to any specific event but were a product of their caregiving experience as a whole. Furthermore, it is important to contextualize this positive side of caregiving: All mothers eventually placed their child with autism due to a number of factors, including their child's maladaptive behaviors increasing drastically, "getting more intense" and more difficult to deal with over time, a failure in the support system that was intended to alleviate stress, and a general inability to cope with the demands of caregiving, leading to mothers experiencing severe distress and feeling that they "couldn't go on" (Corman, 2007a). However, despite this experience of severe distress, all mothers ultimately reflected positively on their caregiving experience as a whole.

For example, one mother explained the learning involved in caregiving where she not only "learned a lot about autism, but I learned a lot about people, and I would have missed that . . . it was a really wonderful thing." Another explained how "the biggest positive is just the learning that came out of that for us as a family, but for me in particular as a person. But I think it's shaped all of us, it certainly has shaped [my husband and daughter] as well as me."

Others described caregiving as making them stronger as a person. One mother mentioned how she "became a fighter, just kind of like an advocate for the family but also for [my child with autism] . . . So, yeah, definitely it makes you stronger. And it makes you tougher in a way." Her experience also made her realize what is "important . . . So, you realize what's really important and don't sweat the small stuff." Another mother described her child with autism as being one of her greatest teachers in life:

I mean, I don't even know who I would be if I hadn't had May . . . it's kind of a weird thing, but in my life, she's been kind of one of my key teachers. She's kind of forced me to kind of examine parts of myself that I don't know if I ever would have got to if I didn't have her. And, she forced [my husband] and I to kind of deal with issues that might have taken us years . . . It's been a struggle, and sometimes I've hated her for it, [but] nobody has taught me so much.

Mothers also discussed how the caregiving experience made them more empathetic:

My husband and I were asked one time about the biggest thing that we got from Sam. I think it was the gift of patience 'cause I have patience unlimited, you know . . . 'cause once somebody's dumping milk out in your front yard [laugh], it's amazing how much patience you have.

Discussion and Conclusion

Despite the demanding aspects of caregiving for children with autism, and it is often very demanding, caregivers experience many positives and joys from their role as caregivers. However, the majority of research focuses on the negative and more stressful aspects of the caregiving experience. Breaking away from this preponderance of research in the field of autism, this article highlights some of the positives of caregiving that mothers experienced during the early years of their child's development and overall reflections on their caregiving experience after their child left home. When asked to discuss the positives of care-giving, all mothers expressed a multitude of positives directly related to their caregiving role (Chappell et al., 2003; Folkman, 1997; Grant et al., 1998; Schwartz, 2003). Others derived positives from finding the "positive essence" in their child (Fleischmann, 2004) and achievements of their child (Grant et al., 1998). More unique positives included discovering what was wrong with their child in the face of not knowing.

Implications for Practice

Many practical implications arise from this study. Although caregiving for children with autism is demanding, this article suggests that the positives and joys that emerge from this role are not only important but also have a specific function. Whereas current research describes the positives of caregiving as a *product* of successful coping—the adaptational function of positives (see Folkman, 1997; Grant et al., 1998)—parents in this study discussed how positives had an impact *on* their stress-coping process, rather than being simply a product of it. In other words, positives also occur outside of the stress-coping process, and interact with it, affecting how mothers experience stressors and negative outcomes, potentially impacting their ability to cope at different times. This finding expands on the function of positives within the caregiving experience; they go beyond adaptational function to being a core aspect of caregivers' experiences.

Furthermore, the importance and function of the positives and joys of caregiving is most apparent when they are not present. In the larger study that contributed to this article, all mothers described severe distress and solely negative outcomes during the time leading up to and immediately following the placement of their child, a time devoid of any positives or joys of caregiving. One mother described it best: "When the stresses got to be too much, the joy of everything started to disappear." Does a lack of positives impact caregiver well-being and a caregiver's ability to cope? Cummins (2001) explained that most caregivers are able to describe positives derived from their caregiving role; when they are unable to do so, the demands of their role are likely to be intolerable. Grant et al. (1998) further explained that without the positives of caregiving, it may not be possible for caregivers to feel as if they are able to continue encountering the stressful circumstances corollary to their role. As such, it might be concluded that the positives of caregiving are an integral part of parents' ability to cope, to the point that when they are not present, parents may not be able to continue caregiving. Policy and practice implications directly follow from these findings in that a lack of positives might be an indicator of the current state of a caregiver's well-being or lack of well-being. It might be an indicator for professional services and supports that additional supports are needed to proactively assist those in crisis or on the brink of crisis. Furthermore, policies need to be developed that are proactively geared toward preventing a crisis or assisting those on the brink of a crisis rather than solely intervening once the crisis emerges. Of equal importance, this examination of positives provides future families of children with autism and other disabilities a better understanding of the experience of caregiving as a whole—an experience that is very demanding at times but also has many positives.

How families cope with the demands associated with caring for a child with autism not only influences the well-being of the family but also possible life gains that an individual with autism can make (Schopler & Mesibov, 1994). Current research on caregiving for children with autism attempts to promote the use of successful coping strategies and resources to improve the quality of life of the caregiver and care receiver (Dunn, Burbine, Bowers, & Tantleff-Dunn, 2001; Gray, 1994, 1998). One practical implication that might inform research, policy, and practice on successful coping is the need to promote and draw attention to the positives of caregiving both within service agencies and for those caregiving for children with autism and other disabilities. If services and supports are able to enhance the positive aspects of caregiving by drawing

attention to them, parents might be able to cope more successfully with the difficulties of caregiving. In addition, it might be beneficial for services and supports to facilitate the joys of caregiving by drawing attention to the strengths of the caregiver and the positive contribution their child with a disability makes to their family (Pierpont, 2004). The strengths-based perspective and active interviewing are two resources that service providers might draw upon to help facilitate and draw attention to the positives of caregiving.

The strengths-based perspective is one orientation that might assist those whose work intersects with individuals with disabilities and their families in drawing attention to and facilitating the identification of the positive and joyous aspects of caregiving. This perspective shifts away from pathological conceptions of persons with disabilities and the experiences of caregiving to more qualitative and holistic understandings, aligned with the positives of caregiving discussed earlier. By focusing on strengths (see Cohen, 1999; Early, 2001), this perspective has the potential to assist service providers in gaining a more complete understanding of the caregiving experience and perceiving their experiences in a more positive light, which has the potential to increase caregivers' quality of life and the quality of care they provide (Berg-Weger, Rubio, & Tebb, 2001).

In addition to the strengths-based perspective, and complementary to it, insights offered by the reflexive and linguistic turns in sociology could be of use to service providers and researchers alike as a resource or tool to draw upon to explore the positives of caregiving and draw attention to them. One approach aligned with this shift is "the active interview," which is a methodological and analytical approach to interviewing that conceptualizes the interview as an active meaning-making process between interviewee and interviewer, who both participate in the coproduction of knowledge. The interviewer (i.e., service provider), in the context of exploring the positives of caregiving, might invite or "incite" the interviewee (i.e., caregiver) to talk about and reflect on the positives of caregiving. Traditionally, this approach might be viewed as leading the respondent, resulting in a social desirability bias (Esterberg, 2002; see also Cummins, 2001). However, the active interview suggests that interviewers are inevitably embedded and implicated in the meaning-making processes of respondents. Holstein and Gubrium (2002) explained:

> This is not to say that active interviewers merely coax their respondents into preferred answers to their questions. Rather, they converse with respondents in such a way that alternate considerations are brought into play . . . encouraging respondents to develop topics in ways relevant to their own everyday lives . . . to provide an environment conducive to the production of the range and complexity of meanings that address relevant issues. (pp. 120–121)

Furthermore, in the context of the positives of caregiving, the active interview is not solely concerned about the positives; it suggests that there is usefulness in inviting individuals to think about the positives and honor participants in the meaning-making process. As such, I suggest that this approach can provide a more fruitful examination of the caregiving experience as a whole by assisting researchers and service providers in exploring and gaining a better understanding and appreciation of the positives of caregiving. This process might also facilitate families and caregivers in talking about and reflecting upon their experiences in a more positive and joyous light (Berg-Weger et al., 2001).

Directions for Future Research

The findings from this study suggest that future research should focus on the factors that lead to positives of caregiving, which might identify and assist in the development of services, supports, and specific interventions that will potentially facilitate improved outcomes for individual caregivers, care receivers, and the family as a whole. As such, there is a need to explore links among positives, social supports, coping, and appraisal processes of caregivers of children with autism and other chronic conditions. Furthermore, future research should investigate these links to determine how the facilitation of positives might affect caregivers' lived experiences. Also, as mentioned earlier, it is important to examine positives and joys not only in relation to stressors but also as a significant factor throughout the entire stress-coping process.

Last, this study focused on the retrospective experience of mothers whose children were under 18 years old. However, for the first time in history, large numbers of people with autism are reaching old age (National Advisory Council on Aging, 2004; Seltzer et al., 2004). As a result, parents now "face a lifetime of caregiving responsibilities" (Kim, Greenberg, Seltzer, & Krauss, 2003, p. 313). However, very little is known about this constellation of caregivers and care receivers. There is need to explore the experiences of individuals with autism, their caregivers, and families as they age over the life course.

Note

1. In British Columbia and Alberta, for instance, institutional services and supports are attached to a diagnosis of autism (see Corman, 2007b).

References

Berg-Weger, M., Rubio, D., & Tebb, S. (2001). Strengths-based practice with family caregivers of the chronically ill: Qualitative insights. *Families in Society: The Journal of Contemporary Human Services, 82*(3), 263–272.

Chappell, N., Gee, E., McDonald, L., & Stones, M. (2003). *Aging in contemporary Canada.* Toronto, Canada: Pearson Educational Publishers/Prentice Hall.

Cohen, B. (1999). Intervention and supervision in strengths-based social work practice. *Families in Society: The Journal of Contemporary Human Services, 80*(5), 460–466.

Corman, M. K. (2007a). *Primary caregivers of children with autism spectrum disorders—An exploration of the stressors, joys, and parental coping before and after out-of-home placement.* (Masters Thesis, University of Victoria, Canada, 2007). Available from the Electronic Theses and Dissertations Web site: http:// hdl.handle.net/1828/1227.

Corman, M. K. (2007b, August). *Panning for gold—An institutional ethnography of health relations in the process of diagnosing autism in British Columbia.* Paper presented at the meeting of The Society for the Study of Social Problems, New York.

Creswell, J. (2002). *Research design: Qualitative, quantitative, and mixed methods approaches* (2nd ed.). Thousand Oaks, CA: Sage Publications.

Cummins, R. (2001). The subjective well-being of people caring for a family member with a severe disability at home: A review. *Journal of Intellectual & Developmental Disability, 26*(1), 83–100.

DeMyer, M. (1979). *Parents and children in autism.* Washington, DC: V. H. Winston & Sons.

Dunn, M., Burbine, T., Bowers, C., & Tantleff-Dunn, S. (2001). Moderators of stress in parents of children with autism. *Community Mental Health Journal, 37*(1), 39–52.

Early, T. (2001). Measures for practice with families from a strengths perspective. *Families in Society: The Journal of Contemporary Human Services, 82*(2), 225–232.

Esterberg, K. G. (2002). *Qualitative methods in social research.* Boston: McGraw-Hill.

Fleischmann, A. (2004). Narratives published on the Internet by parents of children with autism: What do they reveal and why is it important? *Focus on Autism and Other Developmental Disabilities, 19*(1), 35–43.

Folkman, S. (1997). Positive psychological states and coping with severe stress. *Social Science & Medicine, 45*(8), 1207–1221.

Folkman, S., & Moskowitz, J. T. (2000a). Positive affect and the other side of coping. *American Psychologist, 55*(6), 647–654.

Folkman, S., & Moskowitz, J. T. (2000b). Stress, positive emotion, and coping. *Current Directions in Psychological Science, 9*(4), 115–118.

Grant, G., Ramcharan, P., McGrath, M., Nolan, M., & Keady, J. (1998). Rewards and gratifications among family caregivers: Towards a refined model of caring and coping. *Journal of Intellectual Disability Research, 42*(1), 58–71.

Gray, D. (1994). Coping with autism: Stresses and strategies. *Sociology of Health & Illness, 16*(3), 275–300.

Gray, D. (1998). *Autism and the family: Problems, prospects, and coping with the disorder.* Springfield, IL: Charles C. Thomas Publisher.

Gray, D. (2002a). Ten years on: A longitudinal study of families of children with autism. *Journal of Intellectual & Developmental Disability, 27*(3), 215–222.

Gray, D. (2002b). 'Everybody just freezes. Everybody is just embarrassed': Felt and enacted stigma among parents of children with high functioning autism. *Sociology of Health & Illness, 24*(6), 734–749.

Gray, D. (2003). Gender and coping: The parents of children with high functioning autism. *Social Sciences & Medicine, 56*, 631–642.

Holstein, J. A., & Gubrium, J. F. (2002). Active interviewing. In D. Weinberg (Ed.), *Qualitative research methods* (pp. 112–126). Oxford, UK: Blackwell.

Ivey, J. (2004). What do parents expect? A study of likelihood and importance issues for children with autism spectrum disorders. *Focus on Autism and Other Developmental Disabilities, 19*(1), 27–33.

Kaminsky, L., & Dewey, D. (2001). Sibling relationships of children with autism. *Journal of Autism and Developmental Disorders, 31*(4), 399–410.

Kelso, T., French, D., & Fernandez, M. (2005). Stress and coping in primary caregivers of children with a disability: A qualitative study using the Lazarus and Folkman process model of coping. *Journal of Research in Special Educational Needs, 5*(1), 3–10.

Kim, W., Greenberg, S., Seltzer, M., & Krauss, W. (2003). The role of coping in maintaining the psychological well-being of mothers of adults with intellectual disability and mental illness. *Journal of Intellectual Disability Research, 47*(4-5), 313–327.

Lazarus, R., & Folkman, S. (1984). *Stress, appraisal, and coping.* New York: Springer Publishing.

Mansell, W., & Morris, K. (2004). A survey of parents' reactions to the diagnosis of an autistic spectrum disorder by a local service: Access to information and use of services. *Autism, 8*(4), 387–407.

Moustakas, C. (1994). *Phenomenological research methods.* Thousand Oaks, California: Sage Publications.

Moerer-Urdahl, T., & Creswell, J. (2004). Using transcendental phenomenology to explore the "ripple effect" in a leadership mentoring program. *International Journal of Qualitative Methods, 3*(2), 1–28.

National Advisory Council on Aging. (2004). *Seniors on the margins: Aging with a developmental disability.* Canada: Minister of Public Works and Governmen Services Canada.

Pearlin, L., Lieberman, M., Menaghan, E., & Mullan, J. (1981). The stress process. *Journal of Health and Social Behavior, 22*(4), 337–356.

Pearlin, L., Mullan, J., Semple, S., & Skaff, M. (1990). Caregiving and the stress process: An overview of concepts and their measures. *The Gerontologist, 30*(5), 583–594.

Pierpont, J. (2004). Emphasizing caregiver strengths to avoid out-of-home placement of children with severe emotional and behavioral disturbances. *Journal of Human Behavior in the Social Environment, 9*(1/2), 5–17.

Pruchno, R. (2003). Enmeshed lives: Adult children with developmental disabilities and their aging mothers. *Psychology and Aging, 18*(4), 851–857.

Schopler, E., & Mesibov, G. (1994). *Behavioral issues in autism.* New York: Plenum Press.

Schwartz, C. (2003). Parents of children with chronic disabilities: The gratification of caregiving. *Families in Society: The Journal of Contemporary Human Services, 84*(4), 576–584.

Seltzer, M., Shattuck, P., Abbeduto, L., & Greenberg, J. (2004). The trajectory of development in adolescents and adults with autism. *Mental Retardation and Developmental Disabilities Research Reviews, 10*(4), 234–247.

Tomanik, S., Harris, G., & Hawkins, J. (2004). The relationship between behaviours exhibited by children with autism and maternal stress. *Journal of Intellectual & Developmental Disability, 29*(1), 16–26.

Weiss, M. (2002). Hardiness and social support as predictors of stress in mothers of typical children, children with autism, and children with mental retardation. *Autism, 6*(1), 115–130.

Wing, L. (1988). The continuum of autistic characteristics. In E. Schopler & G. Mesibov (Eds.), *Diagnosis and assessment in autism* (pp. 91–110). New York: Plenum Press.

MICHAEL K. CORMAN, MA, is a doctoral student in the Department of Sociology at the University of Calgary and a part-time faculty member in the Department of Sociology & Anthropology at Mount Royal College in Calgary, Alberta. His research and teaching interests include the sociology of health and illness, aging, institutional ethnography, caregiving and autism spectrum disorders, health care work, and critical research strategies. Correspondence regarding this article can be sent to the author at mkcorman@ucalgary.ca or University of Calgary, Department of Sociology, Social Sciences 913, 2500 University drive NW, Calgary, AB, T2N 1N4 Canada.

Author's note—I would like to thank Dr. Neena L. Chappell for her continued support throughout the larger study that contributed to this article and the preparation of this manuscript.

Bereavement after Caregiving

RICHARD SCHULZ, PhD, RANDY HEBERT, MD, MPH, AND KATHRIN BOERNER, PhD

O f the approximately 2.4 million deaths that occur in the United States each year, nearly 70% are the result of chronic conditions such as heart disease, cancer, stroke, and respiratory diseases. The large majority of decedents are older persons suffering from one or more disabling conditions which compromised their ability to function independently prior to death. As a result, a typical death is preceded by an extended period of time during which one or more family members provide unpaid care in the form of health and support services to their disabled relative.[1] A recent survey estimates the out-of-pocket cost of caring for an aging parent or spouse averages about $5500 a year.[2]

Our understanding of bereavement is undergoing fundamental changes as a result of recent prospective studies of bereavement that focus on circumstances surrounding the death of a loved one. One important finding to emerge in recent years concerns the impact of family caregiving on caregiver response to death of a loved one.[3,4] Family members involved in care provision before death show remarkable resilience in adapting to the death of their relatives. Symptoms of depression and grief decline rapidly after the death and return to near normal levels within a year of the death.[5] This may be due to multiple reasons, including having time to prepare for the impending death and life afterward, relief from the burdens of caregiving, an end to the suffering of their loved one, and the absence of guilt over having done the "work of caregiving."

Despite the generally positive prognosis for most bereaved caregivers, a sizable minority continues to experience high levels of stress and psychiatric problems after death. Approximately 10% to 15% of people experience chronic depression.[6] In our own work with caregivers of patients with dementia, we found that 30% of caregivers were at risk for clinical depression 1 year post-death, and 20% experience complicated grief.[4,5] As described below, complicated grief is distinct from both depression and normal grief reactions.

Understanding the variability in response to death and the role of caregiving factors as predictors of bereavement outcomes is critical to developing effective interventions for this group. To address this issue, we distinguish among 2 types of predictors of pathologic depression and grief outcomes among caregivers: Factors associated with the caregiving experience prior to death, and factors associated with depression and grief assessed postbereavement. The rationale for making this

Approximately 20% of bereaved caregivers will experience a variety of psychiatric symptoms including depression and/or complicated grief, a disorder characterized by persistently high levels of distress that impair functioning in important life domains. We identify prebereavement risk factors for poor adjustment after the death of a loved one along with preventive strategies that can be implemented prior to death as well as diagnostic procedures and therapeutic strategies that can be used to identify and treat individuals who develop complicated grief disorder after death.

Schulz R, Hebert R, Boerner K. Bereavement after caregiving, *Geriatrics*, 2008:63(1):20–22.

distinction is that each factor provides a different opportunity for intervention. Identifying which caregiving factors contribute to poor bereavement outcomes provides us with important leads about interventions that could be delivered during caregiving. Likewise, postbereavement factors linked to poor bereavement response may help identify intervention options that can be delivered after death.

Caregivers at Risk for Poor Bereavement Outcomes

The most common finding across multiple studies is that prebereavement levels of mental distress such as depression and anxiety are predictive of postbereavement adjustment. A related finding is that high levels of burden, feeling exhausted and overloaded, lack of support, and having competing responsibilities such as work or caring for younger children are all associated with negative postbereavement outcomes.[3,7,8] The fact that increased burden is a risk factor for poor bereavement outcomes may explain in part the higher mortality rate observed among caregivers of terminal patients who do not use hospice services when compared to those who do.[9] Demographic factors also play a role. Individuals with lower income, lower education, and those who are African Americans are also more likely to exhibit greater depression and complicated grief after the death.

Table 1 Questions to Identify Caregivers at Risk for Negative Postbereavement Outcomes

Do you feel overwhelmed by the responsibilities of providing care to your relative?

Do you feel isolated from family and friends?

Do you feel prepared for the death of your loved one?

In the past month have you felt depressed, sad, or anxious much of the time?

Table 2 Symptoms of Complicated Grief

Trouble accepting the death

Inability to trust others since the death

Excessive bitterness related to the death

Feeling uneasy about moving on

Detachment from formerly close others

Feeling life is meaningless without the deceased

Feeling that the future holds no prospect for fulfillment without the deceased

Feeling agitated since the death

A recent randomized trial of dementia in caregivers showed that psychosocial-behavioral interventions designed to decrease caregiver burden and distress had the added benefit of preventing complicated grief after the death of their loved one.[4] This suggests that adverse effects of bereavement can be addressed through preventive treatments delivered to family caregivers prior to the death of their loved one. Individuals at risk for negative postbereavement outcomes can be identified by asking a few questions to determine how stressful caregiving is, the availability of support from family and friends, how depressed and anxious they feel, and whether or not they feel prepared for the death of their loved one (see Table 1). Treatment options for caregivers thus identified include interventions to reduce caregiver burden, such as hospice care, behavioral and pharmacologic treatment of depression and anxiety, and referral to religious counselors.

Diagnosis and Treatment of Complicated Grief

One of the hallmarks of poor response to death is persistent (ie, 6 months or longer) complicated grief. This disorder is distinct from normal grief reactions or depression. It is characterized by an intense longing and yearning for the person who died and by recurrent intrusive and distressing thoughts about the absence of the deceased, making it difficult to concentrate, move beyond an acute state of mourning, form other interpersonal relationships, and engage in potentially rewarding activities. Complicated grief is a source of significant distress and impairment and is associated with a range of negative psychiatric and physical health consequences.[10]

Formal diagnostic criteria for complicated grief disorder have been proposed for inclusion in the *Diagnostic and Statistical Manual of Mental Disorders, Fifth Edition (DSM-V)*.[11] A diagnosis of complicated grief disorder requires that the bereaved person must have persistent and disruptive yearning, pining, and longing for the deceased. The individual must experience 4 of the 8 symptoms at least several times a day and/or to a severely distressing disruptive degree (see Table 2). Symptoms of distress must endure for at least 6 months and significantly impair functioning in important life domains.

Complicated grief often occurs along with other disorders such as major depression and post-traumatic stress disorder (PTSD) and is associated with suicidality and self-destructive behaviors,[12] but it is a distinct disorder requiring treatment strategies different from those used with major depression and PTSD. A recent randomized trial found higher and faster rates of improvement among persons with complicated grief using loss-focused, cognitive behavioral therapy techniques when compared to rates obtained with a standard interpersonal therapy approach used to treat depression.[13] Components of effective treatment included repeated retelling of the story of the death, having an imaginary conversation with the deceased, and working on confronting avoided situations. In general, although traditional treatments for depression after bereavement such as referral to a psychiatrist or psychologist for medications and/or psychotherapy can be effective in treating depression and to some extent, complicated grief, there is added benefit to treatments that are specifically tailored to address symptoms of complicated grief.[6]

Hundreds of studies carried out in the past 2 decades have documented the negative health effects of caregiving, showing that caregivers are at increased risk of psychiatric and physical morbidity.[14] The challenges of caregiving become even more extreme as the care-recipient nears death. When the death does occur, the caregiver enters bereavement already compromised with high levels of depression and anxiety and sometimes physical exhaustion brought about by the caregiving experience. Even with these vulnerabilities, caregivers, for the most part, adapt well to the death of their loved one. Psychiatric symptomatology typically improves and caregivers are able to effectively reengage in activities that may have lapsed while caregiving.

Opportunities for Intervention

Despite this generally positive picture of caregiver adaptation to bereavement, a minority of caregivers exhibit adverse bereavement outcomes in the form of high levels of depression and/or complicated grief. High levels of burden, physical exhaustion, lack of social support, along with traditional predictors, such as prebereavement anxiety and depression, are all associated with negative postbereavement outcomes. Although empirical support for the efficacy of bereavement interventions to enhance adaptation to bereavement is mixed at best,[13,15] researchers have generally not tested preventive approaches in which interventions are delivered prior to death. In addition, new treatment strategies described above specifically designed to treat complicated grief hold promise for helping individuals who are not able to effectively cope with the death of a loved one.

References

1. Emanuel EJ, Fairclough DL, Slutsman J, et al. Assistance from family members, friends, paid care givers, and volunteers in the care of terminally ill patients. *N Engl J Med,* 1999; 341(13):956–63.

2. Gross J. Study finds higher outlays for caregivers of older relatives. *New York Times,* November 19, 2007:A18.

3. Schulz R, Boerner K, Hebert RS, Caregiving and bereavement. In Stroebe MS, Hansson RO, et al, eds. *Handbook of Bereavement Research and Practice: 21st Century Perspectives.* Washington, DC: American Psychological Association Press; in press.

4. Schulz R, Boerner K, Shear K, et al. Predictors of complicated grief among dementia caregivers: a prospective study of bereavement. *Am J Geriatr Psychiatry,* 2006;14(8):650–658.

5. Schulz R, Mendelsohn AB, Haley WE, et al. End of life care and the effects of bereavement on family caregivers of persons with dementia. *N Engl J Med.* 2003;349(20): 1936–1942.

6. Hensley PL, Treatment of bereavement related depression and traumatic grief. *J Affect Disord.* 2006;92(1):117–124.

7. Hebert RS, Dang Q, Schulz R. Preparedness for the death of a loved one and mental health in bereaved caregivers of patients with dementia: findings from the REACH study. *J Palliat Med.* 2006;9(3):683–693.

8. Boerner K, Schulz R, Horowitz A. Positive aspects of caregiving and adaptation to bereavement, *Psychol Aging.* 2004;19(4):668–675.

9. Christakis NA, Iwashyna TJ. The health impact of health care on families: a matched cohort study of hospice use by decedents and mortality outcomes in surviving, widowed spouses, *Soc Sci Med.* 2003;57(3):465–475.

10. Prigerson HG, Bierhals AJ, Kasi SV, et al. Traumatic grief as a risk factor for mental and physical morbidity, *Amer J Psychiatry.* 1997;154(5):616–623.

11. Zhang B, El-Jawahri A, Prigerson HG, Update on bereavement research: evidence-based guidelines for the diagnosis and treatment of complicated bereavement. *J Palliat Med.* 2006;9(5):1188–1203.

12. Latham AE, Prigerson HG. Suicidality and bereavement: complicated grief as psychiatric disorder presenting greatest risk for suicidality. *Suicide Life Threat Behav.* 2004;34(4): 350–362.

13. Shear K, Frank E, Houck PR, et al. Treatment of complicated grief: a randomized controlled trial. *JAMA.* 2005;293(21):2601–2608.

14. Schulz R, Beach S. Caregiving as a risk factor for mortality: the caregiver health effects study. *JAMA.* 1999;282: 2215–2219.

15. Schut H, Stroebe MS. Interventions to enhance adaptation to bereavement. *J Palliat Med.* 2005;8(suppl 1):S140–147.

Dr SCHULZ is Professor of Psychiatry, Director, University Center for Social and Urban Research, University of Pittsburgh, Pittsburgh, Pa. **Dr HEBERT** is Assistant Professor of Medicine, Division of General Internal Medicine, University of Pittsburgh. **Dr BOERNER** is Senior Research Scientist, Jewish Home Lifecare, Research Institute on Aging, New York, NY.

Disclosures: Drs Schulz, Hebert, and Boerner disclose that they have no financial relationship with any manufacturer in this area of medicine.

Love, Loss—and Love

The death of a young child can devastate a family. How couples decide they're ready to try again.

KAREN SPRINGEN

Two years ago, 5-month-old Cody Schmurr died from multiple congenital myopathy—a rare condition that made his muscles so weak he could not exhale the carbon dioxide from his lungs. Doctors told Cody's parents, Tracy and Steve Schmurr, that there was a one in three chance that their next child might suffer from the same problem. For the Livermore, Calif., couple, it was a risk worth taking. "I didn't want to ever turn back and say, 'I wish we would have'," says Tracy. "Even the five months with Cody were the best five months of my life." In June 2006, 13 months after Cody's death, Tracy delivered a healthy baby boy named Levi.

Every year, about 25,000 kids under age 10 die, most from congenital anomalies, unintentional injury (mainly car accidents), premature birth and cancer. It is the ultimate tragedy: kids aren't supposed to pass away before their parents. But sometimes they do. And then what? "Every family, at some point, evaluates whether they should have another child," says Kristin James, bereavement counselor at Children's Memorial Hospital in Chicago. "When that loss occurs, they're suddenly incomplete. You've defined yourself as a family of five, and now you're a family of four." The fear factor (will another child die, too?) often looms large.

The loss of a child can put tremendous stress on even the best marriages and the closest families. "Losing a kid makes you lose faith in life," says child psychiatrist Alvin Rosenfeld. "To reclaim that faith in living, that it's worth doing this again, is an act of enormous courage." No one knows how many parents gather that courage—or how they fare. It's difficult to study. "You certainly can't randomly assign people to have a child or not have a child," says Douglas Hawkins, a pediatric oncologist at Seattle Children's Hospital. Yet, anecdotally, many experts say parents seem to do better when they try again. "The most profound attachment in human life is mother and child," says John Golenski, executive director of the George Mark Children's House, a residential facility in San Leandro, Calif., for kids with terminal illnesses and their families. "The best adaptation to [the loss of a child] is another attachment."

Still, another attachment is not for everyone. "Some families are willing to risk anything to hold a healthy baby. Some families can't imagine going through that pain again," says James. "It's very hard to convince them that this won't happen again. Their bubble of what they think is safe and normal is forever shattered." Even if they want to conceive again, some couples run into fertility problems. These families may—or may not—decide to adopt.

For one couple, the decision was made easier by their children, including their dying son. On Christmas Day in 1997, Joey Albrecht, 8, died of a rare pediatric cancer. "Two weeks before Joey died, he told us that when he got to heaven, he was going to tell God to send us a baby," says his mother, Cheryl Albrecht. Right after the funeral, Cheryl's daughter, Kelly, now 21, said, "Mom, the house is so quiet. Can we have another baby?" The answer: yes. In January 1999, Cheryl gave birth to Julia, now 8, followed by Nick, now 7. Cheryl remembers seeing Julia's heart beat on the ultrasound. "I thought, 'Oh, my God, my heart is starting to grow again'," she says. "I can love again. There is going to be happiness in my life."

Such feelings cause some parents to feel guilty. "What I do hear a lot is the feeling of, 'Am I betraying my child who died?'" says Barbara Sourkes, director of the pediatric palliative-care program at Lucile Packard Children's Hospital at Stanford. "'How can I throw myself wholeheartedly into a new child and leave the child who died behind?'" Cheryl Albrecht says Julia and Nick have not replaced her Joey. "But they helped us love again and helped us keep happy," she says.

All parents worry about their kids' health and safety—more so when they've lost a child. Michelle and Bill McGowan's daughter Katie died last year, just before her first birthday. (She was born with a blockage in her intestine.) Four months ago, the McGowans, of Glenview, Ill., had a healthy baby boy, John. Michelle still attends a support group at Children's Memorial in Chicago, where moms talk about their fears that other offspring will die. "As a mom anyway, you can be paranoid. Now I'm paranoid to the nth degree," says McGowan. Even her older kids, Kylie, now 4, and Bill, now 6, worry. One day Kylie, concerned about John's getting a cold, said, "We can't touch him. He's going to die." Michelle reassured her that John would be OK. And every week after church, they visit Katie's gravestone, with a small butterfly etched at the top of the cross. (Experts say this sort of ritual is normal.) Michelle tells her kids, "Sometimes butterflies fly away, and you don't see them again." But sometimes they stay—and sometimes new ones are born.

A Family Undertaking

HOLLY STEVENS

When Harriet Ericson died in January 2007 at age 93, she went to the grave in the same manner in which she lived her final years—lovingly tended by her son Rodger Ericson of Austin,Texas. A former U.S. Air Foree chaplain and Lutheran pastor (ELCA), Ericson bathed, anointed and dressed his mother's body, then laid it in a casket he had built himself and named "hope chest" to reflect the family's faith in the resurrection. The next day, with the help of his daughters and grandsons, he lifted her casketed remains into the bed of his pickup truck and secured the precious cargo for a road trek to Minnesota, where a family grave plot was waiting.

Except for the preparation of the grave, Ericson took care of all the details that would usually be handed to a commercial mortician. Ericson was, in effect, his mother's funeral director—and it was all completely legal.

Referred to as home funerals by most who practice them, these homespun arrangements arc protected by law in 44 states. "A home funeral can help people gently integrate the death into their lives and faith." says home funeral educator Donna Belk, who helped Ericson prepare for his mother's passing. "When the body stays at home for up to a few days, family and friends remain connected to the entire process; the gradual changes that occur in the body over this time frame coincide with the family's adjustment to its loss." Even in the six states that require the involvement of a commercial provider—Connecticut, Indiana, Louisiana, Michigan, Nebraska and New York—some families have been able to work with morticians so as to participate more fully in the process.

The term *home funeral* does not mean that a funeral ritual is necessarily held in the home. It refers to an approach to the entire process from the moment of death to final disposition:

A home funeral is a noncommercial response to death.

A home funeral is a noncommercial, family-centered response to death that involves the family and its social community in the care and preparation of the body for burial or cremation and/or in planning and carrying out related rituals or ceremonies and/or in the burial or cremation itself. A home funeral may occur entirely within the family home or not. It is differentiated from the institutional funeral by its emphasis on minimal, noninvasive care and preparation of the body; by its reliance on the family's own social networks for assistance and support; and by the relative or total absence of commercial funeral providers in its proceedings. (From *Undertaken with Love: A Home Funeral Guide for Congregations and Communities,* by the Home Funeral Committee Manual Publishing Group.)

A home funeral can include a religious ceremony in a church. The family may choose to have the body present at the ceremony or not, and may have the casket open or closed. For Christians, a home funeral can address the same religious purposes served by other funeral arrangements carried out within a religious setting: to treat the body with reverence and honesty, to proclaim the hope of resurrection and our risen life in Christ, to commend the deceased into God's care, and to mark our common bond with all who are alive with us and who have died before us.

A home funeral protects the sanctity of the process by removing the material pressures that have shaped American funeral etiquette since the Civil War, when affluent families began paying embalming surgeons to find their fallen sons on the battlefield and inject them with enough arsenic for the body to be preserved for the trip home. At that point a commercial industry began to grow, one that was beholden less to the precepts of the church than to the material and seemingly insatiable whims of consumers—even at life's end.

Is it any wonder that common funeral myths point back to an industry that makes its profits by catering to and encouraging material impulses? In my work as a funeral consumer advocate, families tell me time and again that they had no idea that embalming rarely is required by law or that they can buy an inexpensive casket from a source other than the funeral home or even construct their own.

"I have no problems with people requesting and using the services of funeral homes as long as morticians are not pushing or deceiving the grieving family into expenses that are not necessary," Ericson told me. He said that an employee of Service Corporation International, the nation's largest funeral home chain, told him that every cemetery in America requires an outer liner for cremated remains. When Ericson responded that he knew that was not so, the salesperson qualified his answer:

"Well, not every cemetery, but yes, every cemetery in the country that SCI owns."

Religious leaders are often lured into complacency by the promotional favors they receive from funeral directors. In his book *Does This Mean You'll See Me Naked?* (Rooftop Publishing), funeral director Robert Webster recalls that a former boss, also a funeral director, would welcome a new minister to town with a pen and pencil set. On the next visit, the funeral director would deliver tickets to Cincinnati Reds games; at other times, he'd press a crisp $100 bill into the pastor's hand or send a fruit basket. "These people help us to stay in business," Webster's boss told him. "Go out of your way to treat them well."

In a home funeral involving a parishioner, the pastor can take the lead in helping families integrate the care of the body, the funeral ceremony and the interpretation of the death into a religious context. By contrast, in a typical arrangement with a funeral home, says Ericson. "It was not uncommon for me as a pastor to receive $75 for my services—visitation of the family at the time of death, arranging the religious service with the family, preparing the bulletin, getting the church in order, preparing a personalized yet theologically sound sermon, and conducting the burial/committal service—while the mortician charged an extra $75 to have the service at my church."

In my faith community, New Garden Friends Meeting in Greensboro, North Carolina, a committee assists families in our congregation that want to care for their own dead. We've identified our legal rights and responsibilities in assisting with home funerals. We bring the simple, noninvasive skills involved in caring for the body at home. We bring ease and acquired wisdom to the process, offering families an option for spiritual and emotional closure at life's end.

In Raleigh, North Carolina, the Islamic Burial Society of North America teaches groups of Muslim men and women to care for their dead in keeping with the precepts of the Qur'an. Because Muslim and Orthodox Jewish burial practices are similar, the project has fostered friendships between members of the two faiths as they work together to return death rituals to their religious communities. Death care has a way of reminding us both of our mutual human limitations and of the place of faith as a source for hope and sustenance in the face of great loss.

Granted, even if most families knew that in most states they may care for their own dead without the involvement of a licensed funeral director, home funerals would be unlikely to put any professional undertakers out of work anytime soon. Americans have become so removed from their dead that even in a home funeral they hesitate to touch the body. The practice requires more involvement from the family, although the support of an experienced congregation can greatly ease the load. Occasionally, circumstances prohibit a vigil and make a home funeral impractical.

Families have found the home funeral process to be enormously healing.

Most people who have experienced home funerals tell me that they found the process to be enormously healing; it enabled them to participate creatively in honoring the one who died and to integrate the experience into the context of their faith in ways that commercial funeral homes and crematories cannot replicate. As Ericson says, "Home funerals mean less traipsing behind the undertaker, who is geared toward efficiency and profit."

I see more faith communities embracing home funerals and other less commercial practices at life's end. Some church-owned cemeteries have dropped vault requirements to allow ecologically minded parishioners to simplify their return to dust after death. In the Pocono Mountains, the Eastern Pennsylvania Conference of the United Methodist Church leases a portion of its forests to an organization that creates family burial sites for cremated remains at the roots of selected hardwood trees.

For the first time since embalming surgeons began to set up shop on Civil War battlegrounds, Americans are reassessing how funeral practices relate to congregational life. The growing interest in home funerals and other natural end-of-life practices offers religious institutions the opportunity to support alternatives that are embedded more deeply in community and resistant commercial culture. The home funeral movement calls on religious leaders to honor an etiquette that is simpler, more affordable and ultimately more sacred.

HOLLY STEVENS is a funeral consumer advocate and coordinator of the Undertaken with Love project at homefuneralmanual.org.

From *The Christian Century,* October 6, 2009, pp. 26–27. Copyright © 2009 by Christian Century. Reprinted by permission.

Stressors Afflicting Families during Military Deployment

Gina M. Di Nola

Operation Iraqi Freedom is a stressful time for many military families. Help is available, if one knows where to look. The U.S. Army has implemented a program to address the needs of family members–the Family Readiness Group or FRG. Before any program or group can assist spouses, it is necessary to name and understand the issues families face. In doing so, leaders can be better prepared to help family members handle the stressors associated with the current deployments in support of Operation Iraqi Freedom (OIF) and the Global War on Terrorism (GWOT).

History of the FRG

Involvement of spouses in the military started with the Revolutionary War. In May of 1780, Esther Reed (her husband was an aide to George Washington) and 39 wives started the first wives' club, which became known as "the Association". The Association performed fundraising for supplies, cooking, mending, nursing, and equipment caddying in exchange for rations to feed their families (1).

During World War II, the Association became known as the "waiting wives club", an established support system for family members back home. The club eventually evolved and was institutionalized after the Persian Gulf War (2) to today's family support group known as the Family Readiness Group (FRG). The FRG serves as the link between units and their spouses; it is the support system for family members, especially during wartime or deployment.

Role of the FRG

The FRG plays an important role in the military. The effectiveness of family support groups has been apparent since the Vietnam War (2). After the First Gulf War, the U.S. Army mandated that all units have an established family support group, or FRG (3). "Commanders have an obligation to provide assistance to establish and maintain personal and family affairs readiness . . . . Examples include Family Readiness Groups . . . ." (3). The role of the FRG is to keep families informed and updated during times of deployment, training, or military exercises. Although it doesn't practice the same formalities and structures as the military, the FRG is beneficial during the difficult times that military spouses must face.

Stressors during Deployments

There is no doubt that deployments cause much stress to the service member and the family. Operation Desert Storm/Shield was the largest military mobilization since the Vietnam War (4). Three categories of stressors were identified in a study done during Operation Desert Storm (5): emotional (missing the soldier, safety concern for the soldier), deployment-related (managing budget, Powers of Attorney, and increase in childcare costs), and general life events (non-English speakers, new to installation, etc.). The list of stressors noted at that time were loneliness, financial insecurities, children's discipline, and an overall feeling that the military was not concerned for their well-being. Some spouses did not use programs available to them for fear of being classified as unable to handle their problems. Others were not able to seek family support because they were not stationed near them. Family roles had to be changed and required adjustment by both parents and children.

Other factors affecting spouses during Operation Desert Storm were rumors. In 1992, the US Army War College reported that "family support groups helped, in some cases, to reduce rumors" (6). However, in a subsequent study conducted by the U.S. Army Research Institute (ARI) and the Walter Reed Army Institute of Research (WRAIR), "unit leaders' support for families was strongly related to rumors . . . ." The case study demonstrated that family support groups may facilitate the spread of rumors and any attempts to control rumors actually enhanced them (6).

Another stresser faced by families is spousal aggression. A study done between 1990 and 1994 revealed that there was a significant probability of aggression for soldiers who had deployed than those who did not (7). In 1996 Caliber Associates interviewed 96 couple participants in the Army's Family

Advocacy Programs. Half of the abusers had been deployed an average of 110 days and cited deployment as the triggering stressor (8). Between 2002 and 2004, Fort Bragg, NC alone reported 832 victims of domestic violence (9), which were deployment-related.

Children's reactions to deployments vary with age and developmental stage. Children's system levels are similar to the stress level experienced by their parents or caregiver. One would think the source of the stress would be the immediate family. Instead of being informed by their parents, active-duty children received most of their information from teachers. Media coverage also added to the concerns of safety of the deployed service member. There is an additional stress factor—concern for the service member's safety (10). Active duty children worried that the military parent would die during the deployment (11). Watanabe and Jensen state that children who were not prepared for the deployment fared not as well as those who were (12).

Current OIF Stressors

The National Military Family Association surveyed military spouses in 2005. Stress levels were measured for the various points of the deployment cycle. Fifteen percent experienced heightened stress levels upon notification of the deployment and 18 % upon the departure of the service. During the deployment or absence of the service member, 62 % felt the greatest stress. The respondents emphasized the need for good communication between the unit and the families. Some family members felt that "when entering a second or third deployment, they carry the unresolved anxieties and expectations from the last deployment(s)" (13).

Redeployment and reintegration were also times of much stress for families. The constant deployment left little time for adjustment for each phase of the deployment cycle. Family members expressed an interest in knowing what to expect prior to, during, and after the redeployment phase. Yet few participated in formal training or briefings offered by the installation (13).

Stressors and the FRG

Stressors may vary with each deployment, and everyone copes differently. By establishing family support groups, families were thought to be better equipped to handle the challenges of the military lifestyle, up to the point where the support group becomes a stressor. Whether it is the Army's Family Readiness Group, the Air Force's Key Spouse Program, the Navy's Ombudsman Program, or the Marine Corps's Key Volunteer Network, group dynamics within the support system can affect the coping mechanism of the family members.

The commitment of support group leaders was questioned in a survey conducted recently of 100 family members of deployed soldiers in 2007. Commitment concerns that were stated by the family members included lack of communication from leaders, slow dissemination of information from leaders, cliques within the family support groups (or the FRG), gossip, drama in the group, and limited group activities. Of those who did not like their FRG, 20 % still attended the meetings. Three percent of the participants did not know how to contact their leader in the event of an emergency. One family member suggested that a social worker be present at the meetings. Although 74 % remained on or near the installation, only 54 % attended support group meetings.

Conclusion

According to Webster (2006), readiness is defined as being "prepared mentally or physically for some experience or action." According to the Army's Training and Doctrine Command Public Affairs Office, "Family readiness is the state soldiers, spouses and family members proactively prepare for, and in which they are able to cope with mobilization, deployments and prolonged separations." (14). Independence, financial responsibility, etc. are a few of the attributes of readiness for today's family. Yet, no one knows how ready the family will be until the family separation or deployment occurs.

Deployments are inevitable while serving in the military. Families have many programs or resources available to them to help them cope with the challenges of the deployments, yet many do not use them. The intent of the FRG was to provide families these resources. Unfortunately, the dilemma can stem from the FRG. Addressing the stressors that families face is the first step to attaining readiness. With current and prolonged deployments in support of OIF or GWOT, time is of the essence.

References

1. Crossley A and Keller CA: The army wife handbook: Updated and expanded, Second edition, Sarasota, FL, ABI Press, 1993.
2. Rosen LN, Durand DB: Coping with the unique demands of military family life. In The military family: A practice guide for Human Service providers, ed. Martin JA, Rosen LN, Sparacino LR, Westport, CT: Praeger, 2000; 55–72.
3. Department of the Army: Army Regulation 600–20: Army Command Policy. 2006.
4. Black Jr WG: Military-induced family separation: A stress reduction intervention. Social Work 1993; 38; no. 3.
5. Rosen LN, Durand DB, Martin JA: Wartime stress and family adaptation. In The military family: A practice guide for Human Service providers, ed. J. A. Martin, Rosen LN, Sparacino LR, Westport, CT, Praeger, 2000: 123–138.
6. Schumm WR, Bell DB, Knott B: Predicting the extent and stressfulness of problem rumors at home among army wives of soldiers deployed overseas on a humanitarian mission. Psychol Rep 2001; 89; 1: 123–34.
7. McCarroll JE, Ursano RJ, Liu X, Thayer LE, Newby JH, Norwood AE, Fullerton CS: Deployment and the probability of spousal aggression by US Army soldiers. Mil Med 2000; 165, 1: 41–4.
8. Brannen SJ, Hamlin II ER: Understanding spouse abuse in military families. In The military family: A practice guide for

Human Service providers, ed. Martin JA, Rosen LN, Sparacino LR; 169–183. Westport, CT: Praeger, 2000.

9. Houppert K: Base crimes: The military has a domestic violence problem. Retrieved on February 6, 2008 from http://www.motherjones.com/cgibin/print_article.pl?url=http://www.motherjones.com/news/featurex/2005/07/base_crimes.html

10. Stafford EM, Grady BA: Military family support. Pediatric Annals 2003; 32:2: 110–115.

11. Ryan-Wenger NA: Impact of the threat of war on children in military families. American Journal of Orthopsychiatry 2001: 71; 2: 236–244.

12. Watanabe HK, Jensen PS: Young children's adaptation to a military lifestyle. In The military family: A practice guide for Human Service providers, ed. Martin JA, Rosen LN, Sparacino LR: 209–223. Westport, CT, Praeger, 2000.

13. National Military Family Association: Cycles of deployment: An analysis of survey responses from April through September, 2005: 20. San Diego, Defense Web Technologies, 2005.

14. US Army's Training and Doctrine Command: Family Readiness Group Leader's Command Information Pocket Guide, 2003: Fort Monroe, VA, Headquarters, U.S. Army Training and Doctrine Command, 2003.

Children of the Wars

Students whose parents are called to active duty face challenges and stresses that schools must be ready to address.

LAWRENCE HARDY

"Why does Daddy have to go back?" 7-year-old Tyler kept asking.

It had been three years since Tyler's father, a U.S. Army captain, returned from Iraq after a seven-month deployment. Now he was leaving again—for an even longer tour—and the boy was nervous and upset. "Well, there are other daddies who have been in Iraq, and they have to come home to see their kids," Tyler's mother, Alison Sakimura explained as best she could. "And other daddies have to go" and take their place.

The boy asked: "Will Daddy come back?"

Sakimura answered truthfully: "Daddy wears a helmet to protect his head, and a vest to protect his heart, and carries a weapon. We just have to pray to God to watch over him."

That was in 2006, shortly before Capt. Greg Sakimura, a company commander in the 82nd Airborne, began a 15-month tour of northern Iraq. He returned to Fort Bragg, N.C., last fall; Tyler, who had bravely dubbed himself "Little Dad" to help his mother and two younger siblings in his father's absence, went back to being just another third-grader at Ed V. Baldwin Elementary School.

But Baldwin Elementary is not just another school. More than half its students have parents in the military; and, like similar children attending other schools on or near military bases, they must confront challenges and stresses that most children would never dream of. These include long separations from a parent and fears that loved ones may not return.

"We've had teachers lose spouses," says William C. Harrison, superintendent of the Cumberland County Schools, which includes Baldwin Elementary. "We've had—thank God, not many—students lose parents."

The stresses have intensified in recent years as the military, stretched thin from the ongoing wars in Iraq and Afghanistan, has had to send combat troops back to the war zones multiple times. Downtime has been shortened and deployments extended to as long as 15 months. That can be especially tough for families with school-age children.

"Some people miss two Christmases—that's very hard," says Shannon Shurko, a former science teacher who recently assumed the new position of Military Child Support Liaison for the Cumberland County Schools.

Trauma and Resilience

There are 700,000 children in the United States with at least one parent serving in Iraq, Afghanistan, or other military bases around the world—nearly 40 percent of the 1.8 million military children. According to a July 2007 report coauthored by Stephen Cozza, an expert on the mental health of military children and their families, it is estimated that more than 2,500 children have lost a parent in the Iraq war alone, and nearly 20,000 have had parents injured.

Despite these numbers, Cozza cautions against assuming that military children are uniformly traumatized by the increased stress. Many are extremely resilient, he says, and may even be made stronger by the challenges they face. "To assume either widespread trauma or uniform resilience is harmful to our efforts as concerned professionals," wrote Cozza and coauthor Alicia F. Lieberman, of the University of California, San Francisco. "The truth lies somewhere between these two extremes."

Stress is not the same as psychological trauma, the authors note; it is something we all experience in varying degrees. However, the stress level among military families in this period of extended conflict is substantial.

Last October, Army Secretary Pete Geren alluded to this stress when he said the Army's well-regarded system of family supports could have trouble keeping up with demand.

"For 500,000 spouses and 700,000 children, six years of war is uncharted territory," Geren told a meeting of the Association of the United States Army. "Our family systems . . . did not contemplate the operational tempo our families are experiencing today."

The Front Lines

Alison Sakimura is on the front lines of those family support systems. The wife of an infantry officer who was in charge of 130 soldiers in Iraq, she feels a responsibility to the "Family

Preparing and Supporting Military Children Are Critical

Maybe they develop attention problems, and their grades slip. Or maybe they don't show any signs at all that they are among the "suddenly military" children.

These are children of reservists and National Guard troops whose parents have been sent overseas, says Larry W. Moehnke, chief of staff of the Military Child Education Coalition in Harker Heights, Texas. Moehnke says more than 480,000 children between the ages of 5 and 18 have parents in these service branches, but the coalition has no estimate of the number of these whose parents are deployed.

For schools on or near military bases, the needs of military children are well-known. That may not be the case with children of National Guard members and reservists, who are spread out in school districts across the country. Indeed, some districts may not even know they have children whose parents are deployed, and, even if they do, they may not know how to help them.

The coalition sponsors professional development institutes for school counselors and special education teachers who serve military children. A special institute also trains educators in how to support children with parents in the National Guard and reserves who have been deployed.

"Basically, it's a matter of schools trying to open the lines of communication—letting parents know the schools are supportive and will do what they can to ease anxieties during this period of time," Moehnke says.

An online booklet, *How to Prepare Our Children and Stay Involved in Their Education During Deployment,* is also available for parents and educators (See www.militarychild.org).

Readiness Group" back home. She has a time-consuming volunteer job sending e-mails to its members—parents of soldiers, other relatives, fiancées, and 60 spouses—with information and messages of support.

"We've been in the military for 12 years," she says, using the plural pronoun to describe a commitment that extends to her entire family.

The e-mails let families know about impending deployments, tell them of family-related events on the base, and offer support while they wait for their spouses and loved ones to come home.

When her husband would call from Iraq, he would tell her little more than, "It's hot. It's busy."

"I already know it's hot. I already know it's busy," she recalls telling him. "Will you tell me something else?"

But actually, she didn't want to know too much more, and he was more interested in hearing news from her, things like how the children were doing in school and who got an A on a test.

Kimberly Nieto, a social studies teacher at a Cumberland County middle school, said it helped to keep her children busy and maintain family routines while her husband was deployed in

Iraq for 12 months (his second deployment). Counselors at her now-6- and 7-year-old daughters' elementary school regularly checked on them and the children of other deployed parents.

"That was definitely helpful," Nieto says.

It also helped that her husband, a technical inspector for helicopters, didn't have to travel much during most of his tour and could talk to the family most nights via Internet and Webcam.

The day he came home to Fort Bragg and strode down the "Green Ramp" that has become a symbol of joy to military families, her daughters got excited, and that made now-3-year-old Alexander excited as well—and anxious to meet the parent he'd known only from the Webcam.

"Their Only Memory Is War"

Adrianne Hakes remembers growing up during World War II and the air raid drills that enveloped her hometown of Studio City, Calif. She remembers the darkened windows and the streetlights that gave off a muted yellow glow instead of the bright white light of today. Back then, everyone knew there was a war going on, and everyone was involved. But not now.

"I can go through my daily activities and not give a thought to it," says Hakes, a school board member for the Oceanside Unified School District near the Marine Base at Camp Pendleton. "But for our military families, this is a reality every day of their lives."

Three of Oceanside's elementary schools are located on Camp Pendleton, and the school board has been studying ways to ease transitions for the typically mobile military child. "Just being a military child is stressful," Hakes says, "but having the war is more."

She said deployment is a three-part process, each with its own stressors. There is the anxiety of waiting for the family member to be deployed, the adjustment to life during the parent's absence, and another adjustment when he or she returns. A lot can happen to a family over 12 or 15 months. Children change, take on new responsibilities, and may not relate to their parents as they did when they were younger. This can be stressful and confusing for both the returning parent and the rest of the family.

School can be a place of comfort during wartime. Hakes described a first-grade class in which the teacher read the book *A Long, Long Time* about a parent in the military. Children who thought they were alone realized there were other classmates going through the same thing.

"They each thought they were by themselves," Hakes says. "It was a very poignant moment for the children."

She adds: "There are children in school who were 2 when this war started. Their only memory is war. They don't know anything but war."

"I Hope My Dad Doesn't Die in Iraq"

At Santa Margarita School on Camp Pendleton, 100 percent of the students are children of active duty military personnel, some in the Navy, but most in the Marines. Principal Pat Kurtz says the atmosphere is different than at other schools.

"Just the stress. The stress is just enormous," Kurtz says. "The children really are emotional. And, as anyone would be when there's this kind of stress, they sometimes lose it."

At the same time, Kurtz says she's "always in awe that they handle the stress as well as they do." There are no more discipline problems at Santa Margarita than at most schools, and the students are close to one another. When teachers and administrators do have to discipline students, they try to do so with reason and compassion.

There are many activities to do during lunch and recess. A Japanese club meets in one room (many children's families had been based in Okinawa). There's a Chess Club and a Spirit Club and just quiet spaces to be alone and read. In one class students gather to play LEGOs while the teacher does prep work. ("He's got the mother lode of LEGOs," Kurtz says.)

Kurtz and her staff see their work as a calling and their school as a sanctuary for military children. "As I see it," she says, "we can provide our little piece of patriotism, contribute something to make the families' lives a little better."

Chris Woodard teaches first grade at Santa Margarita. She says the stress level is higher than at the schools "in town." Children sometimes have trouble paying attention, following directions, and getting along with one another.

"'I hope my dad doesn't die in Iraq'—this is something my kids write in their journals," Woodard says.

And yet, she adds, "I'm just amazed that in my class my children operate at or above grade level, which is just, I think, a sign of their resilience."

The children are very interested in geography and want to know just where their parents are deployed. On one wall is a large chart that reads: "I'm a Military Child. My Military Parent is. . . ." The children put sticky tabs on the places, around the world, where they are stationed.

"We're Marines," Woodard says, "so we're based on ships, or headed toward Iraq, or training here." Of her 18 students, nine have a parent who is either on a ship headed toward Iraq, or in Iraq. "That's half my class. It's coming and going time here at Camp Pendleton. We're in transition."

Even on the base, the children are reminded of the conflicts, Kurtz says. They see helicopter flyovers and hear gunfire from the shooting range.

"We're very much children of the wars."

LAWRENCE HARDY (lhardy@nsba.org) is a senior editor of *American School Board Journal.*

From *American School Board Journal,* May 2008, pp. 24, 26–27. Copyright © 2008 by National School Board Association. Reprinted by permission.

A Divided House

In an era of bitter divorce battles, parents often use children as hammers to bash each other, manipulating not only the legal system but also their children's affections. Can a broken parent-child bond be restored?

MARK TEICH

In 1978, after Cathy Mannis and her future husband moved into the same cooperative at U.C. Berkeley, they ran into each other often. She was not immediately smitten. "I detested him at first, and I should have stayed with that feeling," recalls Cathy Mannis of her now ex-husband. "He was overweight and always very critical. Then he lost weight, became cuter, and started paying attention to me. He was going to be a doctor and he seemed so trustworthy; he said he would never desert his family as his own father had done to him." They started dating, and she ultimately cared for him enough to marry him. "I thought he'd be a good father, and I was dying to be a mother. I thought we'd have a good life."

She worked full-time as a legal secretary to put him through medical school. She also bought the two of them a town house with money she'd saved before marriage. When she gave birth to a boy, Matt (not his real name), she was as happy as she'd ever been. Over time, she saw signs that her husband was cheating on her, but she always forgave him.

Their second son, Robby, was born autistic, and things went downhill fast. The boy had speech and learning problems and was frequently out of control. Her husband was appalled. "He's dumber than a fish," he said.

Still, they had one more child, Harry (the name has been changed), hoping to give Matt a sibling without Robby's problems. Harry turned out normal, but he bonded most closely with Robby; they became inseparable.

When Cathy once again became convinced her husband was cheating—he inexplicably never came home one night—she finally threw him out. He filed for divorce before she could forgive him again.

Cathy was granted primary custody of the kids, and her ex soon married the woman he'd been seeing on the side. Because of all she had to do to help Robby as well as her other two kids, Cathy could no longer hold a full-time job. Meanwhile, her ex declared two bankruptcies and, at one point, even mental disability, all of which kept alimony payments to a trickle.

Eventually Cathy was so broke that her electricity was turned off; she and the boys ate dinner by candlelight. Then she became

so ill she had to be hospitalized for life-threatening surgery. She had no choice but to leave the kids with her ex. "He promised to return them when my health and finances improved," she says.

That was almost seven years ago. Her health has long since returned and she has a good job she can do from home, but the only child ever restored to her, despite nonstop court battles, was Robby. In fact, her ex got the courts to rule that the children should be permanently separated, leaving the other two children with him, since Robby was a "threat" to his younger brother's well-being.

Through all those years, Cathy says she faced a campaign of systematic alienation from Matt and Harry. "When I called to speak to them, I was usually greeted with coldness or anger, and often the boys weren't brought to the phone. Then my ex sent letters warning me not to call them at home at all. Whenever the kids came to stay with me, they'd report, 'Dad says you're evil. He says you wrecked the marriage.' " Then he moved thousands of miles away, making it vastly more difficult for her to see her children.

As time has passed, the boys have increasingly pulled away. Matt, now grown and serving in the military, never speaks to Cathy. Thirteen-year-old Harry used to say, "Mommy, why can't I stay with you? All the other kids I know live with their moms," before leaving visits with her. Now he often appears detached from her and uninterested in Robby, whom he once adored. His friends at his new home think his stepmother is his mom, because that's how she introduces herself. "She told me she would take my kids, and she did. The alienation is complete," rues Cathy. "All I ever wanted was to be a mom."

Divorcing parents have long bashed each other in hopes of winning points with kids. But today, the strategy of blame encompasses a psychological concept of parental alienation that is increasingly used—and misused—in the courts.

On the one hand, with so many contentious divorces, parents like Cathy Mannis have been tragically alienated from the children they love. On the other hand, parental alienation has been seized as a strategic tool in custody fights, its effects exploited in the courtroom, often to the detriment of loving parents protecting children from true neglect or abuse. With the impact of alienation so devastating—and false accusations so prevalent—it may take a judge with the wisdom of Solomon to differentiate between the two faces of alienation: a truly toxic parent and his or her victimized children versus manipulation of the legal system to claim damage where none exists.

The maligning of an ex need not be conscious—or even particularly extreme—to inflict lasting damage on a parent-child relationship.

A Symptom of Our Time?

Disturbed by the potential for alienation, many divorce courts have today instituted aggressive steps to intervene where they once just stood by. And with good reason: Alienation is ruinous to all involved. "In pathological or irrational alienation, the parent has done nothing to deserve that level of hatred or rejection from the child," explains University of Texas psychologist Richard Warshak, author of *Divorce Poison: Protecting the Parent-Child Bond from a Vindictive Ex.* "It often seems to happen almost overnight, and neither the rejected parent nor even the rejecting child understands why."

Often, in fact, it's the emotionally healthier parent who gets rejected, Warshak adds. That parent tends to understand that it's not in the child's best interests to lose the other parent. In contrast, the alienating parent craves revenge against the ex—then uses the child to exact that punishment. "It's a form of abuse," Warshak says. "Both parent and child are victims."

The alienating parent could vilify the ex to rationalize the dissolution of the relationship, explains Atlanta family therapist Frank Pittman, MD "Even though they managed to stay married to that person for 10 or 15 years, they now see him or her as the devil's spawn. It's the only way they can justify the breakup of their marriage, because otherwise, it would be their own fault." Once they've convinced themselves of that, it's easy enough to see why their children should be kept away from the other parent.

The maligning of an ex need not be conscious—or even particularly extreme—to inflict lasting damage on a parent-child relationship. "The child can hear negative comments inadvertently," notes Diane McSweeney, a marriage, family, and child counselor for the San Diego Unified School District. "Mom is on the phone with a friend, or Dad is talking to his girlfriend and the child happens to hear negative things. I don't think most people mean to insult the other parent to the child, but they're caught up in their grief for their failed marriage and don't appreciate that the kid can hear everything."

Alienation is especially damaging when one parent can't contain the anger—Mom cheated, or Dad hasn't visited or paid child support—and the wounded parent starts venting to the child. "They're just so desperate to talk to someone, and there's no one else they trust left to talk to. They would never do that to

---

Divorce without Devastating the Kids

Clearly, some parents—those who are physically or emotionally abusive—should be separated from their children. But these are the rarity, and in virtually all other cases, children would do better if their divorced parents stayed amicable partners in raising them. To keep a divorce as healthy as possible for children, follow these rules:

- **Never put** the other parent down. Divorce uproots children's feelings of stability badly enough—trashing or eliminating one of the parents magnifies the instability exponentially.
- **Rather than using** kids as a sounding board, divorced parents who are struggling with each other should seek outside emotional help.
- **Hold any charged** or volatile discussions far out of earshot of the children.
- **Do everything in** your power to accept your ex's next mate, since this person will also play an important role in your child's future stability and happiness.

Parents Who Alienate May Use the Following Tactics

- **Limiting the time** a child can spend with the other parent, and even violating court-ordered visitation schedules.
- **Making false** or unfounded accusations of neglect or abuse, especially in a legal forum. The most damaging expression of this is the false accusation of sexual abuse.
- **Creating fear** of rejection and threatening to withhold affection should the child express positive feelings about the absent parent.
- **Saying negative things** about the other parent in front of or within earshot of the child.
- **Blaming the other** parent for the collapse of the marriage.
- **Moving far away,** making it difficult for the other parent to have a regular relationship with a child.

---

their child in any other situation, but now they are in no shape or form ready to parent," says McSweeney. "The child is then thrown into confusion, feeling the need to take sides. 'I love Mom, but Mom hates Dad, so how can I love them both?' Or, 'I'll make Dad mad if I keep loving Mom, so I have to choose him over her.'"

"I was an adolescent when my parents were divorced," recalls Michelle Martin. "You were either on my mother's side or against her, and if you were on her side, you had to be against my father. She was so angry at him for walking out on her, felt so much shame and betrayal, that you couldn't possibly have a relationship with him if you wanted one with her."

Decades later, Michelle recalls her father (who has since died) as a gentle, caring man. But from the moment he left, her mother systematically worked to convince her that he had been abusive. "She really could not have portrayed him more negatively. 'How can you love him?' she'd say. 'You can't count on him.' He'd call, and she'd tell him my siblings and I didn't want to talk to him, then she'd tell me he didn't want to talk with us."

Afraid to lose her mother's love on top of having had her father walk out, Michelle ended up buying the brainwashing. Eventually, her father married another woman and moved away. At first he came into town regularly to visit, but the ever-renewing hostility gradually became too much for him, and the visits became few and far between.

Her father's reluctance to criticize her mother allowed Michelle's misconceptions to continue unabated, keeping up the walls her mother had created between them. It wasn't until she was 17 that her father finally said to her, " 'You know, a lot of the things you've been told about me were untrue.' It was instantly eye-opening." By her early twenties she'd reconnected with her father, but they only had about 15 years together; he died when she was 38. "I'd lost all those years with a wonderful man, as well as with the members of his family that I loved."

Strategies of War

There's another side to the alienation phenomenon: the hard-edged legal one. Although it is a psychological issue, parental alienation can be truly addressed only in the legal system. Remedy for alienation, say experts, requires an order from a court to allow a manipulated child time to bond with the alienated parent. It is critical, therefore, that there be proof that alienation has in fact occurred. If a parent seeking custody can document the phenomenon, the system—if it is working—will adjust a custody arrangement to promote relationship repair.

The courts worked fairly for Larry Felton, an orthodontist in Detroit (identifying details changed). His wife, an architect who had put her career on hold to raise their daughter, Emily, left Larry and later divorced him. Immersed in his practice, he settled for the once a week plus every other weekend visits the court imposed. "I was devoted and determined to make it work. I wasn't going to let anything keep me from having a relationship with my daughter," he says.

But when Emily grew older and he asked for a little more time with her, things turned ugly. By unilateral decree of his ex, he stopped getting even the limited time that was his due. By the time the court got involved, Emily had grown distant and withdrawn, blaming him for all that had happened. She resisted seeing him at all.

He might have lost his bid for more time with his daughter if not for a key piece of evidence. His ex called to tell him she was canceling yet another weekend with Emily. Then, thinking

she'd disconnected the phone when she had not, she said to the daughter and Felton's answering machine, "Your father is evil, a bad man, but we need him for his money. At least he's good for that."

After hearing the tape, the judge awarded primary custody to Larry in hopes of reversing the alienation that had been ongoing for years. Seven years later, 17-year-old Emily has reaped the benefits. Though it took time to earn her trust back, her father now has a solid relationship with her, and her time with her mother is more positive. "I think it saved her," Felton says.

Things are hardly ever so clear-cut in court. Often, judges don't have access to proof like Felton's incriminating voice mail. In the end, after listening to expert witnesses from both sides, decisions are often based on impressions and even the testimony of the children, the very ones who are brainwashed and may be least reliable of all.

"Even when a judge acknowledges that alienation occurred, the court can end up siding with the alienating parent because of the child's wishes," Warshak says. "Otherwise, they fear, the child in his anger might hurt himself or someone else."

In fact, it takes a sophisticated judge to realize what psychologists might see as obvious: Deep down, the child has never really stopped loving the other parent. He or she has just been brainwashed like a prisoner of war or a cult victim, programmed to accept destructive beliefs until critical thinking can be restored.

"Even if they say they don't want to see the parent, underneath they might be longing to reconnect," says Warshak. "These kids need more time with that parent rather than less. Only then will they have a chance to see that the poisoned thoughts are wrong." In the most extreme cases, children are permitted to see the alienating parent only during therapy sessions until the alienation has been resolved.

Other times judges listen mostly to the parent who says he or she has been wronged—and that too can be misleading. According to John E. B. Myers, a professor of law at the University of the Pacific McGeorge School of Law in Sacramento, California, false accusations of parental alienation do "tremendous harm to many children and their parents, particularly mothers seeking custody in family court."

According to Myers, fathers accused of sexual or other abuse by mothers often hide under the protective mantle of "parental alienation" in court, pitting accusation against accusation. The alleged alienator may be dismissed as manipulative, an assumption not always representing truth. The charge could paint a protective parent as a liar trying to poison a child instead of keeping him from harm.

University of California at Davis law professor Carol Bruch adds that the theory of parental alienation fails to account for the anger often felt by children of divorce, especially the kind of contentious divorce that results in custody fights in the first place. "Sometimes the child's feelings are prompted by the behavior of the noncustodial parent. That parent may not be abusive, but just deficient in some way. A parent can become estranged from a child without any provocation whatsoever from the other parent."

The estranged parent could accuse the custodial parent of alienating behavior through blindness to his or her own role.

It takes a sophisticated judge to realize what psychologists might see as obvious: that deep down, the child has never stopped loving the other parent.

Loss and Repair

With knowledgeable experts and astute judges, real alienation can be discerned from false accusations. When alienation is accurately recognized, appropriate intervention on the part of the court can certainly help families heal the damage.

Without the right intervention, however, the result is a scenario of loss and unresolved grief like that of Cathy Mannis. Ironically it is Robby, Cathy's autistic son, who is most acutely in touch with his pain.

"What his father did, first trying to institutionalize him as dangerous, then separating him from his brothers, gave him a devastating signal that he was not worthy, that he deserved punishment rather than help and love," explains Stephen Stahl, MD, PhD, Robby's psychiatrist and a professor of psychiatry at the University of California at San Diego.

Now 18, Robby feels rejected by both his father and his younger brother, both of whom have very little to do with him anymore. "My father never cared about me, so I don't care about him anymore," he says. "But I loved being with Harry every day and every night. I try to call him a lot, but my stepmom is often mean to me or hangs up on me. I almost never get to see him, and he doesn't call. It all makes me so sad."

Parents' grief is also profound. "The child is alive but still lost to you, so close but yet so far, there but not seeing you, and you're uncertain if you'll ever have the relationship back again," Warshak says. "You can't grieve the final loss, because you can never accept that it's final."

As for Cathy Mannis, she recently had Harry with her in San Diego for a one-week court-ordered visit. She and Robby were both thrilled to have the chance to reconnect with him. But as wonderful as that week was, it only set Mannis up for further heartbreak. "He left on Sunday," she says, "and I won't see him again for four months."

MARK TEICH is a writer in Stamford, CT.

Article 44

Civil Wars

**Psychologists who work as parenting coordinators
help moms and dads keep the peace.**

Christopher Munsey

Research suggest that it's not divorce in itself that most harms children, but the tension between divorcing parents, some of whom repeatedly appear before judges to battle over drop-off times or visitation rights.

One review of studies in *Children and Divorce,* for example (Vol. 4, No. 1, pages 165–182), found that children whose parents bitterly fight over divorces scored as significantly more disturbed on standardized measures of maladjustment.

"In a lot of these cases, the individual parents 'parent' fine. It's when they interface that all hell breaks loose," says Matt Sullivan, PhD, a Santa Clara, Calif., psychologist, who works with many divorcing clients.

But help is at hand: Through the growing practice area of parenting coordination, psychologists are helping feuding parents call a truce, communicate and work out their disagreements with the goal of better-adjusted children and less-burdened courts.

"It can be helpful for parents to have someone who can help them work out how they're going to keep conflict away from the kids, and help them focus on what the kids need, as opposed to what's going on between the two of them," says Judge Judith Bartnoff of the District of Columbia Superior Court, who has seen the benefits of parenting coordination in several custody disputes.

With their communication skills, psychologists are uniquely qualified for parenting coordination, says Robin Deutsch, PhD, of Harvard Medical School who has served in the role and provided training as well. "Psychologists can help people stuck in ineffective communication patterns learn to communicate better," she says. "It's the bread and butter of what [we] know how to do."

A Growing Field

Parenting coordination typically starts with a court-ordered parenting agreement establishing a detailed custody schedule, with exact drop-off and pickup times listed, plus arrangements for vacations and holidays. When a dispute arises—such as which sport a child should play—the parenting coordinator can step in, halt the angry back-and-forth between the parents and gather feedback from all parties involved.

Besides hearing from the adults involved, a parenting coordinator pays close attention to the child's needs. After gathering the different perspectives, the coordinator—depending on the state where the parents live—either makes the decision, or recommends a solution.

Eight states have passed laws setting up parenting coordination procedures since 1989: Minnesota, Oklahoma, Idaho, Oregon, Colorado, Texas, Louisiana and North Carolina. Meanwhile, a number of other states rely on existing laws that give judges leeway to appoint parenting coordinators (see sidebar).

Demanding Work

Sullivan and co-author Karl Kirkland, PhD, recently completed a survey of 54 parenting coordinators. They found that 44 percent of the responding parenting coordinators were licensed psychologists. Other mental health professionals such as master's level social workers and licensed professional counselors also do the work, with attorneys forming the third-largest share.

For all the different ways parenting coordination is carried out, psychologists say common issues arise for practitioners who move into the area of practice: chiefly, the need for balance, and avoiding falling into dual roles, Deutsch says. Parenting coordinators can't become therapists to their clients, and they have to make decisions fairly, Deutsch says.

"Maintaining impartiality is very important," she says.

From a practitioner's perspective, parenting coordination can be lucrative, without the hassle of third-party payers. In most cases, parents pay the parenting coordinator on a fee-for-service basis, says Sullivan, adding that many coordination agreements spell out the hourly cost of the service, how

162

State by State

Here's a snapshot of how parenting coordination works and is developing in several states and the District of Columbia:

- **California:** If both parents agree, a judge can appoint a parenting coordinator, using a statute already on the books. Called "special masters," these coordinators make legally binding decisions when disputes arise between parents.
- **Maryland:** Although efforts are under way to draft legislation to define parenting coordination, judges in several Maryland counties began turning to parenting coordinators several years ago, says Paul Berman, PhD, a psychologist who also serves as the professional affairs officer for the Maryland Psychological Association. If both parties sign off, the judge can name a parenting coordinator once a child custody order has been signed.

    In his work, Berman is empowered to decide what's best, presenting his decision in writing to both parents.
- **Massachusetts:** Legislation establishing a parent coordination program hasn't moved out of committee in the state legislature in the past two years, but judges do appoint parenting coordinators, says parenting coordinator Robin Deutsch, PhD, relying on their traditional discretion to take action in the best interest of children. If both parents agree, the state allows judges to appoint a parenting coordinator at the time of divorce to help resolve disputes that the parties can't resolve on their own.

- **District of Columbia:** As part of a pilot project of APA, Argosy University, the D.C. Bar and the D.C. Superior Court, family law judges can appoint a licensed clinical psychologist as a special master, who works in a team format with advanced doctoral students from Argosy University in Washington, D.C., to provide parent coordinator services to caregivers who otherwise couldn't afford it, says Giselle Hass, PsyD, an associate professor at Argosy who serves as clinical director for the program.

    Besides helping caregivers learn to communicate effectively with each other, the students can help connect them with resources for themselves and their children, Hass says. Those resources might include helping arrange the evaluation of a child for a possible developmental disability, referring a caregiver for treatment of a mental health issue or helping connect with free legal help.
- **Texas:** Under a state statute, a judge can order a parenting coordinator to get involved if parents agree or if there is evidence of high conflict. However, Texas parenting coordinators do not have authority to make decisions, says Lynelle Yingling, a marriage and family therapist in Rockwall, Texas. Instead, parenting coordinators talk with both parents and help parents develop solutions, Yingling says.

—C. Munsey

the parents will split the costs, and what happens if fees go unpaid. Some programs offer pro[[check]] bono parenting coordination to low-income parents, such as one based in Washington, D.C.

The work is also attractive to many psychologists because of its flexible scheduling. And the field is growing, as more judges turn to the idea of using parenting coordinators to help defuse the most problematic cases, several observers say.

It can be very demanding though, judging from the comments of several psychologists experienced in parenting coordination. Getting in the middle of disputes where the parties are often very angry at each other requires a thick skin.

"It's just tough work," says Sullivan. "These are difficult people to work with." He adds that having a "directive, take-charge" personality helps a psychologist succeed as a parenting coordinator. "It takes a particular brand of psychologist to fit this role."

APA's Pilot Parenting Coordination Program

An APA-initiated program enables family law judges in Washington, D.C., to appoint licensed clinical psychologists as special masters who work with Argosy University doctoral students to smooth out disputes between caregivers. Since the program started in January 2005, parenting coordinators have handled 19 cases.

In June, APA's Practice Directorate honored several people who consulted on and helped develop the program including APA's Shirley Ann Higuchi, JD; Dr. Robert Barrett, of the American School of Professional Psychology at Argosy University—Washington, D.C., campus; Judge Judith Bartnoff of the District of Columbia Superior Court; and Dr. Bruce Copeland, formerly of Washington, D.C.

—C. Munsey

Estranged Spouses Increasingly Waiting out Downturn to Divorce

DONNA ST. GEORGE

In the Great Recession, breaking up is hard to do.

With housing values depressed and jobs disappearing, divorce has become a luxury beyond the reach of some couples. There is often not enough money to pay for separate households or to hire lawyers, fight over children and go to court.

What has always been painful is now desperate and confounding, with a growing number of couples deciding to wait out the economic storm while others take new approaches—such as living together as they separate.

"I have lots of files sitting in the drawer, where people can't move forward," says David Goldberg, a divorce lawyer and mediator in Gaithersburg. He has been working in family law for 44 years and says he has never seen a time like this one.

Lately, he said, "I have a lot of clients who have ended up in bankruptcy."

The difficulties of divorce in the downturn are familiar to Paulene Foster, a 42-year-old federal worker from Olney, who says her precarious finances forced her to wait a year. If that wasn't enough, she also shared a house with her estranged husband—him in the basement, her upstairs. Strapped months went by as the couple were saddled with a suburban townhouse that would not sell.

"It was a mess," Foster said.

Her divorce, filed last month with a $105 check after going to a *self-help law clinic* in Montgomery County, comes as the national rate of failed marriages has declined slightly—not necessarily because divorce-minded couples are happier than before but, some experts suggest, because they don't have the money to call it quits.

At one Woodbridge law firm, 20 to 25 percent of clients seeking a divorce live under the same roof as their estranged spouse to save money as they await court action.

Other couples say they are stymied by the grim reality that they owe more on the family home than they could get if they sold it.

How do they start over if debt is all that's left to divide?

Heather Hostetter, who has a divorce practice in Bethesda, said that many couples used to divorce with enough equity in a house so that both spouses could re-create lives not so different from their old ones.

"It used to be you could go own another home," she said. "Maybe it's a little smaller, maybe it's not in the same neighborhood.

"Now you see people who go from homeowners to renters."

Divorce and Bankruptcy

Facing harsher circumstances, Marissa Fuller, who works in child care in Fairfax City, says her husband's job loss and then his underemployment had an accumulating impact. They had relationship troubles. They fell short on bills month after month. She tired of begging utility companies to turn back on the family's water and electricity.

In January, she filed both for bankruptcy and divorce, sure that the economic tension and the discord that came with it took a toll. "That really made the marriage crumble," she said. Fuller found housing through a nonprofit program and is saving for her own apartment, but she says the math of providing for two children on her salary seems nearly impossible.

Experts say that divorce claims slightly more than 40 percent of marriages. *Rates calculated by the National Marriage Project* show a modest decline in divorce during 2008, the first year of the recession, when 838,000 cases were granted in 44 states—at a time when growing economic strain might have produced a spike in divorce. A year earlier, 856,000 divorces were finalized. Scores of studies show a link between tough times and divorce.

W. Bradford Wilcox, director of the National Marriage Project at the University of Virginia, says some families are pulling together amid the economic turmoil, and others that want to split up are postponing until they see a rebound in the economy and in home values. A divorce can cost as little as $100 on a do-it-yourself basis with little in dispute and $10,000 to $20,000—or more—for a divorce that ends up in court.

Still, dividing into two households can prove the more daunting task—the same income being used to cover an extra housing payment, extra utility bills, separate groceries. This can be tricky when a home has no equity or line of credit to draw from.

In Manassas, lawyer Kirk Wilder says that in some cases, the house is so void of value that neither party wants to be stuck with it. "It used to be, 'Well, I want the house,'" he said. "Now it's, 'You take the house.' That's a huge change."

The economics of breaking up are a little better in the District and parts of Northern Virginia, where spouses can live in the same house during the required separation period, as long as they share little more than the space around them. No sex. No meals. No togetherness.

"They don't do each other's laundry, they don't eat together, they don't go to the kids' soccer game together," says Pat Hammond, a lawyer in Prince William County who advises clients with increasing frequency about how to get divorced without moving out of the house. "If they live in a three-bedroom townhouse, and they have four kids, it ain't going to work."

A Place to Sleep

Steve Halbert, an Arlington County resident who divorced in 2008, attests to the difficulty of the proposition.

His wife lived in one bedroom; he lived in another. He tried to work as much as possible to stay out of the house. "If you're in the same room, then a fight is waiting to happen," he said. For all of the struggle, his mortgage is still upside down 18 months later—and he still does not have a way to refinance his house and clear his ex-wife's name from the mortgage loan.

Halbert, a commercial real estate appraiser, says he earns half of what he did in the boom days and now pays alimony. "There used to be a lot of disposable income," he said, "and now it's, 'Be glad you have a place to sleep.'"

Prince William lawyer Larry Fabian says perhaps a quarter of his clients live together while they seek a divorce, which was almost unheard of five or so years ago. "It's really difficult," he says of their experiences. "It's pretty much the worst of all worlds."

Then again, some would say it is even harder in Maryland, which requires a full year of separate residences for mutual and voluntary divorce. That requirement is economically difficult for some; impossible for others.

Jesslyn Haskins, 42, a nurse and mother of three in Upper Marlboro, says a judge threw out her divorce case because she and her ex-husband had shared the same house during their separation. She says she then left, moving in with friends and ultimately getting an apartment, as relations grew more bitter and the mortgage went unpaid. Now divorced, she says she lives in the house and pays the mortgage but is in jeopardy of foreclosure because of missed back payments.

The National Marriage Project's Wilcox says working-class couples, who already have high rates of divorce, are especially vulnerable to a recession-related breakup because they are hit harder by unemployment, which is a significant predictor of divorce. Men, in particular, see themselves as breadwinners and are prone to feelings of worthlessness and depression during lengthy periods without a job, Wilcox says. "We would predict this recession is having a pretty big impact on working-class couples," he says.

In terms of divorce, the recession bears similarities to the Great Depression, says Johns Hopkins University sociologist Andrew Cherlin, noting that in the 1930s, divorce rates fell amid the worst of the economic crisis, only to rise as the country recovered. "Troubled economic times breed troubled marriages," he says. "But whether those marriages end in divorce right away is another thing."

Cherlin said the recession has probably created "a backlog of unhappy married couples who would like to get a divorce soon but can't afford it," and he predicted a surge in cases during the first several recovery years. "The longer this severe economic downturn continues," he said, "the larger the backlog will be."

UNIT 5

Families, Now and into the Future

Unit Selections

46. **Get a Closer Look,** Ira Wolfman
47. **The Joy of Rituals,** Dawn Marie Barhyte
48. **Sustaining Resilient Families for Children in Primary Grades,** Janice Patterson and Lynn Kirkland
49. **Where Is Marriage Going?,** Anthony Layng

Key Points to Consider

- What changes do you see yourself making in your life? How would you go about gathering the information you need to make these decisions?

- What role does spirituality play in the life of your family?

- What is the state of rituals in your family? What rituals might you build in your family? Why? How might you use family gatherings and other traditions to build family integration?

- Marriage clearly is changing, but how, and to what extent will it change? How comfortable are you with the changes that are taking place?

Student Website
www.mhhe.com/cls

Internet Reference
National Institute on Aging
   www.nih.gov/nia

166

What is the future of the family? Does the family even have a future? These questions and others like them are being asked. Many people fear for the future of the family. As previous units of this volume have shown, the family is a continually evolving institution that will continue to change throughout time. Still, certain elements of family appear to be constant. The family is and will remain a powerful influence in the lives of its members. This is because we all begin life in some type of family, and this early exposure carries a great deal of weight in forming our social selves—who we are and how we relate to others. From our families, we take our basic genetic makeup, while we also learn and are reinforced in health behaviors. In families, we are given our first exposure to values, and it is through families that we most actively influence others. Our sense of commitment and obligation begins within the family as well as our sense of what we can expect of others.

Much that has been written about families has been less than hopeful and has focused on ways of avoiding or correcting errors. The four articles in this unit take a positive view of family and how it influences its members. The emphasis is on health rather than dysfunction.

Knowledge is the basic building block of intelligent decisions regarding family relationships. Information is important in planning for our family's future. One way to gather this information is through interviews, and "Get a Closer Look" explains just how this can be done. Family rituals are examined as being a

© BananaStock/PunchStock

powerful force for family cohesion and change, and the nature of family rituals is described in "The Joy of Rituals" and "Sustaining Resilient Families for Children in Primary Grades." Finally, what is understood to be "Traditional" marriage is, in fact, a recent phenomenon. Marriage is an evolving institution, and "Where is Marriage Going?" discusses the direction that marriage may take in the future.

Get a Closer Look
12 Tips for Successful Family Interviews

IRA WOLFMAN

How do you get relatives talking? A good family history interview isn't easy to conduct. You need to combine the best attributes of caring friend, hard-nosed reporter, and sensitive psychologist. But do it well and you may be rewarded with wonderful stories.

Interviews are different from normal conversations. One person has a goal: to get information from another person (let's call him or her the "talker"). You want the talker to feel comfortable, but you also need to direct the conversation to the points you are interested in.

You also have to be flexible. Sometimes an unexpected topic can turn out to be wonderful. Other times you'll need to lead your talker back to the main point—without hurting his or her feelings. This can be difficult, but you will become better at it as you go along—practice will make you skilled. Be patient with yourself and expect some mistakes. To make things easier, keep these tips in mind:

1. Before any interview, give advance warning. Explain what you want to do, why you want to do it, and why the talker is important to you and your research. You can call or write a letter or e-mail. Here's an example of the kinds of things you should say:

> *Dear Aunt Gus:*
>
> *I'm working on a history of our family, and it would be very helpful if I could sit down and talk with you. I'm particularly interested in your memories of my great-grandparents (your mother and father) and the family's early years in Minnesota. I'd also love to look at any old photographs or documents you have.*
>
> *I won't need much more than an hour of your time and would like to hold our talk at your home. Any weekend day would be fine. Can you let me know a date that is convenient for you?*
>
> *Thanks so much for your help.*

By writing this letter, you've given your relative a chance to start thinking about the topics you're interested in, and you may have even jogged her memory. Of course, not all your relatives will be close by, and your arrangements may be more difficult than "any weekend day." That just makes your writing—and planning—even more important.

2. Prepare before your interview. Find out whatever you can about the talker *before* the interview. Where does she fit in the family? What documents might she have? What other genealogical jewels might she have?

Gather as much information as you can ahead of time about her relationship to everyone in your family. Your parents can probably help you with this.

3. Think out all your questions beforehand. Interviewing requires structure. Write your questions on a sheet of paper, organized by subject. One easy way to organize what you want to ask is by year: Start with your relative's earliest years and then move on from there.

"So, Aunt Gus, you lived in the house in a town outside Minneapolis till you were 10—about 1922, right? Then where did you move?" Or "You say Great-grandpa worked as a tailor in St. Paul. Did you ever visit his shop? Where was it? What years did he have the business there?" As this interviewer did, it's a good idea to summarize what you already know so that your subject can verify your facts. Then move on to a request for more detail.

Sometimes the simplest questions can hit the jackpot. I asked my great-uncle Max, "How old were you when you went from Poland to America?" I didn't get an answer; I got a story:

> *I must have been about 15 when I went to Warsaw to get a visa to emigrate. I got the visa, but then the counselor at the examination said, "Listen, boy, you are underage. You can't go without your father." He crossed out my stamp.*
>
> *I went back to our town and told my father. He said, "Don't worry, we'll take care of that."*
>
> *My father was a religious man, but he also knew how to get things done. He called a policeman from our town and asked him to make me older.*

Ready, Set, Research . . .
Your Family Tree

- Interview your parents about their family history. Practice interviewing with them.
- Make appointments to interview other family members.
- Prepare your questions. (For a list of good questions for family interviews, see www.workmen.com/ familytree.)
- Type up your notes from interviews. Ask the relatives you interviewed to review them and correct or add to them.
- Write a thank-you note to every family member you interviewed.

I got new papers. Now I turned from 15 to 18 or 19. I went back to Warsaw, and I was able to leave. And on February 20, 1920, I took the boat Susquehanna *from Danzig to New York.*

Remember to also ask open-ended questions. "What do you remember most about the apartment on Division Street?" or "Tell me about your relationship with your brothers" may yield something unexpected and wonderful.

4. Bring a video or tape recorder if possible.
A small tape recorder usually doesn't disturb anyone, and it catches every bit of information, including the way your talkers sound and exactly how they answer questions. If you plan to videotape, be sure someone comes with you to run the camera. You need to focus on your talker.

5. In any case, bring a notebook and a pen.
Even if you have [an audio tape or video] recorder, always take handwritten notes. Recorders can break down.

During the interview, write down names and dates and double-check them with your subject. Facts are important, but the most important information your talkers offer are their stories. Try to capture the way they talk and their colorful expressions: "That ship was rolling on the ocean like a marble in your hand."

There's another good reason to bring pen and paper with you. You won't have to interrupt when you think of a question; just write a note to yourself so you'll remember to ask it at an appropriate time.

6. Start with easy, friendly questions.
Leave the more difficult or emotional material for later in the interview, after you've had time to gain your talker's trust. If things aren't going well, you may want to save those questions for another time.

It's also a good idea to begin with questions about the person you're interviewing. You may be more interested in a great-grandfather if he is the missing link in your family chart. But first get some background information about your talker—your aunt, for example. This serves two purposes. First, it lets her know she's important to you, that you care about her, and that her life is interesting, too. Second, as she talks, she may reveal some other information that you would never have known about otherwise.

7. Bring family photographs with you.
Look for photos, artwork, or documents that will help jog your subject's memory. Bring the pictures out and ask your talker to describe what's going on. "Do you remember when this was taken? Who are the people? What was the occasion? Who do you think took the picture?" You may be amazed at how much detail your relative will see in a photograph and also at the memories that come spilling forth.

8. Don't be afraid of silence.
You might feel uneasy and want to rush in with another question when your talker stops speaking. *Don't.* Silence is an important part of interviewing and can sometimes yield to interesting results. Because people often find silence uncomfortable, they often try to fill it if you don't—and in doing so, they may say something you might not have heard otherwise.

Sometimes silence is also necessary for gathering thoughts. Don't forget—you are asking your subjects to think back on things they may not have considered for years. Calling up these memories may spark other thoughts, too. Allow your subject time to ponder. You may be thrilled by what he or she remembers.

9. Ask the same question in different ways.
People don't know how much they know, and rephrasing a question can give you more information. This happens all the time. "I don't know," a relative will tell you, sometimes impatiently. They do know—they just don't know that they know. The most common version of this occurs when an interviewer asks, "What was your father's mother's name?" The relative answers, "I never knew her. I don't know." Then a few minutes later, in response to "Whom were you named after?" this answer comes; "My father's mother."

Try to find a couple of ways to ask important questions. You may feel like you're being repetitive, but you never can be sure what you will learn.

10. Be sensitive to what you discover.
Sometimes people become emotional talking about the past. They may remember long-dead relatives or once-forgotten tragedies. If your talker is upset by a memory, either remain silent or quietly ask, "Is it all right if we talk some more about this? Or would you rather not?" People frequently feel better when they talk about sad things; you should gently give your relative the *choice* of whether or not to go on.

11. Try not to interrupt.
If your talker strays from the subject, let him or her finish the story and then say, "Let's get back to Uncle Moe" or "You said something earlier about . . . " By not interrupting, you make the conversation friendlier, and the story may lead you to something you didn't expect.

Of course, there is always the exception to the rule. If a story goes on forever and seems useless, the best way to handle it may be to say, "Gee, Aunt Gus, could you hold the rest of that story for later? I'd like to get the facts out of the way and then come back to that."

12. Ask for songs, poems, unusual memories.
You may discover something wonderful when you ask your subject if she recalls the rhymes she used to recite while jumping rope as a little girl or the hymns she sang in church. Probe a little here—ask about childhood games and memories, smells and tastes and sounds.

From *Writing*, November/December 2005, pp. 15–17. Copyright © 2005 by Weekly Reader Corporation. Reprinted by permission.

The Joy of Rituals
Simple Strategies for Strengthening Family Ties

Reading Bible stories before bedtime, sitting down to Sabbath dinner, and saying grace before each meal brings warmth and joy to many families. Now, researchers are discovering that such activities enhance child development as well.

DAWN MARIE BARHYTE

Rituals are repeated and shared activities that carry meaning and provide an emotional reward to family members. Although routines are also repetitious family behavior and vital to family life, they lack the symbolic content and compelling nature that rituals possess. Unlike rituals, routines are purely instrumental rather than symbolic; they are activities family members *have* to do rather than *want* to do.

Meg Cox, expert on rituals and author of *The Heart of a Family—Searching America for Traditions that Fulfill Us,* believes that a ritual is anything—big or small—that families perform together deliberately. She says they must be repetitious and provide some dramatic flourish that elevates the activity above the ordinary grind.

Even simple activities can be transformed into satisfying and memorable rituals, such as always singing a certain song whenever you give your child medicine, or declaring an evening study break for hot cocoa on cold winter weeknights. Cox writes, "The more we understand [rituals], the more their power will enrich our lives."

William J. Doherty, professor of family social science at the University of Minnesota, and author of *The Intentional Family* adds, "Children are natural ritualists. They crave connection and love predictability. Family rituals give children a sense of steady love and connection, and give order to their lives."

Shared Experience

Rituals are significant not so much for the act itself but for the results they yield; the sense of togetherness that grows out of shared experience and the feeling of rightness that comes from its repetition.

According to research, these repeated positive experiences form strong connections between neurons in the brain and foster a sense of security in children. They also help kids learn what to expect from their environment and how to understand the world around them.

Other studies have shown that young people who are best equipped to face the challenges of life and stay centered are those who feel close to their families. That closeness comes from the routine reassurances and shared experiences found in everyday rituals.

At one time or another, all families experience stress. Rituals have the capacity to provide stability even during trying times. Researchers have found that rituals are integral family resources that can act as a coping mechanism during those challenging moments. Professor Doherty adds that family rituals are what children can fall back on when under stress. He says that regular meals with parents provide emotional protection from every major risk factor.

Little Celebrations

When you think of family rituals, you probably picture the grand annual events such as Thanksgiving, Christmas, Hanukah, birthdays, weddings, or baby dedications. But you may want to consider adding some everyday rituals that can serve as glue that binds families together right in the midst of our harried lives. These common, often repeated happenings can become extraordinarily vital and act as a powerful buffer against this complex world. These rituals will build a bridge that connects the past to the future and allows children to pick up the torch and pass it on to the next generation.

According to Meg Cox, "Scientists tell us that many animals have rituals, and anthropologists report they haven't found any human societies without them, which alone is compelling evidence that rituals must be a human necessity."

Psychologists insist that rituals help us keep track of where we came from and essentially who we are. While this is key for all family members, it's profoundly significant for children who are forming their own identities. Rituals become a road map for kids, offering a comforting sense of predictability and order to life. When children have a clear sense of where they come from, they have a better sense of where they are going. Knowing what to do and being able to predict what comes next helps a boy or girl feel competent, and feeling competent is key to emotional well-being.

Grounded by Constancy

Children delight in rituals, look forward to them, learn from them, and feel comforted and grounded by their constancy. Positive family rituals leave indelible imprints on children's minds and form treasured memories ready to be passed on from generation to generation. For instance, knowing that every fall the family will load themselves into the minivan and go pumpkin or apple picking makes the season something to look forward to and savor.

Knowing that, each night, dad will talk to his child about his or her day and read a story at bedtime gives often-lonely children something to which they can look forward. In fact, developing a bedtime ritual is an excellent way to unwind and quietly embrace the day's happenings.

Whether it's reading a story, saying a prayer, or giving a hug and kiss, these nightly rituals offer security and comfort that fold gently into pleasant slumber.

The challenge, of course, lies in making the decision to create this time and saying no to any intrusions. With the myriad of demands on our time, it will require some effort. But the payoff will be well worth it.

Takes Work

Once you have good family rituals in place, keeping them alive takes work. If it's centered on a specific day, like Sabbath dinner, and you're not able to do it one week, don't let it slip away. Squeeze it in later in the week if you have to do so.

With some attentiveness, your family rituals will survive the demands of life and may endure for generations to come. Know that no matter what life brings, rituals will act as a safety net for your family members. Establishing your own distinctive activities now and faithfully repeating them will offer a much-needed

shelter in unsettling times. Rituals are like keepsakes that live in your heart.

Springboard for Action

If you are inspired but feel at a loss at the thought of starting your own family ritual, here are some ideas to use as a springboard for action.

- If you're like many families today and can't manage family dinners seven nights a week, try for **breakfasts together or special fruit-juice treats in the evening.** These relaxed moments of sharing nourishment and conversation provide a much-needed platform for reconnecting.
- Recognition night. A fun way to celebrate your child's achievements in the classroom or extracurricular activity is to serve an **"Honoree Dinner"** on a special plate reserved for that occasion with all the healthy foods they crave.
- Designate one night a week as **"Family Night"** created solely for family members to connect, interact, and communicate while having wholesome fun. One week you could play board games, another rent a DVD and serve popcorn, and yet another allow various family members to plan the meal and help cook it as a team.
- Hold an **"Unbirthday"** where you surprise your child by unexpectedly celebrating the fact that they exist. Include their favorite foods, a cake, and small tokens of affection.
- Create a **"Give a Helping Hand Day"** to help children cultivate altruism and focus on others less fortunate. As a family, participate in some community service like volunteering at a nursing home or soup kitchen, or collecting food for a local food pantry.

Life is hard. Rituals can help soften the edges and bring a sense of togetherness back into the lives of every family member. Why not start one today?

Freelance writer **DAWN MARIE BARHYTE** of Warwick, New York, is a stepmother of two and grandmother of six. She's a former junior volunteer coordinator at St. Anthony Community Hospital and teacher at the First Baptist Child Care Center.

Sustaining Resilient Families for Children in Primary Grades

JANICE PATTERSON AND LYNN KIRKLAND

The adversities that today's families face are well-documented and staggering (Children's Defense Fund, 2004). Even in the midst of tough times, however, many families are able to display resilience. Family resilience refers to the coping mechanisms the family uses as a functional unit to recover from life's setbacks. The purpose of this article is to provide parents and teachers with guidelines for creating resilient families, thereby helping primary-grade children withstand the challenges in their lives. In this article, we will consider what is known about family resilience, examine the role of protective factors and recovery processes, and suggest specific strategies that families and teachers can use to support resilience.

Family Resilience

Much of the work on family resilience is anchored in studies about the resilience of children. Werner and Smith (1982, 1992; Werner, 1984), authors of arguably the most important study on childhood resilience, spent 40 years studying children on the island of Kauai who were judged to be at risk of living in hardship. The children were born into poor, unskilled families, and were judged to be at risk based on their exposure before age 2 to at least four risk factors, such as serious health problems, familial alcoholism, mental illness, violence, and divorce. By age 18, about two-thirds of the children had fared poorly, as predicted by their at-risk status. The remaining one-third had developed into competent, confident, and caring young adults living productive lives, as rated on a variety of measures. In a follow-up study, the overwhelming majority of this group, now at age 40, were still living successful lives. In fact, many of them had outperformed Kauai citizens from more advantageous backgrounds. They were more likely to be stable in their marriages and fewer were unemployed. The key factors that promoted individual resilience were:

- Caring and support were provided by at least one adult who knew the child well and cared deeply about that child's well-being
- Positive expectations were articulated clearly for the child, and the support necessary to meet those expectations was provided

- Meaningful involvement and participation provided the child the opportunity to become involved in something she cared about and to contribute to the well-being of others

Although it is not impossible for an individual child from a non-resilient family to bounce back from adversity, the child's health and well-being is best supported if the family functions as a resilient unit. When a crisis upsets the life of a primary-grade child, the impact of that crisis on the child is determined largely by the extent to which the family's normal functioning is disrupted. Even when the child is not directly affected by a situation, he or she is touched by the changes in relationships that result from the changes or crises for others in the family.

As we reflect on the image of a resilient family, note how changes in society contribute to that image. Traditionally, the model of a resilient family, those who successfully navigated the ups and downs of life, was the image of a white, affluent, nuclear family led by the breadwinning father and a mother working as full-time homemaker. Enormous social changes in recent decades highlight the fact that resilient families can be non-white, upper or lower income, represent a variety of ethnic and cultural traditions, and include single parents, non-custodial parents, grandparents, stepparents, and same-gender parents. Changes in the definition of family are dynamic. In one landmark court decision supporting the rights of gay parents, the judge recognized changing definitions of "family" by acknowledging, "It is the totality of the relationship, as evidenced by the dedication, caring and self-sacrifice of the parties, which should, in the final analysis, control the definition of family" (quoted in Stacey, 1990, p. 4).

Protective and Recovery Factors

An understanding of family resilience incorporates research on *protective factors* and *recovery factors* (Cowan, Cowan, & Schultz, 1996; Garmezy & Rutter, 1983; Hawley & DeHaan, 1996; McCubbin, Thompson, Thompson, & McCubbin, 1992). Protective factors are behaviors that help give people strength in times of stress (Patterson, Patterson, & Collins, 2003). Examples of such factors include family celebrations, planned family time, consistent routines, and family traditions. In addition, family resilience can be sustained by maintaining open communication within the family and building a solid support network beyond the family.

Recovery factors refer to the family's ability to develop and use adaptation strategies when confronted with a crisis. Families can and do bounce back and adapt by changing their habits, their patterns of functioning, or the situation that has created the problem. Some evidence exists that there may be variation in the nature of the needed recovery factors, depending upon the situation. For instance, families having to deal with chronically ill children (e.g., cystic fibrosis) made use of the following strategies:

- *Family integration.* The mother's and father's optimism and efforts to keep the family together were important to the child's health.
- *Family support and esteem building.* The parents made concerted efforts to reach out to family, friends, and the larger community, thereby helping them to develop their self-esteem and self-confidence.
- *Family recreation orientation, control, and organization.* A family emphasis on active involvement in recreational and sporting activities is positively associated with improvements in the child's health. The greater the family's emphasis on control and family organization, rules, and procedures, the greater the improvement in the child's health.
- *Family optimism and mastery.* The greater the family's efforts to maintain a sense of optimism and order, the greater the improvement in the child's health. Furthering one's understanding and mastery of the health regimen necessary to promote the child's health helps the adaptation process (McCubbin & McCubbin, 1996).

During any family crisis, disruption in the daily routine exacerbates the chaos and confusion. Within the context of divorce, for instance, it is important for the family to establish and maintain routines that provide continuity of family connections, such as Sunday brunch with Dad. Research on children's positive adjustment following their parents' divorce shows that predictability and reliability of contact with the non-custodial parent is as important as the amount of contact (Hetherington & Kelly, 2002; Walsh, 1991). It is also clear that authoritative parenting, which combines warmth and control, is a significant positive protection against family stress that children may encounter (Hetherington & Kelly, 2002).

Strategies to Strengthen Family Resilience

Effective communication, including problem solving and affirmation, is a critical variable for family success in facing routine and extraordinary challenges. Contemporary lifestyles may allow little time for really listening to children, discussing their problems, and affirming their value to the family. A growing number of parents and teachers realize that communication is not something that can be left to chance; they plan for it.

One family reported on the "talk" that took place each night at the dinner table (Feiler, 2004). First, dinner was designated as a sacred time and attendance was mandatory. No television was allowed. Instead, they played a game, "Bad and Good," which began with a moderator asking each person, "What happened to you today that was bad?" Everyone had to respond; respect for others was supported by not allowing anyone to criticize, interrupt, or refute another person's bad experience. It was important that parents participated, to demonstrate that bad things happen to all of us on a daily basis and how we cope is what matters. Next, the rotating moderator asked each person, "What happened to you today that was good?" As family members reported their good stories, others affirmed them and good news begot good news. Primary-grade children in the family learned to celebrate successes. Of course, some events had both good and bad elements; as the family discussed what happened, children learned that everything doesn't fit neatly into good or bad categories. Variations on the theme might be such questions as, "What are you most afraid will happen to you?" or "If you could have one wish, what would it be?" or "What makes you feel really special?"

Problem solving can be nurtured in this context by asking everyone for thoughts on solving family problems. Our daily lives are inundated by e-mail, voice mail, computers, video games, iPods, and other diversions that can replace face-to-face communication, and so we must take conscious steps to let children know we are listening and care about them and their ideas.

These strategies are easily adapted to the classroom. Teachers routinely listen to children during community time, at meals, and in small groups, and can pose questions for all to answer. Class meetings also can provide many venues for children to discuss issues related to their lives and the lives of their families. As part of a class meeting, carefully selected articles from the newspaper can be used to initiate conversation about issues that relate to the lives of the children in the class. For example, children can consider alternative ways of dealing with problems other than those exhibited by individuals acting unlawfully within the local community. As part of routine class meetings, children utilize problems that arise throughout the day in play situations in the classroom, coming up with appropriate resolutions. For example, if a problem has arisen on the playground between children, offering the opportunity for children to defend their position, as well as hear the positions of others, helps them to consider other people and become less egocentric in their reasoning. Hearing others' perspectives encourages the moral development of the child (Piaget, 1997) and encourages flexible thinking, which builds a child's resilience, both individually and within the family.

It is also important that parents and teachers teach children how to ask for help when they need it. One of the biggest predictors of resilience in the Kauai study mentioned earlier in this article was that children knew how to ask for help. We cannot assume that every child (or adult) will, or knows how to, ask for needed help. Today's society places a high value on independent action and neglects teaching collaboration. Parents and teachers can guide children in forming questions and in practicing their help-seeking skills (e.g., "Where would you go if no one was home when you came home after school?").

Within the classroom, teachers can use the writing workshop process to help children write about issues that trouble them. For instance, one teacher found it helpful to encourage a student, from a military family about to relocate, to draft a paper about her fears of moving to a new school. Through the writing and subsequent conferencing that preceded the final draft, the teacher and parent learned that the child's greatest fear was not having someone to sit with at lunch. The parent and teacher in the new school were able to find a "lunch mate" and thus eased the transition. A variation on the writing conference is to establish dialogue journals so that the student is writing to the teacher or parent and the adult responds in writing. Some children will write about fears that are difficult to verbalize.

Another important strategy is to strive to maintain an optimistic outlook, even when the going gets rough. The family that expects to prevail in times of crisis very often will prevail. An orientation toward such hardiness is reflected in the work of Steve and Sybil Wolin, who speak of "survivor's pride"—the deep self-respect that comes from knowing you were challenged and that you prevailed. Children who grew up in families that were *not* resilient and later compared notes reported very similar family experiences, as identified below:

- We rarely celebrated holidays.
- They [parents] hardly ever came to a soccer game, a school play, or a community picnic.
- There were no regular mealtimes.
- They forgot my birthday.
- The house was a pigsty.
- No one had a good word for me; nothing I ever did was right.
- They were always fighting with each other, tearing each other apart in front of us, as if we didn't exist. (Wolin & Wolin, 1993, p. 27)

If we turn this list around, we can see the practices of resilient families for primary-grade children. They *do* celebrate holidays and attend soccer games, school plays, and community picnics as a family. They make time for regular mealtimes and birthday celebrations. The house is clean enough to be functional and pleasant. Love and affirmation are given freely and parental conflict is minimized in front of children. Within the classroom, through conversations, parent meetings, and written communication, teachers can emphasize to parents the importance of participation in these activities as resilience-building strategies.

Importance of Family Traditions and Routines

A family that promotes its own resilience with these strategies takes deliberate steps in building the resilience of the family unit for all members, including the primary-grade child.

The family values traditions, saves mementos, and tells stories about family heroes. Conducting these activities within the family promotes pride in the family heritage and also can provide a link to the present. If the family reflects on the struggles immigrant parents faced in coming to a new country and the strategies they used to survive, the current move across town takes on a different perspective. Children in resilient families see themselves as part of the family unit and take pride in finding ways to contribute to the family's strength. Effective communication and family optimism work to create a resilient family that considers itself to be healthy and is reflected in such statements as:

- We are a good family.
- Home is a safe, welcoming place.
- We have a past that is a source of strength and we have good, sound values that guide our future.
- We are known and respected in the community.
- We like each other.
- Our blood runs thick; we will always be there for one another. (Wolin & Wolin, 1993, p. 40)

Without a doubt, a variety of challenges and crises can tax even the strongest family. Such situations call for all family members to pull together and use their collective strength (all of us are stronger than one of us) to weather the challenge. An attitude of family resilience gives the family a sense of its own competence and control over the outcome.

Deliberately structuring family time and rituals is another important strategy for strengthening resilience in families. Every family has a routine, even if it is one of chaos. Resilient families take control of the routine for the purpose of establishing predictability and stability—critical elements to family balance. Although sometimes difficult to establish, this strategy can make a difference in how the child copes with new events. For instance, a 7-year-old girl was confused by where she was to go each day after school and began crying every morning, saying, "I don't know where to go today." The mother and teacher combined forces to develop a routine in which the mother sent the teacher each Monday a list of where the child was to go every day of the week. She also tucked a note in the child's lunch box that said, "Today, you go to Brownies in the gym after school." The mother used a combination of words and picture symbols to be sure the child understood the message; thus, a stabilizing routine was established.

Family Communication with Children's Literature

Family mealtimes are important venues for communication, as mentioned earlier. They also serve the function of reinforcing family routine. Spending quality time together, including just "hanging out," is important for building family resilience. Family time together does not need to involve money or extensive time commitments. Playing board games or reading together can provide routine and meaning to family relationships.

Children's literature can be used at home or as part of classroom curricula to initiate caring and conversation related to issues that children and families face. When parents and teachers sit and read with children, caring for that child is reinforced and the child feels valued. Discussions of book characters and plots provide meaningful and relevant ways for children to consider the lives of others and begin to look at ways of dealing with problems they face. Resilience in children is promoted through time spent with a caring adult and their participation in retellings and creative dramatizations of story plots.

Table 1 lists examples of good books that promote resilience in primary-grade children. These books were selected because they address, either directly or indirectly, elements of resilience or strategies for strengthening the skills of resilience. For instance, in *Wemberly Worried* (2000), Henkes writes of Wemberly, the little mouse, who worries about everything, especially her first day of school. As Wemberly struggles not to worry, she taps into some basic resilience-building strategies (e.g., telling adults you're worried, finding a friend to share your worries, and building on your strengths by successfully navigating the first day of school and returning for another day). In Faith Ringgold's *Tar Beach* (1991), Cassie Louise Lightfoot, an African American 8-year-old growing up in Harlem in 1939, demonstrates how believing good things will happen and drawing on the love of friends and family can promote a feeling of pride. Critical elements in building resilience include a belief in a positive future and support from a loving community.

Another example of the power of these books is drawn from *Amazing Grace* (Hoffman, 1991). Grace is an African American girl who loves stories and regularly adopts the roles and identities of strong, problem-solving characters, such as Joan of Arc, Hiawatha, and Anansi the Spider, in the plays she writes herself. Grace's grandmother takes her to see a famous black ballerina to encourage her to do "anything she can imagine." That role model encourages Grace to work hard and ultimately achieve her dream of performing the role of Peter Pan in the class play. Grace demonstrates problem-solving skills, emulates successful positive role models, and maintains perseverance—all foundational traits in building resilience.

The literature on individual and family resilience underscores the importance of building strategies to secure a network of social support. Such support begins with a loving relationship between one child and one adult (generally, a parent). Family therapists have likened the resilient family to open systems with clear, yet permeable boundaries, similar to a living cell (Beavers & Hampson, 1993; Satir, 1988; Walsh, 1998a; Whitaker & Keith, 1981).

Boundaries are important for the child and an authoritative parent earns the respect that comes from predictability; "no" means no. Inconsistent reinforcement of family rules undermines trust within the family and is not healthy. In fact, Hetherington and Kelly (2002, p. 130), in their studies of divorcing families, reported that "children of authoritative parents emerged from divorce as the most socially responsible, least troubled and highest-achieving children." Parents building resilient families ask their children for help in maintaining the household.

Examples include setting the table, mowing the lawn, washing dishes, and caring for a younger sibling, all of which can contribute to the resilience, maturity, and competency of a child. Age-appropriate chores are an important aspect of building children's resilience and sense of self-worth.

Family and Community

Resilient families have strength and integrity in their interactions within the family and also know when to reach outside the family circle for satisfying relationships. In an ideal world, the family of a primary-grade child is actively engaged in the broader community and relates to the community and each other with hope and optimism. Family members go out into the community and bring strength and new learnings back into the family circle.

There is a practical element to having relationships outside the family. Other connections can provide information, concrete services, support, companionship, and even respite from difficult situations. A family's sense of security can be enhanced by meaningful relationships with others. Community activities, including involvement in school and extracurricular activities, foster family well-being. Regular participation in sports leagues, faith-based activities, and parent-teacher organizations can bolster protective and recovery processes for the family. Research suggests that there is a highly protective element in belonging to a group and having regular social activity. This is particularly true for those in isolation and depression (Walsh, 1998b).

Because extended family is too often far away or unavailable for other reasons, it is important that families establish connections to meet their life circumstances. In the armed forces, families regularly share meals and child care in support of each other. Some families turn to older people in the community to provide "family" contact and meaningful activities with children at home or school. Both children and elders benefit in these situations. Also, multifamily groups band together in other ways to support single parents or families coping with a chronic illness, and such support can be vital in managing chronic stress or crises.

Conclusion

In this article, we have presented guidelines for creating and sustaining resilient families for primary-grade children and offered strategies for developing effective communication and building an attitude of family hardiness or resilience. We suggested promoting the value of family time, authoritative parenting, routine, and the importance of social support. We offer this work with the caveat that family resilience is an emerging field and we have only touched the surface.

Yet, our research and conversations with teachers, parents, and other child care providers have convinced us that teachers can take particular steps to support children and their families. Work with school administrators to develop sessions for parents on building family resilience during the critical primary-grade years. Invite children to talk about their experiences and say

Table 1   Resilience-Building Books for Primary-Grade Children

Andreae, G. (1999). *Giraffes can't dance.* New York: Orchard Books.

Bottner, B. (1992). *Bootsie Barker bites.* New York: G. P. Putnam Sons.

Bradby, M. (1995). *More than anything else.* New York: Orchard Books.

Brimner, L. D. (2002). *The littlest wolf.* New York: HarperCollins.

Burningham, J. (1987). *John Patrick Norman McHennessy—The boy who was always late.* New York: The Trumpet Club.

Burton, V. L. (1943). *Katy and the big snow.* Boston: Houghton Mifflin.

Cannon, J. (1993). *Stellaluna.* Orlando, FL: Harcourt Brace & Company.

Cannon, J. (2000). *Crickwing.* San Diego, CA: Harcourt.

Carle, E. (1999). *The very clumsy click beetle.* New York: Philomel Books.

Clifton, L. (1983). *Everett Anderson's goodbye.* New York: Henry Holt and Company.

Couric, K. (2000). *The brand new kid.* New York: Doubleday.

Giovanni, N. (2005). *Rosa.* New York: Henry Holt & Co.

Havill, J. (1995). *Jamaica's blue marker.* New York: Houghton Mifflin.

Heard, G. (2002). *This place I know: Poems of comfort.* Cambridge, MA: Candlewick Press.

Henkes, K. (2000). *Wemberly worried.* Hong Kong: Greenwillow Books.

Hoffman, M. (1991). *Amazing Grace.* Boston: Houghton Mifflin.

Juster, N. (2005). *The hello, goodbye window.* New York: Hyperion Books for Children.

Kraus, R. (1971). *Leo, the late bloomer.* New York: Windmill Books.

Kroll, V. (1997). *Butterfly boy.* Honesdale, PA: Boyds Mills Press.

Lester, H. (1999). *Hooway for Wodney Wat.* New York: Scholastic Books.

Lithgow, J. (2000). *The remarkable Farkle McBride.* New York: Simon & Schuster.

McKissack, P. (1986). *Flossie and the fox.* New York: Scholastic Books.

Mora, P. (2005). *Doña Flor: A tall tale about a giant woman with a great big heart.* New York: Alfred A. Knopf.

Moss, S. (1995). *Peter's painting.* Greenvale, NY: MONDO Publishing.

Piper, W. (1986). *The little engine that could.* New York: Platt & Munk.

Puttock, S. (2001). *A story for hippo: A book about loss.* New York: Scholastic Press.

Ringgold, F. (1991). *Tar beach.* New York: Scholastic Books.

Salley, C. (2002). *Epossumondas.* San Diego, CA: Harcourt.

Seskin, S., & Shamblin, A. (2002). *Don't laugh at me.* Berkeley, CA: Tricycle Press.

Taback, S. (1999). *Joseph had a little overcoat.* New York: Scholastic.

Tafuri, N. (2000). *Will you be my friend?* New York: Scholastic.

Tompert, A. (1993). *Just a little bit.* Boston: Houghton Mifflin.

Wyeth, S. D. (1998). *Something beautiful.* New York: Dragonfly Books.

what they believe makes them "bounce back" when bad things happen. Get parents and others involved by creating informational programs and materials about the importance of family resilience. Together, we must do all we can to help families and their children develop and nourish their resilience.

References

Beavers, W. R., & Hampson, R. B. (1990). *Successful families: Assessment and intervention.* New York: Norton.

Children's Defense Fund. (2004). *The state of America's children 2004: A continuing portrait of inequality fifty years after Brown v. Board of Education.* Retrieved August 14, 2004, from www.childrensdefense.org/pressreleases/040713.asp

Cowan, P. A., Cowan, C. P., & Schulz, M. S. (1996). Thinking about risk and resilience in families. In M. Hetherington & E. A. Blechman (Eds.), *Stress, coping and resilience in children and families.* Mahwah, NJ: Erlbaum.

Feiler, B. (2004, August 15). A game that gets parents and kids talking. *Parade.*

Garmezy, N., & Rutter, M. (Eds.). (1983). *Stress, coping and development in children.* New York: McGraw-Hill.

Hawley, D. R., & DeHaan, L. (1996). Toward a definition of family resilience: Integrating life-span and family perspectives. *Family Process, 35,* 283–298.

Hetherington, E., & Kelly, J. (2002). *For better or for worse: Divorce reconsidered.* New York: W. W. Norton & Co.

McCubbin, H. I., & McCubbin, M. A. (1996). Resilient families, competencies, supports and coping over the life cycle. In L. Sawyers (Ed.), *Faith and families.* Philadelphia: Geneva Press.

McCubbin, H. I., Thompson, E. A., Thompson, A. I., & McCubbin, M. A. (1992). Family schema, paradigms, and paradigm shifts: Components and processes of appraisal in family adaptation to crises. In A. P. Turnbull, J. M. Patterson, S. K. Bahr, D. L. Murphy, J. Marquis, & M. Blue-Banning (Eds.), *Cognitive coping research in developmental disabilities.* Baltimore: Paul H. Brookes.

Patterson, J. L., Patterson, J. H., & Collins, L. (2002). *Bouncing back: How your school can succeed in the face of adversity.* Larchmont, NY: Eye on Education Press.

Piaget, J. (1997). *The moral judgment of the child.* New York: Simon & Schuster.

Satir, V. (1988). *Within our reach: Breaking the cycle of disadvantage.* New York: Anchor.

Stacey, J. (1990). *Brave new families: Stories of domestic upheaval in late twentieth century America.* New York: Basic Books.

Walsh, F. (1991). Promoting healthy functioning in divorced and remarried families. In A. Gurman & D. Kniskern (Eds.), *Handbook of family therapy.* New York: Brunner/Mazel.

Walsh, F. (1998a). *Strengthening family resilience.* New York: The Guilford Press.

Walsh, F. (1998b). Families in later life: Challenges and opportunities. In B. Carter & M. McGoldrick (Eds.), *The expanded family life cycle.* Needham Heights, MA: Allyn & Bacon.

Werner, E. (1984). Resilient children. *Young Children, 68*(72).

Werner, E. E., & Smith, R. S. (1982). *Vulnerable but invincible: A longitudinal study of resilient children and youth.* New York: Adams, Bannister, Cox.

Werner, E. E., & Smith, R. S. (1992). *Overcoming the odds: High risk children from birth to adulthood.* New York: Cornell University Press.

Whitaker, C., & Keith, D. (1981). Symbolic-experiential family therapy. In A. S. Gurman & D. Kniskern (Eds.), *Handbook of family therapy.* New York: Brunner/Mazel.

Wolin, S., & Wolin, S. (1993). *The resilient self: How survivors of troubled families rise above adversity.* New York: Villard.

JANICE PATTERSON is Associate Professor, Education Department, and **LYNN KIRKLAND** is Associate Professor, Education Department, University of Alabama-Birmingham.

Where Is Marriage Going?

ANTHONY LAYNG

It was bad enough when the divorce rate in the U.S. reached epidemic proportions and single parenting became commonplace. Now, more and more Americans are developing a tolerance for same-sex marriage. New York recognizes such marriages, and the California and Connecticut Supreme Courts struck down those states' laws banning marriage for same-sex couples, allowing them to join Massachusetts in accepting homosexual unions. Even though Californians recently voted to stop granting marriage licenses to same-sex couples, the sanctity of marriage seriously seems to be undermined and in danger of further deterioration.

Most Americans believe that marriage is an inherently sacred institution, the purpose of which is procreation and the socialization of children. That is why the idea of same-sex marriage, the prevalence of single mothers raising children, and the frailty of modern marriages are considered such a threat to "proper" marriage. Such pessimism particularly is prevalent among biblical literalists and other Christian fundamentalists who feel that any alteration of traditional marriage constitutes a moral decline, and many others agree.

However, examining the history of marriage encourages quite a different conclusion. The ethnographic study of tribal societies suggests what marriage meant to our ancestors thousands of years ago. Obviously, having children is an ancient concern, but most tribal people did not view marriage as something sacred. Many tribes had no ritual to acknowledge the start of a marriage, nothing we would equate to a wedding. Among the traditional Cheyenne, courtship involved a girl allowing a suitor to sleep with her in her parents' tepee, entering stealthfully after dark and leaving before the others in the tepee awakened. All the couple needed to do to be considered married was to have the young man sleep late enough to be discovered by her parents. Similarly, some Pacific islanders, such as the Ulithi, allowed couples to "announce" that they wished to be considered married simply by cohabiting. Coming-of-age rituals were far more common in tribal societies than weddings, and yet marriage was, with very few exceptions, the norm in all these societies.

Somehow, the belief that marriages are arranged in heaven, an extremely romantic idea, has become equated with considering marriage as sacred. Again, taking a historical perspective as provided by our knowledge of traditional societies, marriages frequently were arranged by parents or other relatives. Among the Sambia of New Guinea and the Tiwi of northern Australia, many marriages involved infant brides. In numerous warlike tribes such as the Yanomamo of Venezuela, men obtained wives by capturing them from enemy villages.

Granted, marriage in this country often is associated with religious concepts and usually initiated with a sacred ritual. Yet, from the perspective of the history of humanity, this is a rather recent development. Even newer are our present matrimonial motives. Instead of marrying to ensure that our offspring will care for us when we are too old to provide for ourselves, we now consciously limit the number of children to how many we can afford. No longer does marrying and having children provide assurance that the elderly will be cared for. Understandably, most modern couples, for a variety of reasons, choose to limit their fecundity to one or two children or remain childless. Unlike tribal people, those of us who elect to avoid marriage nevertheless may be admired and influential. However, our tribal ancestors structured their lives around marriage. Who you were, your role in society, and your prestige all largely were determined by your place in the kinship system. Whom you and your kin married could ensure or alter your status in society. One rose and fell in the social order by strategic marriage. Of course, infant marriage and marriage by capture no longer are acceptable. Arranged marriages remain legal, but are considered unsuitable. Now, it seems, the only legitimate motivation for marriage is romantic love and seeking emotional fulfillment. Marriage to enhance status still occurs, but generally is frowned upon. We are quite critical of the wealthy senior socialite who marries her young tennis instructor, or the twentysomething beauty who marries a famous elderly celebrity. Such unions are considered laughable or crass.

Tribal people married to gain prestige by having many children (hopefully, several sons) to ensure their future welfare. Additionally, given the strict sexual division of labor in these societies, at least one man and one woman were necessary components of a normal household. This had been the case since our ancestors lived as hunters and gatherers. Even in traditional agrarian societies, the labors of men and women produced very different things, and both were required for running a successful household and providing for children. Now that men and women are obtaining nearly equal educations and more and more couples are, of necessity, gainfully employed, any domestic division of labor likely is to be dictated by personal inclinations and circumstances rather than gender. No longer is the husband inevitably the breadwinner and the wife a stay-at-home mother. Marriage in the U.S. is a very flexible institution today. The nature of a marital relationship is not determined primarily by custom but is left to each couple to work out according to personal needs and preferences. It no longer necessarily involves a hierarchical arrangement between spouses. Contemporary husbands and wives frequently consider themselves to be equal partners. Even parenting has lost its imperative tie to marriage since it has become acceptable for single people to raise children today.

The nature of a marital relationship is not determined primarily by custom but is left to each couple to work out. . . .

It is under these circumstances, given how marriage has evolved to its present form, that homosexual men and women have begun to find same-sex marriage attractive. Clearly, each marriage is an ever-adapting relationship, altering over time as circumstances change. Similarly, the institution of marriage has evolved and will continue to do so. Since the earliest marriages in very primitive societies, this custom has taken various forms, always adjusting as society evolved. That process particularly is evident today because social change has been accelerating. Current legislative attempts to prohibit such change are understandable, but unsuitable and unlikely to succeed, as our technology, beliefs, and customs have a long dynamic history, and marriage is subject to the same forces of social change as the rest of our culture.

ANTHONY LAYNG is professor emeritus of anthropology at Elmira (N.Y.) College.

Test-Your-Knowledge Form

We encourage you to photocopy and use this page as a tool to assess how the articles in *Annual Editions* expand on the information in your textbook. By reflecting on the articles you will gain enhanced text information. You can also access this useful form on a product's book support website at www.mhhe.com/cls

NAME: DATE:

_____

TITLE AND NUMBER OF ARTICLE:

_____

BRIEFLY STATE THE MAIN IDEA OF THIS ARTICLE:

_____

LIST THREE IMPORTANT FACTS THAT THE AUTHOR USES TO SUPPORT THE MAIN IDEA:

_____

WHAT INFORMATION OR IDEAS DISCUSSED IN THIS ARTICLE ARE ALSO DISCUSSED IN YOUR TEXTBOOK OR OTHER READINGS THAT YOU HAVE DONE? LIST THE TEXTBOOK CHAPTERS AND PAGE NUMBERS:

_____

LIST ANY EXAMPLES OF BIAS OR FAULTY REASONING THAT YOU FOUND IN THE ARTICLE:

_____

LIST ANY NEW TERMS/CONCEPTS THAT WERE DISCUSSED IN THE ARTICLE, AND WRITE A SHORT DEFINITION:

We Want Your Advice

ANNUAL EDITIONS revisions depend on two major opinion sources: one is our Advisory Board, listed in the front of this volume, which works with us in scanning the thousands of articles published in the public press each year; the other is you—the person actually using the book. Please help us and the users of the next edition by completing the prepaid article rating form on this page and returning it to us. Thank you for your help!

ANNUAL EDITIONS: The Family 11/12

ARTICLE RATING FORM

Here is an opportunity for you to have direct input into the next revision of this volume.
We would like you to rate each of the articles listed below, using the following scale:

1. **Excellent: should definitely be retained**
2. **Above average: should probably be retained**
3. **Below average: should probably be deleted**
4. **Poor: should definitely be deleted**

Your ratings will play a vital part in the next revision.
Please mail this prepaid form to us as soon as possible.
Thanks for your help!

RATING	ARTICLE	RATING	ARTICLE
	1. Marriage and Family in the Scandinavian Experience		26. The Fatal Distraction: Forgetting a Child in the Backseat of a Car Is a Horrifying Mistake. Is It a Crime?
	2. The Significant Dynamic Relationship between Globalization and Families		27. Children of Alcoholics
	3. Interracial Families		28. Impact of Family Recovery and Pre-Teens and Adolescents
	4. Family Partnerships		29. Love but Don't Touch
	5. This Thing Called Love		30. Is This Man Cheating on His Wife?
	6. 24 Things Love and Sex Experts Are Dying to Tell You		31. The Opt-Out Myth
	7. Against All Odds		32. Making Time for Family Time
	8. The Expectations Trap		33. Mother (and Father), Can You Spare a Dime?
	9. On-Again, Off-Again		34. Rise of the Desperate House Husband
	10. Fats, Carbs and the Science of Conception		35. Trust and Betrayal in the Golden Years
	11. Not Always 'the Happiest Time'		36. Dealing *Day-to-Day with* Diabetes: A Whole Family Experience
	12. Truth and Consequences at Pregnancy High		37. The Positives of Caregiving: Mothers' Experiences Caregiving for a Child with Autism
	13. Baby Survival Guide: 7 Truths That'll Keep You Sane		38. Bereavement after Caregiving
	14. Contributing to the Debate over Same-Sex Marriage		39. Love, Loss—and Love
	15. Can Marriage Be Saved?		40. A Family Undertaking
	16. The Polygamists		41. Stressors Afflicting Families during Military Deployment
	17. Good Parents, Bad Results		42. Children of the Wars
	18. Do We Need a Law to Prohibit Spanking?		43. A Divided House
	19. Children of Lesbian and Gay Parents: Psychology, Law and Policy		44. Civil Wars
	20. Minding the Kids		45. Estranged Spouses Increasingly Waiting out Downturn to Divorce
	21. Mother, Damnedest		46. Get a Closer Look
	22. The Forgotten Siblings		47. The Joy of Rituals
	23. Four Myths about Older Adults in America's Immigrant Families		48. Sustaining Resilient Families for Children in Primary Grades
	24. Recognizing Domestic Partner Abuse		49. Where Is Marriage Going?
	25. Domestic Abuse Myths		

BUSINESS REPLY MAIL
FIRST CLASS MAIL PERMIT NO. 551 DUBUQUE IA

POSTAGE WILL BE PAID BY ADDRESSEE

McGraw-Hill Contemporary Learning Series
501 BELL STREET
DUBUQUE, IA 52001

ABOUT YOU

Name   Date

_____

Are you a teacher? ❑ A student? ❑
Your school's name

_____

Department

_____

Address   City   State   Zip

_____

School telephone #

_____

YOUR COMMENTS ARE IMPORTANT TO US!

Please fill in the following information:
For which course did you use this book?

_____

Did you use a text with this ANNUAL EDITION? ❑ yes ❑ no
What was the title of the text?

_____

What are your general reactions to the Annual Editions concept?

_____

Have you read any pertinent articles recently that you think should be included in the next edition? Explain.

_____

Are there any articles that you feel should be replaced in the next edition? Why?

_____

Are there any World Wide Websites that you feel should be included in the next edition? Please annotate.

_____

May we contact you for editorial input? ❑ yes ❑ no
May we quote your comments? ❑ yes ❑ no

NOTES

NOTES

NOTES

NOTES

NOTES

NOTES

NOTES

NOTES